# Mental Retardation
# and
# Modern Society

# Mental Retardation and Modern Society

MICHAEL P. MALONEY, Ph.D.

Associate Professor
Department of Psychiatry
University of Southern California, School of Medicine

Psychological Assessment Clinic
Los Angeles County–University of Southern California Medical Center

MICHAEL P. WARD, Ph.D.

Assistant Professor
Department of Psychiatry
University of Southern California, School of Medicine

Psychological Assessment Clinic
Los Angeles County–University of Southern California Medical Center

New York · Oxford University Press · 1979

Library of Congress Cataloging in Publication Data
Maloney, Michael P
Mental retardation and modern society.
Bibliography: p.
Includes index.
1. Mental deficiency. I. Ward, Michael P., 1944- joint author. II. Title.
RC570.M214 362.3 78-16827
ISBN 0-19-502473-7

Printed in the United States of America

To my mother, Gertrude, and to Paige, Mike, Jr., and Jeff

To Helen G. Ward and the late Michael Joseph Ward, my parents

# Preface

We began organizing our thoughts and planning this book approximately 10 years ago, while working in a large state institution for the mentally retarded. Since that time, we have become affiliated with a large psychiatric hospital that serves as the major acute psychiatric facility for much of Los Angeles County. We have remained intrigued by the problems related to low intelligence and mental retardation and have continued to read, work, and teach in this general area. In fact, the change in our place of employment has broadened and deepened our interest and, we hope, our understanding of the difficulties faced by persons of low intelligence in our society. One of our most striking and alarming discoveries was that the problems of mental retardation in particular and low intelligence in general go essentially undetected in many settings. For example, in psychiatric facilities, professionals look so hard for psychiatric symptoms that they often overlook even obvious mental retardation, not to mention the less obvious but far more pervasive instances of mild retardation and low intelligence. We were so impressed with this general lack of awareness and recognition that we began to address this issue in our research and writing. Eventually, we came to the realization that forms the core and the underlying theme of this text: An adequate understanding of the phenomenon and problem of mental retardation is impossible unless we broaden our perspective. Mental retardation is just one part of the general problem of low intelligence. And the problem of low intelligence is intimately related to the characteristics of the society. The crux of the matter is an appreciation of the interaction between low intelligence and the demands of our complex, modern society. From this perspective, it becomes obvious that mental retardation is simply a concept that reflects the coping difficulties that individuals of low intelligence have in a given society. These problems relate both to the complexity of the society and to the individual's intellectual status. Viewed in this manner, mental retardation is not a specific, identifiable phenomenon, some sort of medical condition, as so many people still believe. On the contrary, it is a dynamic and changing idea, which varies as the society and the individual change. Furthermore, this idea is influenced and changed by sociopolitical factors, societal attitudes, developments in technology, and teaching, and a host of other variables.

The realization that mental retardation is essentially an explanatory concept has influenced our approach in writing this introductory text. Since we are dealing with a concept, it seemed both logical and appropriate that the book be conceptually oriented. Our own experience in teaching courses on mental retardation to students reinforced this idea. We had tried a variety of texts and found them wanting. Some were too simplistic; others were good but often so detailed that many students were unable to see the forest for the trees. We felt that there was a need for a more conceptually oriented book that presented the big picture. Specific data and facts are included to illustrate and elucidate the general concepts, principles, and issues. The text, however, is not intended to be a catalog of facts.

As with all authors of books, we owe many debts. The people at Oxford University Press, especially Marcus Boggs and Ellen Fuchs, are appreciated for their assistance, support, and patience with delays. We wish to acknowledge especially Mrs. Eleanor Wash, the librarian at Pacific State Hospital and Developmental Center, for her invaluable help. She is the epitome of what a librarian should be. We also want to thank Shirley Boshard, Betty Valdez, Mary Luben, and Mary Guth for their superb efforts in translating our hieroglyphics into readable and we hope enlightening English. Finally, we wish to thank our families for enduring our late night and weekend vigils.

*Los Angeles, California*
*November, 1978*

Michael P. Maloney
Michael P. Ward

# Contents

There are many both within and without the field who will advise building a program solely around hope. But I cannot do so. We must work for every great gain of which we can think, but we likewise must keep on working in a tiresome way for the little gains alone possible at present. With respect to mental retardation there is no way to run; in our despair, however, let us not stop creeping.

From "On Locusts." By Richard H. Hungerford (1903-1974).
*American Journal of Mental Deficiency*, 1950, 54, 415–418.

Mental Retardation
and
Modern Society

# CHAPTER 1

# Introduction and Orientation

What is mental retardation? How many people are mentally retarded? What causes mental retardation, and what can be done to prevent and treat it? These are some of the questions that an introductory textbook on mental retardation should consider and attempt to answer.

This book would have been much easier to write twenty years ago, when there appeared to be some straightforward answers to these questions. But much has happened in the intervening years to complicate matters. On the one hand, there has been a tremendous upsurge of interest in the field of mental retardation. This has resulted in some dramatic advances and a virtual knowledge explosion—e.g., the discovery of an extra chromosome in a common type of mental retardation called Down's syndrome; the drastic reduction of the severe effects of a disease called phenylketonuria (PKU) through dietary management; and the tremendous training advances brought about by an applied behavioral technology. On the other hand, the inclusion of the "sociological perspective" has revolutionized our theories of mental retardation. Additionally, the field is now plagued with a number of controversies that have sociopolitical implications and ramifications. These issues include the fairness and appropriateness of intelligence tests for minority groups; the role of genetics in intelligence and the related arguments about racial differences; and the issues of labeling, institutionalization, and the rights of the mentally retarded. Paradoxically, a major result of all the increased activity and knowledge over the past two decades is that we sometimes appear to "know" even less. The answers to the above-mentioned questions are no longer simple and straightforward. Furthermore, attempts to answer them often create more problems than solutions. But rather than reflect any real loss of knowledge, the current ambiguity actually indicates a realistic appreciation of the complexity of mental retardation. As such, the field of mental retardation appears to be maturing and acquiring some wisdom.

However, this state of flux certainly complicates the writing of an introductory textbook. Such texts are obviously shaped and constrained by the nature of the field. The usual goal is to distill the essential concepts and data and to present them in a palatable fashion. This would be far easier if there existed a single, unified theory and clearly supporting data. Unfortunately, this is not the case with the field of mental retardation. There is no coherent, inclusive theory, and the mountains of new data are unwieldy and often contradictory. Worse yet, much of the traditional knowledge base has become suspect; for example, the standard estimate that 3 percent of the population is mentally retarded has recently been strongly challenged. This situation involves some hard choices in preparing an introductory text. Do we present a realistic picture of the field, with all of its confusing contradictions and inconsistencies, or do we opt for an unrealistic and simplistic, yet clear and sharply defined "black and white" print? Either approach has its advantages and disadvantages. Should the picture be a panoramic view of the whole field or a closeup with a lot of detail? How many pictures or views must we present in order to adequately cover the subject matter?

There are no simple answers to these questions. To a great extent, the situation is analogous to the old dictum "Damned if you do, and damned if you don't." There are also the more practical constraints, such as page limitations and the amount of material that can be reasonably covered in a typical college semester or quarter. Given such considerations and the nature of the subject, we have decided that the best approach for an introductory textbook in mental retardation is a broad, conceptual overview of the major aspects of this field.

This decision was made for several reasons. First, the conceptual approach seems most appropriate for introducing students to any new area of study, particularly one as complex and ill-defined as mental retardation. Second, given the changing character of the field, a conceptual focus provides a better understanding and has a more lasting value. Finally, the complex and often conflicting and controversial nature of many of the issues demands a solid conceptual foundation. More than anything else, new students in the field need to acquire both the big picture and a sense of direction so that they will be able to discern the forest from the trees and the faddish from the fundamental. We hope that the conceptual orientation of this book will fulfill these needs.

Before presenting the organization of this text, we wish to make several comments regarding the title: *Mental Retardation and Modern Society*. This title reflects in many ways the authors' understanding of and orientation toward mental retardation.

First, we wish to emphasize that mental retardation is primarily and fundamentally a modern phenomenon. This is not to deny, as we shall see in the next chapter, that mental retardation has existed and been recognized for many centuries. But that awareness has been almost exclusively focused on the more extreme forms of mental retardation, those now classified as the severely and profoundly retarded (roughly speaking, IQs less than 50). Aside from gross and obvious intellectual deficiencies, these persons typically manifest significant neuropathology, associated medical problems, and frequently, physical deformities or handicaps. They often look and act much different from normals and are frequently noticeable to the casual observer. They are also the basis for the traditional negative and erroneous stereotypes of the mentally retarded, which often include such notions as repulsive and bizarre behavior (e.g., the "drooling idiot"). What is not recognized by most lay people and many professionals is that this group of the severely afflicted constitutes only a small fraction of persons diagnosed as mentally retarded. Indeed, the vast majority of the mentally retarded (approximately 85 to 90 percent) function at a much higher level and are almost indistinguishable from their normal counterparts in physical appearance and everyday behavior. These are the people who are categorized as mildly retarded (roughly speaking, the 50 to 70 IQ range) according to our modern classification systems. The awareness and recognition of these milder forms of mental retardation is a recent historical event—only one hundred years old. Since the mildly retarded were not "discovered" until modern times, mental retardation is thus considered a modern phenomenon.

Even today, it is the relatively infrequent but more dramatic and severe instances of mental retardation, such as Down's syndrome and PKU, that continue to occupy the limelight. In contrast, the far more frequent but much less dramatic, milder forms of mental retardation have been largely ignored. This is not to imply that we should neglect the more severe and dramatic forms. The problem is that the focus on the dramatic and severe is often incorrectly generalized to all the mentally retarded. According to the popular perspective, mental retardation has a clear physical basis, there is something obviously wrong with the brain (i.e., brain damage), and retardation is thus quite noticeable and detectable. But this is simply not true of the vast majority of the mentally retarded. Mild retardation is rarely associated with any specifiable medical problem or disease; we have been unable to point out anything clearly wrong with the brain; and the condition is neither easily noticeable nor detectable. Thus, while we have no intention of ignoring the more severe forms of retardation, the time has come to downplay their influence on the popular views of mental retardation. Furthermore, as we have stated, most of the mentally retarded are mildly retarded and thus deserve a much greater share of our attention and concern than in the past. Popular conceptualizations and attitudes need to be changed accordingly. The title of this text was chosen to emphasize our focus on the milder but far more pervasive forms of mental retardation.

The second reason for choosing this title derives from the first. Why was mild retardation essentially unknown or unrecognized until approximately 100 years ago? The answer turns on the crucial relationship between mental retardation and society. Severe retardation has a cultural and historical universality; it has been recognized and detected in all societies and at all times. But the situation changes dramatically when we consider the mildly retarded. It was not until the emergence of modern society, with its vast industrial, technological, economic, and sociopolitical changes, that greater intellectual demands were placed on man in his attempt to survive and adapt. In premodern societies and times, the requirements for existence in an essentially agrarian culture were primarily physical. In contrast, existence in our complex modern society is much more determined by man's intellectual skills and abilities.

A striking example of these increased intellectual demands is the system of universal public education that developed concurrently in all emerging modern societies. The purpose was to equip the society's members with the skills necessary for adaption and survival (thus providing for society's survival as well). In the premodern era, education was a luxury and a privilege of the rich; there was no such thing as education for the masses. Only in modern times did mass education become a necessity. The new democracies and the Industrial Revolution required educated citizens and workers. The need for universal education created a situation in which differences, even mild ones, became readily apparent. The resultant increase in academic/intellectual demands was largely responsible for the eventual discovery and recognition of mild mental retardation. Some of the people who were able to adapt in a more agrarian society were now seen as deficient. What we must realize is that it was the changes in society, not changes in the individuals themselves, that brought about the problem. It is in this sense that mental retardation is primarily a modern phenomenon. Moreover, it becomes obvious that mild mental retardation is a condition rather than a disease. The condition exists only under certain circumstances and can change when the circumstances change. Modern society is the circumstance, or precipitating factor, that has created the condition of mild mental retardation. Furthermore, this condition would not exist except for the fact of modern society and its demands on intelligence.

The final reason for selecting the title of this text follows from and is an extension of the other two reasons. The first two reasons state, in essence, that mild mental retardation today is culturally relative. How much intellectual ability is needed to handle the demands of modern society? What is the cutoff point? The current (and traditional) upper limit has been an IQ of 70, although suggestions of an upper limit of an IQ of 85 have been considered and employed in the past. Whatever the case, it must be recognized that any upper limit is both debatable and arbitrary. Does anyone believe that there is a qualitative difference between the person with an IQ of 69 and one with an IQ of 71?

The arbitrary nature of the cutoff point in IQ is closely linked to the cultural relativity of mental retardation. At the upper, or milder, levels of retardation, the crucial factor is not IQ or behavior, but the match between the individual's capacities and the society's demands. This interaction does not allow us to specify precise limits, especially since the culture or society can change rapidly and drastically. (The fact that the person's intellectual status is more "permanent," compared to the possibilities for change in the environment, has important implications for both the meaning and the treatment of mental retardation.) Unlike medical diseases, such as pneumonia, mental retardation is not an all-or-nothing phenomenon. It depends totally on the organism-environment interaction. Given the modern "invention" of mild mental retardation, we must recognize that more "modernity" may cause even more "mild" mental retardation (with an unspecified higher, but equally arbitrary, upper limit). In other words, if we are to take the culturally relative nature of mental retardation seriously, we must avoid focusing exclusively on those we now label mentally retarded. Furthermore, if the trend toward even greater societal complexity is any indication, we can predict that even more people will be affected in the future. Thus, we must instead be sensitive to a continuum of adaptability as it relates to societal complexity. Consequently, we will not limit our discussion to the present. Rather, this book is about mental retardation as it is known and defined today as well as how it may become known and defined tomorrow. Just as today's mildly retarded were unrecognized 100 years ago, today's "borderline" or "low normal" persons may become the "minimally" retarded in the future. The labels and IQ cutoffs, although important from a social-administrative and legal point of view, are irrelevant and actually detrimental to a full understanding of the mentally retarded—namely, people with an undefined lower level of intelligence who manifest impaired adaptive behavior as they attempt to adjust to a complex, modern society.

It is our belief that our society is becoming more complex, posing increased adaptive problems for more and more people. Accordingly, we feel it is imperative that the student be aware of the possible progressive nature of mental retardation.

In summary, the title of this text was chosen to stress the crucial and basic relationship between mental retardation and modern society. To a great extent (i.e., in mild mental retardation), we cannot have one without the other. In thus emphasizing the modern nature of mental retardation, this text is about the past (when it didn't really exist), the present (when it was created and defined), and the future (when it may become even more problematic).

## PREVIEW

As mentioned earlier, the writing of an introductory text in the field of mental retardation involves some hard choices. So that our sins of omission and commission may be understood (if not forgiven), we will now present the organization of the book, pointing out the reasons for some of our choices and making explicit some of our biases. The reader should be aware that many in the field of mental retardation would probably strongly disagree with some or many aspects of our approach.

We will begin our examination of mental retardation by first looking backward in the next chapter, entitled "The History of Mental Retardation and Intelligence." Most introductory textbooks on retardation devote far less space to this topic. We are deviating from traditional practice for several reasons.

First, we find much wisdom in the old adage: "To know where you are and where you are going, you must first find out where you have been." This is particularly true of mental retardation. The current state of this field can be properly understood and appreciated only in the context of the past. Moreover, the past, as it blends into the present, illuminates the possible directions that may be taken in the future. The other major reason for this unusually lengthy historical account relates to the conceptual thrust of the book. Since a broad conceptual overview of mental retardation is our primary goal, the student must first acquire the necessary "sense of history" that will enable him to see the evolution of our modern concepts. The formal, scientific study of mental retardation is a fascinating story, filled with colorful characters (both heroes and villains, with certain pioneers paradoxically playing both roles), alternating eras of great optimism and profound pessimism, and a great deal of politics. One of the most striking features of mental retardation is that it has often been entangled with social and political concerns that have both helped and hampered the study, care, and treatment of the mentally retarded. That entanglement, for better or worse (usually some mixture of both), continues up to the present day and will probably be part of the future. Consequently, the reader should realize that an accurate understanding of mental retardation is possible only with an awareness and appreciation of the complex sociopolitical influences that surround it. Mental retardation has never been a purely theoretical problem that could be leisurely and dispassionately studied. On the contrary, in the last 200 years, and especially since 1900, it has often been viewed as a pressing (and often alarming) social problem.

The other factor to be kept in mind in reading this historical account relates to the title of the chapter. From a historical perspective, it is impossible to talk about either the field of mental retardation or the variable of intelligence without discussing the other, for they have always been inextricably intertwined. Certainly, the most common conceptualization of mental retardation, among both laymen and professionals, is in terms of low intelligence. But the relationship is much more than conceptual. For one thing, the field of intelligence owes a great debt to the mentally retarded. The first successful test of intelligence was the direct result of Alfred Binet's being commissioned by the French Ministry of Education to develop a "screening procedure" that would eliminate "slow learners" (the as yet unlabeled mildly retarded) from the regular public schools. The 1905 Binet-Simon scale proved to be the springboard of the first major scientific inquiry into the nature of intelligence. We thus have an excellent example of how nonscientific forces (the practical problems of mental retardation) are often the greatest impetus to scientific pursuits and productivity.

On the other hand, the results of this scientific inquiry have frequently had dramatic and profound implications for the developing theory and practice of mental retardation. While some of these results have been quite beneficial to the cause of mental retardation (particularly in the last 20 years), our historical review will indicate periods when the implications of the scientific findings were extremely harmful to the care and treatment of the mentally retarded. What will become obvious is that the scientific process is often perverted by intruding sociopolitical attitudes and policy. And it is not just a problem of misuse of scientific knowledge by outsiders; many of the culprits themselves have been scientists who allowed their own sociopolitical attitudes and concerns to prejudice their interpretation of the facts. Nor is this merely ancient history. The entanglement of these two disciplines—the applied field of mental retardation and the more theoretical field of intelligence—continues today, and again often with much controversy (e.g., Jensen's statements regarding racial differences and intelligence; the use of IQ tests to label children mentally retarded, particularly those from minority groups). Chapter 2 thus presents a history of both intelligence and mental retardation because of the clear interactions between these two fields, both yesterday and today.

With this historical review as background, Chapter 3 focuses on one of the central issues throughout that history—namely, the meaning of intelligence and IQ. A more controversial and complex subject is difficult to find. Many professionals working in mental retardation would decry the fact that we are devoting a whole chapter to this topic. For years, the field of retardation has been trying to dissociate itself from the harmful effects of overreliance on and exclusive use of IQ as the defining feature of mental retardation. There has also been a related—and somewhat inappropriate—attempt to disavow the central role of intelligence itself. Unfortunately, the current disgust with IQ is analogous to "throwing out the baby with the bath water." Intelligence is too important to ignore. As we shall argue in Chapter 4, which deals with the concept of mental retardation, the notion of some type of cognitive deficit is basic, although there are several other aspects (e.g., the societal context) that must also be included. To understand the nature of this cognitive-intellectual deficit, one must first understand intelligence itself. Accordingly, the various theories on the nature of intelligence will be examined. Because the IQ test is related to the concept of intelligence (just how poorly will also be discussed) and is the most practical measure of it (despite its many deficiencies), the reader must also understand the concept of IQ, which is the controversial index of these tests. This concept, and some of its problems, is considered in detail.

What will become clear is that much of the controversy about IQ is legitimate, and that the IQ has been misinterpreted and misapplied in the past. However, many of the appropriate criticisms of IQ (the summary index) should not be generalized to the tests themselves. Furthermore, while IQ is definitely *not* synonymous with intelligence, it is related to that concept in some vague and ill-defined manner. The only way to gain a correct perspective on all of these issues and controversies is to understand the concept of intelligence and its particular but limited manifestation as the IQ index. Accordingly, we have included a section on the scientific validity versus the practical utility of the IQ. To put things in perspective, Chapter 3 concludes with a working position on intelligence.

As this conclusion will make clear, although IQ is not critical to mental retardation, intelligence definitely is. Furthermore, while there are no cogent scientific reasons for retaining the IQ index (and in fact, some reasons why we shouldn't), this does not mean that the tests themselves should be abandoned or that the IQ is totally useless. The IQ index has been retained because it is convenient for a variety of bureaucratic, social-administrative, and legal purposes. It is legitimate to question whether these conveniences outweigh the disadvantages of simplistic interpretation and inappropriate application. But if a decision is made to abandon the IQ index, this should not imply that its referent, intelligence, should also be abandoned. To do so would make it extremely difficult to understand mental retardation.

With this discussion of intelligence and IQ behind us, we are now ready to consider what is meant by mental retardation, the topic of Chapter 4. To a great extent, this is the most critical chapter of the book. Mental retardation is here conceptualized as a culturally relative, socially defined, social-psychological, practical problem. Although low intelligence is the defining characteristic, it is a necessary but insufficient condition for mental retardation. There must also be a clear problem with the person's social competence. Most important, as we have seen, mental retardation cannot be fully appreciated without noting its culturally relative nature. Furthermore, by making a distinction between two groups—the severely retarded and the mildly retarded—much of the confusion about mental retardation can be eliminated. Chapter 4 concludes with a discussion of the most widely used definition of mental retardation today.

Chapter 5 discusses the two models of mental retardation that are popular today. The first is the traditional medical or disease-oriented approach, also called the psychological-clinical perspective. According to this model, mental retardation exists in the individual. It will be seen, however, that while this traditional model is appropriate for construing severe mental retardation, it is far less relevant to milder forms of retardation. In terms of sheer numbers, this latter group represents the vast majority of the mentally retarded and is more appropriately viewed from a social system perspective. According to this newer model, mental retardation is inherent in the society, not the individual. Society is seen as having much to do with the creation and definition of mental retardation, which is seen as an achieved social role or status. The implications of these two perspectives for the identification, prevalence, and treatment of mental retardation are discussed. Because the social system approach dominates the field today, this model is reviewed in detail. The results indicate considerable flaws in both the theory and the supporting data. Consequently, the authors conclude the chapter by proposing a third model of mental retardation: the societal perspective. This view, while drawing upon both of the above-mentioned perspectives, goes beyond them. It appears to be the only viable approach to an adequate conceptualization of mental retardation.

After dealing with history and the concepts of intelligence, IQ, and mental retardation, we turn in Chapter 6 to a factual discussion of mental retardation. The "conventional wisdom" about mental retardation will be presented so that the student can become acquainted with the common ground from which all workers in the field operate. The chapter begins by considering the role and purpose of classification and then examines various classification schemes dealing with mental retardation. Particular attention is paid to the most popular behavioral and educational classification systems. We then delineate some basic characteristics and features of persons at the various levels of mental retardation. Finally, the epidemiology of mental retardation is considered, focusing on its prevalence and the various factors that influence prevalence estimates, such as age, sex, and social class.

In Chapter 7, assessment in mental retardation is discussed. How do we decide that someone is mentally retarded? What are the methods and procedures involved? Much of the current controversy about mental retardation centers on the issue of assessment. The chapter begins by presenting a model of psychological assessment. When correctly applied, this approach avoids many of the pitfalls and abuses that have unfortunately plagued this area in the past. Some of the devices for appraising a person's intellectual functioning and level of adaptive behavior are considered, to give the student a general idea of what is done. Some of the difficulties and problems with these procedures will also be explored. Finally, certain new methods and approaches to the assessment of mental retardation will be covered.

Chapter 8 deals with the etiology of mental retardation. Traditional medical causes will be explored, keeping in mind that the more than 250 known medical conditions associated with mental retardation account for only about 10 to 15 percent of all mental retardation. In other words, we still do not know the causes of most types of mental retardation. However, we do know that sociocultural factors are heavily involved. For many mentally retarded persons, there is a mingling of several etiological factors. Consequently, Chapter 8 ends with a discussion of the sociocultural factors involved in the etiology of mental retardation.

The role of certain social-psychological factors in mental retardation is covered in Chapter 9. We will begin by examining social attitudes toward the mentally retarded, focusing on the stigmas, stereotypes, and expectations involved. Next, we will explore the controversial topic of labeling and its real and imagined effects. Although many in and out of the field condemn this practice outright, there is little data to support the allegedly overwhelming, deleterious effects attributed to labels. In fact, several factors suggest that labeling can be beneficial when appropriately and humanely applied. Finally, we will consider what it means to be mentally retarded in our complex, modern society. Very little attention has been paid to this critical topic, and there is a scarcity of relevant research. The considerations and speculations of this section of the chapter are an attempt to correct this situation. In many respects, mental retardation can be viewed as the "unseen handicap." It is hard to imagine a condition more personally devastating in terms of the development and maintenance of self-concept than this one, in a society that places such a premium on intellectual prowess and accomplishments. Furthermore, the implications of a negative self-concept for the intellectual, emotional, and social growth and well-being of such persons can be assumed to be extremely significant and important.

Chapter 10 deals with provisions for the mentally retarded. Volumes have been written on this subject, and it is impossible to summarize this vast literature in a single chapter. What the new student most needs in this complex area is a general orientation and overview. Consequently, the chapter is written at a broad conceptual level, covering only the most important aspects and features of the treatment of mental retardation. Because philosophical, humanistic, and legal concerns have become central to treatment, this chapter will discuss some of these issues and their impact rather than the specifics of the treatment process (e.g., particular approaches or techniques).

The chapter is broken down into several sections. The first one discusses the attitudes and philosophical approaches to the treatment of mental retardation. The cardinal rule, often forgotten in textbook presentations, is to treat the mentally retarded as *persons*. The critical relationship between science and values is explored in this regard. Our assumptions about man, intelligence, and the nature of mental retardation, and their effect on our treatment objectives and procedures, will also be discussed. We will then consider the concept of normalization as both an ideal treatment goal and a methodology. The impact of recent judicial decisions and legislative actions on our treatment philosophy and practices will also be explored. In addition, the difficult, complex and value-laden process of setting goals and allocating limited funds and resources will be considered. Finally, the distinction between the two broad treatment goals of prevention and amelioration will be discussed.

In the final chapter, we discuss the notion of what we call the "adaptive deficit." This refers to a general disability which includes low intelligence but also involves a number of other deficits that relate to adaptation in the modern world (e.g., an inability, based on a lack of knowledge, to use societal resources; motivational deficits; poor coping and problem-solving strategies, etc.). It covers those who are formally recognized and classified as mentally retarded (and who, so labeled, are eligible for services and assistance) but emphasizes the much larger group of people who bear no label (and thus receive no assistance) but who have considerable difficulties adjusting to the demands of modern society.

The concept of the adaptive deficit is a natural, logical, and necessary extension of the concept of mental retardation in the context of our complex modern society. For the general problem of the match or interaction between persons of low intelligence and this society cannot be limited by a set of artificial cutoff points and neatly compartmentalized into the category of mental retardation. The full realization and appreciation of the intricate and intrinsic relationship between mental retardation and modern society demands that the field of mental retardation be prepared to broaden its focus.

# CHAPTER 2

# History of Mental Retardation and Intelligence

Where is the world going?
Look at its past.
What will we learn from it?
That we learn nothing from it.

Don't we learn from history?
Only that we have not learned from history.
Then, we are doomed to relive it again and again.
Or, to begin to learn from history.

*Burton Blatt* (1975)

Unlike such physical or medical conditions as pneumonia or tuberculosis, mental retardation is not a specific disease or entity. As we shall discuss in Chapter 4, mental retardation is simply a concept. Its defining characteristics vary from society to society and have changed radically even over brief periods of time. Our present ideas of mental retardation are rooted in the past and will clearly change in the years to come. Because the concept of mental retardation has evolved, this chapter explores the history of mental retardation in some detail. This overview[1] will provide a basis for the ideas and data presented in the following chapters as well as for the changes that might be expected in the future.

Broadly speaking, the history of mental retardation can be broken down into two periods: the *prescientific*, dating from primitive man up to the nineteenth century, and the *scientific*, from the nineteenth century to the present. The prescientific period merits little discussion, as there was practically no awareness or appreciation then of the concepts of intelligence or mental retardation. With the beginning of the modern period, however, there was a significant change in the thinking about man and his problems. For the first time, people began to examine things with an empirical, scientific approach that eventually yielded dramatic breakthroughs in many areas of human suffering, mental retardation among them. An analysis of this scientific period will dominate this chapter. The reader must keep in mind that the field of mental retardation is actually quite young (less than 200 years old), and some of the most significant developments have occurred only within the last 75 to 100 years. The most dramatic example of this is the fact that mild retardation, which comprises about 80 percent of all of the mentally retarded, was not even discovered or recognized until around the turn of this century.

## THE PRESCIENTIFIC ERA

Primitive man was probably aware of at least gross differences in ability. But the skills required for his existence bore little resemblance to present-day conceptions of intelligence. Primitive man was a nomadic creature who survived by hunting. The most "intelligent" (i.e., adaptive) men were no doubt the best stalkers, the fastest pursuers, and somewhat later, the most accurate spear throwers. All of these abilities or skills may be classified as motor prowess, but it does not appear that primitive societies had any concept of intelligence per se.

Eventually, man changed from a nomadic to a more sedentary-type

[1] Although numerous sources were consulted in writing this chapter, two texts have been particularly helpful: Kanner's *History of the Care and Study of the Mentally Retarded* (Charles C. Thomas, 1964) and *Psychological Problems in Mental Deficiency* (Harper & Row, 1969) by Sarason and Doris. The Kanner book is a clear and charming brief account of the early scientific history of this field. The Sarason and Doris book contains a detailed scholarly exposition of the complex interplay between sociopolitical and scientific factors in the history of mental retardation. We have quoted extensively from both of these sources throughout this chapter. The reader interested in the history of mental retardation is urged to consult them. The authors gratefully acknowledge the permission of these publishers to reproduce some of their materials.

creature. He acquired an agricultural base and added tools of production to those of aggression and protection. Agricultural implements and methods were slowly developed that could be easily used by the masses. The major requirement for existence became long, hard, but basically simple work in the fields. The weather and invading "barbarian" hordes were the major uncontrollable external forces that had to be dealt with. Such a system was probably capable of providing for the welfare of those of lesser ability, although we do not know if this in fact took place.

Much of the above is, of course, speculation. As we enter the age of recorded history, we might expect to learn more about the origins of man's awareness of and response to mental retardation. But such is not the case. Early civilized man had very little to say about either intelligence or mental retardation. In fact, it was not until the golden age of Greece that the concept of intelligence was even vaguely formulated. Aristotle introduced the concept of *nous* (intellect) as a species intellect. This *nous* was the principal factor differentiating man from the animals. But this formal recognition of man's mentality contained no notion of individual differences. Men were seen as different from animals by virtue of *nous*, but not different from each other in terms of the amount or degree of *nous* they each possessed.

The literature of ancient Greece and Rome reveals few references to the mentally handicapped and indicates that they were primarily treated with scorn and persecution. Roman parents evidently threw their blind, deaf, and mentally retarded children into the Tiber River to relieve themselves of the burden of support. Kanner (1964) reports that ancient literature reveals only one use for mental defectives—namely, the role of a fool or jester for the amusement of royalty. References to the retarded can also be found in the Bible, the Talmud, and the Koran, with indications that they were sometimes treated kindly. In summing up the history of mental retardation from ancient literature, Kanner concludes:

> The sum total of all these quotations, however, amounts to little beyond the fact that the existence of such persons was known and that occasionally friendliness toward them was advocated. There is no evidence of specific or organized efforts to do anything for their shelter, protection, or training. Though kind words were said about them from time to time, there was no practical application of any sort throughout many centuries. (p. 3)

It might be expected that with the dawn of Christianity, the example and teachings of Christ would lead to a more humane and responsible approach to the mentally retarded. Although there are increasing references

## BOX 2.1

### Etymology of Some Early Terms for Mental Retardation

The term "fool" was perhaps the first term used to denote mental retardation. In prescientific times, both the mentally retarded and the mentally ill were referents for this term, since there was often little distinction made between the two conditions.

Kanner (1964) notes that there are two possible sources for the meaning of the term "fool." One derivative is from the Latin word *fatuus* (fatuous and fatuity), which is the participle of the verb *fari*, meaning "to speak." According to Kanner, "a fatuus is a person who understands neither what he says himself nor what others say." The other possible source relates to a Roman seeress named Fatua, who was the wife of Faun. "Persons driven to stupefaction by her prophecies were called *fatui*, and this term was then transferred to all without a mind."

The other commonly used term was "idiot." It referred more specifically to mental retardation and was used in both the prescientific and scientific eras. In fact, the formal classification scheme of "idiot," "imbecile," and "moron" was employed even in the early 1900s. While this system is no longer formally used, the terms are part of the vernacular. We will quote from Kanner on the derivation of the terms "idiot" and "imbecile." The word "moron" was invented by Goddard (1910) and will be considered later.

> It is difficult to pinpoint the exact time at which the word *idiot* began to be employed in its present sense. Idiot derives from the Greek term that denotes "a private person." Hence, it came to mean "the common man." It then became reserved for "the unsophisticated layman without professional knowledge." As the next step, it was made to allude to "an ignorant, ill-informed individual." Ultimately, quite a bit later than in the writings of ancient Greeks, it was given the specific connotation of a mental defective.
>
> The term *imbecile* underwent a similar semantic change in the course of time. Originally, imbecillis meant weak and was used by the Roman writers (e.g., Celsus) for any form of debility. Eventually, it was restricted to weakness of the mind, less severe than that of an idiot. (Kanner, 1964, pp. 4–5)

to the kindness accorded some of the retarded, the treatment of the vast majority of the retarded changed little from the pagan to the Christian eras. Indifference characterized the Early Middle Ages. By the end of the Middle Ages, there were a variety of new responses. The retarded were sometimes thought to be "infants of God" and allowed to roam the streets of European cities unmolested. Once again, a select few served as court jesters or fools. They were often regarded with superstition and were thought to be mysterious prophets of God. Barr (1904) reports that the astronomer Tycho Brahe (1546–1601) had as a close companion an imbecile whose babblings he considered to be a form of divine revelation.

In one of the curious paradoxes of history, the treatment of the mentally retarded reached a low point during the age of "enlightenment" and "reform" (the eighteenth century). As Kanner (1964) notes: "It was then that many of them became victims of the prevailing demonism." Both Calvin and Luther denounced them as "filled with Satan." Luther even advocated drowning them because of their alleged possession by the Devil.

In reviewing the prescientific period, several conclusions can be drawn. First, there was little awareness of either intelligence or mental retardation. Second, what little awareness existed was really a recognition of, and response to, *gross deviance* (extreme difference). Mental retardation was often confused with mental illness and was usually associated with physical abnormality and deformity. In modern classification terms, the mentally retarded of the prescientific era were the profoundly and severely retarded of today. These persons often have concomitant gross and obvious physical, medical, and neurological problems. Thus, in the prescientific era, we are talking primarily about an awareness of and response to gross deviance, marked by severe intellectual as well as physical impairment. There was no awareness or recognition of mild mental retardation. The prescientific era is thus marked by a focus on gross deviance, in contrast to the emphasis on more subtle differences in the scientific era.

The final conclusion regarding the prescientific response to mental retardation is that there was considerable variability. At different times and in different cultures, the mentally retarded were considered to be either infants of God or of the Devil, left to die or employed for their entertainment value, and treated either kindly or cruelly. The explanations for retardation were either superstitious or supernatural. The vast majority of these persons suffered a miserable fate. At no time was there any real concern for them or provision for their care and treatment. All this was to change with the dawn of the scientific era.

## THE SCIENTIFIC ERA

The scientific approach to mental retardation began in the nineteenth century. Myriad factors and influences at this time brought about dramatic changes in man's awareness of and response to mental retardation. Most of these influences had nothing to do with mental retardation per se. They served as general antecedent and catalytic agents that produced a humanitarian outlook toward all of the handicapped and oppressed. A rational and empirical orientation was fostered, resulting in dramatic advances in medicine and science. Mental retardation was just one of the many beneficiaries. A brief sketch of these forces and events will be presented here.

### Philosophical and Political Background

Since the existence of severe mental retardation had been known for a long time, why had it taken man so long to deal with it? To answer this question, we must trace the origins and growth of the scientific approach in man's view of himself and his world. Until the emergence of this scientific outlook, no systematic attack on mental retardation was possible.

The scientific approach is rooted in the broad philosophical, religious, economic, political, and sociocultural changes that had taken place in Western Europe before the nineteenth century. We are talking primarily about the transition from the Middle Ages (usually dated from the fourth to the fifteenth centuries) to the modern period (beginning with the discovery of America in 1492). The actual period of transition is known as the Renaissance. A brief look at this transition will help clarify why the understanding of mental retardation was so long in coming.

*The Middle Ages* Historians in the past have often referred to the 1,000 years of the Middle Ages as the "Dark Ages." This pejorative term was applied because of the superstition and intellectual stagnation that allegedly characterized this period. While modern historians consider the appellation "Dark Ages" inappropriate and unjustified, there is no question that in comparison to both classical and modern man, medieval man was somewhat lacking in intellectual curiosity about himself and his world. Modern concepts of science and the whole issue of natural causes and laws were essentially unknown. Medieval man is perhaps best characterized as "otherworldly," more concerned about saving his soul than anything else. Religious concepts permeated and dominated all endeavors and conceptualizations of Western man. Thus, mental retardation, like all other forms of deviance, was considered in either superstitious or supernatural terms; no attempt was made to look at these conditions critically. (The fact that many deviance conditions, such as mental illness and mental retardation, were lumped together shows the lack of a critical focus.) Nature and worldly aims were regarded as temptations of the flesh or impediments to salvation. Given such a religious-philosophical outlook, there was no fertile soil from which a scientific perspective or orientation could emerge. Man had to first shift his focus and preoccupation from the "otherworld" to this world, from God to man. This dramatic change occurred during the Renaissance, preparing the way for the growth and development of science.

*The Renaissance (1350 to 1550)* The Renaissance was a time of reform and rebirth. The previous blind adherence to and reliance upon religious traditions and authorities was replaced by a pervasive skepticism. Man became secularized. He changed from a preoccupation with transcendental questions and problems of the "otherworld" to a devotion to the beauty of nature, the dignity of man, and an attempt to fully develop man's personality and gratify his senses. A pervasive individualism was manifested in business ventures and artistic creations. There was a spirit of free inquiry and curiosity about all things, which, combined with the new penchant for observation and careful description, led to the development of a scientific attitude. The great cultural and artistic achievements in this era engendered a spirit of confidence in man's achievements and possibilities and a desire to perfect and fulfill himself here on earth. For the first time since classical antiquity, man began to look at himself and his environment in a more natural, empirical, and rational manner. This was a striking contrast to the superstitious, supernatural approach of the medieval period.

Two forces had much to do with this revolution. By the end of the Renaissance, it had become clear that the goal of a united European Christendom would never be realized. The dominance and centrality of the Catholic Church in medieval Europe's intellectual, cultural, and political affairs, which accounted for the all-encompassing "religious-otherworldly" outlook, came to an end with the rise of the modern nation-state. Thus, the dominance of religion and religious conceptualizations was broken. Man was free to think instead of this world and himself. The second factor was an even more important ideological change. Copernicus had shocked his contemporaries with his theory that the earth was not at the center of the universe, an idea that had fit in nicely with the religious views of the time. Galileo's invention of the telescope confirmed the correctness of Copernicus' "heretical" allegation. Man was no longer the center of the universe, but rather a mere cosmic speck. Modern man has great difficulty appreciating the tremendous, shocking impact of such a discovery on medieval thinking. This drastic change in world view had immense theological implications and hastened the demise of religious domination. This discovery also increased man's willingness to look at himself and his environment more openly, naturally, and empirically (i.e., scientifically).

The empirical and rational trends of the fifteenth and sixteenth centuries were further emphasized in the seventeenth century. The crowning scientific achievement was Newton's explication of physical laws. Even the philosophers of the day were enamored with the expression of these "natural laws" in mathematical terms. The emphasis on mathematics, logic, and experimentation is the essence of the scientific approach. These trends culminated in the Age of Reason, or Enlightenment, of the eighteenth century. Here man was his most rational, empirical, and scientific. Science reigned over religion, thought over faith, and skepticism over traditional authority. There was the strong conviction that the application of a scientific approach would lead to the discovery of natural laws that would explain all human action and allow for the control and direction of human behavior. To use a mixed metaphor, there was absolute faith in the triumph of rational man and science.

*Humanism* Aside from preparing the ground for a scientific approach, the transition period in many other ways helped to focus attention and concern on various disabling and handicapping conditions. Basic to the cultural achievements of the Renaissance was the philosophy and attitude of humanism. Historians employ the label "humanism" to emphasize that Renaissance man was occupied with things human, in contrast to the theological preoccupations and otherworldly orientation of his medieval predecessor. Humanism stressed the dignity of man and sought to maximize his growth and development. The rise of humanism coincided with the individualism that also emerged during the Renaissance. This combined attitude contributed to the fall of the medieval feudal bondage system and the rise of the modern nation-state. Allegiance to the king was gradually replaced by the idea of a social contract between the individual and the state. The political culmination of this movement occurred during what historians call the Age of Revolution (1775 to 1795). This referred primarily to the American and French revolutions, although the revolutionary spirit was widespread across all of Europe. The essence of these revolutions was the declaration of individual human rights, as embodied in the American Bill of Rights and the French Declaration of Rights. All men were now deemed to be created equal and to have the inalienable rights of life, liberty, and the pursuit of happiness. A more specific humanitarian concern was expressed in the popular French revolutionary slogan: "Liberté, Égalité, Fraternité."

Although it took some time, these revolutionary ideas had definite implications for the afflicted and handicapped of all types. The focus on fundamental and inalienable rights eventually included the less fortunate, who for the first time became real objects of concern. In times past, the fate of these groups was left to the whim of the king, who usually did nothing about them. But now, all men were deemed to be created equal and to be covered by the same social contract. Man now had a legal and constitutional responsibility to his fellow man. When this was combined with the moral and religious responsibility to help the unfortunate, there was an imperative call for reform in man's approach and treatment. Thus, the first half of the nineteenth century witnessed dramatic humanitarian appeals for changes in the treatment of all oppressed, afflicted, and handicapped groups. Citizen advocacy (which will be covered later in this chapter) originated in the impassioned appeals of persons like Dorothea Dix in the United States on behalf of prisoners, poor people, slaves, the insane, and the idiots (as the mentally retarded were then called).

It was largely the force of these humanitarian appeals that was responsible for the application of the scientific approach to problems like mental retardation. Before the tools of science could be applied, however, attention first had to be focused on these people. Thus, while the resulting scientific achievements (and their authors) typically receive acclaim, it must not be forgotten that concerned citizens were largely responsible for setting the tone and direction of these movements.

## Societal Background

Three social trends have been largely responsible for the development of the modern concept of mental retardation. These forces are: industrialization, urbanization, and universal education. Although their influence is obviously interdependent, we will discuss them separately for purposes of analysis.

*Industrialization* Perhaps even more important than the political revolutions of the modern era was the Industrial Revolution. Many historians note that the term "revolution" is inappropriate for a movement that happened so gradually. But the effect was indeed revolutionary in terms of its transformation of the nature of work and the resultant effects on man's life. From the time primitive man became sedentary to his feudal bondage at the end of the medieval period, he was primarily agricultural.

His life and work centered on his or his master's land. The requirements for existence and survival were relatively simple and straightforward, though both his life and work may have been hard and unpleasant. But the severing of his feudal bonds was not too liberating. Although man shifted his political allegiance from the king to the state, he was eventually bound again—this time to a machine. Technological advances made increasing demands on man's adaptability. Life and work became more complex and the requirements for existence and survival more difficult. Specialization of labor increased, but the capricious law of supply and demand provided little security or stability. In general, industrialization demanded a more intelligent and flexible work force. This would eventually have important implications for the adaptability of the less intelligent on a scale never before seen. A more recent offshoot of industrialization, automation, offered the brief illusion that work would become even easier and more simplified. However, the actual result has been to automate the easiest jobs—particularly in agriculture, which has defined man's existence since primitive times. The profound implications of industrialism for life and work in general, and for the less intelligent in particular, cannot be overemphasized.

*Urbanization* Along with industrialization, and to a large extent because of it, man became increasingly urbanized. Industrialism, with its machines and factories, demanded large concentrations of people in cities. This urbanization led to further dramatic changes in life styles. It was more difficult and complex to live in the smaller confines of a city than on the spacious farmlands of the countryside. It was easy to awaken to the rooster's call and walk outside and begin hoeing. It was more difficult for some to have to set a clock (knowledge of how to tell time), at the right time (judgment), so that bus and subway connections (ability to read complicated schedules) would assure arriving on the job (assuming you could fill out the application and possessed the other skills for the job) on time (if you didn't arrive on time, you had to go through the whole process again and learn new times and schedules, etc.). In short, the requirements for existence and survival in an urbanized environment demanded a much different, and in many respects more difficult, set of skills and abilities. The adaptive potentials of less intelligent people are tested more frequently and stringently in a modern urbanized environment than they would ever be in a medieval, feudal, agricultural one.

*Mass Education* Today's student probably feels that education is both universal and perennial. However, such is not the case. Universal education is a modern phenomenon.

In medieval and earlier times, education was essentially a luxury and province of the rich and elite. Recall also that, in general, medieval man was probably less intellectually curious than either his classical or modern counterpart. He was satisfied with a supernatural and/or superstitious view of his world. It is only with Renaissance man and his desire to perfect himself that we see the beginning of an interest in education. The developing attitudes of humanism and individualism furthered this emerging interest. Education was seen as the road to enlightenment. Thus, man became an ardent advocate of formal learning. However, all of these influences were still restricted to the gentry. It was not until the revolutionary pressure of democracy that the importance, desirability, and necessity of universal education was really perceived and sought. For the social contracts of democracy to work, man had to be enlightened and educated. Democracy requires educated citizens for full participation. Thus, education was no longer a privilege or luxury of the rich and well born; it had become a necessity and birthright of all citizens. By the late 1800s, several countries were demanding a universal system of education. The need for education was reinforced by the Industrial Revolution, which required educated workers.

The drastic implications of universal education for the less intelligent seem obvious. The requirements for existence had been changed once again, and again had been made more complex and difficult. Unlike farm life, there were now purely academic demands. It is with the establishment of mass education that the plight of the slow learner first became recognized. Society now became aware of the fact that there were certain children who could not benefit from the standard curriculum. It was this fact that led to the development of intelligence tests and the resulting special education movement. This concept of special education on a massive scale would have never occurred without the prior notion that democracy and industrialism demanded a system of universal education and the fact that such a system could not be universally applied.

In summary, the preparation for the scientific attack on mental retardation was centuries old. It involved sweeping changes in the philosophical, religious, economic, political, and sociocultural fabric of society. In regard to mental retardation, the confluence of all these factors was conclusive. In the transition from the medieval to the modern period, man had not only discovered mild mental retardation, he may in fact have created it. The tremendous changes in society produced or precipitated even greater problems. This was particularly true for the less intelligent in terms of their ability to adapt to an increasingly complex society. Medieval man was unaware of and had no problem with mild mental retardation;

the requirements for existence and survival were simple and primarily physical. But modern man made the requirements for existence and survival a much more intellectual process. In so doing, he created the problem of mild mental retardation. The sociocultural context of mental retardation became obvious. In this sense, historical analysis indicates that mental retardation is truly and primarily a modern problem.

## SCIENTIFIC BEGINNINGS

The formal scientific attack on mental retardation depended on several preceding developments. As noted earlier, by the eighteenth century, enlightened man began to look at deviance in a more rational way. Increasing knowledge about human anatomy and physiology encouraged this new rational and empirical approach. Aside from a general interest in all kinds of medical problems and diseases, there was a new stress on psychopathology, including psychotic emotional disorders and severe mental retardation. In the past, these disorders had been viewed as the bizarre and mysterious workings of the Devil. But modern man began to suspect that something else was responsible. The first big breakthrough came in the early 1800s, when the organic basis of general paresis was discovered. This condition, which is caused by syphillis and results in paralysis, is accompanied by psychotic symptoms (bizarre behavior and thoughts). This was a momentous finding. Part of the mystery of bizarre human behavior was dispelled. There was a rational explanation for some kinds of "irrational" behavior. This discovery opened the door to further inquiry. It reinforced the conviction that scientific investigation would show that all human behavior, even the most deviant, was explainable in natural and rational terms.

However, a second breakthrough was essential before the study of mental retardation could begin. Previously, insanity and idiocy had been confused; neither condition could be studied effectively until they were differentiated. In his new observation and study of nature, modern man began to notice differences among the various mental disorders. Mental retardation had to be separated from the variety of conditions subsumed under the category of mental illness before progress could be made.

Many people had begun to perceive a basic difference between the mentally ill and the mentally retarded. The astute observations of the philosopher John Locke (1623–1704) concerning the difference between "madmen" and "idiots" are still relevant today.

> In fine, the defect in naturals seems to proceed from want of quickness, activity, and motion in the intellectual faculties, whereby they are deprived of reason: whereas madmen, on the other side, seem to

suffer by the other extreme, for they do not appear to me to have lost the faculty of reasoning, but having joined together some ideas very wrongly, they mistake them for truths, and they err as men do that argue right from wrong principles; for by the violence of their imaginations, having taken their fancies for realities, they make right deductions from them. . . .

In short, herein seems to lie the difference between idiots and madmen, that madmen put wrong ideas together, and so make wrong propositions, but argue and reason right from them; but idiots make very few or no propositions, and reason scarce at all. (1905, pp. 276–277)

However, while Locke and others had perceived the basic difference, what was needed was a formal, scientific explanation of this observation. It was the French psychiatrist Esquirol (1772–1840) who provided the essential diagnostic and conceptual breakthrough by pointing out the importance of the developmental factor.

Idiocy is not a disease, but a condition in which the intellectual faculties are never manifested; or have never been developed sufficiently to enable the idiot to acquire such an amount of knowledge, as persons of his own age, and placed in similar circumstances with himself, are capable of receiving. Idiocy commences with life, or at that age which precedes the development of the intellectual and effective faculties; which are, from the first, what they are doomed to be, during the whole period of existence. Everything about the idiot betrays an organization imperfect, or arrested in progress of development. We can conceive of no possibility of changing this state. . . . Dementia and idiocy differ essentially; otherwise the principles of every classification are illusory. . . . A man in a state of dementia is deprived of advantages which he formerly enjoyed; he was a rich man, who has become poor. The idiot, on the contrary, has always been in a state of want or misery. The condition of a man in a state of dementia may change; that of the idiot is ever the same. (1845, pp. 446–447)

Esquirol's developmental distinction has been incorporated in our current definition of mental retardation (Grossman, 1973/1977), in which one of the three criteria for a diagnosis of mental retardation is the requirement that it be "manifested during the developmental period." Note also his belief that mental retardation was "incurable" and "unchangeable."

This important conceptual distinction allowed Esquirol to propose the first classification system for mental retardation. His system was based on the person's use of language and is still relevant today. Esquirol proposed

BOX 2.2

Chronology: 1800 to 1900

1801 Publication of Itard's *De l'éducation d'un homme sauvage*, detailing his five years of intensive work with Victor, the "wild boy of Aveyron." This represents the first systematic attempt to treat a mentally retarded person.

1838 Seguin establishes an experimental class for the mentally retarded at the Salpetriere in Paris, a general asylum for all forms of human illness, misery, and degeneracy. He spent eighteen months trying to educate one particular "idiotic boy."

1841 Guggenbuhl establishes the Abendberg in Switzerland, the first major residential facility for the treatment of mental retardation. Others quickly followed all over the Western world (Berlin, 1842; Leipzig, 1846; Bath, England, 1846; Boston, 1848).

1842 Seguin becomes director of a portion of the Bicetre (the other general asylum near Paris), specifically set aside for the training of mentally retarded persons.

1843 Publication of Seguin's *Hygiène et éducation des idiots*, the first major treatise on the education of the mentally retarded.

1845 Esquirol makes the formal distinction between mental retardation and mental illness.

1846 Publication of Seguin's *Traitement moral, hygiène et éducation des idiots et des autres enfants arriérés*. This book, which spelled out the details of his "physiological and moral" method of instruction, was widely recognized and acclaimed.

1848 Howe establishes an "experimental school for idiots" at the Perkins Institute for the Blind in Boston. This is the first public institution in the United States. Wilbur opens a private school at Barre, Massachusetts, in the same year. Other public and private institutions quickly follow: New York, 1851; Pennsylvania, 1852; Connecticut, 1855; Ohio, 1857; Kentucky, 1860; Illinois, 1865.

1859 Publication of Darwin's *Origin of the Species.* The existence of variation in traits is established, laying the groundwork for the future study of individual differences.

1866 John Langdon Down describes "mongolian type of idiocy" as a separate syndrome of mental retardation.

1866 Publication of Seguin's *Idiocy, and Its Treatment by the Physiological Method.* This is the first major textbook on the treatment of mental retardation.

1867 The first "special class" is formed in Dresden, Germany.

1869 Publication of Galton's *Hereditary Genius.* This book argues for the inheritance of intelligence (and thus, by implication, mental retardation), introduces the method of the pedigree study, and inaugurates the human study of individual differences, particularly in terms of intelligence.

1876 Establishment of the Association of Medical Officers of American Institutions for Idiotic and Feeble-Minded Persons, which was later to become the American Association on Mental Deficiency (AAMD). Seguin was elected the first president.

1877 Publication of *The Jukes, a Study in Crime, Pauperism, Disease and Heredity* by Dugdale.

1877 Publication of William Ireland's *On Idiocy and Imbecility,* the first medically oriented textbook on mental retardation. He proposed 12 etiological subdivisions of mental retardation, thus ending all previous notions that it was a homogeneous condition.

1883 Publication of Galton's *Inquires into Human Faculty and Its Development.* In this work, Galton furthers the notion of individual differences in intelligence and its inheritability and introduces the term and concept of eugenics.

1890 Cattell introduces the term "mental test."

1896 The first special class in the United States is founded at Providence, Rhode Island.

three types of mentally retarded: (1) those making cries only (no speech); (2) those using monosyllables; and (3) those using short phrases but not elaborate speech. In modern terminology, his system includes the profound, severe, and low-moderate levels of mental retardation. Noticeably absent are the mildly retarded. However, this is consistent with the history of mental retardation.

## THE SCIENTIFIC STUDY OF MENTAL RETARDATION

Now that mental retardation was viewed as a natural phenomenon and had been differentiated from mental illness, the scientific study of mental retardation could begin. Modern psychiatry was founded and began to explore the many varieties of mental illness. Mental retardation was to become a discipline in its own right. In addition to the purely scientific concerns, there was the humanitarian desire to do something for all afflicted and disadvantaged groups.

### Early Pioneers

Although he himself made no contribution to the field of mental retardation, *Jacob Rodriques Pereire* (1715–1780) is often credited as the developer of many ideas and methods borrowed by the early pioneers. Pereire was interested in the education of congenital deaf-mutes and created a sensation in Europe by exhibiting a deaf-mute he had taught to speak and read. This had never been done before. He is most famous for introducing and applying the concept of sign language in the treatment of deaf-mutes.

The formal beginning of the scientific approach to mental retardation is usually associated with *Jean Marc Gaspard Itard* (1774–1838) and his efforts on behalf of the "Wild Boy of Aveyron." Itard, a student of Pinel, the father of modern psychiatry, was a young French physician who was working on the staff of the Institution for Deaf Mutes in Paris. (It should be noted that much of the early history of mental retardation is associated with institutions for the blind and deaf.) While he was working there, a boy was brought to the institution. He was about 11 or 12 years old, was naked, unable to talk, and seemed to have been living a wild existence. His hands were calloused and insensitive to extreme heat. Itard noted that he could pick a potato from a boiling pot without evidence of discomfort. There have been numerous reports of such "feral" (wild) children, raised by animals and deprived of human contact. In 1758 Linnaeus included them in his classification of human species as a separate category called "feral man." But before Itard, such cases were objects of speculation and curiosity, and no concerted effort had been made to teach them. As Kanner (1964) notes, the boy stirred the fantasy of the philosophers and scientists of the day. It must be recalled that this was the time of an emerging interest in education. Some people thought of the wild boy as Rousseau's "natural savage," and felt that here was the perfect opportunity to demonstrate the effectiveness and advantages of the new educational methods. Others disagreed. Pinel stated that he was "an incurable idiot, inferior to domestic animals." Itard took issue with his mentor's prognosis. "He believed that the boy was mentally arrested because of social and educational neglect, that he had acquired idiocy through isolation, a sort of mental atrophy from disuse. He undertook to transfer the boy 'from savagery to civilization, from natural to social life'" (Kanner, 1964, p. 14). Seguin (1866) notes that Itard named the wild boy Victor, "doubtless as a sign of the victory which education should achieve in him over brute nature."

Itard worked intensively and almost exclusively with Victor for the next five years. He undertook a long, methodical course of training in an attempt to teach him speech, self-care, manners, and social mores (i.e., to civilize him). While Victor made great strides in his education (he could recognize objects, identify letters of the alphabet, comprehend the meaning of many words, etc.), he never learned to speak, and Itard felt his program of instruction had failed. The French Academy of Sciences, however, did not share Itard's disappointment and applauded his efforts and achievements. In a statement commending him, it was noted:

> This class of the Academy acknowledges that it was impossible for the institutor to put in his lessons, exercises, and experiments more intelligence, sagacity, patience, and courage; and that, if he has not obtained a great success, it must be attributed not to any lack of zeal or talent, but to the imperfection of the organs of the subject upon which he worked.
>
> The academy, moreover, cannot see without astonishment how he could succeed as far as he did, and think that to be just toward Monsieur Itard, and to appreciate the real worth of his labors, the pupil ought to be compared only with himself; we should remember what he was when placed in the hands of his physician, see what he is now; and more, consider the distance separating his starting point from that which he has reached; and by how many new and ingenious modes of teaching this gap has been filled. (Kanner, 1964, p. 16)

There is much wisdom in the Academy's conclusion that "the pupil ought to be compared only with himself"; this applies even today in our efforts with the retarded. While Itard was unsuccessful in his attempt to make the boy "normal," he demonstrated that even a severely retarded person could be considerably improved with training. Finally, Itard's experiment was the first documented systematic attempt to teach a mentally retarded person.

Another pioneer in mental retardation was the Swiss physician *Johann Jacob Guggenbuhl* (1816–1863), who dedicated himself to the study and treatment of cretinism, a thyroid deficiency that results in severe mental retardation. He concluded that residential treatment was the best approach and in 1841 founded the Abendberg, the first residential institution for the mentally retarded. Guggenbuhl designed a comprehensive treatment program that involved medication, diet, and sensory stimulation. As Kanner (1964) notes, "he even introduced into the group two normally intelligent, though neglected, children of a servant who brought life into the institution!" Guggenbuhl's work, hailed everywhere as a major reform, influenced the founding of other institutions throughout the world. While Itard is the originator of an individualized learning approach to mental retardation, Guggenbuhl is the founder of institutional care.

We now turn to the man who probably deserves the title "father of mental retardation"—the French physician *Edouard Onesimus Seguin* (1812–1880). Seguin was a student of Itard and Esquirol. Like Itard, his early career focused on the education of the mentally retarded, despite his other mentor's (Esquirol) declaration that education was useless because "no means are known by which a larger amount of reason or intelligence can be bestowed upon the unhappy idiot, even for the briefest period" (Kanner, 1964, p. 35). Seguin borrowed from and greatly extended, elaborated, and systematized the methods of Itard. He was highly regarded both for his efforts and his educational program. As Kanner (1964) notes: "In 1844, a commission of the Paris Academy of Sciences, appointed at Seguin's request to examine ten of his pupils, declared that he had definitely solved the problem of idiot education." Even the skeptic Esquirol commented that Seguin had "removed the mark of the beast from the forehead of the idiot." In 1866, Seguin published the first textbook on the treatment of mental retardation. In it, he emphasized what he called the combined physiological and moral instruction of idiots. His methods have a clearly modern ring to them, for he was the forerunner of our current emphasis on individualized instruction, sensory-motor training, and even behavior modification. After working in France, Seguin went to the United States where he helped to found several institutions and generally advanced the study and treatment of mental retardation. When the forerunner of the current American Association on Mental Deficiency (AAMD) was founded in 1876, Seguin was elected as its first president.

The primary pioneer in mental retardation in the United States was *Samuel Gridley Howe* (1801–1876). He had visited Guggenbuhl's Abendberg and convinced the Massachusetts legislature to provide funds for a similar institution. As director of the Perkins Institution for the Blind in Boston, in 1848 he set aside a wing of that facility as an experimental school for the teaching and training of 10 mentally retarded children. Other institutions quickly followed. By 1875, there were 25 state institutions with a combined population of approximately 15,000.

The period of the pioneers was an era of great optimism. These highly dedicated and influential men created a movement that quickly spread across Europe and the United States. There was a widespread belief that mental retardation could be cured, a goal that was pursued with almost religious fervor. The enthusiasm generated by these men and their inspired goals had much to do with the rapid spread of the movement. Unfortunately, it also created much disappointment in the next era; the pioneers had raised expectations too high and promised too much.

## Period of Disillusionment and Pessimism

Although the condition of the mentally retarded had improved dramatically under the early pioneers, they were not "cured," as many had been led to believe. The small, well-staffed, nearly ideal institutions began to fill up. Part of the problem was that the expected discharges of residents back to the community rarely occurred. Further, the initial enthusiasm resulted in an increased number of people being referred for help. The besieged institutions were forced to dilute the services they could provide, further weakening the potential for improvement in their clients. The result was institutional expansion, in terms of both number and size, and a corresponding decrease in the quality of care.

A profound pessimism also developed because there were no cures. This was undoubtedly related to the unrealistic optimism of the previous era. People were not satisfied even with dramatic individual improvements; they had been led to expect a return to normalcy. Curiously, the lack of cure was now used to justify the permanent institutionalization of the very individuals who had lived in the community before the institutions were founded. They were now seen as totally unfit for normal living.

In analyzing these early periods of great optimism and profound pessimism, it is important to keep in mind which group of mentally retarded persons was involved. In both cases, we are talking about the severely retarded. The pioneers had contended, implicitly or explicitly, that they could cure the most severe forms of mental retardation. Needless to say, the cards were stacked against them. For as we know today, many of these persons have serious neurological problems. These would preclude full remediation regardless of the quality of education they received.

The disillusionment and pessimism of this period had a profound impact on the treatment of mental retardation. In the optimistic pioneer era, education was seen as the treatment method *par excellence*. There was a clear focus on training and upgrading. Even if cure was impossible, the appropriate educational program could work wonders. All this was to change with the pessimism of the ensuing period. Now that the mentally retarded were clearly "incurable," there was no longer any reason to attempt to educate them. Their condition was seen as essentially static. Since they could never go back to the community, there was no need to train or educate them for this purpose. The notion of custody began to supplant that of education.

Another strong influence on the shift in treatment philosophy was a practical problem. The increased number and size of the institutions caused a considerable financial burden. Added to a sense of futility was the feeling that it was a tremendous waste of money to employ the type of staff that would be needed. Furthermore, if the residents could be trained, the training should focus on service-type tasks that would make the institution self-sufficient and thus less expensive. In other words, the residents should help run the institutions. This idea ushered in the era of vocational rehabilitation and occupational training. While these were introduced under the altruistic guise of providing meaningful work for the mentally retarded, and no doubt did have some beneficial effects, the primary reason was expediency and convenience. The focus had shifted from educating and training the individual retarded person to running the institution as efficiently and cheaply as possible.

Thus, during the era of pessimism, the nature and character of the institutions had changed. The educational philosophies and methods of the early pioneers had been replaced by the notions of care and custody for the most severely deficient and occupational training in the service of the institution for the more mildly retarded. The dehumanization of institutions, so widely publicized today, began in this era of pessimism. The concept of the retarded as both incurable (and thus hopeless) and a financial burden made us lose sight of their dignity and potential as persons. Unfortunately, the worst was yet to come.

### Era of Indictment and Alarm

The era of pessimism was unfortunate but limited in its impact. It had implications for the mentally retarded but not for society as a whole.

While many more people were clamoring for services than in the past, they were still only a small percentage of the mentally retarded. Furthermore, the stress was still on the severe forms of mental retardation, which constitute only a small fraction (approximately 15 percent) of the whole. If these people couldn't be "cured," then they could remain in the institution. While this was expensive, it could be done without too much difficulty and, as we have seen, the mentally retarded themselves could ease the financial burden by providing services. All in all, despite the pessimism, the larger society was not much affected by whatever happened to the mentally retarded. At this time, there was no cause for concern.

All this was to change at the turn of the twentieth century. Society would be shocked out of its complacency, and the mentally retarded would become a cause for grave concern. The story of this dramatic change is a curious mixture of science and politics, starting with the theory of evolution and ending with eugenics. In the process, mild mental retardation was discovered. Many of the current degrading, inhuman, and erroneous ideas and stereotypes of the mentally retarded began in this dismal period of history. Perhaps most discouraging of all, the social indictment of the mentally retarded was brought about by some of the leaders of the mental retardation movement.

To understand this period of history, we must take a look at some of the scientific developments that had been occurring. The early pioneers were so optimistic about curing mental retardation because they perceived it to be environmentally determined. They felt the mentally retarded lacked the proper education. Accordingly, educational remediation was the cure that would make them normal. When the expected cures didn't occur, however, other hypotheses began to be entertained. Chief among them was the suspected role of heredity. Throughout the nineteenth century, there were numerous speculations that "insanity" and "idiocy" were inherited. The major theory was the "degeneration theory," which originated with a Frenchman named Morel, who published works on the subject in 1857 and 1860. Sarason and Doris (1969) describe his theory:

> For Morel degenerations were deviations from the normal human type, which were transmissible by heredity and which deteriorated toward extinction. Deviations from the normal human type included those afflicted with certain physical and psychiatric diseases, for example, the epileptic, the scrofulous, the psychotic, the mentally deficient, the moral deviate, and the alcoholic. The degeneration was subject to the "law of progressivity." The first generation of a degenerate line might be merely nervous, the second would tend to be

> neurotic, the third psychotic, while the fourth consisted of idiots who would tend not to reproduce and so lead to the extinction of the line. (pp. 210–211)

This theory consisted of two parts. First was the belief that the "hereditary taint" was polymorphous; that is, it could be expressed in different forms or diseases, such as mental illness or mental retardation. The second was the famous Lamarckian hypothesis regarding the hereditary transmission of acquired characteristics. This assumption stated that the experiences of parents affect their offspring. Alcoholism was seen as a primary villain. It was believed that alcoholism somehow affected (i.e., "tainted") the germ plasm of the parents, which was then passed on to their offspring, to be expressed in some polymorphous way (e.g., mental retardation). Samuel Howe, the originator of institutional care for the mentally retarded in the United States, firmly believed that mental retardation resulted from the transmission of acquired (usually sinful) traits.

> Suffice it to say now, that out of 420 cases of congenital idiocy examined, some information was obtained respecting the condition of the progenitors of 359. Now, in all these 359 cases, save only four, it is found that one or the other, or both, of the immediate progenitors of the unfortunate sufferers had, in some way, widely departed from the normal condition of health, and violated the natural laws. That is to say, one or the other, or both of them, were very unhealthy or scrofulous; or they were hereditarily predisposed to affections of the brain, causing occasional insanity; or they had intermarried with blood relatives; or they had been intemperate, or had been guilty of sensual excesses which impaired their constitutions. (1848, p. 34)

The degeneration theory, however, was not a cause for pessimism in regard to mental retardation. In fact, it allowed for great optimism since it implied that mental retardation could eventually be prevented. For the theory was ultimately an environmental one. Thus, if individuals were prevented from acquiring negative traits (alcoholism, sexual excesses), these traits could not be passed on to the next generation. This led to calls for social reforms which indirectly affected mental retardation. The future of mental retardation apparently depended on the effectiveness of social reform movements.

By the turn of the twentieth century, the degeneration theory had been discredited by the rediscovery of Mendel's laws of inheritance and the disproof of the Larmarckian hypothesis. However, as often happens, there was a considerable lag between the new knowledge and popular beliefs. Thus, the mentally retarded continued to be lumped together with all other social misfits and outcasts as expressions of "bad blood." It was becoming increasingly difficult to feel sorry for the offspring of such sinful parents. Extremely negative attitudes about them began to develop.

However, another nineteenth century scientific development made the degeneration theory look insignificant. While the physician-teachers (Itard, Seguin, and Howe) were making their pioneering efforts and advances, a scientific theory in the field of biology had far-reaching effects in both the natural and social sciences. It would ultimately have a direct and extremely powerful effect on the field of mental retardation. We are referring to Darwin's theory of evolution.

*Charles Darwin* presented his theory in 1859 with the publication of *Origin of the Species*. The key elements in his theory are the concepts of variation, natural selection, and the hereditary transmission of variation. Darwin stressed that variability among plants and animals exists and that some of this variation is inherited. Furthermore, there is a selective breeding process wherein some members of a species, due to their unique variations, are able to survive longer (and thus breed more) because they are "fitted" to deal with the demands of the environment. In other words, Darwin explained life in terms of a struggle for existence in which the weak members of a species are constantly being eliminated and only the "fittest" survive through the process of natural selection. The doctrine of "survival of the fittest" was to have direct and dire implications for the mentally retarded in terms of society's perceptions and attitudes about them and the resulting reaction to them.

It was Darwin's half cousin, *Sir Francis Galton*, who was primarily responsible for applying evolutionary theory to humans. Galton's impact on psychology and mental retardation (although he had nothing to do with the mentally retarded per se) is profound.

Prior to Darwin, science had ignored individual differences. They were seen as bothersome sources of error. Experimental psychology was interested in discovering universal laws that applied to all persons and situations. Differences or variations were considered anathema. Darwin changed all this. His theory rested on the observation that differences existed and that this fact had important evolutionary implications. For the first time, man began to focus on and to study individual differences.

The notion of individual differences is critical to the history of mental retardation. Without this notion, the discovery of mild mental retardation could not have occurred. Recall that in the prescientific period, there was no awareness of differences in ability. Only gross and obvious deviance was recognized. With this exception, all men were considered to be essentially the same in ability. Differences in performance were attributed to motivation and/or morals, not to some personal characteristic such as intelligence. Darwin taught us to look at and appreciate the fact and significance of variation and difference. Galton took this orientation and focused on human differences, documenting and quantifying them. In this regard, he was influenced by the Belgian statistician Quetelet (1796–1874), who first applied the normal probability curve (the "bell-shaped" curve) of Laplace and Gauss to human data. (Quetelet showed, for example, that the height of French soldiers was normally distributed, as was the girth of their Scottish counterparts.) Galton applied Quetelet's statistics and demonstrated that many human variables, both physical and psychological, were also distributed normally. He suggested that this was particularly true of intelligence. (The distribution of intelligence is discussed more fully in the next chapter.) Even Darwin had not considered the possibility of individual differences in intelligence and told his half-cousin so in a letter:

> You have made a convert of an opponent in one sense, for I have always maintained that, excepting fools, men did not differ much in intellect, only in zeal and hard work. (Pearson, 1914, p. 6)

Galton made one additional important assumption. The theory of evolution stated that much of the variation among a species was inherited. Galton stated that this was also true of intelligence—i.e., that the normal distribution of intelligence was the result of heredity. In doing so, he dispelled the centuries-old notion that men differed because of their efforts or morals.

> I have no patience with the hypothesis occasionally expressed, and often implied, especially in tales written to teach children to be good, that babies are pretty much alike, and that the sole agencies in creating differences between boy and boy, and man and man, are steady application and moral effort. It is in the most unqualified manner that I object to pretensions of natural equality. The experiences of the nursery, the school, the University, and of professional careers are a chain of proofs to the contrary. (Galton, 1869, p. 14)

It must be emphasized that nothing about the normal distribution of intelligence forces this conclusion. A normal distribution could result from purely genetic causes, purely environmental causes, or an interaction between them.

Galton's genetic conclusion was based on the results of his study of genius, published in 1869, just 10 years after Darwin's *Origin of the Spe-*

*cies*, under the title *Hereditary Genius*. His "proof" of the inheritance of intelligence rested on his observation that "genius" has a tendency to run in families. His method (using eminence or reputation as an indication of genius) might be questioned, but he clearly documented that eminent families tended to have eminent offspring. While we know today that these findings can also be explained on an environmental basis, they were considered at the time to be positive proof of the role of heredity. It was only a small step to the related conclusion regarding "feeblemindedness," or mental retardation.

Galton's revolutionary proposal regarding the inherited basis of individual differences in intelligence merits attention. First, it should be noted that Galton's proposition came just 100 years after the revolutionary movements in Europe and the United States had decreed that all men are created equal. Galton was suggesting that this was absolutely and irrevocably false. And whereas many had believed that inequalities were the result of educational differences that could be easily remedied, Galton suggested that such efforts were futile. This had definite implications for mental retardation. The early pioneers had seen it as curable because it was an environmental/educational deficiency. Galton's theory implied that it is inherited and thus not amenable to treatment or remediation. This turn of events shows how our view of intelligence can have drastic implications for our view of mental retardation and its possible prevention or amelioration.

Second, Galton was not afraid to generalize his findings to all mankind and to act upon the implications of his theory. In his 1883 book, *Inquires into Human Faculty and Its Development*, he argued that there were racial differences in intelligence and advocated a program of "eugenics" (he coined the term) to improve mankind. He defined eugenics as "the science which deals with all influences that improve the inborn qualities of a race." The proposed method of racial improvement was selective breeding. In so doing, Galton started the continuing controversy about racial differences in intelligence and provided the impetus for the eugenic alarms of the first two decades of the twentieth century, when the alleged "social menace of the feebleminded" was of great national concern. With issues like race and eugenics as part of the history of mental retardation, it is easy to understand why this field has been and continues to be so sensitive and provocative. It is important to realize that the roots of many of our current controversies go back almost one hundred years. Sarason and Doris (1969) neatly sum up Galton's argument and appeal:

> By contending that intellectual ability was a variable and inheritable trait in mankind Galton had applied to mankind the principle of

> natural selection and hence of evolutionary development of intelligence. He saw the various races of mankind as differing in intelligence in accordance with the degree of civilization that they were capable of developing and sustaining. These differences in races presumably occurred through the slow and chance-like operation of natural selection and led Galton to the converse argument of Darwin's *Origin of Species.* There Darwin opened his argument with observations on the artificial development of races and species of animals and plants under domestication and then proceeded to develop his argument for natural selection. Galton, pointing to presumed intellectual differences naturally occurring between races, nations, and families, argued for artificial selection and breeding of man in order to produce a superior race. And in this proposal for an improvement of the human breed by artificial selection—with a concomitant solution to existing social problems—lies the second and probably more important reason for the ready acceptance of Galton's argument. (p. 236)

Galton left behind one other legacy which had both a general and a specific effect. His interest in the study of individual differences and the attempt to quantify these differences ushered in the school of differential psychology. This school was primarily responsible for the development and growth of psychological tests and testing. The first and most famous of these was the intelligence test, which was to have a profound impact on the field of mental retardation. Most importantly, it was the primary means for the discovery of mild mental retardation.

## Intelligence Tests and the Discovery of Mild Mental Retardation

The credit for the first successful intelligence test goes to the French psychologist Alfred Binet. But perhaps indirectly, the credit should go to the mentally retarded. For it was because of mental retardation that Binet was requested to develop his test.

We must remember that the democratic and industrial revolutions required an educated citizenry. Consequently throughout Europe and the United States, universal education was being implemented. It became quickly apparent, however, that this system could not be applied to everyone. Too many children could not benefit from the standard public school curriculum. Awareness of this fact had already resulted in the development of "special classes" in several countries.

The first special class started in Germany in 1867. By 1905 (the year Binet introduced his test), Kanner (1964) reports that 181 German cities had 583 special classes (81 in Berlin alone), with a total enrollment of

6,623 boys and 5,300 girls. Other countries had also developed such classes, with the first in the United States started in 1896 in Providence, Rhode Island. Although not formerly recognized as such, many of the pupils of these classes were the equivalent of our mildly mentally retarded. As a result of the new educational demands, the problem was beginning to come to society's attention. What was needed was a practical and reliable method for determining who could not benefit from public education and who, therefore, required a special class.

Although France led the mental retardation movement (e.g., Itard and Seguin), it lagged behind other countries in the development of the special class. However, as the French began to institute their own public education system, they also became acutely aware of the problem of "slow learners." However, they felt the selection process was critical, and wanted an objective method for eliminating those who could not benefit from the regular classes. Accordingly, the French Minister of Public Instruction commissioned Alfred Binet to develop a workable screening method. The method he developed was first (in contemporary terminology) a device for screening mental retardation and second an intelligence test.

Prior to Binet, attempts to measure intelligence had focused primarily on simple sensory processes or functions, such as reaction time, two-point discrimination (i.e., the minimum distance on the skin at which two points of stimulation could still be felt), and so forth. It was assumed that these sensory processes were the basis of intelligence and that individuals differed in these abilities. However, numerous studies demonstrated that the measurement of these sensory processes was of little value. Binet agreed. He felt that individuals differ least in these sensory processes and that they had little to do with intelligence. He believed that a scale of intelligence should attempt to measure a wide variety of complex mental processes and that individual differences would be strongest in these "higher" mental areas. It was such complex mental processes as memory, reasoning, and judgment that constituted for Binet the essence of intelligence and that he believed would best differentiate individuals. His definition of intelligence was a practical one:

> It seems to us that in intelligence there is a fundamental faculty, the alteration or the lack of which, is of the utmost importance for practical life. This faculty is judgment, otherwise called good sense, practical sense, initiative, the faculty of adapting one's self to circumstances. To judge well, to comprehend well, to reason well, these are the essential activities of intelligence. (Binet and Simon, 1916, pp. 42–43)

In collaboration with Theodore Simon, a student of medicine and psychology, Binet set about to measure these complex mental functions. The first Binet-Simon scale was published in 1905. In 1908 a revision was published, and with it the concept of "mental age" was introduced. The various test items were arranged according to increasing difficulty, with chronological age used as the criterion of difficulty. In other words, items were grouped according to the age at which children generally passed or failed. Mental age was determined by assessing at what level an individual performed. A child who passed all of the items up to and including those at the six-year level would have a mental age of six, regardless of his chronological age. The use of mental age allowed for comparisons between one child and his age peers. A third and final revision of the original Binet scale was published in 1911—the year Binet died. Binet's scale and his idea of measuring complex mental processes were received enthusiastically and translated into almost every primary language.

Henry Goddard, director of the Training School at Vineland, New Jersey (for the mentally retarded), had visited Binet's laboratory in Paris and brought the scale back with him. After translating it, he began using it at his institution as well as in the public schools. Somewhat later (1916), Lewis Terman and his associates at Stanford University conducted a major revision and standardization of the Binet scale, calling it the Stanford-Binet Intelligence Scale. Along with this revision, Terman introduced the concept of the Intelligence Quotient (IQ). This idea, which had been proposed by the German psychologist, Wilhelm Stern in 1912, was simply a ratio of mental age divided by chronological age ($MA \div CA \times 100 = IQ$). The IQ made individual comparison of intelligence level an easy (albeit somewhat erroneous) matter. Terman's scale and the term "IQ" popularized the idea of psychological tests and assessment. Intelligence tests became widely used in the educational system. The ability to describe someone's mental age was seen as having great "diagnostic-prescriptive" value, for it allowed the teacher to tailor the curriculum to the needs and abilities of the child.

The importance of Binet's work cannot be overestimated. First, he produced a concrete, reliable, and practical method for evaluating a person's mental functioning. Second, this method allowed for the quantitative determination of the differences among people. Darwin and Galton had stated that individual differences exist, but it was Binet's test that concretely demonstrated both their existence and their extent. Furthermore, as Kanner (1964) notes: "It became evident that intellectual inadequacy was not an absolute, all-or-none attribute, as had been previously assumed. There were gradations from the slightest deviation to the most profound state of deficiency" (p. 122). Third, the fine gradations made possible by the use of the IQ test indicated that there were many people whose intelligence fell between the severely retarded and the average. Mild mental retardation was, thus, officially discovered and recognized. The previous special classes suggest that people already suspected that such a group existed. Binet's test not only substantiated these views but indicated that the problem was much greater than anyone had believed.

Goddard (1910) proposed the label "moron" for this group of "borderline" persons. He described the problem and his reasons for the choice of the label as follows:

> I presume no one in this audience, certainly none of the superintendents of institutions need to be reminded that the public is entirely ignorant of this particular group. Our public school systems are full of them, and yet superintendents and boards of education are struggling to make normal people out of them. One of the most helpful things that we can do would be to distinctly mark out the limits of this class and help the general public to understand that they are a special group and require treatment,–in institutions when possible, in special classes in public schools, when institutions are out of reach. Two words have been suggested for this group, the one being the word "proximate" with the underlying thought that these children are nearly normal. The other word proposed is a Greek word, the noun from the Greek word meaning foolish, "moronia," and these children might be called "morons"; fool or foolish in the English sense exactly described this group of children. The Century dictionary defines a fool as one who is deficient in judgment, or sense, etc., which is distinctly the group we are working with. I believe the etymology is correct and the derivatives would be easy. We would have moron for the noun, moronia for the condition, moronic for the adjective, and so it would seem to answer every requirement. (p. 364)

The discovery of the moron was "alarming." It indicated that a significant number of persons were subnormal and needed special assistance. This had the positive effect of awakening the public to a heretofore unknown problem. The result was an increase in the special education movement. However, the main effect of this discovery was negative. The problem appeared to be of overwhelming proportions and was further highlighted by the results of the massive testing that occurred during World War I.

When the United States entered the war huge numbers of men had to be quickly tested to determine their abilities for a wide variety of military demands. The newly developed intelligence tests were quickly chosen

BOX 2.3

| | |
|---|---|
| 1900–1930 | Era of Indictment–"The Social Menace of the Feeble-minded" |
| | *General Characteristics* |
| | –Rediscovery of Mendel's laws of inheritance and the resulting view of mental retardation as a unitary, recessively inherited trait. |
| | –Development of intelligence tests and their use on a massive scale in the schools and military (World War I). |
| | –"Discovery of the moron" (mild mental retardation) through the use of the intelligence tests and alarm over their numbers. |
| | –Series of pedigree studies and surveys "demonstrating" that mental retardation is inherited and associated with all sorts of social ills and evils. |
| | –Resulting anxiety over the "decline of civilization." |
| | –Social Darwinism and the sounding of eugenic alarms. |
| | –Calls for segregation and sterilization of the mentally retarded. |
| 1903 | Formation of the American Breeders Association, which advocated eugenics. |
| 1904 | Publication of Barr's *Mental Defectives, Their History, Treatment and Training*. This is the first general textbook on mental retardation. |
| 1904 | The French Minister of Public Education commissions Binet to develop a method for "screening out the slow learners." |
| 1905 | Publication of the Binet-Simon scale of intelligence, the first successful test of intelligence. Later revisions in 1908 and 1911. |
| 1907 | Indiana passes the first sterilization law. |
| 1910 | Goddard translates the Binet-Simon scale into English. |
| 1912 | Publication of Goddard's *The Kallikak Family*. |

| | |
|---|---|
| 1916 | Reanalysis of Dugdale's 1877 study of the Jukes by Estabrook, in which he concludes that one-half of the Jukes were feebleminded and all of the Jukes criminals were feebleminded. |
| 1916 | Publication of the Stanford-Binet test by Terman, the first standardized test of intelligence. The concept of IQ introduced and popularized with this test. |
| 1916 | World War I and the massive intelligence screening of recruits. |

for this screening and selection. The utility and efficiency of the various intelligence tests that were developed for this purpose did much to put IQ tests and psychological testing on the map. In addition, this massive testing program provided a huge amount of data on tested intelligence, norms, and so forth. The results of the Army testing program were not made available to the public until 1921. In general, the data suggested that Goddard's "moron" was far more prevalent than anyone had expected. As Sarason and Doris (1969) note:

> News of the Army test results had begun to filter out even before the publication of the official report and immediately eugenical alarms arose. Fears began to be expressed for the future of democracy if such was the intellectual level of the mass of its electorate. (p. 300)

In short, the use of the IQ test in education and military settings led to the discovery of the moron. This discovery was "alarming" for two reasons. First, the sheer number of morons discovered was "shocking." Even more important, however, was the growing conviction that the moron was a "social menace." Given this attitude, the problem of their numbers was even more ominous. We will now explore how the mentally retarded came to be perceived as a social menace.

## The Social Menace of the Feebleminded

Many complex factors, acting together, produced a sense of alarm and eventual social indictment of the mentally retarded in the first two decades of the twentieth century. The first factor was the rediscovery of Mendel's laws of inheritance around the turn of the century. Mental retardation came to be viewed as a unitary, recessively inherited trait that followed the simple Mendelian ratios that had been demonstrated with the sweet pea plant. The view of mental retardation, as a unitary—or an all-or-nothing—phenomenon, differed strongly from the view of intelligence derived from the IQ tests and Galton's hypothesized normal distribution. In the latter case, intelligence was construed as the result of the blending of parental traits in the offspring. The Mendelians, however, won out. Part of the "proof" for this unitary conceptualization of intelligence was supplied by the infamous "pedigree studies." Galton had introduced the methodology of these studies in his book, *Hereditary Genius.* Family lines were studied, and the incidence of a particular characteristic (e.g., genius, mental retardation, mental illness) was noted. The two most famous of these pedigree studies were called the "Jukes" and the "Kallikaks."

In 1877, a New York penologist named Dugdale published a genealogical survey titled *The Jukes, a Study in Crime, Pauperism, Disease and Heredity.* Dugdale had discovered six men in the prison system who were all blood relations. He traced their family lineage back to two sons of a backwoodsman. Of the 1,200 descendants of these two sons, information was obtained on 709. Kanner (1964) notes that "of these, 140 had been imprisoned for crime, 280 were paupers dependent on public support, and the majority were of low physical and moral standard" (p. 129). Significantly, however, Dugdale himself made no special mention of mental retardation. The book was reprinted in 1910. In 1916, a man named Estabrook, from the Department of Experimental Evolution of the Carnegie Institution, did a follow-up investigation. Without any attempt at intellectual assessment, he somehow concluded that all of the criminal descendants were mentally defective and that "one-half of the Jukes were and are feebleminded" (Kanner, 1964). Aside from corroborating the alleged hereditary basis of mental retardation, the findings regarding criminality did much to convince people that the mentally retarded were actual or potential criminals. A number of other pedigree studies purported to show that mental retardation was linked with just about every conceivable social evil and ill (e.g., crime, alcoholism, prostitution and promiscuity, immorality, and pauperism). The most famous and influential pedigree study was Goddard's (1912) study of the Kallikak family. As Kanner (1964) notes: "The story of the Kallikaks kindled a spark which soon burst into flames and drove a number of volunteer firefighters to frantic activity" (p. 130).

The family background of one of the "inmates" at the Training School at Vineland, where Goddard was the director, had been traced back to a Martin Kallikak, who was a member of the Revolutionary Army (1776). Sometime during the war, he met a "feebleminded" girl in a tavern and had a son, Martin Kallikak, Jr., by her. After the war, he returned home and married a "respectable girl of good family" and had another line of descendants. Goddard considered this situation to be "a natural experiment of remarkable value to the sociologist and to the student of heredity." As Kanner (1964) notes, Goddard invented the fictitious name "Kallikak" to describe the "good-bad" lines of descendants.

> The name Kalliakak, invented by Goddard, stems from a combination of two Greek words: *kalos,* meaning attractive, pleasing, and *kakos,* meaning bad, evil. Thus the name was to symbolize the two lines of the descendants of Martin Sr., one respectable, intelligent, well adjusted, and the other worthless, a blot on society. (p. 132)

Because of the importance and impact of this study, we have included some of Goddard's reported data and comments in Box 2.4. Deborah Kallikak, the inmate at Vineland, had a mental age of nine years on the "new" Binet scale. She thus represented the new class, the "moron." The data regarding her family background were generalized to all morons, and this helps explain why the discovery of the moron was so "alarming."

The reader today can easily point out the methodological flaws of the pedigree study. The role of the environment is never acknowledged or dealt with. An even more critical problem relates to the method of determining that Martin Kallikak, Sr., did indeed sire the son of this "nameless feebleminded girl" whom he met in a tavern. Goddard's own assertions regarding the promiscuity of the feebleminded should also apply to her. But flaws notwithstanding, the study was accepted uncritically. Why? The reasons have to do with the sociopolitical nature of the times and indicate how "objective science" is often perverted by nonscientific concerns. Sarason and Doris (1969) summarize the situation:

> Goddard's work at Vineland was a major factor in the development of attitudes toward the retardate that prevailed from approximately 1910 to 1920—typified by the catch phrase "the menace of the feebleminded." In this view many of the major social evils of the times were seen as stemming in large part from mental deficiency. The contribution of the mental retardate to crime, prostitution, and pauperism

## BOX 2.4

### Excerpts from Goddard's Published Study: The Kallikak Family

> [This story is] as instructive as it is amazing. We have here a family of good English blood of the middle class, settling upon the original land purchased from the proprietors of the state in Colonial times, and throughout four generations maintaining a reputation for honor and respectability of which they are justly proud. Then a scion of this family, in an unguarded moment, steps aside from the paths of rectitude and with the help of a feeble-minded girl, starts a line of mental defectives that is truly appalling. After this mistake, he returns to the traditions of his family, marries a woman of his own quality, and through her carries on a line of respectability equal to that of his ancestors.

Regarding the descendants from the son born to the feeble-minded girl, he notes:

> From him have come 480 descendants; 143 of these, we have conclusive proof were or are feebleminded while only forty-six have been found normal. The rest are unknown or doubtful. Among these 480 descendants, thirty-six have been illegitimate; there have been thirty-three sexually immoral persons, mostly prostitutes; there have been twenty-four confirmed alcoholics; there have been three epileptics; eighty-two died in infancy; three were criminals; eight kept houses of ill fame. These people have married into other families, generally of about the same type, so that we now have on record and charted 1,146 individuals. Of this large group, we have discovered that 262 were feebleminded, while 197 were considered normal, the remaining 581 being still undetermined.

Regarding the descendants from the lawful "respectable" wife, he notes:

> These now number 496 in direct descent. . . . All of the legitimate children of Martin Sr. married into the best families in their

state, the descendants of colonial governors, signers of the Declaration of Independence, soldiers, and even the founders of a great university. Indeed, in this family and its collateral branches, we find nothing but good representative citizenship. There are doctors, lawyers, judges, educators, traders, landholders, in short, respectable citizens, men and women prominent in every phase of social life.

Some of Goddard's concluding comments on the study:

We have, as it were, a natural experiment with a normal branch with which to compare our defective side. We have the one ancestor giving us a line of normal people that shows thoroughly good all the way down the generations, with the exception of the one man who was sexually loose and the two who gave way to the appetite for strong drink.

This is our norm, our standard, our demonstration of what the Kallikak blood is when kept pure, or mingled with blood as good as its own.

Over against this we have the bad side, the blood of the same ancestor contaminated by that of the nameless feeble-minded girl.

From this comparison the conclusion is inevitable that all this degeneracy has come as the result of the defective mentality and bad blood having been brought into the normal family of good blood, first from the nameless feeble-minded girl and later by additional contamination from other sources.

The biologist could hardly plan and carry out a more rigid experiment or one from which the conclusions would follow more inevitably.

H. H. Goddard. *The Kallikak family: A study in the heredity of feeblemindedness*. New York: Macmillan, 1912.

was exaggerated to fantastic heights. This, combined with the assumed hereditary basis of mental retardation and the further assumption of the higher fecundity of the retardate, led to the frightful prospect of the degeneration of the race and the decay of civilization. . . .

Because of the widespread popularity and the uncritical acclaim with which The Kallikak Family were first greeted, Goddard's view of the social burden of feeblemindedness therein presented was assured widespread influence that contributed much to the growth of the eugenics movement. That view was that feeblemindedness was largely responsible for the social problems represented by paupers, criminals, prostitutes, and drunkards. The Kallikaks were examples of that high grade of feeblemindedness—the moron type—that makes for a massive burden on society. In them [Sarason and Doris now quote directly from Goddard, 1912, pp. 70–71] . . . we have the type of family which the social worker meets continually and which makes most of our social problems. A study of it will help to account for the conviction we have that no amount of work in the slums or removing the slums from our cities will ever be successful until we take care of those who make the slums what they are. Unless the two lines of work go on together, either one is bound to be futile in itself. If all of the slum districts of our cities were removed tomorrow and model tenements built in their places, we would still have slums in a week's time because we have these mentally defective people who can never be taught to live otherwise than as they have been living. Not until we take care of this class and see to it that their lives are guided by intelligent people, shall we remove these sores from our social life.

There are Kallikak families all about us. They are multiplying at twice the rate of the general population, and not until we recognize this fact, and work on this basis, will we begin to solve these social problems. (pp. 255–256 and 259)

One other factor at the time had relevance to the alarm over feeblemindedness. This was racism and the movement for highly selective and restrictive immigration laws:

The growing racist attitudes in America in the latter part of the nineteenth century were expressed in the increasing demands for immigration restrictions which would preserve the blood of the old immigrant stock from northern Europe—the blood that had founded this country and made it great (Haller, 1963). The increasing flood of immigration from southern and eastern Europe with its alien Catholic and Jewish religions, its foreign folkways and strange tongues, alarmed a native population already stressed by the rapid social and economic changes that followed the Civil War. (Sarason and Doris, 1969, p. 291)

The concern over immigration increased in the first two decades of the twentieth century. There was the widespread belief that the more recent immigrants were clearly of inferior quality. Goddard decided to check out this hypothesis by testing the immigrants with the Binet scale. Since many of the new immigrants did not speak English, he used translators to give the test. (The incredible misuse of intelligence tests, so talked about today, was occurring only shortly after their inception.) As one might expect, Goddard "found" that a high proportion of the new immigrants were feebleminded. The post-World War I studies of the massive intelligence data collected on Army recruits were also used to demonstrate the "inferiority" of many racial and ethnic groups. There was a clear movement to demonstrate that any but pure Anglo-Saxons were inferior. The admission of these people to the United States was seen as diluting the quality of society.

> Thus the testing movement in its studies of immigrant groups and in particular through the results of the Army testing program–by charging various racial and ethnic groups with inferior intelligence and proportionately higher rates of feeblemindedness–contributed to both racist and eugenical thought and help to cement the growing alliance between racism and eugenics. This alliance was to insure for eugenics one of its greatest successes in social action programs. This success consisted in furthering the enactment of increasingly restrictive immigration laws throughout the twenties. (Sarason and Doris, 1969, p. 310)

Understanding the attitude toward immigrants is important in helping to put in perspective the alarm over the mentally retarded. There was a general reaction against any defect or difference. All persons deviating from the norm were seen as social misfits who posed serious problems for the future of society and civilization.

## Sounding the Eugenic Alarms

The mildly mentally retarded had been indicted and convicted of practically every social evil. They were immoral, criminal, and parasitic. Ironically, many leaders of the mental retardation movement themselves contributed, albeit sometimes inadvertently, to this indictment. Kanner (1964) relates the mood of the period:

> With so much "evidence" made available within a few years, the eugenic guardians of the race and its civilization came forth with emotionally charged blasts. We shall be lost unless something drastic

## BOX 2.5

The Social Indictment of the Feebleminded
by Experts and Workers in the Field

Dr. Anne Moore, who conducted a widely publicized survey on the feebleminded in New York City, emphasized the causal relationship between feeblemindedness and poverty, immorality, and crime and argued for the segregation of all defectives.

> The feeble-minded at large are dangerous, if not more dangerous, than persons suffering from contagious disease. No consideration of cost, of parental affection and responsibility, or of personal liberty should be allowed to weigh against public safety. (Moore, 1911, p. 93)

Dr. Wilhelmine Key conducted another widely publicized survey of a rural Pennsylvania area. This study was noteworthy because it "documented" the supposed fecundity of defective women and alerted the public to its "disastrous" consequences.

> It is to the unrestrained reproduction of the feeble-minded woman that we owe the disproportionate increase of the socially unfit, with their burden of pauperism, delinquency, and crime. Already this burden is almost intolerable. What will it be a few generations hence? (Key, 1915, p. 38)

Terman was the author of the Stanford-Binet test, the first standardized version of the Binet scales, published in 1916. It was this version that introduced and popularized the concept of IQ. This quotation is taken from his influential book on the measurement of intelligence, published in the same year.

> But why do the feeble-minded tend so strongly to become delinquent? The answer may be stated in simple terms. Morality depends upon two things: (a) the ability to foresee and to weigh the possible consequences for self and others of different kinds of behavior; and (b) upon the willingness and capacity to exercise self-restraint. That there are many intelligent criminals is due to the fact that (a) may exist without (b). On the other hand, (b) presupposes (a). In other words, not all criminals are feeble-minded, but all feeble-minded are at least potential criminals. That every feeble-minded

> woman is a potential prostitute would hardly be disputed by anyone. Moral judgment, like business judgment, social judgment, or any other kind of higher thought process, is a function of intelligence. Morality cannot flower and fruit if intelligence remains infantile. (Terman, 1916, p. 11)

Walter E. Fernald, superintendent of the Massachusetts State School, was a highly respected and influential figure in the field of mental retardation. It should be noted that he later recanted these remarks in the first major follow-up study of persons released from institutions. That study (published in 1919) showed that many of the purported dangers to society emphasized in the quotation here were unfounded.

> The social and economic burdens of uncomplicated feeble-mindedness are only too well known. The feeble-minded are a parasitic, predatory class, never capable of self-support or of managing their own affairs. The great majority ultimately become public charges in some form. They cause unutterable sorrow at home and are a menace and danger to the community. Feeble-minded women are almost invariably immoral, and if at large usually become carriers of venereal disease or give birth to children who are as defective as themselves. The feeble-minded woman who marries is twice as prolific as the normal woman.
>
> We have only begun to understand the importance of feeble-mindedness as a factor in the causation of pauperism, crime and other social problems. Hereditary pauperism, or pauperism of two or more generations of the same family, generally means hereditary feeble-mindedness. In Massachusetts there are families who have been paupers for many generations. Some of the members were born or even conceived in the poorhouse.
>
> Every feeble-minded person, especially the high-grade imbecile, is a potential criminal, needing only the proper environment and opportunity for the development and expression of his criminal tendencies. The unrecognized imbecile is a most dangerous element in the community. (Fernald, 1912, pp. 90–91)

All of these quotations were taken from the secondary source of Sarason and Doris (1969), pp. 284–286.

> is done. Mankind stands at the crossroads, East of Harvard warned in 1923, after Grant had predicted "the passing of the great race" in 1921 and Stoddard had written in 1922: "In former times, the numbers of the feebleminded were kept down by the stern processes of natural selection, but modern society and philanthropy have protected them and have thus favored their rapid multiplication." In 1928, Pitkin invited the public to worry with him about the "twilight of the American mind." In Germany, von Behr-Pinnow went even farther and, in a popular booklet published in 1929, spoke of the "dusk of mankind" (*Menschbeitsdämmerung*). (pp. 133–134)

The presumed danger of mental retardation was seen in even more drastic terms in light of evolutionary theory. As Sarason and Doris (1969) note:

> The Darwinian theory put the implications of the degeneration theory in a new light. If the evolution of a species is the result of variation in traits among members of the species, hereditary transmission of the variants, and natural selection of those variants most fit to survive in the struggle for existence, then the theory of degeneration is placed in a broader context. The "degenerates," the physically and mentally ill, are no longer seen as the unfortunate victims of environment and/or hereditary taint—of whom one might say "there but for the Grace of God go I"—but rather as those who are demonstrably members of an inferior race of mankind which in accordance with natural law ought to be allowed to die out as quickly as possible. This then would be an indirect but powerful effect of Darwinism on the perception of the mentally retarded. (pp. 223–224)

This variant of evolutionary theory which advocated eugenic solutions is known as Social Darwinism. This theory states essentially that the principles of biological evolution should be strictly translated and applied to human society. The doctrine of "survival of the fittest" made philanthropy, compassion, and humanism a fault because it violated the natural law of elimination of the unfit. In attempting to help the unfortunates, we are actually diluting and ultimately destroying the future of the race. The force and appeal of the argument is aptly demonstrated in this quote from Darwin himself:

> With savages, the weak in body or mind are soon eliminated; and those that survive commonly exhibit a vigorous state of health. We civilized men, on the other hand, do our utmost to check the process of elimination; we build asylums for the imbecile, the maimed, and

> the sick; we institute poor-laws; and our medical men exert their utmost skill to save the life of every one to the last moment. There is reason to believe that vaccination has preserved thousands who from a weak constitution would formerly have succumbed to small-pox. Thus the weak members of civilized societies propagate their kind. No one who has attended to the breeding of domestic animals will doubt that this must be highly injurious to the race of man. It is surprising how soon a want of care, or care wrongly directed, leads to the degeneration of a domestic race; but, excepting to the case of man himself, hardly any one is so ignorant as to allow his worst animals to breed. (Darwin, 1874, p. 149)

The proposed solution to the problem was eugenics. Before the 1900s, and following Galton's lead, a program of positive eugenics—which consisted of improving the breed by increasing the productivity of the best members, such as by early marriage—was advocated. But after 1900, and because of the alarm over the problem, programs of negative eugenics—improving the breed by limiting or decreasing the productivity of the worst members—became increasingly popular.[2] The situation, rationale, and proposed solutions are succinctly summarized by Sarason and Doris (1969):

> But by 1915 . . . mental deficiency was in the focus of public attention as perhaps the largest and most serious social problem of the

[2] The reader may have some difficulty appreciating or even believing the sense of alarm and hysteria during this period. However, two observations should help quell any skepticism. It was during the 1920s that prohibition (of alcohol) was attempted. This crusade was fueled partly by the scientifically discredited but still popular belief in some form of degeneration theory; alcohol was viewed as a primary cause of the "hereditary taint" that resulted in conditions like mental illness, mental retardation, criminality, and general immorality. It is no wonder that there was an almost religious fervor to rid society of this evil. It was considered to be both a cause of many social ills and a symptom of their existence.

However, the clearest example of the force and impact of the "eugenic alarms" is Nazi Germany. The racist philosophy that led to the most extreme eugenic reaction in the history of mankind stems from the same eugenic issues considered during this period in the United States. In addition to the 6,000,000 Jews who were considered racially inferior, the Nazis also eliminated mentally ill, physically handicapped, and mentally retarded persons. The first law allowing for this eugenic solution was passed in 1933. As Rosen et al. (1975) note: "In his obsession with homogenization of the 'race,' Hitler carried what he considered to be the tenets of Social Darwinism to their incredible extreme. In 1933, Nazi Germany saw the passage of the Act for the Prevention of Hereditarily Diseased Offspring. Under this act a program of sterilization and 'mercy killings' of mental defectives, physically deformed, and incurables was initiated. Selection procedures were formulated by physicians working for the dreaded SS. It is estimated that approximately 100,000 persons were exterminated in Germany under the 'euthanasia' program" (Grunberger, 1971, p. XXII).

time. Conservative estimates placed the number of defectives in the country at over 400,000. With mental defect seen as underlying all sorts of social maladjustment and antisocial behavior, the implications were grim.

Since mental retardation was viewed as basically a biological condition determined by a defective central nervous system, for the most part hereditarily transmitted from one generation to the next, the solution to the problem was naturally seen to be in the realm of biology. And as defective neural tissues could not be replaced or improved the major attack on the problem could only be preventive and not curative.

In 1911, the Eugenics Section of the American Breeders Association appointed a special committee "commissioned to study and report on the best practical means for cutting off the defective germplasm in the American population." The reports of this committee appeared in the Eugenics Record Office Bulletin in 1914.

Although the committee recognized many groups presenting problems for eugenical study such as paupers, alcoholics, criminals, epileptics, the insane, and the deformed, it was forcefully maintained that, "The greatest of all eugenical problems in reference to cutting off the lower levels of human society consists in devising a practical means for eliminating hereditary feeblemindedness" (Laughlin, 1914, p. 18).

Various alternative solutions were considered from laissez-faire to euthanasia. The committee concluded that the two most socially acceptable and effective remedies were life segregation–or at least segregation during the reproductive period–and sterilization. Other remedies, such as restrictive marriage laws, were seen as ineffective. As for euthanasia, the committee, while deprecating Sparta's custom of exposing undesirable offspring to the elements, could not but "admire her courage in so rigorously applying so practical a system of selection." But for modern eugenics, the committee felt that the aim must be, "preventing the procreation of defectives rather than destroying them before birth, or in infancy, or in later periods of life." (pp. 286–287)

In essence, the committee's recommendations were carried out. Segregation in institutions for the mentally retarded was the primary method advocated and employed. The eventual folly of this approach, however, was later highlighted by the discovery of the moron. The great number of morons made total segregation impossible. This led many states to enact restrictive laws that forbade the marriage of two mentally retarded people. Sterilization laws were also passed (beginning with Indiana in 1907), but they were applied almost entirely to the institutionalized mentally retarded.

By 1926, 23 states had such laws. The practical effect of these laws, however, was minimal. By 1958, the total number of people sterilized was about 31,000 (Sarason and Doris, 1969).

In the final analysis, there was considerably more talk than action. The sociopolitical hysteria of this dismal period of history gradually subsided. In the process, however, the mentally retarded had acquired a strongly negative public image. Many lay people continue to think of the mentally retarded as dangerous, promiscuous, and subhuman and we are still attempting to counteract these erroneous, stereotyped images.

### The Great Lull (1930 to 1950)

The period of indictment and alarm had lasted for 30 years (1900 to 1930). However, even at its height, people had begun to perceive the hysteria and excesses of this reaction. The view of mental retardation as a unitary, recessive, inherited trait began to fade as the science of genetics grew in scope and precision. In addition, new clinical studies demonstrated the significance of other, non-hereditary, sources of mental retardation, such as trauma, infection, and endocrine disturbances. The methodological flaws and biased interpretations of the pedigree studies were becoming more and more apparent. Other surveys of institutional populations indicated that over one-half of them had intellectually normal parents, further weakening the singular heredity view and associated calls for eugenic solutions. The older research studies that had linked mental retardation with every conceivable social ill were critically reanalyzed and found wanting. Newer, better controlled, and more objective studies failed to reveal the dramatic links of the previous era. Even Walter Fernald, a leading America figure in the field, who had earlier condemned the mentally retarded as a "predatory, parasitic class," reversed himself on the basis of the first major follow-up study of 1,500 residents released from institutions. His reports were generally optimistic and did not support the social-menace view. The sociopolitical storm over mental retardation began to subside. The Great Depression following the stock market crash of 1929 had much to do with this. There was little point in focusing on the "unfortunates" and "social misfits" when everybody had become destitute and disadvantaged. Worry about the "future decline of civilization" was superseded by worry over survival in the present.

Mental retardation received little attention during the 1930s and 1940s. The nation had other priorities: The Depression and its aftermath in the 1930s and World War II and its effects in the 1940s. This lull was to some extent necessary and beneficial, since it provided time for a dissociation from the previous era's attitudes and ideas.

BOX 2.6

1930–1950 *The Great Lull*

- –Advances in the science of genetics that questioned the simplistic view of mental retardation as a unitary, recessively inherited trait.
- –Awareness of the methodological flaws of the pedigree studies.
- –New research studies that failed to find significant links between mental retardation and criminality, immorality, and other social ills.
- –Rise of psychoanalytic theory and emphasis on personality rather than intelligence (emergence of the mental hygiene and child guidance movements).
- –The Great Depression and its aftermath, resulting in the New Deal, whereby the state took on greater responsibility for the welfare of all of its citizens.
- –World War II and the massive screening of intelligence, resulting in the rediscovery of mild mental retardation.

–The Nature-Nurture Debate

Twin studies, mainly emphasizing the role of genes.
Bayley's longitudinal investigations pointing up the inconstancy of IQ.
Spitz's studies on the effects of deprived environments.
Iowa studies (Skeels, Dye, Skodak) demonstrating the effects of changes in environment.

1934 Folling of Norway discovers the metabolic disturbance in PKU.

In one particular area, however, there was no lull: the "nature-nurture" debate continued in academia. There was a great deal of research on this issue, with contradictory findings resulting in claims for the preeminent effects of heredity or environment. A long series of "twin studies" suggested that heredity was clearly predominant (e.g., comparison of identical and fraternal twins, comparison of identical twins reared apart). On the environmental side were the longitudinal investigations of Nancy Bayley (1933), who retested the same children at various intervals. These tests indicated that the IQ was not fixed or constant, as implied by the heredity view. Spitz's classic work (1945, 1947) on institutional environments and the importance of mothering to children's intellectual development corroborated Bayley's findings. Other research, most notably that of an Iowa group (Skeels and associates), demonstrated that environmental stimulation and early intervention could influence the development of mental traits previously thought to be entirely hereditary. The landmark study in this series was that by Skeels and Dye (1939). Their subjects were 25 one- to two-year-old mentally retarded children living in an orphanage. Thirteen of this group was transferred to an institution for the mentally retarded, where female residents used as surrogate mothers played and worked with them. The other 12 children remained in the somewhat deprived orphanage environment. On retesting, there were dramatic changes in IQ for both groups. Of the 12 children remaining in the orphanage, all but one showed a decrease in IQ ranging from 18 to 45 points, with five children exceeding 35 points. Of the 13 children transferred to the institution for the mentally retarded, all had increases in IQ. The minimum was seven points, with one child gaining 58 points. All but four of the children gained more than 20 points. This study dramatically showed both the good and bad effects of environment on the development of intelligence. In so doing, it also demonstrated that the old hereditarian view, with its notion of a fixed and constant IQ, was no longer tenable. Although the genetic evidence from the twin studies could not be discounted, the dramatic effects of environment shown by the Skeels-Dye studies overpowered the heredity view and paved the way for the environmental approach of the 1950s.

One other important factor contributed to the neglect of mental retardation. In the field of psychology, the 1920s and 1930s saw the rapid rise and pervasive influence of Freud's psychoanalytic theory. Although we cannot go into his theory at this time, its emphasis is on the importance of the early years of life for later psychological growth and emotional wellbeing. This focus on early childhood created the mental hygiene and child guidance movements. The issues of intelligence and mental retardation were lost in the overwhelming concern for the social-psychological growth, development, and adjustment of children. The crucial issue became personality, not intelligence.

Thus, for different reasons both the general society and the academic community became indifferent and neglectful of the field of mental retardation.

## Resurgence of Interest in Mental Retardation (1950s)

With the 1950s came an upsurge of concern for mental retardation that culminated in the 1960s and continued on, slightly abated, into the 1970s. Prior to the 1950s there had been no *positive* national concern or policy regarding the mentally retarded. They had been important only when they were seen as a social menace. Perhaps the most significant historical event in the field since the 1950s is the emergence and development of a national policy and commitment to the problem of mental retardation.

This national concern and policy originated in the impact of the Depression and World War II. The cataclysmic effects of the Depression forged a new definition of the relationship between the individual and the state. The individual was seen as powerless to deal with the complex, overwhelming economic and political forces that determined his destiny. It was up to the state to provide safeguards against them. Thus began the social security system, which provided some protection against any future economic downturn. There were also safeguards built into the financial system and labor force (unions). The major factor in the development and implementation of these new safeguard systems was the federal government. Washington was seen as the logical source of reform because the size and complexity of the problems overwhelmed the resources of the states. Thus, once again, the legal-constitutional imperative of providing for all citizens was reestablished. In fact, the responsibility to the less fortunate was seen as even more pressing, given the nature and scope of the problem. The government responded by offering everyone, including the handicapped, a New Deal.

Now that the general obligation to help and provide had been reaffirmed, it was still necessary to focus attention on the needy. Once again, it was a war that brought the problem of mental retardation to national awareness. The massive selection and screening demands of World War I had been partially responsible for the discovery of mild mental retardation. The problem now was that after the "great lull," this phenomenon had to be rediscovered. The nation had forgotten about the extent and size of the problem. World War II brought the matter to acute public attention; mild

## BOX 2.7

1950s Reemergence of Interest in Mental Retardation

*General Characteristics*

- –Interactionist resolution of the nature-nurture debate, but with emphasis on the environment.
- –Discovery of Piaget's developmental (environmental) theory of intelligence by American psychology.
- –Emergence of the sociological perspective on mental retardation and the resulting indictment of society.
- –Tremendous advances in medical science, particularly in the field of genetics.
- –Emerging national concern for the mentally retarded.
- –Formation of parent groups of the mentally retarded.
- –Debate over whether public schools had responsibility for educating TMR children.

| | |
|---|---|
| 1950 | Founding of the National Association of Retarded Children. |
| 1953 | Discovery of DNA by Watson and Crick. |
| 1954 | Supreme Court decision against school segregation (the impact of this decision on mental retardation would not be felt until 1971). |
| 1956 | Discovery of the exact number of chromosomes in a human cell by Tjio and Levan. |
| 1958 | Publication of *Mental Subnormality* by Masland, Sarason, and Gladwin. This book emphasized the social-psychological and cultural determinants of mental retardation and espoused the sociological perspective. |
| 1958 | Public Law 85–926. First piece of federal legislation specific to mental retardation. Provided for the training of professionals and teachers in special education for the mentally retarded. |
| 1959 | Publication of new AAMD definition (Heber manual), emphasizing the dual criteria of low IQ *and* adaptive behavior. In addition, the upper IQ cutoff was raised from 70 to 85. A revision of this manual appeared in 1961. |
| 1959 | Discovery of the extra chromosome (trisomy #21) in Down's syndrome. |

mental retardation was rediscovered on a massive scale. As Ginzberg and Bray (1953) note regarding the testing of recruits:

> Hidden within these startling figures is the still more startling fact that during World War II, 716,000 men were rejected on the grounds that they were "mentally deficient." At the peak of mobilization the Army had eighty-nine divisions. Those rejected for mental disabilities were the equivalent in manpower of more than fifty divisions. (p. 3)

There was, however, a crucial difference between the discoveries of these two world wars. The initial discovery was "alarming" because of the prevailing negative attitudes about the mentally retarded and a total lack of compassion or sense of obligation to help them. The situation after World War II was much different. The changed relationship between the state and the individual created a sense of obligation and compassion. There was both a moral and a legal imperative to help, and the nation gradually resolved to do something about the problem. Although the fruits of these labors would not be forthcoming until the 1960s and 1970s, the seeds had been sown.

During the 1950s, there were other movements as well. Perhaps the most important nonscientific aid to the mentally retarded came from the newly organized parent groups (see Box 2.8). These parents had become fed up with the neglect and indifference of both science and society toward their retarded children. From their beginning in 1950 to the present time, they have become a powerful force in the field of mental retardation. Their first goal was to obtain public school education for TMR (trainable mentally retarded, IQs between 30 and 50) children. Many professional educators had believed that these children were not educable in terms of traditional academic instruction. While they admitted that the mildly retarded were entitled to special education, they were unwilling to assume responsibility for more severe degrees of mental retardation. The parents argued that all citizens, regardless of their ability, had a right to public education, and that it was the school's responsibility to change its educational curriculum to meet their needs. The situation was not formally resolved until a Supreme Court decision of 1971. However, the debate over this issue in the 1950s served to focus attention on the mentally retarded and forced people to think about what society's response should be.

A number of scientific developments in the 1950s also helped to increase interest in mental retardation. Perhaps the most dramatic was the discovery of the genetic error that results in mongolism, or Down's syndrome. In 1959, Dr. Jerome Lejeune discovered that Down's children have an extra chromosome—trisomy #21, as the condition is now officially

## BOX 2.8

### The National Association for Retarded Citizens (NARC)

This association originated with a small group of parents of mentally retarded children in Minneapolis, Minnesota, in 1950. The idea of parent groups quickly spread, and in that same year, representatives from 20 local parent groups formed the National Association of Parents and Friends of Retarded Children. In 1952, they changed their name to the National Association for Retarded Children, and in 1973 to the National Association for Retarded Citizens.

As Dr. Philip Roos, executive director of the Association notes (1975):

> The growth of the NARC has been impressive. From 125 member organizations with approximately 13,000 active members, it has grown to over 1,600 state and local units and a membership of approximately 250,000 in 1974.
>
> Membership has not been restricted to parents of the retarded, although parents have played a major role throughout NARC's history. There has been a gradual trend toward increasing involvement of nonparents as members and as leaders within the organization. In general, however, parents have continued to play a key role at the local, state, and national levels of NARC. (p. 348)

This organization has been extremely effective in promoting the welfare of all mentally retarded persons. Over the years, it has sponsored multiple research and demonstration projects, set up special classes for TMRs, day care, sheltered workshops, and other service programs through its local units, and has been a politically powerful force through its advocacy in the courts and legislatures across the country. The rise of interest in mental retardation during the 1950s and its progressive climb to national priority in the 1960s and 1970s can be largely attributed to the leadership and activism provided by this organization. The NARC represents one of the best examples of the power, influence, and effectiveness of a relatively small, but extremely organized and dedicated group of people, in bringing about drastic societal changes in the promotion of the welfare of a previously neglected group of persons.

known. This discovery resulted in a flurry of activity to find the causes of other forms of severe retardation. Finding the cause of a problem always leads to the hope that someday, somehow, the condition may be prevented or corrected. Lejeune's discovery raised many hopes and made mental retardation research interesting and respectable. Many more scientists would now enter the field.

Two general scientific developments had important implications for the field of mental retardation. The first concerns the conceptualization of intelligence. The nature-nurture debate of the 1930s and 1940s finally subsided in the 1950s. It was resolved by the *interactionist* position, which stated that both nature and nurture were critical to the development of intelligence. Intelligence was seen as the product of the interaction between the genotype (the genetic inheritance) and the environment. The discovery of Piaget by American psychology (the majority of his work, done in the 1920s, was not translated until this time) helped bring about the interactionist resolution. However, it must be emphasized that Piaget's theory, while acknowledging the role of the genes, is essentially environmentally oriented. (Piaget's theory is discussed in the next chapter.) Thus the interactionists favored the environmental side, which stressed the malleability of intelligence. This was in sharp contrast to the previous rigid, hereditarian views which, by definition, implied that there could be no cure for mental retardation. The new environmental view was the source of renewed hope about the prevention and alleviation of mental retardation. The early pioneers had had just such an environmental orientation. Once again, people began to believe that something could be done about mental retardation.

The other general scientific development related to the field of mental retardation was the emergence of the *sociological perspective* on a host of social problems. It was in the field of mental retardation that this new perspective was to have its most profound impact. It resulted in a dramatic reconceptualization of the problem of mental retardation.

The field of sociology owed a debt to the mentally retarded. It was the emerging field of sociology that had contributed to the "alarming surveys" of the era of indictment and helped create the myth of the "social menace of the feebleminded." In the 1950s, however, sociology was to make another critical indictment. Whereas in the early 1900s the mentally retarded were seen as the root of all social ills, by the 1950s sociologists were saying that many social conditions appeared to be causing or contributing to mental retardation. This new perspective has its strongest impact on the mildly retarded, of whom it can be contended that the condition inheres in society rather than in the individual. In other words, perhaps the society, with its increasing complexity and demands, creates mild mental retardation (this position will be discussed further in Chapters 4 and 5). The important thing is that this new perspective was a virtual revolution in terms of the conceptualization of mental retardation. Furthermore, this view had strong implications for the issues of prevalence and treatment possibilities and approaches. Finally, this view had much to do with the "War on Poverty" in the 1960s.

The immediate effect of the new sociological perspective was reflected in the new 1959 (Heber) definition of mental retardation by the American Association on Mental Deficiency. (A revised manual was published in 1961. However, there were no major changes, and the definition remained essentially the same.) The new definition was:

> Mental retardation refers to subaverage general intellectual functioning originating during the developmental period and associated with impairments in adaptive behavior.

This definition contained a number of critical new ideas which merit further discussion.

First, and most importantly, the new definition stated that the past practice of relying on IQ as the sole criterion of mental retardation should be abandoned and condemned. The new definition stated that there are two essential requirements for a diagnosis of mental retardation: (1) low IQ and (2) associated impairments in adaptive behavior. In other words, unless the person can be shown to have trouble adapting, he cannot be called mentally retarded regardless of his IQ. The effect was to shift the emphasis from a predictor index (IQ) to a social-criterion measure—namely, a demonstrated impairment in adaptive behavior. This new criterion was added for two reasons: (1) a person with a low IQ who was adapting successfully could not logically be labeled retarded, and (2) many people were thus unfairly labeled because of a low IQ. This latter factor was related to the whole issue of the validity of IQ tests for disadvantaged and minority groups. In making poor adaptation a requirement for diagnosis, the new definition firmly established the social context and the cultural relativity of mental retardation. That is, it recognized that a person could be considered mentally retarded in one social or cultural context but not in another. The environment was now seen as an integral aspect of the problem of mental retardation.

The second characteristic of the new definition follows from the first. Now that mental retardation was seen in a social context, the old conceptualization of it as a medical condition had to be abandoned. While a medical model had undeniable relevance to many forms of severe mental retardation (e.g., PKU, Down's syndrome), it is clearly inappropriate for mild mental retardation. Furthermore, given the social context of the problem, the old notion of incurability associated with the medical model had to be abandoned. In short, mental retardation was no longer seen as a static condition. It was dynamic and developmental, and closely related to the social environment. To the extent that it was culturally relative and socially defined, it was also potentially curable.

One final aspect of the new definition deserves notice. Prior to 1959, people had always used an IQ of 70 as the upper limit for mental retardation. The 1959 and 1961 definitions raised the cutoff to 85, thus increasing the number of the potentially mentally retarded (such people would also have to manifest adaptive impairments). The upper limit had been raised because of the growing recognition that adaptation was becoming increasingly difficult in our complex modern society. In other words, taking the newly recognized "social context" seriously, it was felt that even more people might be having problems adapting.

## The "Heyday" of Mental Retardation—Another Era of Optimism (1960s)

The 1950s had seen an end to the indifference and neglect of the 1930s and 1940s. Both professionals and lay people began to take an active interest in mental retardation. The interactionist resolution of the nature-nurture debate, as exemplified and influenced by the discovery of Piaget's writings, provided a foundation for hope and an urgency for intervention. The conceptual revolution brought about by the sociological perspective further changed the perceived "nature" of mental retardation and clarified society's role in the creation and maintenance of mild retardation. An emerging national compassion and sense of obligation toward the less able created a favorable climate for a major attack on the problem. But a national policy had not yet been formulated; a spark was needed. That spark was provided by the election of President John F. Kennedy. As Crissey (1975) aptly observed:

> Through the kind of coincidence that occurs when an idea's time has come, the President of the United States had the same reason to be involved as did most of the founders of the parents movement: He had a close relative who was retarded. With his interest, federal support became available. All kinds of encouragement flowed from previously indifferent sources. Mental Retardation became a viable field, a rallying ground for a noble endeavor and a promising career ladder for many kinds of professions and people. (p. 805)

In 1961, President Kennedy established the President's Panel on Mental Retardation, which in 1962 produced a highly influential report entitled "National Action to Combat Mental Retardation." An official national policy was born. Crissey states:

> One can think of few governmental reports and recommendations that have had such an impact and that have served so well as a guideline. . . . The impetus from the report and the financing of the several recommendations are essentially the story of today and a guiding outline for tomorrow. (p. 805)

Among the recommendations included in this report were the following: (1) establishment of research and training centers in mental retardation, (2) development of a comprehensive, community based service system, (3) availability of an appropriate educational system for all children, including the most severely retarded, and (4) a call for the improvement of welfare, health, and general social conditions of all people, and especially the disadvantaged. All of these recommendations have now been carried out to a significant degree. Today there are 12 university-based centers specializing in research and training in mental retardation. An even greater number of university-affiliated centers provide professional diagnostic, treatment, and consultation services. There has been an almost mass movement to depopulate the institutions and treat the mentally retarded in the community. Accordingly, community-based services have greatly expanded in recent years. Increased education has been made available to more and more mentally retarded at all degrees of severity. This movement culminated in the historic "Right to Education" decision of the Supreme Court in 1971. Perhaps the most far-reaching effect, however, concerns the fourth recommendation, which deals with improving the situation of all disadvantaged people. This recommendation flowed naturally from the insights of the 1950s regarding the new environmental view of intelligence and the new sociological perspective on mental retardation. Since mental retardation was now seen as a developmental phenomenon, certain social conditions were seen to have an adverse effect on healthy development. The Report summarizes this view:

> The majority of the mentally retarded are the children of the more disadvantaged classes of our society. This extraordinarily heavy prevalence in certain deprived population groups suggests a major causative role, in some way not yet fully delineated, for adverse social, economic, and cultural factors. These conditions may not only mean absence of the physical necessities of life, but the lack of opportunity

## BOX 2.9

1960s The "Heyday" of Mental Retardation

*General Characteristics*

–Formation of a national policy and commitment to mental retardation.
–Influence of President Kennedy.
–Huge influx of federal money for facilities, services, and training of professionals.
–Era of great optimism and belief that mental retardation could be cured or at least greatly alleviated and/or prevented.
–View of mental retardation as a developmental phenomenon.
–Advent of behavioral technology in the treatment of mental retardation.
–Civil rights movement and eventual implications for all handicapped persons, including the mentally retarded.
–War on Poverty–Project Head Start. The first large-scale (though indirect) attempt to prevent the occurrence of mental retardation.
–Emphasis on community treatment of mental retardation and outrage at institutional conditions.
–Discovery of the devastating effects of maternal rubella.
–Dietary management of PKU and newborn screening of PKU.
–Further dramatic advances in medicine and genetics.

| | |
|---|---|
| 1960 | Election of John F. Kennedy. |
| 1961 | Publication of J. M. Hunt's *Intelligence and Experience*. This extremely influential book emphasized the critical role of experience in the development of intelligence and further popularized Piaget's developmental view of intelligence. |
| 1961 | Formation of the President's Panel on Mental Retardation. |
| 1962 | Publication of the President's Panel report, *National Action to Combat Mental Retardation*. This report became the guiding national policy on mental retardation for the next two decades. The impact of this report and its accomplishments cannot be overestimated. |
| 1966 | Establishment of the President's Committee on Mental Retardation (PCMR). Assures continuing national attention, leadership, and policy direction for the field of mental retardation through the publication of its annual and special reports. |
| 1966 | Publication of Blatt and Kaplan's *Christmas in Purgatory: A Photographic Essay on Mental Retardation*. This book graphically portrayed the blight and degradation of our institutions for the mentally retarded and was just one of the many exposés that began to appear. |
| 1968 | Declaration of the General and Specific Rights of the Mentally Retarded. |
| 1968 | First International Special Olympics. |
| 1969 | Publication in the *Harvard Educational Review* of Jensen's controversial article: "How Much Can We Boost IQ and Scholastic Achievement?" |

> and motivation. A number of experiments with the education of presumably retarded children from slum neighborhoods strongly suggests that a predominant cause of mental retardation may be the lack of learning opportunities or absence of "intellectual vitamins" under these adverse environmental conditions. Deprivation in childhood of opportunities for learning intellectual skills, childhood emotional disorders which interfere with learning, or obscure motivational factors appear somehow to stunt young people intellectually during their developmental period. Whether the causes of retardation in a specific individual may turn out to be biomedical or environmental in character, there is highly suggestive evidence that the root causes of a great part of the problem of mental retardation are to be found in bad social economic conditions as they affect individuals and families, and that correction of these fundamental conditions is necessary to prevent mental retardation successfully on a truly significant scale. (pp. 8–9)

In many respects, the "War on Poverty" during the Administration of President Lyndon B. Johnson was an attempt to carry out this last recommendation. Project Head Start was the program designed for disadvantaged children who were at high risk to become mildly mentally retarded. This was the first large-scale (though indirect) effort to prevent mental retardation.

The impact of the President's Panel's report cannot be overestimated. It brought the field of mental retardation into national prominence. We now had both national concern and a national policy. In a historical sense, this establishment of an active, comprehensive, forward-looking national policy may be the most important event in the history of mental retardation. It is primarily for this reason that the 1960s are considered the heyday of the mental retardation movement.

The energy and enthusiasm generated by the national program were reinforced by the successful use of behavioral technology in treating mental retardation. Rather than viewing mental retardation as a personal deficit or failure, advocates of this approach saw it as a program failure. The person was retarded because he had not been properly trained in the first place. Retardation could be cured or prevented by designing appropriate training programs based on learning theory. While the expected cures didn't occur, dramatic gains were made. This was most apparent in the training of the severely and profoundly retarded (IQs from the mid-30s and under). In the past, it had been believed that these people could do practically nothing for themselves. They were considered to be custodial cases; public responsibility consisted only of assuring their comfort and safety. But the applied behaviorists, who believed that they could cure mental retardation, reversed this defeatist attitude and self-fulfilling prophecy. Suddenly, with the use of behavior modification, these persons were now found to be capable of many things, such as dressing, eating, toilet use, and even simple work skills. For example, even the severely and profoundly mentally retarded can learn to assemble bicycle brakes (Gold, 1972) and operate a drill press (Crosson, 1969) when these tasks are broken down into simplified steps. The 1960s were reminiscent of the era of the early pioneers, such as Itard and Seguin. In their attempt to do the impossible, they accomplished much more than was thought possible. The comment of the French Academy of Sciences regarding Itard's disappointment over his inability to cure "Victor" is still relevant today: "the pupil ought to be compared only with himself."

The 1960s, then, was a period of great optimism. The nation had finally made a commitment and forged a vigorous policy to do something about mental retardation. On the scientific level, there was renewed hope that the problem could either be prevented or greatly ameliorated. The sense of possibility and optimism of this period was poignantly reflected in an event that occurred at the Joseph P. Kennedy, Jr., Foundation awards banquet. The reader should recall the landmark Skeels and Dye (1939) study involving the mentally retarded orphans who were transferred to an institution for the mentally retarded and cared for by female residents. Crissey (1970), one of the researchers involved in the study, notes: "The stirring presentation ceremonies on April 28, 1968, reached their dramatic climax when Senator Edward Kennedy turned the Steuben crystal trophy over to Louis Branca for presentation. In a moving speech, the poised young man identified himself as one of the children in Dr. Skeel's landmark study (p. 3)." Mr. Branca was the holder of a master's degree. One could hardly ask for a more concrete and effective symbol for the possibilities of treating and preventing mental retardation.

There were, of course, many other developments in the field of mental retardation during the 1960s. The causes of many severe forms of retardation were discovered. The tragic rubella epidemic of 1963 and 1964 led to intensified research efforts with rubella and other birth defects. The dietary treatment of PKU was formulated, and public prevention programs were instituted (e.g., newborn screening for PKU; measles vaccination). The vocational rehabilitation movement expanded, leading to the development of work adjustment centers and sheltered workshops. Mental retardation also became an international concern. Several scientific congresses on the subject were held, and the parent group movement spread to most of the Western world. Many other developments that culminated in the 1970s (and will thus be discussed later) began in the 1960s. Chief among them was the civil rights movement. Civil rights became a topic of grave national concern, initially for racial minorities and eventually for all types of minorities, including the mentally retarded. The movement was to have a profound effect on the field of mental retardation, particularly in terms of approaches to treatment. The mentally retarded would finally be liberated, afforded full citizenship, and receive a long overdue "due process." Furthermore, mental retardation itself would again become politicized.

## The Mentally Retarded Citizen (1970s)

If any one event symbolized the state of affairs in the field of mental retardation during the 1970s, it was a simple change of name. In 1973, the National Association for Retarded Children, that influential and politically powerful parents group begun in 1950, changed its name to the National Association for Retarded *Citizens*. This act was symbolic of what was to happen throughout the field. The reason for this particular change was simple. In 1950, these parents had been fighting for their young children. Throughout the 1950s and 1960s, the field was child oriented. Theoretically and practically, the focus was on the need for early childhood intervention to prevent and ameliorate mental retardation. But by 1970, these children had grown up. And it suddenly became apparent to their parents that the provisions for the mentally retarded adult were either nonexistent or grossly inadequate. Consequently, the parents began to fight for their now-adult children. The struggle took place in the context of social concern and turmoil over the whole issue of civil rights. Discrimination on the basis of race, religion, age, and sex had all been ruled unlawful. The rights of all kinds of "different" persons had been reaffirmed and guaranteed. But there remained the difference of intellect, and more importantly, the rights of those intellectually different. Concern for these persons' rights was to become the rallying point of the 1970s. Many of the burning issues of this period (e.g., labeling, normalization, deinstitutionalization, IQ testing) relate either directly or indirectly to the broader topic of civil rights.

Another attempted name change also occurred. Beginning with a major federal funding bill in 1970, the term *developmental disability* became popular. This term is defined as follows:

> Developmental disability means a disability attributable to mental retardation, cerebral palsy, epilepsy, or another neurological condition of an individual found by the Secretary [of Health, Education, and Welfare] to be closely related to mental retardation or to require treatment similar to that required for mentally retarded individuals, which disability originates before such individual attains age eighteen,

> which has continued or can be expected to continue indefinitely and which constitutes a substantial handicap to such individual. (Hobbs, 1975b, p. 83)

Of the three categories mentioned in the definition (mental retardation, cerebral palsy, and epilepsy), the mentally retarded constitute the overwhelming majority. For this reason, the term "developmental disability" is gradually replacing "mental retardation" in some circles. For example, many institutional and community clinic facilities have changed their names to some variant of "center for the developmentally disabled." However, while the term has some limited use, it is unlikely that it will formally replace the label "mental retardation." Nevertheless, the emergence of this term reflects a growing attitude about the nature of mental retardation. It serves to underscore the developmental orientation and conceptualization, with its optimistic focus on the possibility of change. Learning theory-based formulations of mental retardation are also congruent with this developmental view; retardation is seen as the result of a history of inadequate or negative learning experiences. Whether the term "developmental disability" is eventually formalized or forgotten, it gives official notice that mental retardation is now clearly seen as a developmental condition.

During the 1970s, the formal definition of mental retardation also changed. In 1973, the American Association on Mental Deficiency published a revised manual on mental retardation. (This manual was also slightly revised in 1977.) The definition in both editions is very similar to the one used in the 1959 and 1961 manuals. There is, however, one major difference. Prior to 1959, an IQ of 70 had always been the traditional upper cutoff point for mental retardation. However, with the new sociological perspective of the 1950s, which suggested that our increasingly complex society was making it difficult for more and more people to adapt, the 1959 definition raised the upper IQ cutoff point to 85. By the 1970s, many people began to suggest that this had been a mistake. Certain new data implied that the vast majority of persons in the 70-to-85 IQ range had no real problems in adaptation. Some data even suggested that people in the 55-to-70 IQ range were also adapting. The net result was a strong presure to return the upper IQ limit to 70. The new 1973 definition did just that. This change also occurred amid intense concern over labeling and civil rights. These issues and the resultant social pressures may also have influenced the decision to lower the upper limit for mental retardation.

In general, the field of mental retardation slowed down a bit in the 1970s. This was most evident in government leadership and financial sup-

BOX 2.10

1970s The Mentally Retarded Citizen

*General Characteristics*

–Nonscientific issues transcend scientific ones.
–General and pervasive concern with the rights of mentally retarded persons.
–Numerous court decisions affirming the rights of mentally retarded persons.
–Development of citizen advocacy programs.
–The principle of normalization as a philosophy of human management. Specifies both the goals and means of treatment for mentally retarded persons.
–The Jensen affair.
–Controversies about IQ testing and labeling.
–Campaign to depopulate the institutions.

1970 Developmental Disabilities Act. Major new policy and funding legislation. Introduces term "developmental disability" as a synonym for "mental retardation." Provides for a range of services in terms of the lifetime needs of the developmentally disabled. Beginning of the movement toward a non-categorical approach to disability.

1971–1972 *Pennsylvania Association for Retarded Children* vs. *Commonwealth of Pennsylvania*. Historic "right to education" decision of the Supreme Court. Affirms that all mentally retarded children, no matter how severely disabled, have a right to public education.

*Wyatt* vs. *Stickney*. Right to "appropriate and effective treatment" decision of the Supreme Court. Establishes the principle of "least restrictive alternative."

1973 The new Grossman AAMD manual, which changed the definition of mental retardation. The main difference between this definition and the Heber (1959/1961) definition is the lowering of the upper IQ cutoff from 85 to 70.

| | |
|---|---|
| 1973 | National Association of Retarded Children changes its name to National Association of Retarded Citizens. |
| 1973 | National Conference on The Mentally Retarded Citizen and the Law. |
| 1975 | Project on the Classification of Exceptional Children. Strongly recommends non-categorical approach in providing funds and services. Emphasis on the needs of the individual regardless of diagnostic category. |
| 1975 | The Education for All Handicapped Children Act (Public Law 94–142). This landmark legislation attempts to carry out the Supreme Court's "right to education" decision by making education-for-all the official policy of the federal government and encouraging states to develop programs accordingly by providing funds. |
| 1977 | Revision of the Grossman AAMD manual. (There is essentially no difference between the 1973 and 1977 definitions of mental retardation.) |

port. Although the continuation of the President's Committee on Mental Retardation and its yearly reports assured the field some definite priority and national leadership, the country's preoccupation with and divisiveness over the Vietnam War, along with a general anxiety and concern about the economy and energy problems, served to dilute some of the previous era's focus, commitment, and enthusiasm. This dissipation was furthered in the late 1970s by the so-called "tax revolt," spearheaded and symbolized by the passage of California's Proposition 13 in 1978. There arose a general reluctance to propose or fund any new types of service programs, no matter how noble the cause. It became difficult to even maintain the status quo in light of the pressure for cutbacks in government spending. Other more specific developments regarding handicapped people in general reduced the prominence that the field of mental retardation had enjoyed in the 1960s.

Largely as a result of the intense concern regarding the rights of the mentally retarded, the civil rights of all handicapped persons now became important. This was dramatically illustrated by the passage of the Education for All Handicapped Children Act (PL94-142) in 1975. This landmark legislation establishes four basic rights for all handicapped children:

1. *The right to due process,* which protects the individual from erroneous classification, capricious labeling, and denial of equal education.
2. *Protection against discriminatory testing in diagnosis,* which ensures against possible bias in intelligence tests used with ethnic minority children.
3. *Placement in an educational setting that is the least restrictive environment,* which protects the individual from possible detrimental effects of segregated education for the handicapped.
4. *Individualized program plans,* which ensures accountability by those responsible for the education of the handicapped. (Macmillan, 1977, p. 1)

While the mentally retarded are at the heart of all of these concerns and will greatly benefit from these guarantees, the fact that the focus is on *all* handicapped children dilutes the prominence of any one group. We are not implying that this is bad; we are merely pointing out why the field of mental retardation is not as much in the spotlight as it was during the 1960s.

Two other related developments are also important. We have mentioned the new term "developmental disabilities." While this refers mainly to the mentally retarded, it also includes those individuals with cerebral palsy, epilepsy, autism, and other neurological conditions. This grouping effect, as we have noted, reduces the prominence of any one group. Perhaps the most important factor is the growing pressure to change the way governmental funds for handicapped children are appropriated. In the past, funds have always been handed out on a categorical basis (i.e., for the blind, deaf, mentally retarded, etc.). It was this approach that allowed mental retardation to rise to prominence in the 1960s. The effect of President Kennedy and the 1962 President's Panel report was to pump an unprecedented amount of money into the field, with obvious beneficial effects. However, such an approach also has some problems. Whichever category happens to be in the spotlight gets the most attention, often to the detriment of other groups. Worse yet, the categorical approach has never been able to meet the needs of multiply handicapped children, of whom there are many. The new recommended approach to funding (Hobbs, 1975b) is based on services needed rather than categories. This is in line with the emerging attitude and mandate to provide for all handicapped children, regardless of their disability. In short, concern for any one group has been superseded by concern for all.

The 1970s has also witnessed some dampening of the optimism of the 1960s regarding the prevention and amelioration of mental retardation. This optimism had two sources: (1) Piaget's developmental view of intelligence, which suggested that early intervention could have dramatic preventive effects, and (2) learning theory, which suggested that mental retardation represented a "program failure" and could therefore be treated. Data from a variety of sources showed that the optimism of these "environmental" formulations had to be tempered. Most disheartening were the results of Project Head Start, which was the first large-scale (though indirect) attempt to prevent mental retardation by improving the intellectual environment of disadvantaged children. While initial gains were made, later research demonstrated that these gains did not hold up over time. In fairness, according to many observers, this "early" intervention was not early enough. Heber and others (see Chapter 8) believe this and, at the same time, are optimistic that a successful prevention program can be designed. Nevertheless, Head Start had largely failed, and enthusiasm was somewhat dampened. In addition, the applied behaviorists, for all their ingenious methods and dramatic accomplishments, failed to reverse the alleged "program failures" and "cure" mental retardation, as some had believed they could. There did indeed appear to be some limits to what could be done. This was further corroborated by the animal studies of the behavior geneticists, which demonstrated that there were clear genetic components and limits to some behaviors. All of these new data put the unbridled environmentalism of the 1960s in a more limited perspective. Naive enthusiasm was replaced by a more realistic, cautious optimism.

One other factor helped to dampen the optimism of the 1960s and reopened the old nature-nurture debate. In 1969, Arthur Jensen published a provocative article entitled "How Much Can We Boost IQ and Scholastic Achievement?" In it, he documented the failure of compensatory education programs, such as Project Head Start, to achieve any significant, lasting gains in intellectual functioning. On the basis of this and other data from his own research, Jensen argued that there was convincing evidence of the heritability of intelligence. What caused the furor was his assertion that there are substantial racial differences in intelligence. While this is a controversial and complex issue, Jensen's statements and data have been severely criticized but not demolished. The argument continues and has had great impact on the field of mental retardation. As we have noted, many influences had already tempered the extreme environmental optimism of the 1960s and forced a more realistic recognition of the role of the genes. The Jensen controversy reinforced this view, and in some extreme circles served to harden it. Certainly, an extreme genetic focus contradicts the prevailing developmental view of mental retardation.

The main concerns of the 1970s have been nonscientific, principally related to the civil rights of the mentally retarded. However, these issues spill over into the more scientific ones, often with marked emotional overtones. The topics of IQ testing, labeling, and deinstitutionalization illustrate this interplay of factors.

*Problems with IQ* Ever since the introduction of IQ testing, the question has been, are these tests fair and appropriate for members of disadvantaged and minority groups? This is a legitimate concern, since the norm groups for even some of our best and most popular tests are admittedly not representative of the entire population. Furthermore, there is clear evidence that the tests have been misapplied and misinterpreted in the past. However, with the civil rights movement of the early 1960s, the attack on IQ tests has become vocal and vitriolic. The IQ has been condemned as unreliable, invalid, and discriminatory. Many have called for its abandonment, particularly as a screening device for mental retardation. (This is the precise reason why Binet developed his initial test of intelligence.) The main problem is that the IQ test identifies a far greater proportion of minority group children as mentally retarded compared to their Caucasian peers. Because the minorities are primarily racial, the IQ is therefore accused of being racist. The result has been a number of legal challenges to its use in determining mental retardation. For instance, lawyers representing six black elementary school pupils in one city in California placed in educable mentally retarded (EMR) classes on the basis of their low IQ scores argued that such tests were racially and culturally biased. The federal judge was given data showing that while blacks account for only 9.1 percent of the population, they constitute 27.5 percent of students in EMR classes. The judge supported the lawyers' view and ordered a statewide moratorium on certain IQ tests for evaluating minority students. Other court decisions have similarily limited the use of IQ tests for "tracking" students and placing them in special classes. One decision disallowed heavily verbal tests, such as the Stanford-Binet, with pupils of Spanish surnames. Although many of the above-mentioned cases are on appeal or in various stages of the legal process, IQ testing is clearly on trial and the courts may make some far-reaching decisions regarding its use.

*Labeling* The issue of labeling also involves civil rights. (This will be discussed more fully in Chapter 9.) Aside from the alleged detrimental effects to the person being labeled, a central issue is suspected racial discrimination. That is, more minority group children are labeled as mentally retarded than their Caucasian peers. The calls to abandon this practice have been extremely emotionally charged.

*Institutionalization* Perhaps the most highly publicized recent issue in mental retardation has been the massive campaign to empty the residential care institutions. The reasons behind this movement are many. The nature-nurture studies of the 1930s and 1940s depicted many of these institutions as warehouses of deprivation. The emphasis on the environment in the development of intelligence during the 1950s and 1960s brought them under even more intense scrutiny. It was easy to find both objective and subjective data revealing horrible, often inhuman, conditions in these facilities. Both professional and lay people wrote books exposing the degradation of such places. A 1972 nationwide television broadcast (Rivera, 1972) on the inhumane and barbaric conditions of one state institution did much to coalesce the public outrage. There were immediate demands for swift reform. This movement was aided by the clear policy statement in the report (1962) of the President's Panel on Mental Rertardation, which advocated and emphasized community treatment. At the same time, the newly discovered Scandinavian principle of *normalization* was advocated for the treatment of mental retardation. (This principle will be discussed later.) More recent court decisions about the mentally retarded person's right to appropriate and effective treatment provided a legal mandate for swift change. The result was a twofold attack on the problem: (1) to get as many people as possible out of the institutions and into the community, and (2) to transform these "custodial warehouses" into real treatment facilities for persons who must remain. At the very minimum, there was a call to break up the large institutions and replace them with smaller, more effective, and more humane ones.

The movement away from institutionalization continues today. However, now that some of the emotion has been discharged, people are taking a more critical look at the situation. One thing became immediately clear: many previous decisions were made in the absence of any relevant data. Some communities were not prepared to take the discharged residents and had no appropriate housing or treatment programs. Some of the residents merely moved from a large, impersonal, nonenriching institution to a small community facility with similar characteristics. Also, not all institutions were horrible; some, in fact, provided excellent service. More importantly, it gradually became apparent that only a fairly large facility with centralized services could supply the many forms of treatment that many severely mentally and physically handicapped residents required. While there is still a clear movement to deinstitutionalize wherever possible, such decisions are now made with less haste. Furthermore, given the many services required to serve all the mentally retarded, it is now recognized that there may still be a place for a large, well-run, multipurpose institution.

## Normalization

As mentioned earlier, the overriding principle of the 1970s for the treatment and organization of services for the mentally retarded is *normalization* (Wolfensberger, 1972). This philosophical principle serves both as a means and an end. It tells us where we should be going and how we should be getting there. Aside from the general concern for the rights of the mentally retarded, it is the major feature of the field of mental retardation in the 1970s. It is directly related to the concern over rights. However, it is also much more. It is the ultimate expression of the humanism that workers in the field have hoped for since the humanitarian appeals of the early 1800s. It asks not only that we accord the mentally retarded their constitutional rights of citizenship, but more importantly, that we give them the humanity they deserve as members of the human community. Because of the importance of this principle, an extended statement by one of its leading exponents (Nirje, 1969) is presented:

> My entire approach to the management of the retarded, and deviant persons generally, is based on the "normalization" principle. This principle refers to a cluster of ideas, methods, and experiences expressed in practical work for the mentally retarded in the Scandinavian countries as well as in some other parts of the world. The normalization principle underlies demands for standards, facilities, and programs for the retarded as expressed by the Scandinavian parent movement. . . .
>
> To discuss human endeavors to create wholesome programs, facilities, and life conditions for other human beings in terms of one unifying principle might seem preposterous, especially when the mentally retarded are involved, a group which is characterized by wide variations in age, degree of handicap, complicating physical and emotional disorders, social backgrounds, and educational and personality profiles. Nevertheless, in the Scandinavian countries, a general principle which expresses the aims, attitudes, and norms implied in quality work for and with the mentally retarded has been found of value. As expressed by N. E. Bank-Mikkelsen of Denmark, this principle is

> given in the formula "to let the mentally retarded obtain an existence as close to the normal as possible." Thus, as I see it, the normalization principle means making available to the mentally retarded patterns and conditions of everyday life which are as close as possible to the norms and patterns of the mainstream of society.
>
> This principle should be applied to all the retarded, regardless whether mildly or profoundly retarded, or whether living in the homes of their parents or in group homes with other retarded. The principle is useful in every society, with all age groups, and adaptable to social changes and individual developments. Consequently, it should serve as a guide for medical, educational, psychological, social, and political work in this field, and decisions and actions made according to the principle should turn out more often right than wrong. (p. 363)

The impact of this principle on the field of mental retardation has been significant. Normalization has profoundly influenced the organization of programs and services, even down to minor details. (This will be discussed further in Chapter 10.) For now, we will focus on just one important change.

There has been a long, controversial debate on the value of special versus regular classes in educating the mentally retarded. Much data have been gathered on the advantages and disadvantages of each approach, with no conclusive proof. Yet, the principle of normalization, as expressed through the concept of "mainstreaming" (placing retarded with nonretarded children for all or most of the school day) in educational services, has provided a philosophical answer: it is preferable to leave children in the regular classes whenever possible. Even if there was hard data to demonstrate the advantages of special classes, normalization would disallow it on philosophical, nonscientific grounds.

This is just one example of the significance of normalization in treating the mentally retarded. It demonstrates that many of our decisions on program planning and treatment will be made on philosophical grounds. This orientation is of overriding importance. This does not mean that relevant data will be disregarded. It does mean, however, that certain issues are based on values rather than on scientific answers. Finally, while normalization can and at times has been carried to ridiculous extremes (e.g., even the severely retarded should vote, make major decisions affecting their life, etc.), its overall effect has been extremely beneficial. When the humanity of the mentally retarded is stressed, intellectual differences are seen to be of secondary importance.

The principle of normalization has also helped us to recognize how our erroneous good intentions for the welfare of the mentally retarded have actually created even more problems. Nowhere is this more evident than in the matter of the "dignity of risk" or the "right to fail." The mentally retarded have been grossly overprotected from failure and negative experiences; we do not allow them a chance to fail, make mistakes, or take normal risks. For instance, to prevent their being harmed or taken advantage of in the community, we keep them in institutions. This policy creates a self-fulfilling prophecy as well as violating their right to try and fail. Without the chance or possibility of failure, these persons will never be able to succeed. Respect for their dignity demands that we allow them a normal and reasonable chance of risk.

In general, concern over the civil and legal rights of the mentally retarded is the most significant characteristic of the field in the 1970s. Although normalization is the moral and humane corollary to these legal concerns and represent the spirit of the law, it was first necessary to have the letter of the law clearly specified and reaffirmed. While many factors were responsible for the success of the civil rights movement, judicial decisions and laws provided the real impetus. Without them, the principle of normalization might have had little impact. It was necessary for the courts to assert the full citizenship of the mentally retarded before their humanity would also be recognized and responded to.

In short, the recent dramatic changes in our treatment philosophy and practices with respect to the mentally retarded are largely the result of court decisions and legislative actions in response to or in anticipation of these rulings. Some of the initial impetus came from the parent groups, which decided to pursue legal means of redressing the grievances against their children. The mentally retarded themselves have issued their own Bill of Rights (International League of Societies for the Mentally Handicapped, 1969). However, because of the nature of their handicap, they have been unable to assert their own cause. In this sense, they are the most handicapped of the handicapped groups—some of which have been very effective in their protests and demands. The result has been a new movement called "citizen advocacy." According to Wolfensberger (1975), citizen advocacy is defined as follows: "an unpaid competent citizen volunteer, with the support of an independent citizen advocacy agency, represents—as if they were his own—the interests of one or two impaired persons by means of one or several of many advocacy roles, some of which may last for life" (p. 15). The essence of this program is the one-to-one relationship by which a volunteer, free from conflicts of interest (e.g., including the "good intentions" as an administrative or service agency set up to "help" the mentally retarded), relates to an impaired person and looks out only for this person's best interests. The advocate may play a variety of formal and informal roles, such as helping with day-to-day problems of living, administering property and income, representing the client's interests vis-à-vis agencies and the law, and providing friendship and support during crises. This program was started in 1971 in Nebraska and has spread rapidly to other states. It is also an international movement, with the Scandinavians again providing the initial impetus and model. This program has been instrumental in safeguarding the rights of the mentally retarded and making all who deal with them more aware of those rights.

As a result of the concern over human and civil rights and the program of citizen advocacy, the field of mental retardation is no longer the exclusive province of professionals. The opinions, judgments, and decisions of the "experts" no longer go unchallenged. Parents or citizen advocates participate in all program planning and decision making. The field has become even more multidisciplinary than in the past. Lawyers, judges, parents, and lay advocates are now an integral part of the team that provides for the mentally retarded. Even the mentally retarded themselves, to whatever extent they are able, participate in planning and decision making.

In summarizing the situation in the 1970s, it is clear that nonscientific issues have transcended scientific ones. Concern over etiology, classification, treatment methods, and so on has been superseded by a concern with treatment of the mentally retarded as persons and citizens. Mental retardation has become politicized (legal rights) and humanized (the principle of normalization).

History reveals curious paradoxes and twists. Before the discovery of mild mental retardation, the mentally retarded were full-fledged citizens. But their "alarming discovery" in the early 1900s set off a chain reaction. They were considered parasites, the source of all social evils and ills, the harbingers of the decay and downfall of civilization. As a result, society took away their legal and civil rights as well as their humanity. We forbade them to marry and propagate and attempted to segregate them into institutional warehouses. Even their right to life was questioned with the advocacy of various eugenic solutions. A small but significant minority were actually sterilized. They became both dehumanized and disenfranchised.

The situation is drastically different in the 1970s. Many scientific gains and achievements have occurred since that dismal period of history. But none of these is as important as the redress of their unspoken grievances regarding their rights and humanity. The courts and legislatures have reaffirmed their citizenship and the principle of normalization has restored their humanity. A 1973 statement of the American Association on Mental Deficiency on abortion is of considerable historical significance when seen in the light of the previous eugenic alarms:

> It is [our] position that the existence of mental retardation is no justification for the terminating of the life of any human being or for permitting such a life to be terminated either directly or through the withholding of life sustaining procedures.

While the 1960s represent the heyday of the *field* of mental retardation in terms of national concern and commitment, scientific knowledge, and treatment advances, the 1970s represent the heyday of mentally retarded *persons* as full-fledged human beings and citizens.

## CONCLUSION

Two conclusions emerge from the history of mental retardation. First, mental retardation is primarily a modern phenomenon and problem. The vast majority of mentally retarded persons—namely, the mildly retarded—were not even discovered until 75 years ago. To a large extent, modern society both created and caused this "discovery." The second conclusion concerns society's reaction to this discovery. Mental retardation became politicized. In addition to its "scientific" history, mental retardation now has a sociopolitical history. More importantly, these two histories have become inextricably intertwined. To study and examine only one of them is to miss the essence of mental retardation. The problem cannot be considered in scientific isolation; it is a social problem as well. Accordingly, the history of mental retardation is the story of people and their reactions to being different or perceiving difference. The "alarming" quality about the discovery of mild mental retardation and its aftermath says much more about "us" than it does about "them." Fortunately, the 1970s have put "us" in a more positive light than in the past. In the final analysis, the history of mental retardation is not just "their" history; it is our history. Ultimately, it is a story about all of us. So it will be in the future.

# CHAPTER 3

# The Concepts of Intelligence and IQ

Traditionally, mental retardation has been viewed almost exclusively in terms of low intelligence. More recently, however, intelligence has been de-emphasized, with more importance given to such factors as social competence, motivation, and learning potential. The new term "developmental disability," which is replacing "mental retardation," underscores this change. However, while this shift in attitude draws needed attention to many important neglected factors, low intelligence is still necessary for a diagnosis of mental retardation. Consequently, it is important to understand what intelligence is and how it is measured. In general, the material in this chapter will provide the student with a necessary framework for a full understanding of the concept of mental retardation.

## INTELLIGENCE: THE PROBLEM OF DEFINITION

Most persons can readily offer some definition of the term "intelligence." Lay or colloquial definitions typically incorporate such ideas as how smart a person is, how much a person knows, or how fast he is able to learn. Such attempts at definition are imprecise and tend to replace one vague term ("intelligence") with another (e.g., "smart"). Professional/scientific definitions are more precise, but there remains considerable disagreement as to what intelligence actually is. The scientific approaches fall into two general categories: operational and theoretical.

### Operational Approaches

The term "operational approach" refers to any attempt to explain intelligence by describing related behaviors. Thus, definitions that include the ability to learn or the amount of accumulated knowledge would be considered operational. These approaches are distinguished from theoretical approaches in which there is an attempt to infer or speculate on the basis of intelligent behavior.

Even a cursory review of the literature indicates a great variety of operational definitions. A comprehensive summary would go well beyond the scope of this text. However, many of the differences among these definitions are merely a matter of emphasis—that is, what is considered primary or essential. Thus, we can summarize the operational approaches using a few categories or behaviors.

Cattell (1971), for example, indicates three major approaches which focus on different fields of endeavor. Thus, educators use the "capacity to learn" as the essential feature of intelligence. Philosophers and mathematicians focus on the "ability to think abstractly," and comparative psychologists stress "adaptability to new situations." Other authors (e.g., Robinson and Robinson, 1965) discuss other common operational approaches. The "amount of accumulated knowledge" is often used to define intelligence, since it is believed that brighter persons, in general, retain more information. In recent years, the idea of "general problem-solving ability" has received more attention. It must be reiterated that the differences among these definitions are a matter of emphasis. The educator who focuses on the ability to learn does not deny that the ability to adjust or adapt is also a facet of intelligence. He simply emphasizes learning ability.

While all of these operational approaches define intelligence in terms of behavior, they do so in a very general way. They refer to broad classes of behavior but do not enumerate what specific behaviors make up, for example, "general problem-solving ability." The generality of such a term becomes apparent when we ask some obvious questions. What is the difference (in intelligence) between one person who can solve many problems rapidly and another person who is much slower but ultimately solves more difficult problems? Is the *how* of problem solving as important as *how many?* How do we account for the fact that some persons easily solve one type of problem (e.g., numerical) while doing relatively poorly on another type (e.g., mechanical reasoning)? As these questions indicate, most operational approaches lack scientific rigor. Nevertheless, they do have some value in showing what general behaviors are considered intelligent.

One attempt to clarify the meaning of many psychological terms, including "intelligence," is the strict *operational definition.* This attitude grew out of the philosophical-scientific movement called "logical positivism" (see, e.g., Bergmann, 1951), where concepts are defined solely in terms of the operations, or measures, used to identify them. In this approach, intelligence is simply defined as what intelligence tests test (Boring, 1923). In this rigorous definition, the term "intelligence" has no other meaning. However, while this definition has more scientific rigor than those discussed above, it has less general communication value. Moreover, it raises the issues of what test was or should be used, what should be on an intelligence test, and so forth. Thus, what the strict operational definition gains in scientific rigor it loses in practical utility.

The foregoing discussion illustrates two facts regarding definitions of intelligence. First, the term refers to a variety of behaviors. There is no single agreed-upon definition, and there probably never will be. Spiker and McCandless (1954) comment that "intelligence" is a word taken by psychologists from the common language:

> Its common-sense meaning, like that of many similar concepts, is complex and indefinite. An unequivocable characterization of the common-sense notion is probably both impossible and unprofitable. (p. 260)

A second conclusion is that the general operational definitions of intelligence simply describe a class or type of behavior. Thus, intelligence does not exist as an entity. It is merely a hypothetical idea to explain the behavior we see or describe. Most psychologists do agree that intelligence is a *hypothetical construct.* It has no concrete physical basis, nor is it a process that can be found or located in the body. Conger (1957) summarizes this popular view:

> It is purely a hypothetical construct, a scientific fiction, like the concept of force in physics. We invent it because it helps us to explain and predict behavior. That is the first fact to be grasped in attempting to understand the word intelligence: namely, that it is a hypothetical attribute of the individual. The second fact to be grasped is that this hypothetical attribute is assumed to vary in amount from one individual to another. In other words, we assume that it makes sense to say that one individual has more intelligence than another. (p. 11)

## Theoretical Approaches

Thus far, we have determined that "intelligence" is simply a term used to represent something about human behavior. It is a shorthand way of classifying or grouping a set of behaviors which may be broadly labeled intelligent. It is only when we attempt to define this hypothetical construct that the real problem begins. While the operational approaches describe intelligent behavior, the theoretical approaches attempt to explain how or why intelligent behavior occurs. There are four theoretical approaches to intelligence: (1) learning theory, (2) neurological-biological, (3) psychometric, and (4) developmental. The first two are considered minor (Maloney and Ward, 1976), since they are less well developed and have had less impact (i.e., less researched).

The *learning theory approach*, associated with such writers as Staats (1970), considers "intelligence" an unnecessary, superfluous, and even detrimental term. Within this approach, intelligence can most adequately be described in the context of learning theory terms. All people have generally the same biological and neurological equipment (excepting extreme cases of brain damage) and are essentially equal in their ability to learn intellectual skills. Additionally, it is assumed that the brain, as the basic mechanism of learning, is more than adequate to handle all the levels of problem complexity. Given this assumption, the crucial factor in intellectual development is the quality and quantity of environmental experiences (learning opportunities) that the individual receives during his development. Early in development, certain "basic behavioral repertoires" are learned; these, in turn, become the basis for learning in a new situation. For Staats (1970), the extent and quality of prior learning experiences constitute intelligence:

> . . . children inherit, as members of the human species a biological structure that fits them for the most complex intellectual learning and accomplishment. What they become then depends upon the nature of their learning circumstances and the behavioral repertoires they acquire. (p. 276)

The *biological-neurological approaches* (see, e.g., Halstead, 1961; Hebb, 1972) explore the neurological, neurochemical, or biological basis of intelligence. These approaches start with the assumption that the brain is the basic organ of intelligence and adaptive behavior. Defining intelligence then becomes a matter of describing which processes, functions, or attributes of the brain underlie intelligent behavior. Research in this area has encountered many serious problems. There are neither enough data nor a sufficiently comprehensive theory to present an adequate neurological-biological definition of intelligence. However, this research area holds great promise; under study are neurotransmitters, hemisphere functioning of the cortex, and so forth. If breakthroughs do occur, the idea of intelligence could become quite tangible and definable in terms of specific brain processes.

The *developmental theory approach* is best illustrated by the work of Jean Piaget (Flavell, 1963), who became interested in intelligence while working on refinements of the Binet scale. While observing children's answers to trial test questions, he became intrigued with the types of wrong answers given. He noticed that children of the same age generally give the same type of wrong answers and that similar kinds of wrong answers are given at different age levels. These observations led him to suspect that different modes of thinking were employed at different ages. Piaget then began to observe the behavior of his own and other children to gain insight into these thought processes that, for him, are the essence of intelligence. Based on his observations, he went on to develop one of the most influential theories of intelligence. Piaget's is called a developmental theory because intelligence is presumed to change as the individual matures. At different developmental stages, intelligence is quantitatively and qualitatively different. Piaget proposes three periods of intellectual development. In the *sensory-motor period,* which lasts from birth to about two years of age, intelligence is primarily action oriented. The child learns by doing. He interacts with his environment and develops what Piaget calls "schema" as a function of his experience (see, e.g., Flavell, 1963, for further elaboration of these stages). During this first stage, intelligence is defined by these sensory-motor operations: how the infant interacts with and incorporates motor feedback from the environment.

The second phase of intellectual development, the *period of concrete operations,* lasts from about two years of age to 11 years. During this time, the child acquires the use of symbols and language and learns to think logically and "representationally." The latter term refers to the child's ability to think about objects without having to deal with them directly; that is, he is able to maintain an image of them in his mind. However, while less dependent on the perceptual dimensions of the environment (i.e., the seeable, touchable, etc.), he still thinks of the real world in its actual, concrete form. This can be illustrated by an informal experiment similar to those conducted by Piaget. Young children are presented with two identical large pitchers of liquid. The contents from one pitcher are poured into a flat, shallow pan. The children are then asked which (pan or pitcher) has more liquid in it. Children in the early phase of the period of concrete operations choose the pitcher, since it "looks bigger." They are unable to think abstractly and cannot appreciate how an object can change greatly in appearance but remain the same.

The final stage of intellectual development, the *period of formal operations,* represents adult intelligence and occurs from about age 11 onward. In describing how the person with formal operations deals with his world, Piaget uses the analogy of a scientist. In solving a problem, the scientist approaches it logically, looking at all possible alternative solutions and eliminating them systematically until he has arrived at one solution. At this stage of intelligence, all possible solutions can be considered, not only those that are immediate, obvious, and concrete.

For Piaget, the essence of intelligence lies in these changes of structure (i.e., sensory-motor, concrete operations, formal operations). Intelligence is qualitatively different at different ages and is not an entity that grows in height or width. From the developmental point of view, intelligence can never be represented by a number like IQ. It is not so much measured as described.

The *psychometric approach* rests on the assumption that individual differences in intelligence do exist and that these differences are measured or reflected in intelligence tests. The term "psychometric," in fact, refers to the measurement (metric) of psychological traits. Psychometric theorists attempt to understand and define intelligence by evaluating how persons perform on intelligence tests: what problems they get right and wrong and how these relate to each other. Two statistical procedures, correlation and factor analysis, are the primary tools. They are used to answer such questions as, Is intelligence a single global trait or are there many different discrete traits (e.g., memory, spatial visualization, perceptual speed, word knowledge, etc.) which comprise it? Spearman (1927) emphasized the general or global nature of intelligence, referred to as "g." Guilford (1967), however, contends that intelligence is composed of many discrete abilities. In his system, referred to as the Structure of Intellect (SI), he theorizes some 120 such abilities.

It is now widely accepted that intelligence is composed of many separate abilities or components (called multidimensional). (The exact number remains unspecified, but both Spearman's and Guilford's proposals are considered too extreme.) Given this multidimensional concept of intelligence, assessment is focused on patterns of ability rather than on a single level of ability, as implied by IQ.

## THEORIES OF INTELLIGENCE: SOME COMPARISONS AND CONTRASTS

Our brief review has illustrated the wide diversity in thinking about intelligence. Let us further compare these theories on several dimensions. This will provide a basis clarifying the relationship between these theories and the concept of mental retardation.

*Process-Content Differences* The *content* of intelligence typically refers to "what" or "how much" an individual knows. The *process* of intelligence, on the other hand, refers to "how" an individual knows. On this dimension, the psychometric approach stands in sharp contrast to the other three approaches. It specifically focuses on test responses or results as the empirical base for the various theories (e.g., Guilford or Spearman). In this approach, there is almost no concern with how the problem was solved. The focus is on the response and how it can be classified (right or wrong). In contrast, the learning theory and the neurological and developmental approaches have relatively little interest in the content of intelligence; they emphasize the processes by which a person solves problems or learns. They are concerned, respectively, with the learning, neurological, or developmental structures or processes that indicate how intelligence functions. The process-content difference is most striking when the developmental and psychometric approaches are contrasted. With the developmental approach, the focus is on the processes of thinking and knowing and how these processes change over time.

*Measurement versus Description* In measurement versus description, the contrast once again is between the psychometric and the other three orientations. The basic issue here is the idea of individual differences. The psychometric approach assumes that individuals do differ in intelligence and that such differences can be measured (i.e., IQ). None of the other three approaches focuses on such differences; in fact, the opposite is true. The learning, neurological, and developmental theories delineate or describe the *common* or *universal* processes of intelligence. Thus, they focus on the similarities in intellectual processes among people rather than on differences. Individual differences are not denied but simply ignored. It is important to note that the very concept of mental retardation (less intelligence) flows directly from the psychometric attitude, which focuses on the differences between people.

*Homogeneity versus Heterogeneity* The psychometric view quantifies the heterogeneity of intelligence. From this perspective, people do differ in terms of intelligence, often markedly. This view contrasts sharply with the implicit homogeneity of intelligence of the other three approaches. To illustrate, Piaget emphasizes stages of intellectual development which the vast majority of people proceed through. While the thinking characteristic of these stages appears to be similar for all people, can we assume that everyone at, for example, the stage of formal operations, is equally intelligent? The important point is that, while such theories lead to much information on the processes of intelligence, they may imply that intelligence is a fairly homogeneous trait. From a practical point of view this is not the case, as will be explored later in this chapter. One solution may be to apply the idea of individual differences to the learning or neurological and developmental approaches. For example, while people may be similar in learning mechanisms or neurological or developmental structures, there may be differences among multiple related factors (experience, nutrition, etc.). These latter variations may account for differences in the efficiency of the basic systems (e.g., learning mechanisms). The application of the idea of individual differences to these other theories may lead eventually to a comprehensive and systematic theory of intelligence.

*Intelligence as a Trait* The term "trait" in psychology refers to a personal attribute that is fairly ingrained and permanent. Of the four theoretical approaches we have discussed, only learning theory does not treat intelligence as an individual trait. This is because, from the learning theory perspective, intelligence is seen as an attribute of behavior rather than of the person. While the learning model does postulate that there is some neurological substrate (learning mechanism) for intelligent behavior, it minimizes any inter-individual differences in such a mechanism. All intelligence differences are assumed to be the result of the person's learning history or the parameters of the learning situation. Such differences are not considered to inhere in the individual.

In contrast, since the other three approaches view intelligence as a personal attribute, definite structural or trait features are postulated. The developmental approach hypothesizes the existence of underlying psychological structures and assumes that they have a neurological analogue. The neurological-biological approach is the ultimate in the structural aspects of intelligence, with its focus on the nervous system. However, the epitome of the trait notion is found in the psychometric approach. The very concept of individual differences assumes the idea of traits as personal attributes. These differences in the intellectual trait between persons have been quantified as the IQ.

## THE RELATIONSHIP BETWEEN THEORIES OF INTELLIGENCE AND IQ TESTS

It might seem logical to assume that tests of intelligence somehow stem from theories of intelligence. Such, however, is not the case. Intelligence tests evolved from an applied-practical orientation. Consequently, they were not based on any specific theory. Early test developers, faced with the necessity of making decisions about educational potential, or the like, developed practical measures to aid them. Alfred Binet, for example, was under contract to the French Ministry of Education to develop a method for determining which children would profit from public education. He tackled this task in an empirical manner, experimenting with various procedures to see what would work. At the onset, he had no theory of intelligence. In fact, his original goal was not to develop an intelligence test. What was later to become the Stanford-Binet intelligence test evolved over time, with no guidance from any systematic theory of intelligence. As it turned out, the intuitive and quasi-theoretical ideas of the early test developers worked out quite well from a practical point of view, and IQ tests are among the most reliable and valid psychological tests available.

Although the development of intelligence tests predates any systematic theories of intelligence, it might be expected that these theories could now provide some theoretical justification or explanation for the success of IQ tests. Unfortunately, this has not proved to be the case. The mere fact that we have four diverse theories suggests that there is little relationship or congruence between them and intelligence tests. It is instructive to explore the theories and how, if at all, they relate to intelligence tests and the concept of IQ.

With the learning, neurological-biological, and developmental approaches, the lack of relationship to IQ is clear and understandable. As noted earlier, these orientations are concerned with the intellectual structures or processes that are common to all people. In contrast, tests of intelligence are designed to determine how much a *given* person knows or how intelligent he is. Only in a very general sense can such test results be related to these theories. In learning theory terms, for example, IQ might be thought of as a broad indication of the effectiveness of an individual's learning mechanism. In this sense, IQ can be considered the "results" of past learning. Similarly, intelligence test results could be thought of as a rough approximation of the efficiency and soundness of the neurological basis of behavior. In both of these cases, however, the relationship between IQ tests and theory is quite strained, very general, and of little theoretical or practical value. With the developmental approach, there is practically no relationship whatever. Piaget's developmental theory describes psychological processes and structures (stages) that change qualitatively over time. The concept of qualitative stages is totally at variance with the notion of a continuous quantitative index such as IQ.

With the psychometric approach, the relationship is paradoxical. Intelligence tests were the impetus and empirical foundation of this approach. Intelligence is theoretically measured by how persons perform on tests—whether they answer correctly, and so on. Thus, one would expect to find considerable congruence between the psychometric approach and the tests. However, there is actually little relationship between the tests and the various psychometric theories. Spearman's idea of "g," or a single general factor of intelligence, initially seems to be directly related to the concept of IQ. However, while there is some actual relationship between these concepts (IQ and "g" do correlate), Spearman theorizes that "g" is a pure factor and IQ is not. In other words, IQ tests tap many different factors or mental processes in addition to a "g" or general factor. Thus, although there is some relationship between IQ and "g," Spearman and others contend they are basically different.

At the other extreme from Spearman's "g" concept is Guilford's Structure of Intellect (SI) model. This model proposes that intelligence is composed of 120 separate abilities. In discussing the relationship of this model to tests of intelligence, Guilford and Hoepfner (1971) note that our predominantly verbally oriented IQ tests (e.g., Binet-type scales) strongly emphasize only two of these abilities. For the Wechsler scales (which have 11 subtests), they point out that 11 of the SI abilities are sampled but in a very imperfect and inadequate manner. The obvious implication is that the standard tests ignore most of the aspects of intelligence as defined by Guilford, while emphasizing others much too strongly.

In summary, intelligence tests either do not relate to the four theoretical approaches or do so in a very vague and ill-defined manner. While the tests provided the empirical base for the psychometric approach, this approach does not provide a scientific or theoretical basis for the tests.

## THE MEANING OF IQ

All tests of intelligence have one thing in common: their results are expressed as a quantitative index called the intelligence quotient, or IQ. The IQ summarizes a person's performance, or level of general intellectual functioning, on a given test. It is this index that most people think of and refer to when talking about intelligence. Perhaps no other notion in the field of psychology has engendered so much, and often heated, debate. Much of the controversy concerns interpretation. There are, however, some misunderstandings about the meaning of IQ that must be clarified. Further, many of the theories of intelligence were proposed as rivals to the vague and implicit theory represented by the IQ. Thus, an understanding of IQ is necessary before we can fully appreciate the differences between the theoretical views and the actual tests. Let us first consider the historical development of the IQ concept.

The first Binet scales of the early 1900s did not include the IQ. Binet developed an age-graded scale and used the concept of mental age (MA) as an index of mental functioning. The MA is defined as the general mental ability of the average child of a particular chronological age (CA). Thus, an eight-year-old child with an MA of four years is considered to function on an intellectual level of the average four-year-old child. Binet used the difference between a child's MA and CA to talk about deficits or exceptionality. The eight-year-old child with an MA of four would have a deficit of four years. There is, however, a serious problem with such an approach. A difference of one year between MA and CA does not mean the same thing at age two that it does at age twelve. The child who is one year behind at age two is far more deficient than the child who is one year behind at age twelve. This is the result of the absolute changes in mental development that occur in the growth process. Stated simply, as with most growth characteristics, the greatest absolute changes usually occur in the early years. Bloom (1964) has reviewed the data from numerous longitudinal studies of intelligence and has computed figures that demonstrate this effect. In discussing the implications of Bloom's data, Sattler (1974) notes:

> He [Bloom] concluded that the variation in intelligence at age 17 can be accounted for by the following developmental pattern: 20% is developed by age 1, 50% by age 4, 80% by age 8, and 90% by age 13. This pattern shows differentially accelerated growth, with very rapid growth of intelligence in the early years. As much development takes place during the first 4 years of life as in the next 13. (p. 16)

Bloom thus argues that intelligence should be viewed as a developmental phenomenon similar to height, weight, or strength. The greatest absolute changes in all of these characteristics occur in the early years. With this in mind, it can be seen that the use of the absolute difference between MA and CA would lead to very erroneous interpretations if the "absolute" growth curve of mental development is not taken into account.

That curve (see Figure 8.5 in Chapter 8) is negatively accelerated. That is, it has a sharp, steep rise in the early years, gradually tapering off to some asymptote later on.

Even without such empirical data, Stern (1912) intuitively perceived the problem of the absolute difference between MA and CA. To attempt to solve this dilemma, he was the first to propose the IQ concept. Since the absolute difference between MA and CA meant different things at different CA levels, he suggested that the ratio of MA to CA (MA ÷ CA) would provide a much better index of mental functioning. In his revision of the Binet scales for American use, Terman (1916) employed Stern's IQ index and thus established its use in all future intelligence tests.

The formula for this ratio is: IQ = MA/CA × 100. Thus, an eight-year-old child with an MA of eight years has an IQ of 100. That same eight-year-old child would have an IQ of 50 if his MA was four (4/8 × 100) or 150 if his MA was twelve (12/8 × 100). If we reconsider the radically different implications of the same one-year difference for a two-year-old and a twelve-year-old child, the former has an IQ of 50 (1 ÷ 2 × 100) while the latter has an IQ of 92 (11 ÷ 12 × 100).

As implied by the ratio concept, IQ was thus thought to indicate the rate of mental development. Consequently, a child with an IQ of 50 was thought to be developing mentally at a rate half that of a normal child. For each year of advancing CA, that child would presumably gain only one-half year of mental development. An additional early assumption was that the rate of development as measured by the IQ was constant. Thus, for every chronological year the child gained only one-half year of mental age, and thereby continued to have an IQ of 50. Such notions, of course, reflected the prevailing hereditarian view of intelligence as a completely genetic and unchanging trait. There has been considerable research on this assumption of a constant IQ, but the supporting data have not been particularly conclusive. Longitudinal studies, for example, which retested the same children at various CA levels, often revealed marked inconstancy.

The ratio method of computing IQ was the only method available until the appearance of David Wechsler's (1939) Wechsler-Bellevue Scales. In constructing this test, Wechsler abandoned the Binet strategy of an age-graded scale and the mental age concept. The primary reason was the inherent problems in the MA concept as employed in the Binet scales. In such an age-graded scale, data indicate that mean MA scores increase with advancing CA up to approximately 13 or 14 years of age. Beyond that age, mean MA leveled off. The implication was that mental development had reached its peak. In other words, as with height, the individual had "topped out." Testing for intelligence of adults beyond this level was thus impossible with the age-graded approach. Consequently, Wechsler developed a test in which all adults received the same test items and IQ was computed in a manner much different from the ratio method (with its reliance on MA).

Several other problems with the MA concept point up Wechsler's wisdom in abandoning it. One of these has already been alluded to in our discussion of the different absolute changes in mental growth over the developmental years. The greatest absolute changes occur in the early years, gradually tapering off in adulthood. The obvious implication of this fact is that the MA units for the different CA levels are not equal. For example, one year of MA growth between ages two and three involves far more absolute mental development than one year of MA growth between ages twelve and thirteen. This inequality of MA units across the developmental span seriously undermines this concept as an absolute indicator of mental development.

Another problem with MA lies in the method of computation. On a Binet-type scale, each MA-year level is composed of six tests. For example, Year VII on the Stanford-Binet has tests of "picture absurdities," "similarities," "copying a diamond," "comprehension," "opposite analogies," and "repeating digits." Each of the tests at each year level is assigned two months' credit. Thus, at year seven, there are six tests with two months' credit each, resulting in a total of twelve months, or one year of mental age credit. Under ideal conditions, and if the scale was a natural ordinal scale, a child with an MA of seven years should get all the tests right at each year level up to and including the year seven level, with no further successes beyond that point. In practice, however, the ideal rarely occurs. Rather, there is considerable scattering (children fail some easier items and pass other more difficult ones). Because credit over all year levels is added together in arriving at the MA level, an MA of seven can be obtained in a variety of ways (e.g., all six tests passed at year six, none at seven, but all at year eight; three of six tests at year seven and three of six tests at year eight, etc.). Consequently, two children with the same MA may differ greatly in a qualitative sense in terms of the types of skills they can successfully use. This aspect of MA computation also makes it very difficult to consider MA as an absolute indicator of mental development. People at both the same and different CA levels can come up with the same MA in very different ways, with consequently very different qualitative meanings for their mental development. This becomes especially apparent for the mentally retarded adult who receives, for example, a mental age of three although he manifests few actual behaviors similar to a normal three-year-old.

Wechsler constructed his test of adult intelligence to deal with the fact that mean MA scores leveled off in the early teens. Because of the additional problems regarding the inequality of MA units and the way the MA was computed, he also developed a test for children (WISC) modeled after his adult test. As with the adult test, it was not an age-graded scale like the Binet type, which employed different tests at different age levels. Instead, children at all ages were given the same set of items. Since no MA was computed, the ratio IQ method was also not utilized.

Because of the problems with the MA concept, Wechsler replaced the ratio IQ method with the *deviation IQ* method. The logic behind the deviation IQ, along with the many problems with the ratio IQ, has resulted in a broad acceptance of the deviation IQ. The only disadvantage of this method is the loss of simplicity and clarity implicit in the ideal MA and its use in the ratio IQ. However, we have seen that the actual MA is a gross distortion of the ideal and leads to more problems of interpretation than it solves.

The deviation IQ method, while avoiding many of the serious problems of the ratio IQ, is much more difficult to interpret, particularly for the nonprofessional. It requires a knowledge and understanding of the normal curve (the theoretical distribution of intelligence) and the standard deviation. It is important to note, however, that the two methods of IQ computation yield similar results; the deviation method is more scientifically valid and precise. When explaining the IQ to lay persons, the examiner will often find it more meaningful to revert to the older ratio IQ rationale, noting that somewhat different procedures are actually employed.

The interpretation of the deviation IQ is based on the assumption that the theoretical distribution of intelligence can be described by the normal curve (see Figure 3.1). (This assumption, and the empirical distribution of intelligence, will be discussed later.) For now, let us assume that intelligence for the population is "normal"; that is, the IQs of most people cluster around a central point (IQ 100), and progressively fewer people have IQs that are increasingly higher or lower. Given this assumption, the interpretation of the deviation IQ is quite straightforward. What it tells you is the relative position of the person compared to his age peers in terms of the normal curve. Relative position is described in terms of standard deviation units. The essential feature of the deviation IQ is that its meaning is derived through a relative comparison of performance—that is, how one person compares to the population. It is not, in any sense of the word, an absolute measure of performance. The deviation IQ method gives each individual IQ meaning by referring it to the distribution of all relevant IQs and telling you where in that distribution this particular IQ is located.

One advantage of the use of the normal curve and standard deviation units is that they have easily understood and interpretable percentile equivalents. Thus, the meaning of the deviation IQ can be thought of in the same terms as SAT (Scholastic Aptitude Test) or GRE (Graduate Record Examination) scores. The SAT and GRE scores do not indicate in absolute units how much verbal or quantitative ability a person possesses. The total meaning of these scores is derived by comparing the individual's performance to that of the appropriate norm or reference group. These comparisons are usually made in terms of percentiles (see Table 3.1). For instance, a person in the 99th percentile on the verbal portion of the test has performed better than 99 percent of those taking the test or the appropriate norm group. The use of such percentile ranks thus allows the individual score to be interpreted in terms of relative, not absolute, performance. The same is true of the IQ as computed by the deviation method. An IQ of 100, which is arbitrarily set as the mean of the distribution, indicates that the individual is at the 50th percentile and that, compared to his peers, his performance is better than approximately 50 percent and worse than approximately 50 percent. An IQ of 70, which is the upper limit for mental retardation, tells you that the person is in the bottom 2 percent of his age peers in terms of performance on this test, and that 98 percent of his peers perform better than he does. These IQs do not

TABLE 3.1

Percentile Ranks of IQ Scores

| Percentile Rank | IQ | Percentile Rank | IQ |
|---|---|---|---|
| 99 | 135 | 50 | 100 |
| 98 | 130 | 40 | 96 |
| 95 | 125 | 30 | 92 |
| 90 | 119 | 25 | 90 |
| 85 | 116 | 20 | 87 |
| 80 | 113 | 15 | 84 |
| 75 | 110 | 10 | 81 |
| 70 | 108 | 8 | 75 |
| 60 | 104 | 2 | 70 |
| 50 | 100 | 1 | 65 |

indicate an absolute level, as with height in inches, but only a relative comparison to one's age peers. Thus, IQ does not really indicate how much intelligence a person has, only how well he performed relative to others taking the same test. However, some general qualitative statements can be made, given the knowledge of a person's IQ. On the basis of experience with people at given IQ levels and the types of test content such people are typically able to answer correctly, probabilistic statements about an individual's ability (the kinds of things he can and cannot do) can be made.

One difference between the ratio and deviation IQ methods concerns the issue of rate of development. To review, it is implicitly assumed that the ratio IQ is an indicator of the rate of mental development, given the ratio of MA to CA. Since the deviation IQ has nothing to do with MA, such rate issues are, technically speaking, not applicable. However, the constancy of IQ still applies, since it is widely assumed that one's relative position among one's age peers (rather than one's ratio) will not change from year to year. However, the same data regarding the constancy of IQ in the longitudinal studies mentioned before also apply here.

Another issue with the deviation IQ method is similar to the problem of the way MA is computed in the ratio IQ method. In computing deviation IQs, the raw test scores are transformed to some standard score. However, the way that raw score is determined is crucial to the ultimate meaning of the deviation IQ. Just as with the old MA concept, these raw scores are arrived at by merely summing up all the correct items for a given person. Consequently, the same raw score can be obtained in many different ways, thereby masking the potential qualitative differences among persons being tested. Thus, although relative performance might be identical for two people (i.e., both have the same IQ), important differences in the pattern of intellectual abilities are lost.

A final problem with the deviation IQ method also applies to all psychological measurement. Tests of intelligence, like almost all psychological tests, fall somewhere between ordinal (A is better than B is better than C, with no indication of the magnitude of the differences between A and B and B and C) and interval (A is better than B is better than C, and the magnitude of difference between A and B is exactly the same as that between B and C) scales. Thus, while IQ tests are able to rank people in terms of relative performance (better or worse), the units between intervals are only assumed to be equal. In fact, we have no idea whether or not IQ units are equal. Consequently, although an IQ is a quantitative index, it does not function like a ratio scale of height, with an absolute zero and equal units between intervals. This fact is often forgotten. Thus, while it is correct to say that a six-foot person is twice as tall as a three-foot person, it is incorrect to state or imply that a person with an IQ of 100 is twice as smart as a person with an IQ of 50. Such absolute statements are not permissible because the IQ scale has neither an absolute zero (what would constitute zero intelligence?) nor equal units (is the difference between IQ 90 and 95 the same as the difference between 60 and 65?). The only really permissible statement, given the ordinal nature of the scale, is that the IQ is merely a measure of relative performance in terms of the rank-order of the individuals involved.

As mentioned above, the meaning of the deviation IQ rests on the assumption that the theoretical distribution of intelligence is normal. This theoretical distribution, by definition, is unknown. Because of empirical data demonstrating that the distribution of many human characteristics (e.g., height) is approximately normal, the assumption of normality of intelligence is considered at least tenable. Given this assumption, tests are designed to yield a normal distribution. The success of these efforts can be examined by looking at investigations on the distribution of tested IQ.

Figure 3.1 presents the expected theoretical distribution of intelligence, using an arbitrary mean of 100 with a standard deviation of 15 points. (Standard deviation is simply a measure of the amount of variability in the distribution.) The figure indicates the standard deviation units, the corresponding IQ scores for those units, and the percentage of cases (rounded off) that fall between successive standard deviation units. It can be seen that the normal or bell-shaped curve is symmetrical, and that the percentage and breakdown of cases is the same both above and below the mean. It should be noted that almost 70 percent of the population is expected to fall within plus or minus one standard deviation unit (IQ 85 to 115), and that in moving away from the mean in either direction, there is a progressive reduction in the percentage of cases expected to fall between the standard deviation units.

Studies based on large samples suggest that the shape of the obtained distributions closely approximates the expected theoretical distribution. There are, however, discrepancies. In summarizing some of these data, Haywood (1974) indicates that, in general, there are more cases in both "tails" of the curve and fewer in the middle portion than expected. In other words, there are slightly more persons of significantly above- and below-average intelligence than would be expected and slightly fewer in the middle range.

One final consideration merits attention: IQ has been defined as a quantitative index of a person's *general intellectual functioning* as measured by a test of intelligence. But what is the meaning of the term "gen-

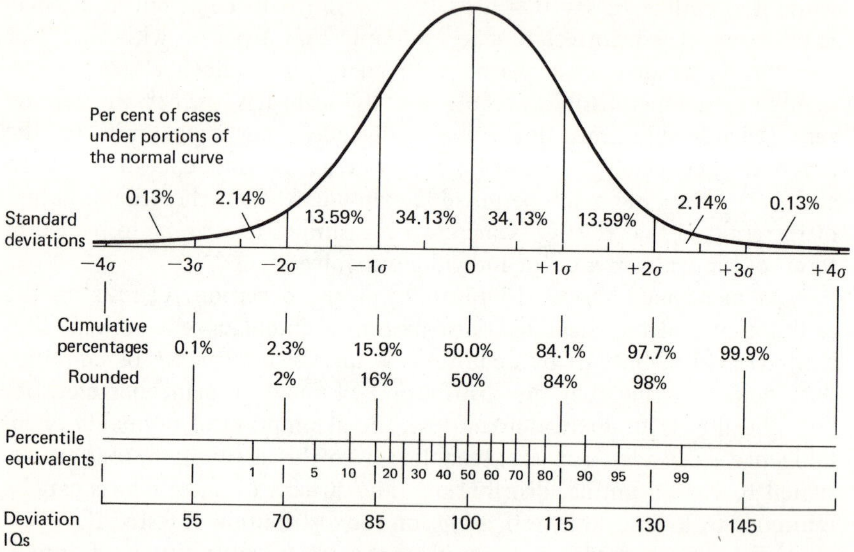


FIGURE 3.1

Theoretical Distribution of Intelligence Based on IQ. (Adapted from *Test Service Bulletin*, Psychological Corporation, 1954–55, Nos. 47–49.)

eral intelligence"? Let us refer to the thinking of the two most prominent test developers.

Alfred Binet conceived of intelligence as a composite of various "faculties," or abilities. Consequently, his test was designed to sample these faculties. By sampling a wide variety of complex mental processes, Binet felt he could arrive at an index of general mental functioning. Although never explicitly stated, his formulation implies that general intelligence is a weighted average of these faculties.

Wechsler (1971) also believed that intelligence is composed of separate abilities, but that it could also be described as a global capacity. However, he expanded the notion to include non-intellective factors, such as drive and incentive, which necessarily combine with the various abilities in the expression of intelligent behavior. In addition, Wechsler notes that the obtained scores are not identical with intelligence, but neither are they separate from it. Wechsler briefly summarizes his thinking about general intelligence:

> I personally prefer to look upon general intelligence as a global capacity that manifests itself in different ways, depending upon the chal-

> lenge presented and the assets which the individual possesses to meet it. But the question of a global versus special kinds of intelligence turns out to be primarily a theoretical one. In practice, i.e., when it comes to devising instruments or tests for appraising intelligence, it generally plays a minor role. Notwithstanding their theoretical views, authors of intelligence scales tend to make use of the same sort of tasks and items. Procedures may vary, but the tests themselves do not differ very much. The reason is that basically there are really not very many different ways of appraising intelligence. One is limited by the kind of reasonable tasks that can be set and the suitable questions that can be asked.
>
> . . . But the abilities called for to perform these tasks do not, per se, constitute intelligence or even represent the only ways in which it may express itself. They are used and can serve as tests of intelligence because they have been shown to correlate with other more widely accepted criteria of intelligent behavior. (p. 52)

In summary, the term "general intelligence," as represented by the IQ, is probably best thought of as a weighted average of the separate or qualitatively different aspects of intelligence. The IQ is thus an index or summary term. Its meaning is further amplified by referring the obtained score to a distribution of such scores and noting the relative performance indicated.

## SCIENTIFIC VALIDITY AND PRACTICAL UTILITY OF THE IQ

The intelligence quotient (IQ) has been technically defined as the summary index that indicates a person's relative position among a distribution of such scores. However, the ultimate meaning of this concept remains problematic, given the lack of relationship between any of the previously discussed theories of intelligence and the intelligence tests themselves. There is simply no adequate theoretical explanation for the acknowledged practical success of these tests. The most tenable conclusion is that theory and practice have little in common.

One possible solution to this problem is related to the scientific validity versus the practical utility of intelligence tests. The Binet test of intelligence, as we have seen, was constructed with a practical purpose in mind. Binet was asked to develop an objective, standard procedure for screening out the mentally retarded from regular public school instruction. He was not asked to develop a scientifically valid theory of intelligence as well. His concern was purely pragmatic, and by this criterion his efforts were eminently successful. Today, these practical, intuitively constructed mixture of items called intelligence tests have consistently proven their value in terms of certain practical affairs such as the prediction of school achievement. It is thus in terms of these practical effects that the tests are designated "successful." They are concerned with performance. Emphasis must thus be placed on their practical utility rather than their scientific validity in any rigorous theoretical sense.

What is the practical utility of intelligence tests? The scores on these tests are related to a number of criteria of success. It is important to note that the definition of success is social and cultural rather than scientific. Thus, tests are simply a tool of a given society to be used for certain practical purposes. As already mentioned, tests of intelligence have always been the best predictors of school achievement. School achievement is highly valued in Western cultures because it is typically a prerequisite to later success as an adult. The marked verbal emphasis in most intelligence tests denotes the importance of verbal facility in the culture as a measure of successful adjustment and adaptation. The tests are thus useful because they reflect the important demands that are made by the society and culture. Rather than attempting to assess all aspects of intelligence, they tap only those that are most important to societal success. For instance, in talking about the relationship of the Stanford-Binet to Guilford's Structure of Intellect model, it was noted that only two of the one hundred and twenty hypothesized abilities were adequately represented, and in fact, that these two were overrepresented. But therein lies the practical utility of the tests. They ignore theoretical aspects or components of intelligence that are necessary to a comprehensive scientific conceptualization because many of these aspects have little relevance to practical daily living. They grossly overemphasize other aspects of the theoretical model because these components are considered to be crucial to societal success.

Thus, when the issue is practical utility, there is little concern with scientific validity from a theoretical perspective. The tests are valid in the predictive sense. They relate to performances or criteria that are socially defined and presumably require or reflect intelligence. But the tests are not valid expressions of any of the major theoretical notions about the nature of intelligence. However, they were never intended to be. In fact, if the tests had to conform to some theoretical conceptualization, the likely result would be useless from a practical standpoint. Scientific or theoretical validity has been and must be sacrificed for practical utility. The reverse also holds.

What has been suggested is that the dilemma between the scientific validity and practical utility of IQ tests is legitimate and necessary. The tests and theories have been developed with different purposes. As mentioned, it is doubtful that a test modeled strictly after a theory of intelligence could properly serve its "applied" functions. However, this does not imply that theories are useless in test construction. The tests we are discussing are tests of general intelligence, whose use is restricted to certain applications. For other goals and practical purposes, devices constructed along more theoretical lines might be more widely applied. For instance, a Guilford-type theoretical model has great potential practical value in situations where fine differentiations of intellectual functioning are necessary. Such would be the case in higher academic, industrial, and military settings. Likewise, such a model would be useful in assessing people's particular strengths and weaknesses, as well as determining and delineating learning disorders. Another example of the potential usefulness of theoretical models comes from Piaget's developmental theory of intelligence. This approach allows for the development of a natural ordinal scale of intellectual development. This scale can serve as a practical guide in curriculum design, prescriptive teaching, and qualitative assessment or description of intellectual functioning. Thus, while the current tests of intelligence can be expected to continue their successful predictive functions in certain limited areas (e.g., academic achievement), future advances in the assessment of intelligence for both much boarder and more specific applications will depend on continued development and refinement along diverse theoretical lines.

An important point about the utility of current intelligence tests in diagnosing mental retardation must be noted. In general, the greater the intellectual deficit, the more useful these tests are. At the lower levels of intellectual functioning, intelligence is crucial in determining behavioral adequacy and adjustment. This is because a minimum level of intellectual competency is necessary for daily living. At the higher intellectual levels, other factors, such as motivation, interests, and personality variables, become increasingly more influential in determining behavioral performance and outcome. In addition, the role that intelligence does play at these higher intellectual levels necessitates a greater degree of ability differentiation so that specific intellectual aspects can be examined and related.

At this point, it is important to recall Wechsler's view of intelligence. Wechsler (1971) expanded the notion of general intelligence to include nonintellectual factors, such as personality and motivational variables, which combine with the various abilities in the expression of intelligent behavior. In other words, he maintains that the tests tap these other areas as well, since a test is a behavioral performance. You cannot assess intellectual functions in a vacuum or get a "pure" or "abstract" measure of an ability; the person's personality and motivation interact with his cognitive functions in producing his responses. In essence, the test gives you a measure of a person's *effective* intelligence, which is the product of the interaction of all of these variables. This fact relates directly to the issue of the scientific validity versus the practical utility of intelligence tests. Not only do the tests focus primarily on those abilities most relevant to socially defined success, but they also touch upon the personality and motivational correlates of such success. It is precisely because the tests do tap all of these factors (i.e., effective intelligence) that they have such predictive value. Unfortunately, this very mixture also complicates the attempt to study the theoretical structure of intelligence (i.e., scientific validity).

## INTERPRETATION OF IQ: USE AND ABUSE

Intelligence testing has been one of the most productive and successful enterprises in the field of psychology. However, its main derivative, the notion of IQ, has generated more controversy than perhaps any other psychological concept. The debate has centered on the role of genetics in the determination of IQ scores. The nature-nurture debate of the 1930s and 1940s has resurfaced in the 1960s and 1970s preoccupation with the possible genetic aspects of racial differences in intelligence. Other concerns have been the detrimental effects of labeling and misclassification on the basis of IQ, particularly regarding the diagnosis of mental retardation in minority groups. As the result of several court decisions, various school districts have recently either forbidden or greatly restricted the use of all or certain IQ tests. The illegal use of the IQ test in furthering job discrimination has also been terminated as the result of a Supreme Court ruling. In short, the scientific concept of IQ has at times been politicized and used for nonscientific purposes. This has resulted in a general furor, with numerous calls for its abandonment. Although it is beyond the scope of this text to comment on or add to these controversial issues, a few remarks on the abuses of the IQ concept itself are necessary. They are appropriately placed at the end of this chapter on intelligence, since IQ is the most common lay conceptualization of intelligence.

### Heredity—Constancy

The concept of IQ was introduced into the United States at a time (1916) when hereditarian notions about intelligence were pervasive. This period culminated in the warning from eugenicists to spare society from the so-called "social menace of the feebleminded" (see Chapter 2). At this time, too, the IQ was assumed to be *constant*. This followed logically from the simplistic notion that intelligence (i.e., the IQ) was inherited in terms of a simple Mendelian formula. The implication here is that a person's IQ at any point is predictive of his IQ throughout his life. Although our ideas about the inheritance of intelligence have changed greatly (e.g., a polygenetic model with consideration of environmental factors), the notion of the constant IQ remains fixed in the minds of most lay people and even some professionals. This is so despite the overwhelming evidence of considerable shifts in IQ scores after retesting at various intervals. The longer the interval between testing and the earlier the initial assessment, the more dramatic the shift. It should be recalled that many placement decisions about children are made early in their school careers. Given the great variability in IQ scores, the potential for misclassification when basing decisions on IQ *alone* is frightening. This is especially true when we consider the serious implications for the lives of the people affected.

## Problems of Tests

One problem with the notion of IQ is related to the testing of intelligence. Most lay people and many professionals are unaware of the many factors that can affect performance on such tests. First, there are possible examiner errors or biases which can affect both the administration and scoring of the tests. This is especially true with new or poorly trained examiners. As Maloney and Ward (1976) note, there has been an unfortunate trend toward using less trained and less experienced persons for psychological assessment. Second, there are a host of nonintellective characteristics (e.g., lack of motivation, anxiety) which can negatively affect test performance. Other factors, such as cultural differences and language barriers, may also affect test performance but not reflect intelligence per se. The experienced examiner will take such factors into account and qualify the obtained IQ score accordingly. However, others utilizing these reports often tend to focus only on the IQ score rather than on interpretations, qualifications, or cautions. Further, it is the number that stays with the person's file, not necessarily the entire report. When such procedures are combined with the idea that IQ is constant, the potential detrimental effects are obvious.

## Precision of IQ

Most persons perceive IQ as a precise, "scientific," quantifiable measure of intelligence. To the unsophisticated, mere quantification is the essence of science and creates an impression of believability and exactness that is not justified. The rigid use of particular IQ scores and exact IQ cutoffs for legal and administrative purposes is ridiculous in light of the known standard errors of IQ tests (3 to 5 points; see Chapter 7 for explanation) and the relatively indirect and imprecise nature of all psychological measurement. It would make much more sense to describe a person's intellectual level in terms of broader ranges (e.g., subnormal, average, or superior) than in terms of specific IQ scores.

### Meaning of IQ and Intelligence

It is commonly believed that IQ and intelligence are synonymous. However, we have seen that this is untrue. Intelligence tests ignore most theoretical aspects of intelligence (e.g., Guilford's model) while overemphasizing certain limited traits that are most relevant to cultural and social success. Also, the current conclusion of the psychometric viewpoint is that intelligence is multidimensional, although the exact number of dimensions is left unspecified. Yet, we continue to focus on and emphasize a single IQ score, rather than at least a number of such scores. More importantly, however, as pointed out by Wechsler, the practical success of our tests is partially due to the fact that they tap nonintellectual (e.g., motivation) factors in addition to intellectual ones. However, this is done in such an unsystematic manner that the two types of factors (intellectual and nonintellectual) cannot be separately measured. This fact, along with the diversity of theoretical approaches to intelligence, strongly suggests that the tests are related to intelligence in a very vague and ill-defined way. Thus, although these devices measure intelligence—or, more correctly, certain aspects of intelligence—the IQ cannot be considered synonymous with intelligence itself.

### IQ and Simplistic Interpretation

The basic problem with the IQ is that it is extremely vulnerable to misuse and misinterpretation. Because it is so simple, most people use the term and believe they know what it means. In fact, it represents an extremely complex and ill-defined phenomenon. Nevertheless, while we try to understand the nature of intelligence, practitioners and consumers of psychological techniques continue to make important decisions on the basis of a two- or three-digit number that supposedly represents intelligence.

It cannot be denied that the concept of IQ has performed certain useful selection, placement, and diagnostic services (e.g., the prediction of academic achievement) in the past and will continue to do so in certain limited settings. However, this restricted usefulness serves to perpetuate its misuse and misinterpretation in other areas. It is time to recognize that the reputation of IQ has exceeded its usefulness and that it would be perhaps better, from an overall perspective, to abandon the IQ concept altogether. This is not to suggest that we stop trying to improve or refine either our theories or our tests. Good assessment demands these advances. But it does suggest that the psychological assessment of intelligence should take a more multifaceted, descriptive approach that allows for a more in-depth view of intellectual functioning. We need both theories and tests of intelligence. We do not need the concept of IQ. Its pragmatic utility is perhaps outweighed by its susceptibility to misuse and misinterpretation.

An analogy to the area of personality is useful. There is no single two- or three-digit number that describes or measures the whole personality. The acknowledged complexity of this phenomenon will not tolerate such an approach. Likewise, the simplistic idea of intelligence as expressed in the IQ is grossly at variance with the complexity of the concept of intelligence, as indicated by the diverse theories and continuing arguments about its essence.

## WORKING POSITION ON INTELLIGENCE

Despite its complexities and problems, intelligence is a useful and important concept. Robinson and Robinson (1965) present a working position, modified and extended here by the present authors, which provides a good basis for the practical understanding and use of the concept of intelligence.

1. Intelligence is a hypothetical idea which refers in general to cognitive capacity. It is a description, not an entity.
2. From a practical point of view, intelligence is a useful idea, especially in terms of behavioral description and assessment.
3. Intelligence is an elastic concept which refers to very different behaviors at different ages and under different conditions.
4. Intelligence, as reflected in IQ tests, refers only to present performance under a specific set of conditions.
5. Intelligence refers to a wide variety of abilities and traits. Although it is clear that it is not a single factor, the specific number of abilities that make up intelligence remain a matter of debate.
6. Intelligence must be viewed in the context of a specific sociocultural system. What is considered intelligent behavior may vary from one culture to another. This is especially critical when con-

sidering the results of an IQ test—which, we have seen, is simply a tool of society.

7. Intelligence is a dynamic, developmental phenomenon. Because of the importance of this last characteristic, we will elaborate on the several meanings conveyed by this term.

As noted earlier in this chapter, and Chapter 2, since the discovery of Piaget by American psychology in the 1950s, the developmental view has become the most prominent theory in the area of intelligence. This theory states that intelligence develops dynamically; this is in striking contrast to previous views of intelligence as fixed and static. Furthermore, the development of intelligence is seen to be a function of the interaction between the genetic inheritance and the environment. In other words, one is not born with a certain amount of intelligence that develops at a fixed and constant rate to a predetermined level. On the contrary, both the rate of development and the final level of attainment depend on the quality of the interaction between the organism and the environment. The new term for mental retardation—"developmental disability"—flows directly from this conceptualization of intelligence.

The term "dynamic-developmental" also means that both the development and the expression of intelligence are closely related to personality and motivation. When talking about intelligence, scientists tend to discuss it as a separate, distinct, isolated entity. This is done primarily for purposes of convenience. In actuality, however, intelligence cannot be divorced from the total functioning of the whole person. It is not expressed in a vacuum, nor can it be studied in a vacuum. We cannot observe intelligence per se; we can only observe intelligent behavior. We then infer that this behavior is due to some underlying trait called "intelligence." But as noted above, intelligence is a hypothetical, descriptive idea; it is not an entity. More importantly, it is dynamic and interactive, and must be viewed in a developmental framework. Each of the factors involved (i.e., intelligence, personality, and motivation) are seen to affect the growth and development of the others.

An appreciation of the dynamic-developmental nature of intelligence is essential in understanding mental retardation. It indicates that mental retardation is not just a "mental" or "low IQ" problem. Because personality and motivation are involved in the development and expression of intelligence, the same is true regarding mental retardation. Consequently, a focus on low intelligence alone is grossly inappropriate. We must also consider the personality and motivation of the mentally retarded. If there is a problem in one of the three components of intelligent behavior, there may also be a problem in the other two. In short, if intelligence is a dynamic-developmental phenomenon, then mental retardation must be a dynamic-developmental disability. Accordingly, our study of mentally retarded persons must also focus on the personality and motivational characteristics that affect the development and expression of their intelligence.

# CHAPTER 4

# The Concept of Mental Retardation

This chapter addresses itself to the question "What is mental retardation?" Although there is a generally accepted definition (i.e., the AAMD definition, discussed later in the chapter), there is really no simple, adequate answer to this question. In fact, the meaning and value of the concept of mental retardation has always been more pragmatic than scientific. The pressing practical problems of mental retardation necessitated an immediate, practical response. Thus, over the years, a consensus on various working definitions has been arrived at, despite the ambiguities and vagueness in the concept itself. As such, these practical definitions have served a variety of legal, economic, social-administrative, and bureaucratic purposes. Accordingly, the concept of mental retardation has been primarily legal and social-administrative. The courts needed a concrete set of criteria on which to base critical decisions on issues like competency to stand trial, culpability for criminal acts, and when institutionalization could be ordered. School systems needed to set eligibility requirements for admission to their special classes. The legislators, social planners, and bureaucrats charged with providing services for this population needed a practical set of guidelines so that laws could be formulated and funds made available. It was ultimately a question of expediency; the "scientific" nature of the concept was of secondary importance.

This practical emphasis is further illustrated by the use of many different upper IQ cutoffs. For instance, while an IQ of 70 has been the traditional limit, many school systems have used 75 or even 80 for admission to special classes. This situation makes for some interesting problems. A child enrolled in a special class in one school district may be ineligible in a neighboring school system which uses a lower cutoff figure. A further complication occurs in the interactions across various institutional systems. For instance, a boy with an IQ of 75 who attends a special class (and thus is considered to be mentally retarded by some educational systems) would not be considered mentally retarded under the legal system, in which the upper limit is typically 70. The most striking discrepancy between the scientific and pragmatic aspects of the concept of mental retardation is the change in the 1959/1961 AAMD formal definition. Scientists and professionals in the field had decided that the upper IQ cutoff for mental retardation should be 85 rather than 70. While this definition was widely accepted and employed at the time, there were several areas where the change had little impact. The courts, state legislatures, and many school systems never changed their laws or policies to conform. Thus, there can be a major difference between the scientific conceptualization of mental retardation and the practical use of the concept in everyday affairs.

Despite the stress on the pragmatic aspects of the definition and concept of mental retardation, its ultimate scientific meaning still remains quite relevant and important. Whatever the practical inconsistencies, the definition of mental retardation has a clear scientific basis. The practical criteria represent a translation of this underlying concept. In this chapter, we will examine the scientific concept behind these operational criteria and explore its various aspects and meanings. This is necessary to evaluate the appropriateness of the practical translation as manifested in the formal definitions.

We will demonstrate that mental retardation is not a specific disease, entity, or syndrome but rather a vague, complex, and *indefinite* concept. This is best reflected by the fact that the concept is used to describe an extremely heterogeneous group of people who differ greatly among themselves in terms of the causes, degrees, effects, and treatment implications of their retardation. A unitary idea of mental retardation is both a myth and a misrepresentation of the actual state of affairs. Furthermore, as we have seen, the scientific concept of mental retardation has evolved over time. New formulations continue to emerge; and while many of these are short-lived, a few have been so provocative and potent as to force broad reconceptualizations of the whole field. The issue is by no means resolved, and further evolution of the concept can certainly be expected. We must assess the current thinking in this area, bearing in mind that the concept of mental retardation is still fluid. More importantly, it will become clear that by its very nature, mental retardation will always be an indefinite concept.

Since all concept formation starts with the classification of specific instances, we shall begin by examining one mentally retarded person. We shall call her Carrie. The case was chosen because it illustrates dramatically how a person of limited intellectual resources can "survive" in our modern society. Carrie, however, is not a typical mentally retarded person living in the community. First, she is moderately retarded (IQ range of 40 to 55), while the vast majority of the mentally retarded are mildly retarded (IQ range of 55 to 70). As such, they possess more adaptive and coping skills than Carrie and have a correspondingly better prognosis. A second atypical feature of this case is Carrie's sexual promiscuity. It is important to note this because many of the older stereotypes of mental retardation erroneously included notions of promiscuity, crime, and degeneracy as intrinsic and inevitable concomitants of this "disease." We do not wish in any way to further such misconceptions about the mentally retarded. Carrie's sexual behavior does not typify that of a mentally retarded female. Her behavior, in this respect, is clearly extreme.

## THE CASE OF CARRIE

As with the vast majority of the mentally retarded, if you met Carrie on the street, you would not suspect she is retarded. Carrie is a 29-year-old, fairly attractive, plainly and casually dressed Caucasian female. If you engaged her in conversation, you would find her to be pleasant, friendly, unassuming, and possessing a certain charm. After a while, you might begin to perceive her as a somewhat naive or simple person, but you would not suspect low intelligence unless you went beyond the ordinary niceties of casual conversation. The most striking physical feature you would observe is the absence of her two upper front teeth, which is quite noticeable given her tendency to smile. If you asked her what happened, she would tell you in a matter-of-fact manner that an old boyfriend "knocked them out."

I[1] first met Carrie about seven years ago, when I began working at an institution for the mentally retarded. While I had no professional contact with her there, I saw and talked with her briefly on numerous occasions

[1] M.W.

on the facility grounds or at the canteen. Carrie was friendly, likeable, and fairly well known around the institution.

Prior to her placement in 1964, Carrie had lived at home with her family. Her father was a painter, her mother a housewife. Both parents had an eighth grade education. Carrie was the youngest of six children. Of her five siblings, one had graduated from high school, one had finished the tenth grade, and three had left school after the eighth grade. None had ever been labeled mentally retarded or had attended special classes in school. All her siblings are now married and working as housewives or in various unskilled or semi-skilled jobs. According to Carrie, they are doing "okay."

Carrie's early developmental years were unremarkable, with the exception of two or three unexplained "seizure episodes" when she was two years old. Her parents never suspected anything abnormal and reported that she developed "about the same as the other children." She attended first grade in a school in the East and was promoted to second grade. However, in the interim summer, the family moved to California. Carrie was enrolled in the second grade of a Catholic school. After several months, school officials reported to her parents that Carrie "would not pay attention and had a short attention span." This was the first time her parents ever suspected that something might be wrong. Carrie was transferred to the second grade of a local public school, where after several months, school officials told her parents essentially the same thing. In addition, however, the school had obtained a psychological evaluation and informed the parents that Carrie was moderately mentally retarded (she had received an IQ of 46 on the Stanford-Binet test). The parents eventually had Carrie placed in a special school for the trainable mentally retarded (TMR).

Carrie was generally described by her parents and teachers as "a good child" until approximately 11 years of age, when she began to run away from home. From that time on, school records describe her as a poor student, resentful of authority, frequently running away, and "misbehaving" with boys. Carrie's behavior worsened considerably after the death of her father, when she was 15 years old. Her mother became overwhelmed with the burdens of caring for her other children and trying to deal with Carrie's runaway behavior and sexual activity. In desperation, her mother reluctantly had Carrie placed in an institution for the mentally retarded when she was 17 years old.

Carrie stayed at the institution from 1964 to 1971. She was classified as moderately retarded on the basis of a 1963 Stanford-Binet IQ of 40. However, the examiner's report contained several relevant comments. He observed that her IQ of 40 was relatively low in comparison to her level of conversation and that her mental age of six years and four months was not consistent with her obvious adolescent interests and identification. But he also noted that her score was consistent with previous psychological evaluations and her extremely low level of academic achievement, manifested by her inability to read any letters or count to ten accurately. "She appears to have developed superficially more mature ways of relating to people than would be predicted on the basis of her intellectual level. However, her retardation still shows in her poor judgment and inappropriate social behavior."

Carrie's institutional diagnosis was listed as: "Mental retardation, moderate, due to uncertain cause, with the functional reaction alone manifest." What this means is that Carrie satisfies the intellectual, adaptive, and developmental criteria for a diagnosis of mental retardation, but that the cause of her retardation is uncertain. While in the institution, Carrie was generally considered to be a model resident. In fact, she functioned so well that she was virtually treated as a junior technician in the "token economy" unit in which she resided. She did, however, run away on numerous occasions. Carrie states simply that she "likes to travel." Her typical pattern was to hitch a ride to a truck stop near the institution, where she would "hang around" in the coffee shop until she got a ride. She has seen most of the Western United States several times from the window of a truck cab. Occasionally, as might be expected, she has been stranded far from home. She has also been arrested and jailed several times for vagrancy (walking the streets with no money or identification) and joy riding. The latter offense was not deliberate; she had been picked up by men with stolen cars, and she was not aware that the car had been stolen.

In an effort to deal with this runaway problem, several community placements in family care homes were tried. Predictably, she continued to run away. She was also tried on several leaves to her own home over the years, but with the same result. On one of these home visits, she met a foreign student who was attending a local junior college. Within three weeks, he gave her an engagement ring worth several hundred dollars. A week later, she pawned the ring for $3.50 and ran away with a man she had just met. A social worker later contacted the student and noted that he appeared to genuinely care for Carrie. However, to the worker's surprise, he was totally unaware of her intellectual limitations. Although cultural and language barriers may have been an important factor, this attests to Carrie's ability to "pass" as normal in many situations despite her low IQ.

Carrie's excursions from her home, family care settings, and the institution lasted from a few days to several months. The longest was her last absence from the institution—from August, 1970, to April, 1971. When found, she was six months' pregnant (father unknown), had never seen a doctor, and had an untreated venereal disease. She was discovered by an alert welfare worker, who became suspicious when she realized Carrie was unable to read or write while applying for financial assistance. She had been traveling all over the West Coast, staying in various towns for short periods, and then hitching a ride with a trucker for a new destination. At the time of discovery, she had been living with a man and his family in a commune. Reports indicated that the man was associated with motorcycle gangs, and drugs were present in the home. Carrie admitted to some drug usage but could give few details. She apparently had been treated well and on their advice had sought financial assistance because of her pregnancy.

Carrie was returned to the institution to have her baby, which she insisted she wanted to keep. Her mother agreed to take both Carrie and the baby into her home (most of the other children were now married). The mother also gave her consent for Carrie to have a tubal ligation following delivery.

Carrie gave birth to a physically normal and healthy boy. Things went quite well for the first month. Carrie's mother made her take full responsibility for the baby (changing diapers, bathing, fixing the formula, etc.), and Carrie seemed to enjoy the situation. However, one social worker on a home visit noted that she had "the unpleasant feeling it was like a little girl playing with a new doll, and I wondered when the novelty would wear off."

Carrie was counseled on the implications of her runaway behavior now that she had a baby. She was informed that such behavior would lead to a foster home placement of her child. She stated that she understood this and assured everyone that her traveling days were over. Unfortunately, the lure of the highway proved stronger than that of her son. She ran away once during the second month and twice in the third. Her mother, however, had decided by then to keep the child, so no placement was necessary. Carrie began to leave home more frequently and for longer periods, returning only for brief visits. The mother finally legally adopted the baby.

Nobody saw Carrie or knew much about her from 1971 to 1975. I was now working in a large emergency psychiatric unit of a county hospital. One day in late 1975, I went into the waiting room to pick up the next patient's chart. It was Carrie's. We recognized each other immediately, and she seemed pleased to see a familiar face. She had come to get a refill of "my nerve pills" which she had received a month previously, when a boyfriend brought her because she was "upset and nervous." The report from that first visit indicated a diagnosis of "anxiety neurosis" and made no mention of an intelligence problem.[2] We talked briefly about the old days at the institution. She reported that she "really liked" the people there but was glad to be on the "outside." She then spent most of her time talking about the difficulties she was having with her family. She had not seen her son in over a year and couldn't locate her mother. Her mother's inaccessibility was evidently by design. Several people in the past had helped her call her brother, who lived in a nearby suburb. He refused to tell Carrie the whereabouts of her mother and son, indicating that her mother did not want to see her. She reportedly kept calling him, "begging" for this information, but he would just hang up and eventually had his telephone number unlisted. Carrie was initially unable to understand or explain why her family was treating her this way. However, over the course of several visits, it became apparent to me that the family highly disapproved of her life-style and were realistically fearful that she might try to take the baby on one of her trips (she had wanted to do this on several occasions). Carrie's proposed solution to her inability to reach her brother was simply to take a bus to the suburb in which he lived (a large one), walk around the streets until she recognized the house, and then "demand" that he give her the information.

During our first appointment, Carrie was given a refill of her medicine, and a second appointment was set up for the following week to make further service and treatment arrangements. She failed to show up. I have seen Carrie five times since our first session. She has yet to show up at the scheduled time, arriving anywhere from three days to three months late. I have learned a lot about her from these infrequent visits. The intervening four years between her discharge from the institution and our recent reacquaintance have been busy ones for Carrie. She has lived with a succession of men on Skid Row. She has been married twice, but never obtained a divorce from her first husband. The longest she has lived with any one man is approximately four months, including both of her marriages. On the average, she has run away from these men at least three or four times for several weeks at a time, stating, "I just get the urge to be on a truck going somewhere." Most of these Skid Row men and truckers have been fairly good to her in terms of basic support (food, shelter, companionship). However, as might be expected, a few have not. She has been beaten severely a couple of times and left stranded several times when on the road.

[2] The lack of recognition of mental retardation and low intelligence among mental health professionals will be discussed in Chapter 11.

But on the whole, these men constitute her sole means of support. She has never received welfare assistance in these four years. Thus, while her relationships with these men can be accurately described as promiscuous, they are from another perspective quite adaptive.

We have talked about a number of other things in our infrequent and unscheduled visits. Carrie never tells anyone she was in the institution "because then they think I'm stupid or retarded, and I'm not." However, with a tactful approach, she will freely admit that she has great trouble learning things and could use some help. She is embarrassed and frustrated over her inability to read and write and expresses a strong desire to learn to do so. However, she fails to recognize that any remedial program would require her to stay in one place. She is also embarrassed about her inability to use money (make change, etc.). Thus, the men in her life must usually do the shopping. When she is attached to a man, she spends most of her day in the apartment watching television, doing minor cleaning, or preparing simple meals. Occasionally she will do some waiting on customers at a bar (she has lived with several bartenders). When unattached, or when bored with her current relationship, she will hang around bars or pool halls in the Skid Row area until she meets a new companion. Of course, when the urge hits her, she will eventually go to a truck stop and take another trip.

On one unscheduled visit to my office, Carrie surprised me by asking if I could readmit her to the institution, telling me how much she liked the technicians (she really did) and her unit. I jokingly reminded her that we spent more time looking for her than helping her, that institutionalization wasn't appropriate or necessary, and that I felt she was running away from something. She finally told me that she wanted to leave her second husband, a bartender 30 years her senior. He had been fairly good to her, and she didn't want to hurt his feelings ("I just can't tell him"). In the four months of their marriage, she had run away (trips) three times for a total of eight weeks. I suggested she have him come in, and we could all talk about the problem and see what could be done. She showed up three months later. She had left her husband, taken several more trips, and was now living with a new boyfriend, a bartender only 10 years her senior.

On several of her visits, she requested that I write a note which she could give to her boyfriends indicating that she did come here and that we gave her the pills. Evidently a number of the boyfriends threw out her pills because they thought they were street drugs. The issue of validating her visits was related to their general mistrust of Carrie.

The last time I saw Carrie was about four months ago. She came in because her teeth hurt (she has poor dental hygiene, in addition to missing front teeth). We also talked about her son, her inability to read and write, and the possibility of financial assistance. I told her that she first had to stabilize her life before dealing with some of these problems. Welfare assistance could be provided, but a guardian (to manage the money) was necessary. She agreed. An appointment was made for her to return in two days to fill out the necessary papers and obtain a referral to a dental clinic. I also promised her that if she would take care of these things, I would make some arrangements for help in reading and writing. She left smiling.

I haven't seen Carrie since. When she didn't show up for her scheduled appointment two days later, I called the bar where her current boyfriend was employed (she usually has her boyfriends write their phone number on a piece of paper so that she can have someone help her call if she's in trouble). Her boyfriend stated that he hadn't seen her since the day of her visit to my office. When I called back a few days later, he told me that he still hadn't seen or heard from her and had no idea where she might be. I visualized her in a truck cab somewhere in the Western United States, flashing that toothless smile and talking about her difficulties in finding her mother and son.

Like many other people, I genuinely like Carrie and am concerned about her. But she is also very frustrating and makes it difficult for one to help her. She is mentally retarded, but she is much more than this. The label doesn't define her essence. Aside from having a low IQ and adaptive deficits, she is also a mother, a daughter, a sister, a divorcee, a girlfriend, a roommate, and a casual lover. She's promiscuous or adaptive, depending on your point of view. She can't read or write, tell time, or make change, but she is evidently good company on a long truck trip. Like everyone else, she worries and gets nervous and upset. She loves to travel and has been "taken for a ride" both literally and figuratively. Her main concern in life now is finding her son, although she is easily diverted from this mission. I don't know if she will ever find him. I do know that the odds of her completing her dental work, much less a remedial reading and writing program, are poor.

With the case of Carrie in mind, it is instructive to go back and examine our original question—What is mental retardation?—from the perspectives of the different people involved. For Carrie, mental retardation is a label she detests and refuses to acknowledge or admit. It means going to a special TMR school and eventually to an institution. It's being called "stupid" or "dumb" by people because of what you can or cannot do. It's the everyday embarrassment and frustration of being unable to read and write, tell time, or make change. It's telling people that you cannot do these things because you were bad, crazy, or lazy in school—anything but admitting that you just couldn't learn like everyone else. It may lead to being dependent on a succession of men for survival and ostracism from your own family. It's having a tubal ligation when you don't really understand what that means. It's watching television or going to the movies, often without really understanding what is going on. It's seriously planning to walk around a large suburb in a futile attempt to locate a brother's house. It's often being "taken for a ride," usually without even knowing it. For people at Carrie's level of functioning and above, it's having the worst of all possible handicaps in our intellectually oriented society, without any of the advantages that the physical stigmata of many other handicaps offer, such as easy recognition and the often accompanying support, help, and understanding. For many of the retarded, it is a life full of frustration and failure, an awareness of being unacceptably different and unequal, and the constant fear of being discovered.

For Carrie's parents, mental retardation wasn't even suspected until school officials informed them when she was seven years old. For Carrie's mother, mental retardation meant a daughter who ran away and "misbehaved" with boys. Eventually, it was the trauma of institutionalizing someone she had worked so hard to help. Finally, it was unexpectedly becoming a grandmother, legally adopting and knowing she had to take full responsibility for her grandchild, and ultimately hiding from Carrie to prevent her from taking her son on some unknown journey.

Parents' reactions to mental retardation are quite varied, depending on the onset and severity of the condition and the family's social class and value structure, orientation, and expectations. For some, mental retardation is a challenge; to many more, it is an extreme burden, often associated with undeserved guilt feelings. It is often a lifelong task of trying to make the necessary arrangements for proper care and treatment. It may also be a source of embarrassment with neighbors, friends, and relatives. Curiously, for the parents of the largest group of the mentally retarded (i.e., mild retardation associated with adverse sociocultural factors), there may be little suffering. They may perceive (often correctly) that their children are no different from themselves and thus be unaware that there is a problem. However, even they may have to deal with a hurt son or daughter who comes home and tells them that other children at school make fun of them because they are in "that special class."

To the average person, mental retardation is usually unrecognized. However, the cashier or bus driver may get angry and frustrated at the person who can't seem to give the correct amount of money, or keeps asking, "Has my street come up yet?" When retardation is recognized, the response can vary from con artists who take advantage to "do-gooders" who overprotect and dominate the lives of their self-appointed charges.

For many people, however, including some of Carrie's truck driver and Skid Row friends, it is an opportunity to be genuinely helpful, supportive, and human. It may also be a brief but satisfying relationship, perhaps even receiving more than they give.

To many physicians and biological scientists, mental retardation means a search for the "cause" and the discovery of methods of treatment and prevention. It is primarily a diagnostic challenge. In the vast majority of cases, however, this quest is futile; approximately 85 to 90 percent of the mentally retarded (mostly those at the mild level) have no known organic pathology. But with the more severe forms of retardation, there are innumerable physical handicaps and problems associated with or responsible for the severe intellectual defect that require medical intervention. Finally, it should be noted that physicians often have the painful duty of breaking the tragic news of severe mental retardation. They are also usually the first professionals consulted by anxious parents when a young child is not developing properly.

To many psychologists, particularly in the past, mental retardation was equated with IQ. Schools often asked them to use their tests to determine whether retardation was present and, if so, how much. In more recent times, the focus has expanded to include the developmental and sociocultural determinants of this index, with its implications for treatment and prevention. In addition, the discovery and application of learning laws (e.g., behavior modification) in the last two decades has helped revolutionize the care, treatment, and future of the mentally retarded. In general, the psychology of mental retardation is now a vast research enterprise attempting to describe and understand the ability, learning, motivational, and personality characteristics of the mentally retarded. IQ is no longer the sole preoccupation.

For the sociologist and anthropologist, mental retardation raises issues about both the mentally retarded and society in general. Since much of mild retardation is considered to be a sociocultural problem, they focus on the society that does the defining and labeling as well as on those who are defined and labeled. They view mental retardation as a deviance condition with many of the characteristics of other deviance conditions (e.g., other handicaps, minorities, etc.) A cross-cultural perspective has demonstrated that much of what we view as intrinsic to the problem is often nothing more than a cultural response or consequence. There is a focus on the social role of the mentally retarded as a function of societal attitudes and expectations rather than a mere expression of personal defects. In recent times, there has been much concern with the detrimental effects of labeling on the self-concept of the mentally retarded. In addition, the often inappropriate, unfair, and discriminatory way that these labels have been applied is becoming more apparent. By shifting the focus from the individual retarded person to the society, anthropologists and sociologists have helped force a dramatic reappraisal of our concept of mental retardation.

Of all the professionals, it is the educators who bear the greatest responsibility for the care and treatment of the mentally retarded. The widespread use of the terms "custodial, trainable, and educable" reflects the implications and goals of retardation from an educational perspective. Retardation is primarily a treatment challenge and it is considered to be mainly a problem of learning. It involves the discovery and development of the most effective educational techniques and curricula. The education of the mentally retarded has become "special education," which involves much more than teaching the three R's. It includes training in self-help and social skills, vocational education, and help with practical everyday affairs. The goal is a complete preparation for life, and this often requires a lifelong educational effort.

The mentally retarded pose a very difficult and often intriguing problem for our legal and justice system. As a group, they tend to get into slightly more trouble than the average, although their involvement is typically of a minor or "accessory" nature. What can and should be done about this? How can we establish whether they are mentally competent to stand trial, to discern right from wrong, or to understand the consequences of their actions? Is there an IQ level that will provide the answers to these questions? If convicted of a crime, should they go to jail or be placed in an institution for the mentally retarded?

There are other complex issues regarding their legal rights. Several recent Supreme Court rulings have implications for the legality of IQ testing, special class placement, and the whole issue of the "right to treatment." This last factor could upset many of our current institutional provisions if fully enforced in terms of the quality of treatment that must be available. No longer can institutionalized mentally retarded persons be required to wear only "state gowns"; they have a right to their own clothing and personal belongings, such as a toothbrush. The whole spectrum of institutional care has come under intensive scrutiny in recent years. State and federal courts are also becoming more involved in the legality of our institutional commitment procedures.

On another front, citizen advocacy groups are forming to protect and ensure the often neglected rights of the mentally retarded. Even the mentally retarded themselves have become involved, as reflected in the "bill of rights" recently drawn up by a group of mentally retarded persons at an international conference. And there are many extremely important issues that must be dealt with. It is instructive to list a few of these. Should the mentally retarded automatically be entitled to disability income or welfare assistance? Should they be allowed to own property, enter into legal and financial contracts, drive a car, or vote? Do they have the necessary judgment to exercise many of these rights? What about the issue of sterilization? Who should decide if people like Carrie should have a tubal ligation? What influence should her feelings or wishes have on the decision? Should the retarded be allowed to marry? Even if they have the right to bear children, is it unethical for professionals in the field to counsel them against it because of a presumed lack of personal, emotional, social, and financial resources? Again, on what basis are all of these decisions made? Is there a particular IQ level that can be used as a guideline? Does that IQ level change for the particular issue involved? Most importantly, who shall make all of these important decisions, with their moral, ethical, and legal overtones? Finally, is it possible that in our attempt to afford the mentally retarded full citizenship status, we may give them more responsibility than they can carry? Who shall balance the protection of their legal rights with their legal right for protection?

Mental retardation is clearly a complex and variable *practical problem*. The problems differ greatly not only among the mentally retarded themselves but also among all of those who must deal with them either directly or indirectly. It is not just a matter of low IQ, and the problems are not simply "mental" ones. A second point, illustrated by the case of Carrie, is that the concept of mental retardation is truly *multidisciplinary*. There is no single profession or discipline that can encompass the myriad problems of mental retardation. The understanding, treatment, and prevention of mental retardation demands the cooperative expertise and participation of an extremely large and diverse group of scientists and professional practitioners. This appears to be more true of mental retardation than of any other health problem.

Based on our discussion of Carrie, it becomes clear that mental retardation involves a complex mixture of theoretical and practical concerns. As such, it cannot be viewed simply as low intelligence. An understanding of the scientific concept of intelligence alone is not sufficient to clarify the concept of mental retardation. Intelligence is primarily a theoretical construct; mental retardation is basically a practical one. It presents concrete problems which individuals, families, and other societal institutions must deal with. In the remainder of this chapter, we will explore the concept of mental retardation and its implications.

## PERSPECTIVES ON MENTAL RETARDATION

Thus far, we have used such terms as "complex," "vague," "multidimensional," and "variable" when referring to mental retardation. These terms are not meant to imply that the concept of mental retardation is nonfunctional, but rather that it is not absolute. One can focus on different dimensions or aspects of the problem.

### Focus on Low Intelligence

We have noted that mental retardation covers an extremely diverse group of people in terms of the causes, degrees, effects, and treatment implications of their retardation. It is this very diversity that makes it so difficult to define the concept. But the question still remains: In what way or ways are all of these people similar, such that the same label can be generally applicable? This can be viewed from several different perspectives. First, from a logical point of view, it would seem that the essential feature of mental retardation is some kind of mental defect or inefficiency, which manifests itself as low or subnormal intelligence. This is typified by such lay descriptions as "dumb," "stupid," "moronic," "slow," and so forth. Moreover, most professionals in the field would agree that low intelligence is the common denominator of mental retardation.

From a more practical, clinical point of view, the concept of low intelligence is summarized in the IQ index derived from tests of intelligence. The traditional and still most widely used criterion of mental retardation is an IQ below 70. At first glance, therefore, it might appear that mental retardation could simply be defined in terms of low intelligence. This, in fact, has historically been the case. But simply using low IQ, however, does not really clarify the nature of mental retardation. In the preceding chapter, we saw that the IQ is merely a description of a person's *relative* position among his age peers along a vague and ill-defined intellectual continuum. It is not an absolute intellectual yardstick. Also, an analysis of intelligence tests has revealed that the IQ is an unspecified weighted average of a number of different abilities. But it is extremely difficult to say just what is being measured and therefore what the IQ really means. However, despite these problems, the IQ does have practical value and can be used generally to indicate the presence and severity of mental retardation. Typical IQ tests sample only a small number of the abilities that are theoretically involved in some psychometric view of intelligence (e.g., Guilford's SI model). But herein lies the practical value of these tests; for it is these very abilities that are most needed, required, and valued by our culture. Since we have already established that mental retardation is, above all, a practical problem, it makes good sense that the tests chosen to measure intelligence have this practical rather than theoretical orientation. Given this practical utility of the IQ, we should not, perhaps, abandon the intelligence tests altogether. As noted earlier, if these tests were more scientifically valid, they would lose much of their practical value.

The discussion in the last chapter on the nature of intelligence also relates to mental retardation. Despite the differences among the four theoretical approaches reviewed, there is a general, albeit vague, consensus on the basic nature of intelligence. Intelligence is viewed as an active, creative process that depends on a continuing interaction between the genetic givens (nervous system, soundness of the brain and nervous system, etc.) and the environment. Future growth depends on the quality of that interactive process. Thus, intelligence is ultimately a developmental phenomenon. The preeminence of the developmental theory is obvious.

This general consensus has much relevance for our understanding of mental retardation. In fact, it is the major reason why many people are now advocating the replacement of the term "mental retardation" with "developmental disability." The current view of intelligence as dynamic and developmental allows for much greater modification of the expression of intelligence. It helps us understand the normal progression and development of intelligence, as well as the possibilities of regression or fixation and the implications for treatment. There is a much broader concept of reversibility and an appreciation of training and experience in influencing the rate and final level of intellectual development. Accordingly, there is much more cause for hope and optimism in terms of the cause, prevention, and treatment of much (especially mild) retardation. This change represents a revolution in the concept of mental retardation.

## Focus on Social Competence

Another way of examining the nature of mental retardation is to look at the definitions of this concept. Although low intelligence is generally seen as the core concept, the definitions of mental retardation have usually emphasized such concepts as social competence or social adaptation as the ultimate criterion. This appears to be the result of the practical concerns of most definitions. As Robinson and Robinson (1965) note:

> There has been relatively minor controversy about whether mental retardation when it is considered as a more general concept should be defined in theoretical or in applied practical terms. The problems of

> mental retardation are very practical problems for every society; and traditional definitions have therefore tended to emphasize practical criteria. In one way or another, most definitions have equalled the concept with social adaptation, with the ability of the individual to make his way alone in the world of normal persons. (p. 28)

For example, Tredgold (1937) defined mental retardation as:

> A state of incomplete mental development of such a kind and degree that the individual is incapable of adapting himself to the normal environment of his fellows in such a way to maintain existence independently of supervision, control, or external support. (p. 4)

One of the most famous early definitions is that of Doll (1941), who lists six basic elements of mental retardation, beginning with social incompetence. The reader should also note the emphasis on the presumed constitutionality and alleged incurability of mental retardation that obtains in his definition, which was widely used in the 1940s and 1950s:

> We observe that six criteria by statement or implication have been generally considered essential to an adequate definition and concept. These are (1) social incompetence, (2) due to mental subnormality, (3) which has been developmentally arrested, (4) which obtains at maturity, (5) is of constitutional origin, and (6) is essentially incurable. (p. 215)

Haywood and Stedman's (1969) definition focuses on the person's ability to function adequately in society. They relate the inability to an impaired efficiency of learning.

> In terms of its current usage, mental retardation is a global term encompassing over 200 etiologic conditions with one common manifestation: impaired efficiency of learning, both in academic and social areas, which results in the inability to function adequately in society.

The tendency to deemphasize low IQ is perhaps best reflected in a recent position statement by the Division on Mental Retardation of the American Psychological Association (Ellis, 1975). This statement makes it clear that although low intelligence is the common denominator, the foremost problem is behavioral inadequacy:

> The term mental retardation is applied to persons who exhibit *behavioral inadequacy* that appears early in life and persists. There are

> many causative factors involved: disease, injury, inheritance, cultural environment, or combinations of these. Patterns of inadequacy differ from individual to individual, with low intelligence as a common denominator. Those more severely affected frequently suffer physical and health problems as well. However, mental retardation is, in the main, a behavioral problem. The individual's behavior cannot cope with everyday problems; normal adaptation does not occur. (p. 1)

It is clear that the various definitions have a practical orientation. However, there is also a confusion of theoretical and practical concerns which blurs the actual concept of mental retardation. The definitions emphasize the practical *manifest* problem—namely, social incompetence or behavioral inadequacy—while most of the lay and professional thinking focuses on the presumed *latent* factor responsible for it—namely, low intelligence. Thus, the question, What is the nature of mental retardation? has at least two answers, depending on which problem you want to consider. The relationship between these two criteria—overt and covert—is extremely difficult to specify. However, an appreciation of this relationship is crucial to an understanding of mental retardation.

The current (1973/1977) and previous (1959/1961) AAMD definitions of mental retardation state that there must be a deficit of adaptive behavior "associated with" (1959/1961) or "existing concurrently" (1973/1977) with subaverage general intellectual functioning. This adaptive behavior criterion was added precisely because there is no one-to-one relationship between intelligence and social competence, as was often thought or assumed in the past. For example, Doll states that social incompetence is *due* to subnormal intelligence. The assumption of a perfect relationship led to the reliance on IQ as the sole criterion of mental retardation, since social competence was presumably directly related to intelligence. This assumption proved to be false. Over the years, it was found that many people with IQs below 70 manifested no significant adaptive impairments. Calling them mentally retarded on the basis of a test score alone contradicted the practical orientation of most definitions, which focused on behavior.

On a commonsense basis, most of us would agree that brighter people tend to be more socially competent. But we all are familiar with numerous exceptions to this rule. The standard jokes about extremely intelligent people lacking common sense or practical skills are based on fact. There are also the "bright but immature" people whose social judgment and skills are not on a par with their level of intelligence. Finally, there are also numerous examples of people of low intelligence who are mature, responsible, and socially capable. In other words, there are many factors other than IQ or intelligence that determine social competence.

Consider the example of Carrie. Was her runaway behavior and sexual acting out strictly a function of her low intelligence? The answer is a definite "no." For there are many mentally retarded people at Carrie's intellectual level who manifest no such behavior. While coping ability is strongly related to level of intelligence, the general quality and content of behavior has many other determinants. It is for this reason that two people with the same IQ score can be so different in terms of their general behavior, skills, personality, and social competence. Thus, IQ alone cannot explain the tremendous behavioral differences found among the mentally retarded.

However, as noted in the previous chapter, there is a useful rule of thumb regarding the relationship between intelligence and social competence. At the lower levels of intellectual functioning, intelligence is much more important in determining behavioral adequacy and adjustment. At the higher intellectual levels, other factors, such as motivation, interests, personality variables, experiential history, and environmental circumstances, become more important. Thus, there appears to be a minimum intellectual level essential for social competence. However, beyond that level, social competence is multidetermined, with intelligence playing an important but not exclusive role.

For the mentally retarded, therefore, the relationship between intelligence and social competence is stronger for the profoundly and severely retarded than for the moderately and mildly retarded. However, even at the lower intellectual levels, the relationship is never perfect. There are, for example, vast behavioral differences among the severely retarded. What causes such differences is difficult to specify, but they appear, at least in part, to be a function of training and experience. This was dramatically shown in the 1960s, when great advances in the skill levels of the severely and profoundly retarded were made using behavior modification techniques. Years ago, their IQ levels were assumed to render them helpless. Yet, we now know that these severely handicapped people can be taught to feed, dress, and groom themselves. Recently, they have even been shown to be capable of such complicated tasks as assembling bicycle brakes and working on other vocational tasks formerly thought to be totally beyond their range. The point is that IQ alone can never explain the total behavior in mental retardation and therefore should not be the sole criterion for its determination.

The imperfect relationship between social competence and intelligence is the reason mental retardation is no longer considered irreversible or incurable. We are now more optimistic about the treatment of the mentally retarded for it is recognized that their behavior is a function not only of their IQ but also of the quantity and quality of their training and experience as well as their personality and motivational characteristics. While their level of intelligence cannot be significantly changed, their level of social competence definitely can.

The issue of social competence, especially for the mildly retarded, implies that the diagnosis of mental retardation *may* be temporary. For if the individual can be trained to a higher level of social competence, in a practical sense he would no longer be mentally retarded. It must be remembered that both an intellectual *and* an adaptive deficit are needed for a diagnosis of mental retardation.

Regarding this issue, Zigler (1975) notes that "a deficiency in cognitive functioning is the essential defining feature of mental retardation." But he laments the fact that our preoccupation with the intellectual deficit has led us to try to explain all their behavior on this basis, ignoring the obvious fact that their behavior is multidetermined. His research suggests that some of the behavioral differences between the retarded and the nonretarded may be due to motivational and personality factors rather than to intellectual ones. As such, these are not necessarily intrinsic to mental retardation. By implication, therefore, behavior and social competence may be changed or improved by modifying the environmental effects on motivation and personality.

> This point becomes an especially crucial one when dealing with the everyday social competence of the retarded individual. No amount of change in his motivational structure will make it possible for him to become a nuclear physicist. However, rather circumscribed changes in his motivational structure may make the difference between successful and unsuccessful employment at an occupation whose cognitive demands fall within the limits of his cognitive ability. . . . Thus a concern with motivational factors in the performance of the retarded holds no promise of a dramatic cure for mental retardation when such retardation is defined in terms of its essential cognitive foundation. A motivational approach does hold promise of informing us how we might help the mentally retarded utilize their intellectual capacity optimally. Although not terribly dramatic, such a goal is not only realistic, but is of the utmost social importance in light of the now well-documented evidence that the everyday adjustment and/or competence of the bulk of the retarded residing in our society is more a function of the retarded individual's personality than it is of his cog-

nitive ability. Such evidence bolsters a recurring theme in my thinking; namely, that as important as the formal cognitive processes are, their roles have been overestimated, especially with respect to those minimal daily demands of society which we consider when assessing individual social competence. (pp. 378–379)

Zigler's comments are extremely relevant and important to a general understanding of the concept of mental retardation. A person's social competence is a function of his intelligence as it interacts with his personality and drive. Nor is this just a matter of the current expression of behavior. These interactive influences must also be evaluated from a developmental framework. Consider the dynamic-developmental nature of intelligence, described in the previous chapter. According to this formulation, intelligence, personality, and motivation are separate but interactive factors. Changes in any one of them can affect the development and manifestation of the others. Thus, any conceptualization of mental retardation must include all these factors, not merely the problems of low intelligence.

## Focus on Social Dimension

Perhaps the greatest revolution in the concept of mental retardation has occurred in the last 20 years. It was caused by two disciplines that never had much to do with mental retardation: sociology and anthropology. The resulting change of perspective on mental retardation will be covered in more detail in the next chapter. For now, we will present the basic thesis and its implications for a concept of mental retardation.

The traditional view of mental retardation is what Mercer (1973a) has called the "psychological-clinical perspective." The basic idea here is that retardation is a problem, defect, or some other characteristic *of the individual*. He "has it," and it is this condition that accounts for his behavior and performance. The newer view of mental retardation is the "sociological-social system" perspective. Here, retardation is considered a social role, created, enforced, and maintained by the societal context. The focus of study is no longer the defined (the mentally retarded) but the definers (society). Retardation is thus something that inheres not in the individual but in the society. For example, agrarian societies have little need for formal intellectual skills (e.g., facility with language and symbols, abstract thought and reasoning). The size of one's biceps is far more important to adaptive functioning than the size of one's vocabulary. The inability to read and write is not really problematic or stigmatizing. However, in a complex, technological society, the reverse is often true. There is a need and demand for more formal intellectual skills. By virtue of the different competencies needed or valued, society has created the problem of mental retardation. It is the societal demands or expectations that have changed. Retardation "inheres" in the society, not the individual.

Another example of the influence of the social context is the "six-hour retarded child" (President's Committee on Mental Retardation, 1970). This refers primarily to the plight of many mildly retarded children. They are classified as mentally retarded by the schools because of low intelligence and poor academic performance. However, many of these children are seen as mentally retarded only in the social system of the school (i.e., 9 A.M. to 3 P.M.). For the rest of the day, at home and in their neighborhoods (other social systems), they appear to be functioning normally or adequately because few if any intellectual demands are made of them. These facts are difficult to integrate with the old concept of retardation as a permanently disabling personal condition. We are now talking about a condition that changes with the individual's social environment. The most important conclusion is that IQ alone can no longer be the sole determiner of retardation, for it is only a description of the individual's competencies. Now, the competencies demanded by the social context must also be taken into account. In fact, according to the newer perspective, the social context is seen to be the essential feature of mental retardation.

We have already noted the emphasis on social competence as the ultimate criterion of mental retardation. With the inclusion of the social system perspective, the problem of definition becomes even more difficult. Social competence is a value-laden and variable concept that is difficult to specify and define. When we add the fact that different social contexts may demand different levels of competence, the problem increases. How can we define mental retardation, knowing the many cultural and social class variations in what is considered competent and incompetent behavior?

The inclusion of the social dimension includes both benefits and problems. On the one hand, it emphasizes the relativity of mental retardation. Since mental retardation is a practical problem, to understand it we must take the social context into account. However, the social dimension has also complicated the task of assessing, measuring, and determining mental retardation. What do you call someone who is "mentally retarded" from 9 A.M. to 3 P.M. but essentially "normal" the rest of the day? What are the implications of all this for a theory of mental retardation? Obviously a true theory of mental retardation cannot be limited to the characteristics of the retarded themselves; it must include the social or cultural dimension. The person with an IQ of 65 may be considered mentally retarded in one culture and normal in another. Above all, the past practice of relying solely on the IQ to determine mental retardation must be abandoned.

Furthermore, it is also apparent that a comprehensive theory of mental retardation will not be just some aspect of the general theory of intelligence. Even if we knew all there is to know about intelligence, we could not begin to understand the practical problem of mental retardation without taking the social dimension into account. And this social context is a primary reason why the concept of mental retardation is relative. By including it as an intrinsic part of mental retardation; retardation itself must remain an indefinite concept.

## Pathological and Statistical Models of Mental Retardation

Is mental retardation a qualitative or quantitative difference from normalcy? This issue has been discussed throughout the history of mental retardation, turning on the issue of intelligence in general and IQ in particular. Does the mentally retarded person just have a lower IQ (question of degree), or is there a qualitative difference in his intelligence (question of kind)? Although the IQ, with its emphasis on numbers, leads to a quantitative interpretation, much of the professional thinking is qualitative. This view is furthered by the fact that the term "mental retardation" is a diagnostic label, with all of the medical-disease-defect associations of the diagnostic process. It is an orientation toward pathology. The focus is on finding the agent or mechanism responsible for the pathological condition and its symptoms. As we shall see in Chapter 8, a formal medical classification system is widely used. And there are now more than 250 medical conditions that are known to cause or be associated with mental retardation. This lends much credence to a pathological model of mental retardation.

The second major model of mental retardation is called the statistical model. It is quantitative in nature and based on the normal distribution of intelligence discussed in the previous chapter. However, there is a definite arbitrary quality to this model in its use of an IQ of 70 as the cutoff point. This cutoff is simply a statistical convenience, since an IQ of 70 is exactly two standard deviations away from the mean (IQ 100) of the intelligence distribution. It is important to note, however, that the 1959/1961 AAMD definition used an IQ cutoff of 85, which is exactly one standard deviation below the mean. This illustrates the capriciousness of a statistical model and criterion. The problem is always one of "where to draw the line."

The issue of whether mental retardation is a pathological-abnormal condition or a statistical phenomenon has major implications for a theory of mental retardation. If it is just a question of "less than," then much of the work and research on "normals" can be directly applied. If it is a question of "different from," then work on the specific pathological processes and their treatment must be undertaken. Although the pathological model avoids the arbitrariness of the statistical model, it also has significant problems. Perhaps the biggest stumbling block is the fact that approximately 85 to 90 percent of the mentally retarded have no known or identifiable organic or medical pathology. (Most of this 85 to 90 percent consists of the mildly retarded.) Thus, we have a model that is unable to detect pathology in the vast majority of cases. Furthermore, the biggest problem group in terms of detectable pathology—the mildly retarded—are also the persons about whom the question of the social dimension is so relevant (i.e., is it their problem or society's problem?).

An example from medicine is illuminating. The diagnosis of most medical diseases is a fairly straightforward, albeit often difficult, process. For instance, cancer and pneumonia both have specific effects and symptoms; both are clearly the result of pathological processes. It is difficult to imagine calling 90 percent of cancers or pneumonia "functional" problems. Yet, if we use a pathological model, this is what a diagnosis of mental retardation means. Finally, there is no such thing as a person who has cancer in one culture or social context and not in another. This kind of medical pathology is cross-cultural. Yet, despite this contradiction, we often think of mental retardation in medically oriented terms. The fact is, while some mentally retarded persons do fit the pathological model, the vast majority do not. What is important to keep in mind is that neither the statistical nor the pathological model is "right" for all mentally retarded persons. Mental retardation is not a definite process or disease but an indefinite and relative concept signifying problems generally associated with low intelligence.

One of the basic problems with the concept of mental retardation is that it attempts to cover an extremely diverse group of people. By dividing the mentally retarded into two basic groups, much of the conceptual confusion can be cleared up. This idea is not new. Many people have proposed such a separation, and we believe this is wise, particularly from a conceptual point of view. The division is based on the presence or absence of neuropathology (a defect in the central nervous system), which has crucial implications for the cause, treatment, and prevention of mental retardation. The mentally retarded can thus be placed into one of two groups: (1) those with neuropathology, whose IQs are generally in the 0 to 50 range, and (2) those without detectable organic pathology, whose IQs generally fall into the 50 to 70 range. It is important to note the relationship of this division to the normal distribution of intelligence. Although the first group covers an IQ range two and one-half times that of the second group, the second group includes approximately twelve times (estimated prevalence) as many people. In other words, there are about twelve times as many mildly retarded people who have no detectable pathology as the more severely retarded people with neuropathological conditions. The 50 to 70 IQ group tend to be the "functionally" mentally retarded. They are considered to be natural variants of the normal distribution of intelligence or those whose intellectual development was adversely affected by psychological or sociocultural factors. This group is often labeled "the culturally deprived" or "cultural-familial." With this conceptual breakdown, we can now resolve several of the theoretical issues confronting us.

*The 0–50 IQ Group: Presence of Neuropathology* For this group, mental retardation is best thought of in medical, disease, diagnostic, or pathological terms, since neuropathology is usually detectable and obvious. They appear to be truly "different from" rather than "less than" the norm. Also, the IQ is so low that low intelligence is the most pervasive influence on their behavior and social competence. The social context is negligible in defining their mental retardation. They will be seen as mentally retarded in all social contexts and cultures. In the past, this group was often considered to have "mental deficiency" in contrast to "mental retardation," reflecting the organic nature of their problems. They are the "24-hour mentally retarded," for whom the defect or clinical perspective is most appropriate. Retardation inheres in them; they "have it."

*The 50–70 IQ Group: Absence of Neuropathology* For this group, mental retardation is best thought of in terms of "less than" rather than "different from" the norm. They are considered mentally retarded rather than mentally deficient. Intelligence (IQ level) is not considered to be the sole factor in their behavior and social competence. Two other factors come into play. On the personal level, their motivations, interests, personality characteristics, and personal experiences are important in determining their social competence. On a much broader level, their retardation is seen to be a function of their social context. Accordingly, they may pass back and forth from retardation to normalcy, depending on the setting they are in. Mental retardation does not so much inhere in them as in their society.

By making this conceptual division between the mentally retarded, on the basis of neuropathology and its implications for intelligence, much of the conflict about the concept of mental retardation is dissipated. However, by the same token, it illustrates why trying to fit the entire group into one general concept is so problematic. We are really talking about two very different groups of people.

One additional point: Since the 50 to 70 IQ group accounts for about 90 percent of the mentally retarded, any single concept of mental retardation should be oriented to this group. This will in fact be the focus of the next section, which presents a general summary concept of mental retardation. But realize also that this is the very group which raises so many definitional problems, especially those related to social competence and social context.

## The Concept of Mental Retardation: Summary

Although the concept of mental retardation is vague and indefinite, there is a general consensus about what it should cover. The relevant issues are summarized below.

*Social-Psychological, Practical Problem* Above all, mental retardation is a practical problem. It is this fact, and this fact alone, that has generated the intense theoretical and practical interest in the subject. But the problem has two main aspects: social and psychological. The social is placed first because the practical definitions tend to stress the manifest problem of social incompetence as the ultimate criterion. However, the authors are in firm agreement with Zigler that a cognitive deficit must be seen as the essential defining feature of mental retardation. The latent problem is, therefore, a psychological one. Thus, mental retardation is a practical problem that manifests itself in social incompetence. From a theoretical point of view, there is also the underlying latent psychological deficit.

*Socially Defined* Because mental retardation is, first, a practical problem, we must recognize the role of the social context. This becomes crucial when dealing with the largest group of the mentally retarded: the mildly retarded. Although many tend to think of mental retardation in strict medical terms (e.g., disease, pathology), this model is clearly inappropriate for the majority of the retarded. The problem is not so much a matter of individual disease, defect, or pathology as of something the society tolerates, demands, and defines as competent or incompetent.

*Culturally Relative.* Social competence is a highly complex, value-laden, and variable concept. Different cultures make different demands and have different expectations and levels of tolerance. Since mental retardation is ultimately seen as a practical problem, its extent will vary with the cultural context. Consideration of mental retardation as a medical disease becomes even more incongruous under these circumstances. The individual must be matched with his environment. Thus, retardation becomes a temporary rather than a permanent condition (relatively speaking, and primarily in terms of the mildly retarded). The same person can be mentally retarded or normal, depending on the social system of which he is a part.

In conclusion, the concept of mental retardation has gone through great changes. The old, simplistic notions of the past no longer hold. It is not just a matter of low IQ, it is not just inherited and genetic, and it is not seen as irreversible and incurable. However, the newer concept, while much more optimistic, is also much more complex, vague, and indefinite. Mental retardation is seen as a dynamic, not a static, phenomenon. It depends on many personal, social, and societal factors. We cannot conceive of such a significant practical problem in simple, precise terms. The concept of mental retardation is indefinite because its nature is not specific. They are both difficult to pin down, identify, and specify. However, we are making progress in understanding the phenomenon and clarifying the concept. At the present time, mental retardation is best conceptualized as *a culturally relative, socially defined, social-psychological, practical problem.*

## THE AAMD DEFINITION OF MENTAL RETARDATION

Despite all the problems with the concept, the fact of mental retardation has necessitated an immediate practical response. Thus, while there are many differences of opinion regarding theory, workers in the field have always appreciated the need for a practical working definition. The most widely used definition in the United States and Canada is that of the American Association on Mental Deficiency (AAMD), which publishes the "Manual on Terminology and Classification in Mental Retardation." In its basic form, this definition has also been accepted and utilized by the World Health Organization.

The most recent AAMD manual (Grossman, 1977) is the seventh compendium of classification and terminology since the appearance of the first manual in 1921. Since 1959, there have been four revisions (1959, 1961, 1973, and 1977). Because students frequently find the references to these various manuals confusing, the following discussion should prove helpful.

In 1959, the AAMD published a new manual edited by psychologist Rick Heber. In 1961, a minor revision was published, also under Heber. Because there were no substantive changes between the two editions, and the formal definition remained the same, these two manuals are referred to as the "Heber manual" and the definition as the "Heber definition." The definition used in both of these manuals was as follows:

> Mental retardation refers to subaverage general intellectual functioning originating during the developmental period and associated with impairments in adaptive behavior.

In 1973, the AAMD published another revision of the manual, this time edited by physician Herbert Grossman. In 1977, the latest revision was published, again with Grossman as the editor. As with the two Heber manuals, there are no major differences between the 1973 and 1977 editions, and the formal definition is the same. Accordingly, these two manuals are known as the "Grossman manual" and the definition as the "Grossman definition." The newest definition of mental retardation is as follows:

> Mental retardation refers to significantly subaverage general intellectual functioning existing concurrently with deficits in adaptive behavior, and manifested during the developmental period.

As the reader can observe, the Heber and Grossman definitions are essentially the same, except for minor changes in wording and the arrangement of terms. This is true with one notable exception. The addition of the word "significantly" in the Grossman definition has drastically different implications from the Heber definition in terms of who can potentially be called mentally retarded. This critical difference will be discussed later. First, let us consider the Grossman definition in some detail.

The Grossman definition of mental retardation, as well as the Heber definition, consists of three criteria which must be present before a diagnosis of mental retardation can be made. We shall now discuss each of these criteria in the order stated in Grossman's definition.

### Significantly Subaverage General Intellectual Functioning

This first requirement relates to the person's level of general intelligence. This level is operationally defined and measured by performance on an individually administered, standardized test of intelligence. The IQ index derived from these tests serves to quantify the general level of intellectual functioning and is used as the practical criterion.

The word "significantly" is included in the definition for a very specific reason. It refers to the fact that the IQ cutoff for mental retardation is two or more standard deviations below the mean or average IQ of 100. Since most tests of intelligence have standard deviations of 15 or 16 points, this means that the upper cutoff for mental retardation is an IQ of 68 or 70, depending on the standard deviation of the test being used. Thus, all persons with IQs below this cutoff point satisfy the first requirement for a diagnosis of mental retardation—namely, significantly subaverage general intellectual functioning.

In making this intellectual determination, as noted above, only individually administered, standardized tests of intelligence may be employed. Group tests are specifically excluded, along with any poorly standardized instrument (issue of appropriate norms). Of course, such measures can be very useful for screening or detection. But once a potential problem is detected, an individualized test must be administered before an actual diagnosis of mental retardation can be made. The most commonly used accepted tests that satisfy all of the requirements are the Stanford-Binet and the various Wechsler scales, which will be covered in Chapter 7.

### Existing Concurrently with Deficits in Adaptive Behavior

This second essential ingredient for a diagnosis of mental retardation represents a major historical shift in the diagnostic process. In the past, IQ alone was considered the sole and sufficient criterion for mental retardation. For many reasons already discussed, this practice is no longer appropriate. There must now be a manifest impairment in adaptive behavior as well. If a person has no difficulty adapting to his environment, it is meaningless to consider him mentally retarded just because of a test score.

Adaptive behavior is defined as the degree to which the individual meets the standards of personal independence and social responsibility expected for his age and cultural group. Since these standards are age-related and culturally variable, this criterion is difficult to specify and, consequently, to measure reliably. This is particularly true for the cultural factor. Fortunately, we have some fairly good normative developmental data regarding age, although good, reliable, practical measuring instruments are not yet available. Currently, such scales as the Vineland Social Maturity Scale or the more recent AAMD Adaptive Behavior Scales are employed. However, considerable clinical judgment is still necessary, and only broad guidelines are available. The problems and methods of adaptive behavior assessment will also be covered in Chapter 7. However, it is instructive, at this point, to list some general age-related guidelines.

While the criteria vary with age level, there is a general expectation for increasing independence, self-mastery, and conformity to societal demands and conventions as the person progresses from one developmental level to the next.

*Infancy and Early Childhood* During this period, the focus is on the development of sensory-motor (e.g., crawling, walking, gross and fine motor coordination), communication (receptive and expressive language), self-help (eating, dressing, personal grooming, and hygiene), and socialization (ability to deal and interact with peers and adults) skills. Deficits in the maturational process or lags in the appearance of developmental milestones are evidence of adaptive impairment.

*Later Childhood and Early Adolescence* The primary focus during this period is school performance in general and learning in particular. Difficulty in school, low achievement, and being behind two or more grade levels are signs of potential adaptive impairments. In addition to academic pursuits, the person in this age group should be developing more sophisticated social skills, such as forming interpersonal relationships and participating in group activities.

*Late Adolescence and Adult Life* During this period, the primary focus is on vocational and social responsibilities. The ability to obtain and maintain employment, to handle financial matters with judgment and foresight, to meet the practical requirements of daily living, to develop close interpersonal relationships, and to be cognizant of, and abide by, conventional social mores are areas of particular concern. In short, the ability to conform to community standards and to maintain an independent existence is assessed.

The mere presence of deficits at any of these age levels does not, by itself, imply mental retardation. Such deficits can occur for a variety of reasons (e.g., situational or emotional problems). It is only when these deficits are manifested by a person with an IQ below 70 that they constitute criteria for mental retardation. At that point, the adaptive impairment is considered to be related to the intellectual deficit.

### Manifested during the Developmental Period

This third requirement is included primarily to distinguish mental retardation from a variety of other disorders where low IQ and adaptive impairments are present. For example, a bank president suffering from "brain damage" secondary to an automobile accident may score well below 70 on an IQ test and manifest all sorts of adaptive impairments. Likewise, people with acute emotional disturbances are often quite impaired behaviorally and unable to perform well on the IQ test. However, although both of these examples satisfy the first two requirements of the definition, such people cannot be called mentally retarded. The best way of eliminating such cases is to require that the low IQ and behavioral deficits be initially manifested during the developmental period. Recall that the recent concept of mental retardation includes the notion, as well as the formal label, of "developmental disability." Thus, the people in the above examples are not mentally retarded because their condition did not originate or exist in the developmental period; presumably they developed in a normal fashion. It is important to distinguish between those people who had ability but lost it (permanently or temporarily, due to accidents and situational or emotional distress) and those who never really developed it. The "developmental period" refers to the time during which the growth of intelligence is presumed to occur. Practically, this is considered to be from the time of birth until 18 years of age, although the upper limit is arbitrary and debatable (e.g., the Heber manual used 16 years of age as the upper limit).

It is important to remember that there are *three* criteria which *must* all be satisfied before a person can be diagnosed as mentally retarded. This is in direct and purposeful contrast to the past practice of relying solely on the IQ in making this determination. It is now essential that the person with low IQ have a clear, concomitant adaptive impairment and that this deficit be traced to the developmental period.

Several important implications of this definition of mental retardation deserve emphasis. First, the definition says nothing about cause. Although there are now more than 250 known etiological conditions associated with mental retardation, the definition ignores them in favor of a purely functional description. Mental retardation is considered to be a state of behavioral impairment or social incompetence that has many causes. It is reflected in low measured intelligence and manifest adaptive impairments.

The second and most important implication of this definition is that it describes the *current functioning status* of the individual. No prognostic statements are implied. Again, this is in sharp contrast to past attitudes and practice, wherein the notions of "permanence" and "incurableness" were associated with the diagnosis of mental retardation. The current view gives much greater recognition to the notion of changeability. Prognosis is now much more related to such factors as associated medical conditions, motivation, treatment and training opportunities, and the environmental context. An extract from the AAMD Manual will serve to reiterate this extremely important point:

> Within the framework of the definition of mental retardation, an individual may meet the criteria of mental retardation at one time in life and not at some other time. A person may change status as a result in changes or alterations in his intellectual functioning, changes in his adaptive behaviors, changes in the expectations of the society, or for other known and unknown reasons. (Grossman, 1977, p. 15)

The third and final implication of the definition is the formal endorsement of much of what has been considered in this chapter about the concept of mental retardation. In proposing this tripartite definition, the field has asserted that IQ alone is no longer sufficient for a determination of mental retardation. As mental retardation has come to be seen as a culturally relative, socially defined, social-psychological problem, the formal definition specifically includes adaptive behavior as a criterion. This attests to the field's awareness and recognition of the changing concept. The inclusion of this dimension, with its implications for a concept of mental retardation, is perhaps the most significant feature of the definition.

## The Grossman and Heber Definitions

As stated earlier, the Grossman and Heber definitions of mental retardation are essentially the same, with one notable exception. The addition of the word "significantly" in the Grossman definition has major implications for the number of people who could be potentially diagnosed as mentally retarded.

Under Heber, subaverage general intellectual functioning was operationally defined as *one* or more standard deviations below the mean or average IQ of 100. Grossman defines "*significantly* subaverage general intellectual functioning" as *two* or more standard deviations away from the mean. Thus, Heber had an upper IQ cutoff of 83 or 85, while Grossman has an upper cutoff of 68 or 70 (depending on the standard deviation of the test used). To fully appreciate the significance of this change, the reader should refer back to the discussion of the normal distribution of intelligence in Chapter 3. There we saw that an IQ of 70 (two standard deviations below the mean) represents approximately 2.25 percent of the population, while an IQ of 85 (one standard deviation below the mean) represents approximately 16 percent. For a United States population of 220 million, this means 5 million versus 35 million people—quite a difference! Of course, it must be stressed that even under the Heber definition, these people would also have to show deficits in adaptive behavior before any label would be applied. And it does appear reasonable to assume that people in the 70 to 84 IQ range may have a greater chance to adapt than those in the 55 to 69 IQ range. Thus, in practice, the potential 35 million may be considerably reduced. Nevertheless, this does represent a rather dramatic shift in the potential pool. Why was such a change made?

The 1973 Grossman manual had very little to say about this change. It recommended that persons in the 70 to 84 IQ range, formerly called "borderline mental retardation," now be called "borderline intelligence." The only rationale presented for this change was that it "reflects changing concepts regarding the social capabilities of persons with low intelligence" (p. 5). In the 1977 Grossman revision, a comment was added regarding the 1973 change.

> The deletion of the borderline level in the 1973 revision was based on data indicating that the large majority of persons in the borderline range of intellectual functioning are not significantly impaired in adaptive behavior. (p. 19)

Although the borderline category was formally deleted in the Grossman manuals, both manuals allow for the fact that a few borderline individuals may still qualify for a dignosis of mild retardation. We quote from the 1977 manual:

> However, a small minority of persons with IQ's up to 10 points above the guidelines are so impaired in their adaptive behavior that they may be classified as having mild mental retardation. (pp. 19–20)

Despite such comments, however, the clear intention of both the 1973 and 1977 manuals is to eliminate the borderline category of mental retardation. It was precisely for this reason that the word "significantly" was added to the Grossman definition. And although the manuals allow for the fact that a few borderline persons may still qualify, more often than not, the definition is being rigidly interpreted to exclude them.

The present authors suggest that the social pressures and emotional overtones of such issues as individual rights, concern over labeling, and so forth may have been important in changing the formal diagnostic criteria. Furthermore, we also seriously question the conclusion that many people in the 70 to 84 IQ range do not have a serious intellectual-adaptive handicap in our modern society. We concur with the reservations and concerns of Robinson and Robinson (1976) on this matter:

> The 1959 position recognized explicitly that within the highly urbanized, technologically oriented culture of the United States, even minor deficits in intellectual capacity may constitute a substantial handicap. Yet the criterion also led to classifying persons as mentally subnormal who fitted unremarkably into their communities. A change of definition does not change reality, of course, and many persons of borderline intelligence do experience considerable difficulty in mastering the responsibilities demanded of them in a competitive society. It will be unfortunate if the revised definition tends to discourage society from offering supportive services to members of this group. (pp. 31–32)

We shall have much more to say about this critical issue in the final chapter. For now, we merely wish to point out that the deceptively minor differences between the Heber and Grossman definitions are potentially quite significant.

CHAPTER 5

# Psychological, Social System, and Societal Perspectives on Mental Retardation

As we indicated in the last chapter, the idea of mental retardation is somewhat illusory. Most lay persons have some notion of what mental retardation is and, if pressed, could probably define it. Upon scrutiny, however, such definitions are typically vague and usually refer only to the stereotyped characteristics of profound or severe retardation. If we examine professional or expert definitions, the concept *appears* much clearer and more specific—especially since there is an agreed-upon definition (AAMD) that enjoys widespread usage and popularity. It would seem that if we agree on the essential features of mental retardation, and can measure and quantify them, we must then have a good grasp of the concept. However, this is more apparent than real. The concept of intelligence presents many theoretical problems. Mental retardation, on the other hand, involves practical problems (e.g., dealing with retarded persons) which press for some agreed-upon definition of intelligence. Consequently, we use the AAMD definition of mental retardation, which utilizes the IQ in defining intelligence. A gap still exists, however, between the AAMD definition and solving such critical problems as "Who are the mentally retarded in the community?" and "How many persons are mentally retarded?" The difficulty in drawing the line between mental retardation and normalcy goes beyond a simple and static definition; it depends on our interests and perspectives. Thus, mental retardation can be viewed in extremely different ways. Based primarily on Mercer's work (1965, 1973a,b), two contrasting perspectives on mental retardation have been delineated. These are the "clinical" and the "social system" perspectives.

## THE CLINICAL PERSPECTIVE ON MENTAL RETARDATION

Traditionally, mental retardation has been viewed from a clinical perspective, with the primary focus on the individual. That is, mental retardation is viewed in terms of the "defect" or "medical" model. This reflects the early roots of mental retardation in medicine (A.P.A., 1970). The person was considered to have a medical or organic defect, and any change or cure was dependent on changing the faulty mechanism responsible for the inadequate (retarded) behavior. While this defect was typically considered to be of genetic (but not necessarily hereditary) origin, it could also be nongenetic (i.e., the result of trauma, infection, or deprivation). In either case, the clinical perspective views the individual as handicapped and defective. Cure or treatment based on this model has been woefully inadequate. Indeed, lack of medically based improvement or cure was so predominant that some authors (e.g., Doll, 1941) concluded that if a person did improve, the condition was not true "feeblemindedness" (the common diagnostic term several decades ago). They retrospectively referred to the condition (before improvement) as "pseudo-feeblemindedness."

One ultimate consequence of this clinical model was that treatment consisted of removing mentally retarded persons from society. They were placed in institutions, where treatment essentially amounted to custodial care.

The clinical model dominated professional thinking in mental retardation until the 1930s, when several issues forced a partial change in professional attitude. As Crissey (1975) states:

> . . . there was increasing evidence that the IQ was not fixed, that children could move from retardation to normalcy, or normalcy to retardation. A sober look at the correlates of poverty suggested that poor nutrition, inadequate health care, prematurity, multiple sensory and neurological defects even though minor, and an impoverished environment, were at least as deleterious as genetic factors. Evidence also suggested that continuing deprivation, especially at crucial points in development, could and would institute damage which was evident in succeeding generations. (p. 805)

Thus, in the 1930s and 1940s, it was becoming obvious that a host of environmental factors, as well as genetic or organic factors, could be critical in substandard intellectual development. Intelligence was thus seen (e.g., Hunt, 1961) as the result of the interaction of the genotype with the environment. The rate of development was set by this interaction, not by the genes alone. Thus, while genetic factors admittedly set broad limits, the quality of the environment and experience was considered by many to determine the final level of intellectual functioning. This change in focus has been so dramatic that some people now believe we have overemphasized the environment. Zigler (1970) emphasizes that genetic differences are necessary for a true interactionist position. He contends that this consideration is lacking on the part of many professionals.

Acceptance of the importance of the environment has served to change the clinical model of mental retardation into a *developmental* model. Thus, except in the case of obvious biological damage, mental retardation is viewed as a developmental failure, which results from inappropriate or inadequate environmental conditions. It is important to stress that this developmental model is still subsumed under the clinical model. There is still some defect in the individual, but its implications are quite different. With the clinical model, the individual has some organic deficit (genetic, traumatic, etc.), which is typically seen as irreversible. With the developmental model, the condition is not seen as irreversible. If a poor environment is partially or totally responsible for inadequate intellectual or adaptive behavior, the solution becomes a matter of reprogramming the environment and experiences.

The change in emphasis from the clinical to the developmental model is illustrated by the work in short-term memory. In the clinical model, mentally retarded persons were considered to have some physiological deficit in short-term memory. Something was wrong with the memory trace, either with the amplitude or the duration of underlying nervous impulses (Ellis, 1963). More recently, however, it has been hypothesized that the memory difficulty may be more accurately viewed as a motivation-behavior problem (Belmont and Butterfield, 1971). According to the developmental model, the mentally retarded are not deficient in a physiological sense but rather were never adequately programed in memory rehearsal strategies or not sufficiently motivated to use them.

The clinical approach to mental retardation has greatly expanded its focus in recent years. Numerous nonintellective factors have been evaluated as contributing to mental retardation. Zigler (1967) contends, for example, that many of the deficits commonly associated with mental retardation are more accurately seen as motivational rather than cognitive.

Zeaman and House (1963) stress the role of poor attention in the low learning ability of retarded persons. Gray and Miller (1967) state that attitudes toward achievement are just as important as aptitudes. As already indicated (see Crissey, above), sociocultural determinants of mental retardation are now the object of more and more research. In a related manner, increasing emphasis is being given to the child's "significant others" and how they link the child to his environment. Both the objective (how things actually are) and the effective (intellectual stimulation provided by others in the child's interaction with the environment) facets must be adequate for healthy intellectual development (McCandless, 1964). Feuerstein (1970) contends that inadequate or insufficient mediated learning experiences are the chief deficiency of the mildly retarded. He has developed a promising program based on assessment of "learning potential," which is geared to the development of learning strategies. These strategies or sets are acquired through interaction with a mediating adult who selects, focuses, and feeds back environmental experiences for the child. Thus, the environment is mediated for the child as he, in turn, learns to mediate for himself.

This expanding view of the developmental approach is summarized by Benton (1970), who has developed a fairly inclusive model to predict the intellectual level of a child. Intelligence is considered to result from the interaction of many variables, each of which has several gradations. Benton's model includes consideration of cerebral, sensory, motor, emotional, and cultural statuses. While other variables may have to be added (e.g., motivation and possibly some measure indicating the presence and effectiveness of mediating agents), such a multivariate approach to intelligence seems potentially promising in terms of prediction. But it is even more important in a conceptual sense, for it suggests that no one variable alone (with the possible exception of severe cerebral damage) necessarily leads to mental retardation. Benton's model suggests, for example, that a combination of low cultural status and mild cerebral defect may be deleterious to cognitive growth, whereas low cultural status with superior cerebral growth may pose no problem. It is the interaction among these multiple variables that is important and that should be the focus of developmental research.

A number of points should be kept in mind regarding the evolution and current status of the clinical approach to mental retardation. First, while there has been a shift from the clinical to the developmental model, the focus is still on the individual. While the environment has assumed almost overriding importance, the emphasis is on its impact *on the individual.* Second, from Hebb's (1949) cell assembly theory to Haywood's

(1967) concept of dynamic intelligence, the argument is essentially reductionist. The environment influences the nervous system of the individual, and it is this nervous system which mediates all behavior. In essence, we are still talking about the clinical model, only now in a developmental sense. There is *still* something different about the mentally retarded person; his nervous system has been altered by the developmental programs to which he has been subjected. While mental retardation is now viewed developmentally, and while the environment may be the cause of much retardation, the resulting condition does indeed exist in the individual. Such a reductionist view, however, is no longer considered a cause for pessimism. It is now believed that adequate programs effectively applied at the "critical periods" of development will prevent the development of the maladaptive behaviors known as mental retardation. Finally, in terms of remediation or treatment, there is a broader concept of reversibility. For many persons, mental retardation or developmental disability can be altered.

## THE SOCIAL SYSTEM PERSPECTIVE ON MENTAL RETARDATION

From the sociological perspective, mental retardation is a subcultural phenomenon or a deviance condition defined within the context of the dominant culture. In contrast to the clinical approach, mental retardation is not viewed as an individual trait but as a role or function of a specified group in society. Mental retardation is, thus, a cultural phenomenon rather than a characteristic of a given individual. Some professionals have even suggested that mental retardation is not a problem of the individual at all, but only of society. Society, and society alone, is responsible for the creation of a group called the mentally retarded. Dexter (1958) states: "A substantial proportion of the cost and trouble resulting from the presence of mental defectives in our society is a consequence, not of the biological or psychological characteristics of mental deficiency, but of their socially prescribed roles or statuses" (pp. 920–921).

Viewing mental retardation as a deviance condition in the dominant culture, Dentler and Erikson (1959) suggest that the mentally retarded may help to maintain social group and class structures by helping to define the limits, standards, sanctions, and boundaries of the group. Farber (1968), with a similar view, considers the mentally retarded as part of an organizational surplus population. This surplus population is maintained and reinforced by the dominant culture, but it is an amorphous group which plays no integral role in the organization of society. Instead, society must divert much of its energy and resources to the maintenance of this group, which is unproductive in the institutions of economics, politics, the arts and sciences, or the family. Society could function without this surplus population, but the mentally retarded do contribute to the maintenance of the social structure. This is done by creating the need for institutions for their treatment and care; by facilitating the operation of social institutions (by providing increased freedom in selecting and more efficient filling of organizational positions); and by helping to perpetuate social classes.

Although numerous investigators have considered the mentally retarded from the social system perspective, the work of Jane Mercer (1965, 1972, 1973a,b) most clearly distinguishes between the clinical and social system models and is largely responsible for the recent interest in the social system perspective and its implications. Mercer contends that while the clinical model may be adequate for considering the profoundly retarded, it is less satisfactory for mild retardation. Here, the social system model is more appropriate. Because this perspective stems from the sociological tradition and the study of deviant behavior, we must examine several specific terms before this approach can be fully understood and appreciated.

The social system perspective is based on an analysis of the social structure, which is viewed as a number of interrelated and interacting social systems. Each system is composed of *social statuses, social roles, role expectations, and social norms.*

"Social statuses" are the positions in a given social system. In the family, for example, the positions of mother, father, son, and daughter are names for the formal positions. The term "social role" refers to the socially determined behavior of the person occupying a given status. This is the part played by that position in the group. Thus, the father's role in the family has generally been to provide a steady income, give direction to the children, and so forth. (The social roles change with changes in the general society.)

Statuses and roles can be either "ascribed" or "achieved." The former term refers to a role that is determined at birth, such as sex or race. Achieved status is earned; it is determined by one's behavior and how it is evaluated by the group. A prime example of achieved status/role is occupation.

"Role expectation" refers to the attitudes and beliefs about how occupants of various statuses ought to play their roles or how they ought to behave. Thus, sons have general expectations regarding fathers, and so on. Role expectations involve certain obligations and privileges for the occupant of each status in relation to other statuses in the system. The father, for example, has the obligation to provide a steady income, but has the privilege of deciding what to do with extra money. Mutually shared expectations are the "norms" of the social system; they are shared by most of the people.

The term "normal behavior" refers to role performance that conforms to the norms and expectations of the social system. Deviant behavior is defined (Mercer, 1973a) as behavior that varies sufficiently from the group norms to trigger group strategies to deal with it. Deviance, however, can vary on several bases: (1) norms can vary for different social systems (a behavior might be normal at home, but not at school); (2) the norm can focus on different aspects of behavior, even if social systems share the same norm (e.g., probation officers focus on legal behavior while deemphasizing academic achievement); (3) the level of expectation may vary from one system to another even if norms and focus are similar (one system demands a higher level of performance); (4) norms vary in their degree of formality (the norm of neighbor is informal and flexible, while the norms for civil service employment are titled, codified, and explicit); (5) tolerance of deviation from the norms can vary greatly, depending on the social system involved (the school may view a student's C average as acceptable, while the middle-class family may not).

In the context of the above ideas, mental retardation can be defined in social system terms:

> From a social system perspective, "mental retardate" is an achieved social status and mental retardation is the role associated with that status. . . . A mental retardate is one who occupies the status of mental retardate and plays the role of the mental retardate in one or more of the social systems in which he participates. To clarify this point, let us consider the public school system. In addition to such statuses as teacher, principal, and custodian, the school system also has statuses for children: the status of children in a regular class; the status of accelerated student; the status of retained student; the status of educable mental retardate; the status of trainable mental retardate; and so forth. Children achieve these statuses just as adults achieve the status of teacher, principal, or custodian. . . . From a social system perspective, the term mental retardate does not describe individual pathology, but rather refers to the label applied to a person because he occupies the position of mental retardate in some social system. (Mercer, 1973a, pp. 27–28)

Mercer makes a distinction between what she calls "labeled mental retardate" and "clinical mental retardate." The latter are persons who have failed some clinical measure—for example, low IQ. The former are playing the role of mental retardation and fill the expectations of that role. In this case, clinical symptoms are considered to be irrelevant. Obviously, however, one individual may well fit both cases.

From a social system perspective, mental retardation exists only in the context of a specific social system. Mental retardation thus cannot be comprehended as an abstract category; it has meaning only in terms of a status and role in a given system. Since an individual participates in numerous social systems simultaneously (e.g., family, neighborhood, church) and moves in and out of social systems over time (e.g., school), he may achieve the status of mental retardate at one time and drop it at a later time. For example, a child may be considered normal by his family, but be labeled retarded when he enters school. When he leaves school, he may again be regarded as normal.

## COMPARISON OF THE TWO PERSPECTIVES

Mercer (1973a) notes a number of differences between the clinical and social system perspectives and suggests some different implications which stem from them. Several of her points simply summarize what has already been discussed in this chapter. Others, however, go beyond what we have discussed and have broad implications.

### Prevalence: Theoretical Considerations

On the issue of prevalence, Mercer compares the clinical and social system perspectives. First, regarding the social system perspective, she states:

> A person is "normal" if he meets the expectations of the social system in which he is operating. Prevalence rates, in the traditional epidemiological sense, are meaningless. Sociocultural factors are intimately involved in the labeling process, i.e., the clinical diagnosis. . . . The prevalence rate for mental retardation will be relative to the content, focus, level, formalization, and tolerance limits of the norms of a particular social system, and the extent to which the status of "mental retardate" is differentiated within the structure. (p. 36)

From a strict social system perspective, these comments are operationally correct. But this may represent theoretical validity and not practical utility. To illustrate what we mean, let us take the case of a lower-class family with poorly educated and barely literate parents. Within this social system, a child of significantly below average intelligence and with adaptive deficits might not be considered mentally retarded. From the social system perspective, he has not achieved the status of mental retardate and, by definition (from this perspective), is not retarded. But does this mean that he does not have, or will not have, problems related to low intelligence in attempting to cope with our complex, competitive, industrialized society? The point is that the norms for many social systems may have little value in predicting adequacy of coping with other systems or with society in general. The relationship between intelligence and social competence will be explored in more detail in the last chapter. What needs to be underscored here is that to assess the prevalence of mental retardation within the social system perspective, we must first evaluate the social system itself. Again, taking the family as the index social system, even if all members were moderately retarded (IQ below 55, with a clear adaptive deficit) from a clinical perspective, none would be retarded from a social system perspective.

Regarding the clinical perspective, Mercer (1973a) states: "If a person has the symptoms of mental retardation, he is mentally retarded. Prevalence and incidence rates can be calculated by determining the number of persons with symptoms. *Sociocultural factors* need not be taken into account in making a clinical diagnosis" (p. 36; italics ours).

If we accept the AAMD definition of mental retardation, both intelligence and adaptive behavior must be significantly below average before a person is diagnosed as mentally retarded. Except for very young children, it is difficult to imagine how adaptive behavior could be evaluated without using a sociocultural context and norms. In fact, a primary reason for including an adaptive behavior deficit as a criterion of mental retardation is that it does control for possible sociocultural biases in IQ. Thus, contrary to Mercer's statement, sociocultural factors are not ignored with a clinical perspective diagnosis.

## Prevalence: An Empirical View

Thus far, we have discussed prevalence from a hypothetical point of view. Let us now take an empirical view and evaluate some of the actual data on the number of mentally retarded persons in the community. (The whole issue of prevalence will be discussed more fully in the next chapter.) Traditionally, the prevalence of mental retardation has been estimated on the basis of the normal curve. Using an IQ of 70 (based on the AAMD definition) as the upper cutoff, it is estimated that roughly 3 percent of the population could be mentally retarded. (The word *could* must be stressed, since an adaptive deficit must also be documented before a diagnosis is made.) Recently, this traditional estimate has been challenged. Based on an extensive field study in Riverside, California, Mercer (1973a,b) contends that the 3 percent estimate is too high; the actual prevalence is closer to 1 percent (1973b). She displays this sentiment in the title of one of her papers (1973b), "The myth of the 3% prevalence." The Riverside study and Mercer's conclusions have been widely disseminated and well received. Mercer has also explored the problems and apparent inequities in labeling the mentally retarded. These issues and this type of data (i.e., lower prevalence estimates) appear to have influenced the AAMDs (Grossman, 1973) decision to lower the IQ cutoff score for mental retardation from 85 (Heber, 1961) to 70. The result was to eliminate the category of "borderline mental retardation" (now referred to as "borderline intelligence").

Due to the great impact of Mercer's study, the basis for her opinion (the Riverside study) must be carefully scrutinized to determine if her conclusions are warranted.

The purpose of the Riverside study was to "comprehend the nature and extent of mental retardation in an American community" (Mercer, 1973a, p. 38). At the time of the study (1960s), Riverside was a community of some 85,000 persons, located approximately 50 miles east of Los Angeles. Although the city has a large military base, a university, and small industries, its economic history is agricultural and the community still has a strong rural and agricultural component.

The Riverside study was a complex, multifaceted endeavor, which is difficult to summarize in a few pages. Moreover, Mercer's (1973a,b) own description of the study is unclear, making it difficult to develop a precise overview. Consequently, we will explore only a few critical features of her investigation and attempt to appraise its overall generalizability.

One method of the study was to assess a representative sample of two informal social systems (neighborhood and family) to determine the extent of mental retardation. The city was stratified on the basis of geographic region and socioeconomic level (as determined only by housing cost). The actual sample was slightly biased in favor of the upper socioeconomic deciles.

This sample was assessed using a field study wherein 41 graduate students were trained (for 44 hours) to conduct an interview regarding adaptive behavior and physical disability and to collect certain demographic data regarding the family. An interviewer would go to the sampled housing unit and interview one family member, who would provide data about all of the members. Although the sample size is reported as 6,998, only 26 percent of these persons answered questions about themselves. The respondent was "any member of the household eighteen or more years of age and/or married, who was mentally competent to answer" (Mercer, 1973a, p. 279).

The methodology of this phase of the study has some potentially serious problems. First, no data are presented regarding the reliability of the interviewers. How do we know that the various interviewers were using the same methods and gathering the same information? To address this issue, 165 units were revisited by supervisors. They reported no significant discrepancies regarding such data as composition of the family, number of years in Riverside, and occupation, place of birth, and education of head of the household. It is fortunate that such data were generally consistent. Indeed, if they were not, the entire study would be meaningless. However, no reliability data are supplied regarding the adaptive behavior levels of family members, information which is critical to the study. Two points are of merit here. First, as we have already indicated, the reliability of the interviewers is important. Of even greater importance, however, is the fact that data regarding 74 percent of the sample were obtained through informants (other family member). Again, we have no idea of the reliability of these informers and the information they provided.

The actual sample used in the study presents other problems. Mercer (1973a) reports that 234 housing units, or 7.9 percent of the sample, refused to participate in the study. While obtaining data from over 92 percent of the housing units is commendable, it is impossible to determine the potential bias from the housing units that failed to respond. This is especially important since Mercer argues about changes in prevalence rates from 3 percent to 1 percent. It is reasonable to question whether families with retarded members would be more prone to refuse cooperation. The Riverside study did not adequately deal with this issue.

The Riverside sample also poses a problem of generalizability. In other words, can we apply the results of this study to other areas, cities, and so on? Wouldn't we expect to find a much larger proportion of identified (labeled) mentally retarded persons in large urban centers, such as New York, Los Angeles, and Chicago? A multitude of differences, including such diverse factors as job availability, presence of ghettos, available resources, residential stability, and general level of complexity, suggest potentially higher estimates than those found in Mercer's study. As will be discussed in Chapter 11, the incidence of low intelligence in large urban areas may be significantly higher even than the 3 percent estimate suggests.

A subsample of the Riverside study was selected for psychological testing to determine IQs. The selection of this subsample was quite complex, and its representativeness can be questioned. Additionally, the use of different measures and psychometrists raises questions regarding both the reliability and validity of the IQ data. Because of the complexity of the study's IQ testing procedures, it is not feasible to summarize all of the possible methodological problems here. One point, however, deserves mention. Mercer (1973a, p. 283) states that "In the opinion of the psychometrists, 66.7% of the tests were very reliable, 29.6% percent were somewhat reliable, and only 3.7% were unreliable." It is difficult to speculate about the meaning of "somewhat unreliable," but it is clear that if one-third of the IQs of the subsample were somewhat or very unreliable, great caution should be taken in interpreting these scores. This is especially true when we recall that Mercer uses the Riverside data to argue for a 1 percent versus a 3 percent prevalence of mental retardation.

In another phase of the study, social system epidemiology was formally assessed by contacting various organizations and government agencies ($N = 241$) and asking them to indicate what persons served by their agency were mentally retarded. This approach was used since mental retardation (from the social system perspective) is defined as achieving the status of mental retardate. This is done through identification by an agency (school, State Department of Mental Hygiene, and so on) that is concerned with and labels persons as mentally retarded (gives them the status of mental retardate). Although Mercer stresses the differences between the clinical and social system perspectives, it is interesting to note that the social system epidemiology identifies only persons who have previously been identified through the clinical approach. When agencies are surveyed to determine how many mentally retarded persons they serve, they typically identify persons who have been tested and diagnosed as mentally retarded according to the AAMD (clinical) criteria. In the social system perspective, mental retardation is an achieved social status, but the achievement process (identification through assessment) is paradoxically done from the clinical perspective. The social system perspective, then, only identifies persons who are clearly mentally retarded and has no relevance for persons of low intelligence who have not previously been diagnosed. This seems contrary to Mercer's contention that the clinical perspective is more appropriate for the more severely retarded, while the social system perspective is more appropriate for the mildly retarded. It appears that the social system perspective simply ignores the intelligence-related problems of many persons whose IQ would be in the mild range (55–69) and who also have an adaptive deficit—that is, persons who fit the AAMD criteria but who have not been formally labeled.

## INTEGRATION OF THE CLINICAL AND SOCIAL SYSTEM PERSPECTIVES

The clinical and social system perspectives at first appear to be totally disparate. In a practical sense (e.g., who are labeled mentally retarded, how many retarded persons are there), as we have seen, this difference is more apparent than real. The theoretical bases of these approaches, however, are quite divergent and seemingly incompatible. This situation is reminiscent of Niels Bohr's (1934) "theory of complementarity," which sprang from the experimental observations that a light ray at times presents the characteristics of wave motion and at other times of particle motion. Bohr reasoned, despite this apparent contradiction, that the wave and particle characteristics were complementary and not mutually exclusive; each simply described light from a different point of view. This principle of complementarity has had a tremendous impact on the theory of knowledge. It is now recognized that science can accommodate different but equally valid perspectives in the study of a single phenomenon. In fact, by recognizing that different perspectives complement each other, the phenomenon in question can be more readily understood.

The idea of complementarity can be applied to the viewing of mental retardation from the clinical and social system perspectives. It would be difficult to contend that either of these approaches is wrong or even that one is generally superior. Both contribute to an understanding of mental retardation—an understanding which is furthered by their complementarity. This complementarity, however, is not generally recognized by professionals in the field. This is especially true of many of the strong adherents of both perspectives. Unfortunately, such a proprietary attitude restricts our understanding of mental retardation, both as a general construct and as an individual diagnosis. By integrating these approaches, we can view the individual, with his unique traits, deficits, and so on (clinical perspective) in the context of a given social system or systems with varying statuses, roles, and expectations. However, to gain maximum understanding of the concept of mental retardation, additional factors must be considered—factors which are not adequately covered by either the social system or clinical perspectives. Neither system takes into account a broader conception of society and how facets of the society relate to intelligence and to mental retardation.

## SOCIETAL CHARACTERISTICS AND INTELLIGENCE

Due to the inherent complexity and flux of any cultural system, it is impossible to list all the societal variables which relate to the intellectual ability of its members. The following factors are offered as guidelines to the types of societal characteristics which may influence the intellectual demands on its members.

### Societal Complexity

An individual's effectiveness in coping with the demands of a society is obviously multidetermined. Such personality variables as motivation, stability, and need patterns, and other variables such as physical constitution all play important roles. However, the factors that become preeminent are largely a function of the specific society. This is especially important when assessing the coping ability of persons with low intelligence. Edgerton (1970) stresses this point:

> No matter the definition nor the discipline doing the defining, mental retardation is everywhere seen as a social and cultural phenomenon. Mild mental retardation is generally taken to be fundamentally social and cultural in every respect, and it is equally widely agreed that even severe and profound mental retardation cannot be understood, much less responded to effectively without knowledge of the social and cultural system in which it occurs. I should think it safe, therefore, to insist that the study of mental retardation calls for a broadly social and cultural view. (p. 524)

In other words, different societies demand different levels of intellectual ability. This fact is illustrated in an unpublished study by Albizu-Miranda (discussed by Haywood, 1971). Here, IQ ratings and a measure of economic success were made in six types of communities in Puerto Rico, which varied from urban to rural. Predictably, persons with low IQs were poorer than persons with high IQs. However, this study also indicated that as complexity of the community setting increased, the percentage of poor persons among the mentally retarded grew consistently larger. In the more agrarian and peasant-like communities, intelligence was less important because of the minimal intellectual demands of such societies. As the communities become more complex (urbanized), intelligence becomes more relevant. Edgerton, citing Ginzberg (1965), states that "complex industrial societies demand greater intellectual competence than do small, technologically simple societies. In vulgar terms, the understanding reads as follows: 'simple people for simple societies'" (Edgerton, 1970, p. 525). Conversely, we might add, more intelligent persons for more complex societies! Consequently, it is necessary to consider the salient features of the society before assessing what demands it makes on its members and what abilities or skills are needed to cope with these demands.

## Cultural or Societal Stability

It is logical to assume that under static conditions, more could be learned about a given phenomenon since there would be more time available for learning. Moreover, change adds the dimension of complexity. Thus, we would expect an increase in intellectual demand as the rate of change increases. American society continues to become more complex, technology continues to advance, and change continues at an *accelerated* rate. Toffler (1970), for example, dramatizes the rapidity of change in society by summarizing the evolution of speed in transportation. In 6000 B.C., the fastest long-distance mode of transportation available was the camel, which traveled at an average speed of eight miles an hour. Not until the advent of the chariot some 4,400 years later (1600 B.C.) was the average speed raised—to 20 miles an hour. So impressive was this speed that almost 3,500 years later, in 1784, the first mail coach in England averaged a mere 10 miles an hour; the first steam locomotive, introduced in 1825, attained a speed of 13 miles an hour, while the great sailing ships of that time cruised at one-half that speed. Not until the 1880s, with an improved steam locomotive, did man attain a speed of 100 miles an hour. This accomplishment took man millions of years, but it took only 58 additional years to quadruple that record with a 1938 airplane that broke 400 miles an hour. In another 20 years this new record was doubled; and by the 1960s, rocket planes approached a speed of 4,000 miles an hour. In 1971, American astronauts traveled through space at a speed of 18,000 miles an hour. Plotted on a graph, the line representing progress in transportation speed would jump off the page (Toffler, 1970, p. 27).

Transportation is not an isolated example. Indeed, similar changes can be noted in almost any aspect of science, economics, medicine, and in society itself. Technology feeds on itself, making more technology possible. This results in an increasing rate of development and, consequently, of complexity and increased intellectual demand.

## Economic Variables

A variety of economic factors appear to be related to intelligence and, in turn, to occupational performance. For example, during periods of economic recession or depression, increases in unemployment result in higher competition for jobs. Generally, persons of lower intelligence are less capable of successfully competing in the job market and thus constitute a higher proportion of the unemployed. Under these conditions, such persons are more apt to manifest an adaptive impairment. A further consideration of this issue is presented in Chapter 11.

### Automation

Automation has a unique and direct effect on persons of low or marginal intelligence. The general effects of automation have been discussed by numerous writers (e.g., Dexter, 1958; Greenberger, 1962; Diebold, 1964; Simon, 1965). The relationship between intelligence and the effects of automation, however, has not been emphasized. The majority of jobs that have been "automated out" were within the capacity of marginal or less intelligent persons. Despite a small increase in service positions, the job possibilities for persons who are uneducated, unskilled, and of low intelligence are rapidly disappearing. Again, this variable is closely related to adaptive ability and to the concept of mental retardation.

Thus far, it has been contended that in a modern industrial society, intellectual level is strongly related to social competence. In this regard, social competence has been implicitly defined as the ability to maintain steady employment and to live independently within the society. It is reasonable, however, to expect that in such a society the effects of low intelligence would be more widespread—that is, not simply limited to difficulty with employment. The increasing complexity in American society, for example, permeates our daily life. Recent concern with consumer rights, truth in lending, and the like attest to the complexity involved in common sales contracts and in everyday consumer purchasing. Insurance contracts, tax computation and reporting, legal restrictions, and so forth all offer similar problems. Even freeway systems and printed bus schedules in metropolitan areas are so complicated as to confuse persons of even average or above-average intelligence.

## THE SOCIETAL PERSPECTIVE

We have considered mental retardation from the clinical perspective, where the focus is on traits and defects of the individual, and from a social system perspective, where the focus is on achieved statuses and roles in a given system. However, both of these approaches, considered either individually or together, do not provide a complete understanding of mental retardation. In general, such terms as "mental retardation" simply indicate that an individual has problems related to low intelligence. The nature and significance of these problems, however, can be adequately appreciated only in a societal context. In other words, low intelligence is a problem because of the demands and expectations of the society. Thus, before we can fully understand mental retardation, we must consider the characteristics and demands of the society, as well as those of the individual and his immediate social milieu (family, school, etc.). This is known as the "societal perspective."

Initially, the societal perspective may appear similar to Mercer's social system approach. The similarity, however, is superficial. Mercer uses a sociological approach wherein *one* social system (e.g., family, school) is viewed in terms of statuses, roles, norms, and so forth. While Mercer readily agrees that an individual could be in several different social systems simultaneously, the social system perspective focuses on one system at a time. This is why Mercer contends that an individual may be mentally retarded at one time (e.g., while in the school system) and not at another (i.e., at home).

The social system perspective is myopic; it focuses on a specific social system but fails to consider the sociocultural context in which that system exists. The clinical perspective might initially seem even further removed from the societal context. The AAMD's two-dimensional definition of mental retardation, however, clearly reflects a societal perspective. That is, both IQ and adaptive behavior, in some degree, reflect societal norms and demands. With IQ, both the content of the tests (test items) and the method of test construction reflect societal conditions and demands. In the first case, test items from such measures as the Stanford-Binet and the Wechsler scales deal with social comprehension (i.e., what to do in various problem situations) and directly reflect sociocultural conditions. Such test content is often criticized as "culturally biased" precisely because it does reflect the attitudes and conditions of the society.

Measures of adaptive behavior also reflect the societal context, since they stipulate what is considered normal behavior for persons of various ages. For example, children are rated on their school performance, adults on their ability to hold a job and be self-sufficient, and so on.

Although the clinical and social system perspectives partly reflect societal variables, neither system adequately considers them. Conversely, we obviously cannot attempt to understand mental retardation by focusing completely on societal or cultural attributes. Thus, to clearly appreciate the nature and problems of mental retardation, we must consider both individual social system and societal factors. The perspectives are complementary and a failure to appreciate this can only serve to decrease the level of our understanding of mental retardation.

# CHAPTER 6

# Classification, Description and Prevalence

In this chapter, the "common ground" from which most professionals in the field of mental retardation operate, is discussed. The first section presents the role, importance, and problems of classification systems. Past and current attempts at developing such systems in this field are then briefly reviewed, especially the current behavioral classification system of the AAMD. The classification system used by educators in this field is also discussed. The behavioral characteristics of persons at the four levels of mental retardation—profound, severe, moderate, and mild—are then described. This material will give the student a general idea of what persons at the various classification levels can and cannot do. The final section of the chapter deals with the epidemiology of mental retardation, focusing on the complex issue of its prevalence. This important topic has relevance both for the theoretical understanding of mental retardation and the more practical problems of developing public policy and planning programs.

## THE ROLE OF CLASSIFICATION

The classification of adults, and especially children, in all areas of exceptionality (a term used for all handicapped conditions, such as blindness, deafness, emotional disturbance, and mental retardation) has become an extremely important and controversial subject. Hobbs (1975a,b) reports on a landmark study, entitled the "Project on Classification of Exceptional Children," which is the culmination of several years' work by 93 experts from many fields of exceptionality. This project was initiated because of the widespread concern over the inappropriate labeling of children, and the serious consequences for the child because of classification even when appropriate. Mental retardation has been at the heart of this concern, both in terms of mislabeling and the alleged detrimental effects of labeling (this issue is discussed in Chapter 9). The purpose of the Project was to determine ways of mitigating the ill effects of classification while preserving its value in providing or obtaining specialized services for exceptional children.

In general, the Project participants were quite critical of our current classification schemes and procedures. Present systems were seen to be too general, vague, imprecise, and deficit-oriented (focusing only on weaknesses rather than including the strengths of a person). Also, present systems tend to group together too many different types of persons, thereby creating an artificially homogeneous view of the handicapped. Furthermore, these rigid systems are almost totally unable to deal with the multiply handicapped individual (of whom there are many), with the result that these persons are "bounced around" from agency to agency. Perhaps the strongest criticism, however, is the fact that our systems have little to offer or suggest in the way of treatment or prescriptions. These experts stressed repeatedly that diagnosis and classification should lead to improved services, not merely to labeling. Nevertheless, despite all of these criticisms and the belief that the disadvantages of our current classifications may outweigh their advantages, the Project did not recommend abandoning them. In fact, the Project report strongly concluded that the classification of children is essential. As Hobbs (1975b) states:

> We do not concur with sentiments, widely expressed, that classification of exceptional children should be done away with. Although we understand that some people advocate the elimination of classification in order to get rid of its harmful effects, their proposed solution oversimplifies the problem. Classification and labeling are essential to human communication and problem solving; without categories and concept designations, all complex communicating and thinking stop. We shall address abuses in classification and labeling, but we do not wish to encourage the belief that abuses can be remedied by not classifying. In fact, we shall argue for more precise categories and for more discriminating ways of describing children in order to plan ap-

> propriate programs for them, and we shall advocate safeguards to decrease the deleterious effects of classification procedures that can, in fact, have many beneficial outcomes. (p. 5)

Part of the problem with our present classification systems is that they serve a wide variety of scientific, clinical, legal, social-administrative, and political purposes. It is almost impossible to cover so many areas equally well. The general and vague categories that are essential from a social-administrative point of view are woefully inadequate in treating the individual case. Still, there is no denying that "without categories and labels, there would be no programs or services." Classification schemes provide the necessary statistical data upon which to base program planning, funding, and legislation. As Robinson and Robinson (1976) note: "At all levels of public and private planning and decision making, objective criteria are needed to determine the extent of the population needing services, the kind of services needed, and, therefore, the amount and manner of funding" (p. 25). Thus, it is important to distinguish between the policy-making aspects of classification systems and their practical or clinical utility. Serving one goal well may preclude serving the other. Of course, certain improvements in our current systems would probably increase both the policy-making and clinical functions of these systems. However, this would be true only up to a certain point, beyond which one of the purposes of classification is sacrificed. At present, the policy-making value of our classification systems far outweighs their clinical usefulness. The latter could probably be improved without doing too much damage to the former. But there will always remain a certain tension between the two goals. The hope for a perfectly satisfactory single classification system is simply unrealistic.

## CLASSIFICATION SYSTEMS IN MENTAL RETARDATION

When Esquirol (1845) made the distinction between mental illness and mental retardation (see Chapter 2), the field was ready to begin classifying the mentally retarded. Esquirol himself proposed the first classification system, which was based on language usage (e.g., those with no speech, those who could say a few words, and those who could speak in simple sentences). Since mental retardation was then viewed as a homogeneous condition, classification according to severity seemed the most appropriate. However, with new developments in medicine and pathology, it became obvious that there were multiple causes of mental retardation. Accordingly, a need for an etiological classification system was felt. As the physician Down (who presented the first formal description of mongolism) noted (1866): "The best classification of idiocy, the one which most assists in the prognosis and treatment, is that which is based on etiology." Down described three etiological groups: congenital idiocy, developmental idiocy, and accidental idiocy. In 1877, the first well-organized medical textbook on mental retardation (Ireland) listed 12 etiological subdivisions of mental retardation. However, as Kanner (1964) aptly observes:

> While Down and Ireland established a new direction of the quest for an etiological grouping of mental defectives, the desire for a classification according to degree was by no means abolished. We thus witness two parallel groupings, which Weygandt characterized as follows: 1) from the practical viewpoint of educability and social behavior; 2) from the viewpoint of a purely scientific consideration of the nature of the manifold conditions. (p. 106)

This dual classification system for mental retardation has been maintained over the years. For example, both the Heber (1959/1961) and Grossman (1973/1977) classification manuals present both a biomedical classification system (based on etiology) and a behavioral classification system (based on severity of behavioral deficit as manifested by levels of IQ and adaptive behavior). The biomedical system is presented in Chapter 8. Here, we will be concerned solely with the more popular and widespread behavioral system. Blanton (1975) states why this system has greater prominence:

> While the development of the biological sciences permitted the differentiation of the retarded on an etiological basis, the primary social need was for functional classification which could be used for educational and legal decisions. (p. 167)

## Behavioral Classification System

Since the advent of the intelligence test, the classification of mental retardation has been based almost exclusively on IQ levels. Over the years, a number of such systems have been developed, each with its own labels and IQ cutoff points. Table 6.1 presents some of the past and present classification systems. The oldest formal system utilized the categories of "idiot," "imbecile," and "moron." The current system (Grossman, 1973/1977) employs the terminology of "mild," "moderate," "severe," and "profound," as did its predecessor, the Heber (1959/1961) manuals. As noted before, the major difference between the Heber and Grossman sys-

Table 6.1: Classification Systems of Mental Retardation

<table>
<tr><th rowspan="2">System</th><th rowspan="2">Generic term</th><th colspan="20">Intelligence quotients</th></tr>
<tr><th>95</th><th>90</th><th>85</th><th>80</th><th>75</th><th>70</th><th>65</th><th>60</th><th>55</th><th>50</th><th>45</th><th>40</th><th>35</th><th>30</th><th>25</th><th>20</th><th>15</th><th>10</th><th>5</th><th>0</th></tr>
<tr><td>Amer. Assoc. for the Study of the Feebleminded (1921) (Old name of Amer. Assoc. on Mental Deficiency–AAMD)</td><td>Feebleminded</td><td colspan="4"></td><td colspan="5">Moron</td><td colspan="5">Imbecile</td><td colspan="6">Idiot</td></tr>
<tr><td>Amer. Psychiatric Assoc. (1952)</td><td>Mental deficiency</td><td colspan="2"></td><td colspan="3">Mild or slightly mild</td><td colspan="4">Moderate</td><td colspan="11">Severe</td></tr>
<tr><td>World Health Organization (1954)</td><td>Mental subnormality</td><td colspan="5"></td><td colspan="4">Mild</td><td colspan="6">Moderate</td><td colspan="5">Severe</td></tr>
<tr><td>Sarason and Gladwin (1958)</td><td>Mental subnormality</td><td colspan="5"></td><td colspan="4">Mental retardation</td><td colspan="11">Mental deficiency</td></tr>
<tr><td>Mental Health Act (1959) Great Britain</td><td>Mental subnormality</td><td colspan="5"></td><td colspan="4">Subnormality</td><td colspan="11">Severe subnormality</td></tr>
<tr><td>Educational Systems (General)</td><td>Mental retarded or mentally handicapped</td><td></td><td colspan="3">Dull—normal or educationally handicapped (EH)</td><td colspan="5">Educable (EMR)</td><td colspan="5">Trainable (TMR)</td><td colspan="6">Custodial, dependent, or profound (PMR)</td></tr>
<tr><td>AAMD (Heber, 1959/1961) Also: Amer. Psychiatric Assoc., 1968 (DSM–II) and WHO, 1968</td><td>Mental retardation (adaptive behavior not included)</td><td colspan="2"></td><td colspan="3">Borderline mentally retarded</td><td colspan="3">Mild</td><td colspan="3">Moderate</td><td colspan="3">Severe</td><td colspan="6">Profound</td></tr>
<tr><td>AAMD (Grossman, 1973/1977) Also: Amer. Psychiatric Assoc., 1979 (DSM–III)</td><td>Mental retardation (adaptive behavior not included)</td><td colspan="2"></td><td colspan="3">Borderline intelligence</td><td colspan="3">Mild</td><td colspan="3">Moderate</td><td colspan="3">Severe</td><td colspan="6">Profound</td></tr>
</table>

tems is the inclusion or exclusion of the 70 to 84 IQ group, called the "borderline mentally retarded" in the Heber manuals and "borderline intelligence" in the Grossman manuals.

Two features of the Heber and Grossman classification systems merit further discussion. The first is a technical matter related to the way IQ tests are constructed and standardized. Most IQ tests are made so that the average score equals an IQ of 100, with a standard deviation (statistical index of variation) of 15 or 16 IQ points. The various levels of retardation (e.g., mild, moderate) are separated in terms of these standard deviation units. Thus, mild mental retardation is two to three standard deviations away from the mean. If we use a test which has a standard deviation unit of 15, then the IQ levels for mild mental retardation are 55 to 69. However, if we use a test that has a standard deviation of 16, then the IQ levels for mild mental retardation become 52 to 67. Most of the popular tests of intelligence (e.g., the Wechsler scales) have a standard deviation of 15 IQ points. However, several tests, most notably the Stanford-Binet, use 16 IQ points. Thus, the IQ cutoffs used for the four levels of mental retardation depend on whether a standard deviation of 15 or 16 IQ points is employed. The resulting differences are most evident in the area of profound mental retardation, where an IQ of 19 or below is the cutoff for a standard deviation of 16, in contrast to an IQ of 24 and below with a standard deviation of 15. Thus, a person with an IQ of 21 could be classified as either profoundly (Wechsler scale) or severely (Binet scale) retarded, depending on which type of test is used. Table 6.2 presents the standard deviation units and IQ cutoffs for the various levels of mental retardation for both types of tests. It should be noted that in discussing mental retardation, most people use the "easier" Wechsler (standard

TABLE 6.2

IQ Ranges for the Levels of Mental Retardation

| | | IQ Ranges: Tests with Different SDs | |
|---|---|---|---|
| | | SD = 15 (Wechsler Scales) | SD = 16 (Binet Scale) |
| Borderline intelligence | −2.00 to −1.01 | 70–84 | 68–83 |
| Mild retardation | −3.00 to −2.01 | 55–69 | 52–67 |
| Moderate retardation | −4.00 to −3.01 | 40–54 | 36–51 |
| Severe retardation | −5.00 to −4.01 | 25–39 | 20–35 |
| Profound retardation | Below −5.00 | Under 25 | Under 20 |

deviation of 15) system. This will be our practice in the present text. However, the reader must be aware that a second system does exist and must be utilized when tests with a standard deviation of 16 are employed.

A second important point is that our present system of classification refers to IQ only. As we have pointed out before, however, IQ is no longer the sole criterion of mental retardation; there must also be a manifest impairment in adaptive behavior. Consequently, this scheme is merely a guideline for determining the level of intellectual deficit. Unless the person also has an adaptive deficit, the formal classification cannot be applied.

The Heber and Grossman manuals also present levels of adaptive behavior that correspond to the intellectual categories of mild, moderate, severe, and profound. The behavioral characteristics of persons at these levels are presented in the next section of this chapter.

The dual set of criteria (IQ and adaptive behavior) for the behavioral classification system does pose some problems. For example, a person with an IQ of 15 is classified as profoundly retarded on the intellectual dimension. However, this same person may be considered severely retarded in terms of adaptive behavior. What, then, would be his official classification? There is no straightforward answer; a clinical judgment must be made. Reflecting the current emphasis on manifest behavior, many professionals feel that in cases of discrepancy, the official designation should reflect the level of adaptive behavior. However, it should be noted that for statistical reporting purposes (in terms of program planning and social-administrative concerns), the IQ levels are almost exclusively used.

As noted, almost everyone is dissatisfied with the clinical utility of the present classification system. Knowing someone's IQ or level of retardation does not really tell you what that person can or cannot do. In this area, experienced workers in the field develop their own set of guidelines. The behavioral characteristics of persons at the four levels of severity, presented in the next section of this chapter, also provide a set of helpful guidelines. However, this is a rather cumbersome way of actualizing vague terms like "mild" and "moderate." The main problem is that the current labels themselves give no clues as to what kinds of treatment are indicated; hence the dissatisfaction with the AAMD system. A partial solution to this problem is represented by another type of classification system that is widely used by educators in this field. We will now discuss this more clinically useful approach, at least with children.

### Educational Classification System

In essence, mental retardation is a psychosocial and educational problem. Educators bear the heaviest responsibility for treating the vast majority of the mentally retarded. It is for this reason that the educational classification system is so prominent. In carrying out their task, educators have always been most concerned with the "educability," or learning potential, of their charges. They want to know whether the child can learn and at what level. Thus, a child's IQ was only of limited importance. In the early days of the special education movement, educability was primarily defined in terms of the child's ability to master the "three R's." Consequently, the education classification system is couched in these terms. However, while these older terms are still used, the current notion of education for the mentally retarded goes far beyond this basic concern. It now includes such things as practical daily skills and personal and social growth and adjustment.

From the educator's perspective, there are three basic categories or levels of mental retardation. This system is also based on severity, although learning ability rather than IQ is the primary criterion. IQ ranges for the three categories have always been employed, but these are intended as general guidelines only. Furthermore, there is considerable overlap in these IQ ranges. Finally, progress in an educational program, not IQ, is the primary factor in placement decisions.

The three categories in the educational classification system are known as EMR (educable mentally retarded), TMR (trainable mentally retarded), and PMR (profoundly mentally retarded). The reader may have heard of the first two categories; the last, PMR, is a recent term and is not as descriptively meaningful or treatment relevant as the other two. (It is, of course, exactly like the AAMD category "profound," with all of its "noninformative" problems.) We will now consider each of these categories in turn.

The EMR group consists of children in the IQ range of 50 or 55 to 75 or even 80 in certain school systems. The term "educable" refers to the fact that these children are capable of academic instruction. In other words, while they may gain little from regular school programs, they are still able to learn basic academic skills such as reading, writing, spelling, and arithmetic. They are also able to provide for most of their personal needs. Educational programs for these children thus stress academic skills as practical tools for daily living as well as the enhancement of social competence, personal adequacy, and occupational skills.

The TMR group consists of children with IQs somewhere between 25 and 35 up to 50 or 55. The term "trainable" means two things. First, it specifies that the child is not educable in terms of formal academic subjects—reading, writing, and arithmetic skills. Second, the child is still considered capable of learning a great deal in terms of practical daily living skills. "Trainable" means that the child can indeed benefit from such training. The goal of the educational program is to teach the child to provide for most of his personal needs. The focus is on self-care skills and personal and social adjustment.

The PMR group consists of children with IQs below 35 or so. In the past, these children were not served by educational agencies. They were often known as the "custodial" or "totally dependent" mentally retarded. It was assumed that they could not benefit from any type of education or training. However, as a result of recent judicial decisions that have established the right of every child to appropriate public education or training, educators now have a mandate to develop programs for this group. Since the majority of these children live in institutions or group homes, formal training programs will probably be carried out there rather than in the public schools. The advent of applied behavioral technology in the last 15 years has drastically altered our expectations regarding these children. While they will never achieve independence and will always require constant care and supervision, we now know that they can be taught, at least partially, to perform many basic self-care skills. They are also "trainable," but to a much smaller degree than the TMRs.

The value of this educational classification system over the AAMD system is that the category labels are much more meaningful and treatment relevant. Knowing that a child is "mildly" retarded tells you nothing about his abilities and deficits and what kind of treatment approach would be appropriate. However, knowing that the child is "educable" immediately tells the educator what type of educational intervention is indicated. In other words, the label is not just a label; it is also a treatment recommendation. It describes the general problem and how one might deal with it. Mild, moderate, etc., refer primarily to IQ levels and tell us little about the child. In contrast, EMR and TMR refer to the types of educational programs in which children are placed. These shorthand terms have much more communication value and treatment relevance. Of course, even they are rather crude and general. But they do represent some improvement over the AAMD system, at least in terms of clinical utility.

In conclusion, we mentioned earlier that the search for a single satisfactory classification system was unrealistic. The AAMD has provided a fairly objective behavioral classification system. This scheme separates mental retardation into four levels of severity based on intellectual level and adaptive behavior. However, this system is most useful from a policy-making and social-administrative point of view. In terms of clinical utility, it is simply too general, vague, and uninformative. The other widely used classification scheme is the educational system. This approach, while still rather general and vague, has far greater clinical utility than the AAMD system. However, it is restricted to children and formal educational environments. These two classification systems serve different purposes and should be retained. However, both can be improved and refined.

## BEHAVIORAL CHARACTERISTICS OF THE MENTALLY RETARDED

In this section, we will consider the behavioral characteristics of the mentally retarded at the four classification levels. The "borderline intelligence" category will also be described. This material is presented as a set of general guidelines to familiarize the student with the various levels of mental retardation; it is neither comprehensive nor exhaustive. In addition to our own comments, material from the Grossman (1973/1977) manuals indicating the adaptive behavior levels by age will be included. However, regarding this material, the reader must keep in mind that the *highest* degree of competency at each level is presented. Many, if not most, of the people in these categories will not be functioning at this level. One other point must be emphasized: Adaptive behavior requirements change with age. Thus, what may constitute profound mental retardation at age fifteen may correspond to mild mental retardation or even normality at three years of age and younger. For convenience, our discussion of the levels of mental retardation will concern only what can be expected of an adult functioning at each level. The descriptions from the AAMD manual are based on persons 15 years of age and older.

### Profound Mental Retardation

Profoundly retarded persons have a Binet IQ below 20 or a Wechsler IQ below 25 (extrapolated; the norms for the Wechsler tests do not go below an IQ of 40), with an estimated adult mental age of three years and eight months or less. The probability of concomitant neurological damage is high, and many are nonambulatory. They are often multiply handicapped. They may learn to walk (usually awkwardly) and to speak a few words. Until recently, most of these persons were unable to feed and toilet themselves. The widespread use of behavior modification has been effective in increasing the number who have such skills. For this group, total supervision is required. Little learning beyond simple motor tasks is possible. They may, however, recognize and respond to familiar faces and objects and follow simple commands. The mortality rate in this group tends to be high.

The following material, taken from the AAMD manual, gives a more specific description of the kinds of skills that might be found in the highest-functioning profoundly retarded individuals.

> *Independent functioning:* Feeds self with spoon or fork, may spill some; puts on clothing but needs help with small buttons and jacket zippers; tries to bathe self but needs help; can wash and dry hands but not very efficiently; partially toilet trained but may have accidents.
>
> *Physical:* May hop or skip; may climb steps with alternating feet; rides tricycle (or bicycle over 8 years); may climb trees or jungle gym; play dance games; may throw ball and hit target.
>
> *Communication:* May have speaking vocabulary of over 300 words and use grammatically correct sentences. If non-verbal, may use many gestures to communicate needs. Understands simple verbal communications including directions and questions ("Put it on the shelf." "Where do you live?"); (Some speech may be indistinct sometimes.) May recognize advertising words and signs (Ice cream, STOP, EXIT, MEN, LADIES). Relates experiences in simple language.
>
> *Social:* Participates in group activities and simple group games; interacts with others in simple play ("Store," "House,") and expressive activities (art and dance).

We must reiterate that the AAMD descriptions indicate the highest level of functioning for that category. For example, the vast majority of profoundly retarded persons have little, if any, speech and are certainly nowhere near the 300-word speaking vocabulary or "grammatically correct sentences" specified in the manual.

### Severe Mental Retardation

Severely retarded persons have a Binet IQ ranging from 20 to 35 or a Wechsler IQ from 25 to 39 (extrapolated), with a mental age roughly from three years and nine months to six years. Although neurological damage is common in this group, they are more apt to be ambulatory than the profoundly retarded. Unlike profound retardation, special training can teach them to talk and care for simple personal needs. Academic training, however, is not effective. The focus of training is on self-care skills, and little independent behavior occurs. These individuals need constant supervision and care. And, as Robinson and Robinson (1965) mention, severely retarded adults are apt to be openly friendly, in the manner of little children, and attach themselves to persons with whom they come in contact.

According to the AAMD manual, some specific abilities of the highest-functioning severely retarded persons are as follows:

*Independent functioning:* Feeds self adequately with spoon and fork; can butter bread; (needs help with cutting meat); can put on clothes and can button and zipper clothes; may tie shoes; bathes self with supervision; is toilet trained; washes face and hands without help.

*Physical:* Can run, skip, hop, dance; uses skates or sled or jump rope; can go up and down stairs alternating feet; can throw ball to hit target.

*Communication:* May communicate in complex sentences; speech is generally clear and distinct; understands complex verbal communication including words such as "because" and "but." Recognizes signs, words, but does not read with comprehension prose materials.

*Social:* May participate in group activities spontaneously; may engage in simple competitive exercise games (dodge ball, tag, races). May have friendship choices which are maintained over weeks or months.

*Economic activity:* May be sent on simple errands and make simple purchases with a note; realizes money has value but does not know how to use it (except for coin machines).

*Occupation:* May prepare simple foods (sandwiches); can help with simple household tasks (bedmaking, sweeping, vacuuming); can set and clear table.

*Self-direction:* May ask if there is "work" for him to do; may pay attention to task for 10 minutes or more; makes efforts to be dependable and carry out responsibility.

## Moderate Mental Retardation

The moderately retarded person has a Binet IQ of from 36 to 51 or a Wechsler IQ from 40 to 54, with an approximate mental age of from six years and one month to eight years and five months. Although much less dramatic than with the profoundly and severely retarded, these individuals often have some observable physical features which indicate abnormality. They frequently look as though something is wrong with them. Some of them do maintain full-time jobs, and many others have part-time or odd jobs. The chief focus of training is on self-care and other practical skills, and the majority become fairly proficient in such skills as dressing, toileting, eating, and grooming. As children, they may well have attended TMR classes. The moderately retarded adult is roughly equivalent intellectually to normal second- or third-grade children. However, although the moderately retarded may be able to recognize some written words or even read some simple sentences, they are essentially functionally illiterate. Very few of these persons marry or become independent. They have few friends outside the immediate family, and any employment they obtain is usually of a repetitive, unskilled nature, perhaps in a sheltered setting where income is not dependent on production.

The AAMD manual lists these specific skills as typical of the highest-functioning persons in this category.

> *Independent functioning:* Feeds, bathes, dresses self; may select daily clothing; may prepare easy foods (peanut butter sandwiches) for self or others; combs/brushes hair; may shampoo and roll up hair; may wash and /or iron and store own clothes.
>
> *Physical:* Good body control; good gross and fine motor coordination.
>
> *Communication:* May carry on simple conversation; uses complex sentences. Recognizes words, may read sentences, ads, signs, and simple prose material with some comprehension.
>
> *Social:* May interact cooperatively and/or competitively with others.
>
> *Economic activity:* May be sent on shopping errand for several items without notes; makes minor purchases; adds coins to dollar with fair accuracy.
>
> *Occupation:* May do simple routine household chores (dusting, garbage, dishwashing; prepare simple foods which require mixing).
>
> *Self-direction:* May initiate most of own activities; attend to task 15–20 minutes (or more); may be conscientious in assuming much responsibility.

## Mild Mental Retardation

Adults functioning in the mild range of mental retardation have a Binet IQ of from 52 to 67 or a Wechsler IQ of from 55 to 69. The typical mental age ranges from about eight years and six months to ten years and ten months. These persons usually look and act normal; there is nothing obvious about their retardation. In fact, many are not even suspected of any retardation until the age of six, when they encounter the intellectual demands of school. Consequently, many in this group are referred to as the "six-hour mentally retarded." As adults, they are frequently able to find and keep a job, but often need supervision in social and financial affairs. Intellectually they are at the level of a fourth- or fifth-grade child. However, their academic achievement is usually below this level. Many of these persons attended EMR classes in school. Vocational training is the major educational emphasis rather than proficiency in academic skills. In addition, the training focuses on the personal-social skills necessary for job success (e.g., dress, personality, being on time) rather than on specific job tasks (although this is also done). Mildly retarded persons are very vulnerable to occupational displacement by adverse economic conditions ("last hired, first fired") or automation. Motor slowness and lack of reading skills make competitive employment difficult for them. Mildly retarded women are more capable than men of successful marriage, since the homemaking and social skills required of them are less demanding than the public work skills required of men. One of the most common problems with mildly retarded adults is their inability to handle leisure time. Post-school programs for socialization and recreation, as well as for supplying guidance with their personal and career problems, are extremely important.

According to the AAMD manual, the highest-functioning mildly retarded persons should be able to perform many of the following skills.

> *Independent functioning:* Exercises care for personal grooming, feeding, bathing, toilet, may need health or personal care reminders, may need help in selection or purchase of clothing.
>
> *Physical:* Goes about hometown (local neighborhood in city, campus at institution) with ease, but cannot go to other towns alone without aid; can use bicycle, skis, ice skates, trampoline or other equipment requiring good coordination.
>
> *Communication:* Communicates complex verbal concepts and understands them; carries on everyday conversation, but cannot discuss abstract or philosophical concepts; uses telephone and communicates in writing for simple letter writing or orders but does not write about abstractions or important current events.
>
> *Social:* Interacts cooperatively or competitively with others and initiates some group activities, primarily for social or recreational purposes; may belong to a local recreation group or church group, but not to civic organizations or groups of skilled persons (e.g., photography club, great books club, or kennel club); enjoys recreation (e.g., bowling, dancing, TV, checkers, but either does not enjoy or is not competent at tennis, sailing, bridge, piano playing, or other hobbies requiring rapid or involved or complex planning and implementation).
>
> *Economic activity:* Can be sent or go to several shops to make purchases (without a note to shopkeepers) to purchase several items; can make change correctly, but does not use banking facilities; may earn living but has difficulty handling money without guidance.
>
> *Occupation:* Can cook simple foods, prepare simple meals; can perform everyday household tasks (cleaning, dusting, dishes, laundry); as adult can engage in semi-skilled or simple skilled job.

*Self-direction:* Initiates most of own activity; will pay attention to task for at least 15–20 minutes; conscientious about work and assumes much responsibility but needs guidance for tasks with responsibility for major tasks (health care, care of others, complicated occupational activity).

### Borderline Intelligence

Persons in the borderline range of intelligence have a Binet IQ of 68 to 83 or a Wechsler IQ of 70 to 84. These persons have a mental age from about ten years and eleven months to about thirteen years and three months. Their level of intellectual development can be compared to that of a normal child of similar age. Adults in the borderline range are frequently able to achieve adequate vocational and social adjustment if they have the proper training and reasonable employment opportunities. As a rule, they are employed in unskilled and laboring positions, although they are capable of attaining some skilled and semi-skilled levels. Many of these individuals blend into the normal population and have never been identified or labeled as having difficulty related to intelligence. They are most often of low socioeconomic status, which possibly causes more difficulty than intellectual level. However, low intelligence clearly compounds the problems of low socioeconomic level, preventing the individual from rising above the poverty line.

Based on mental age, we would expect that adults of borderline intelligence would perform academically like normal sixth- to eighth-grade students. Gunzburg (1968), however, suggests a lower level of achievement. His data indicate that the average reading level of borderline persons is at about the age nine level, rather than between ages eleven and thirteen (as we would expect from their mental age).

There are no AAMD adaptive behavior descriptions for these persons. In contrast to the Heber (1959/1961) manuals, they are no longer considered mentally retarded.

## EPIDEMIOLOGY OF MENTAL RETARDATION

In this section, we will consider the epidemiology of mental retardation. Epidemiology is defined as "a science concerned with the study of factors that influence the occurrence and distribution of disease, defect, disability, or death in aggregations of individuals" (Clark, 1953, p. 31). The unit of study in epidemiology is the group, not the individual. Epidemiology involves making a determination or estimate of the number of cases of some condition in a population. In addition, the epidemiologist attempts to relate this estimate to other classifications of the population, such as age, sex, and social class. Thus, the epidemiologist studies the occurrence of a condition in both the general population and specified segments of that population.

Good epidemiology depends upon the definition of the condition in question. If the condition is poorly or vaguely defined, there will be problems with the estimates of its occurrence. This is particularly true of mental and emotional disorders, which are often much more difficult to define than many medical diseases. The discussion in Chapter 4 on the concept of mental retardation suggests that epidemiology in this field is quite problematic. The cultural relativity of this condition makes it extremely difficult to pinpoint cases and to make any generalizations across cultures. There is also the problem that different cultures and different social institutions within any given culture often employ different IQ cutoffs for mental retardation (e.g., the AAMD uses an IQ of 70; some public school systems use an IQ of 75 or even 80). Even more striking in this regard is the difference between the Heber (1959 /1961) and Grossman (1973/1977) AAMD definitions; the former used an upper IQ limit of 85, while the latter has reverted to the traditional IQ of 70. Needless to say, such situations and variations make epidemiology a complex and difficult task.

## Prevalence of Mental Retardation

Epidemiologists use two statistical methods for estimating the occurrence of a condition in a population: the incidence rate and the prevalence rate. "Incidence" refers to the number of new cases in a population during a specified period of time. "Prevalence" refers to the total number of cases in a population group during a specified period of time. In the literature on mental retardation, these two indices are often used interchangeably, despite the fact that they refer to two different types of estimates. This has resulted in some confusion regarding the overall estimation of mental retardation. We shall return to this problem after discussing the traditional prevalence estimates in widespread use. It will become apparent that what the field has always called prevalence is more correctly labeled incidence.

As might be expected, given the vagueness and variations in the definition and criteria for mental retardation, there is considerable discrepancy in the estimates of mental retardation. In a review of 60 studies from 1894 to 1958, Wallin (1958) reported estimates of from .05 to 13 percent of the populations surveyed. Most of this variation, however, was related to methodological differences, particularly in terms of the criteria (e.g., IQ cutoff) employed. In commenting on the results of more recent European and American surveys, Farber (1968) noted that a modal figure of 2 to 3 percent was consistently found. This is in agreement with the traditional prevalence estimate of 3 percent, which is the standard figure reported in almost all textbooks and articles on mental retardation.

On the basis of the 3 percent figure, it is estimated that in a United States population of 220 million people, there are 6.6 million mentally retarded persons. This 3 percent figure is based on three factors: (1) the theoretical distribution of intelligence, (2) sampling surveys of the distribution of IQ, and (3) an excess of cases at the lower end of the distribution of intelligence. We shall discuss each of these factors in turn, in demonstrating how this 3 percent prevalence figure is arrived at.

*Theoretical Distribution of Intelligence* As discussed in Chapter 3, scientists have assumed that intelligence is normally distributed. Therefore, we can consider the theoretical distribution of intelligence in terms of IQ scores and specify what percentage of the population would fall above and below any particular score. As shown in Figure 3.1, approximately 2.27 percent of the population is expected to have an IQ below 70. In a population of 220 million, this means that 4,994,000 persons satisfy the psychometric criterion (IQ below 70) of mental retardation. This figure of 2.27 percent thus accounts for most of the traditional 3 percent estimate. But we are still left with almost 1.6 million people ($3.00 - 2.27 = .73 = 1.6$ million). The other two factors are responsible for these additional persons.

*Sampling Surveys* It was also noted in Chapter 3 that according to sampling surveys, the actual distribution of IQ closely approximates the theoretical normal distribution. However, as Haywood (1974) has noted, there are slightly more people at both ends of the distribution and fewer in the middle than expected. Thus, just on a sampling basis, more than 2.27 percent of the population has an IQ below 70. This sampling effect also occurs at the high end of the distribution of intelligence; more than 2.27 percent have IQs above 130. However, there is a pooling at the lower end of the distribution that causes even more of a sampling excess.

*Excess Cases: The Actual Distribution of Intelligence* The greatest distortion between the theoretical and actual estimates occurs at the low end of the distribution of IQ. This is dramatically illustrated in Table 6.3.

As the table shows, the lower the IQ, the greater the proportionate excess of actual to expected cases. The explanation for these empirical findings revolves around the presence of severe pathological conditions that have pronounced effects on the normal expression of intelligence. In other words, these people are not really part of the normal curve; rather, they are individuals with biologically depressed intelligence. There are no corresponding biological phenomena that enhance intelligence; thus, there is no such excess at the high end of the intelligence distribution. This problem is peculiar to the low end of the distribution and is thus particularly relevant to mental retardation.

An analogy used by Jensen (1969) should clarify this important point. Height is normally distributed; most people fall near the average, with progressively fewer and fewer as we move farther away from the mean. Neither short nor tall persons are abnormal; they are merely at the extreme ends of this distribution. However, Jensen has noted that the situation is very different for midgets and dwarfs. They are not part of the normal distribution. Rather, their stature is a function of pathological factors that override the usual biological determinants of height. This is exactly the case with the severe forms of mental retardation. These people are not part of the normal distribution; they represent a different group that results from pathological factors. The reader should recall the discussion in Chapter 4, where it was stressed that the mentally retarded could be divided into two groups based on the presence or absence of neuropathology. The "excess" of persons we have been talking about here are the neuropathological group. This much smaller but more dramatic group

TABLE 6.3

Prevalence of Mental Retardation

| IQ Range | Theoretical Expectations | Actual Estimated Prevalence | Excess | Percent Excess |
|---|---|---|---|---|
| 0–20 | 57 | 100,000 | 99,943 | 175,339 |
| 20–50 | 177,747 | 400,000 | 222,253 | 125 |
| 50–70 | 5,970,577 | 6,030,577 | 60,000 | 1 |
| Total (0–70) | 6,148,381 | 6,530,577 | 382,196 | 6 |

* Data on theoretical expectations from normal curve and the actual prevalence estimates from sampling surveys taken from Haywood (1974). Data are based on an assumed United States population of 200,000,000.

of persons differs qualitatively from the much larger but milder group of mentally retarded persons that do fit the normal distribution. This situation has given rise to a bulge at the lower tail of the distribution of intelligence. Persons with significant neuropathology constitute their own group, with their own mean and standard deviation. This pathological group is often superimposed on the normal distribution to demonstrate the effect, as illustrated in Figure 6.1. It can be seen that the neuropathological group (the "excess" over theoretical expectations) has a mean IQ of 32 and a standard deviation of 16. It is this neuropathological group in particular that dispels any notion of mental retardation as a homogeneous condition.

By combining the three above-mentioned factors, we arrive at the traditional 3 percent prevalence estimate. We start with the theoretical expectation of 2.27 percent. To this is added a certain excess factor. Part of this excess (mostly for the 50 to 70 IQ range) is simply the result of sampling; the other part (mostly for the 0 to 50 IQ range) is due to the effects

FIGURE 6.1

The frequency distribution of intelligence quotients, based on an assumed total population of 220 million. (Adapted from Dingman and Tarjan, 1960.)

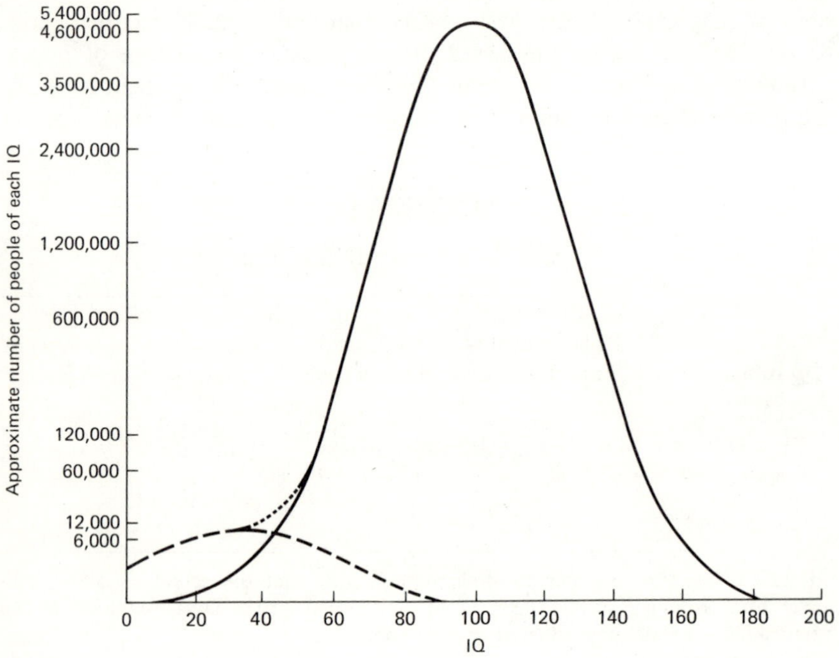

of various pathological conditions. The net result is a 3 percent estimate for the prevalence of mental retardation.

There is, unfortunately, one major problem with all of these estimates based on IQ. As we have stated repeatedly, the diagnosis of mental retardation cannot be made on IQ alone; there must also be clear evidence of an adaptive impairment. Accordingly, unless we can assume that all persons with an IQ below 70 also manifest adaptive deficits, these estimates will be inflated. Many people in the field are unwilling to make this assumption. Hobbs' (1975b) comments in this regard are quite relevant:

> Many individuals whose IQ's are below 70 are not significantly impaired with respect to an adaptive behavior criterion; in spite of low IQ's, they hold jobs, marry, raise families, and participate in community life. At present there is no satisfactory way of estimating the number of persons with low IQ's who are functioning in a satisfactory manner in vocational or social settings. What can be said is that the number of persons estimated on psychometric criteria alone to be retarded must be reduced by an unknown number to take account of such normally functioning low-IQ persons for the purpose of determining how many are functionally mentally retarded. (p. 52)

In recent years, this situation has given rise to investigations employing the "double screen" (low IQ and adaptive behavior) to diagnose mental retardation. Perhaps the most famous of these is Mercer's (1973a) Riverside study, reported on in the previous chapter. As noted there, Mercer concluded that the prevalence of mental retardation in that community was closer to 1 percent than to 3 percent when the double screen was employed. While a number of other factors contributed to this 1 percent estimate (some of which will be covered later), the most prominent was her contention that a good portion of those with IQs below 70 were adapting. However, both the present authors (see Chapter 5) and other investigators (e.g., Robinson and Robinson, 1976) have seriously questioned this study's methodology, particularly the assessment of adaptive behavior—which is the critical issue here. Mercer's assessment of adaptiveness seems quite liberal; more realistic and stricter criteria would have revealed a much smaller percentage of the low-IQ people "making it."

The correspondence between IQ and adaptive behavior is an extremely difficult issue. While all investigators agree that these two measures do not correspond, most believe that they are highly correlated, particularly below IQ 70 and increasingly so as the IQ drops. It is at the higher levels of intelligence that the relationship breaks down. The correspondence issue was much more relevant and critical under the Heber

(1959/1961) definition of mental retardation, which included the "borderline" category (IQ 70 to 84). A strong case can be made that many of these people are adapting. In fact, it was just such reasoning and supporting data that led to the dropping of the borderline category in the Grossman (1973/1977) manuals. Furthermore, it should be noted that Mercer's Riverside data were already known when the 1973 Grossman revision was prepared. Her indication that many mildly retarded people were adapting no doubt influenced the decision to drop the borderline category. Given these data, there seemed to be no basis for including this even higher (borderline) category of mental retardation.

Obviously, more research is needed to resolve this issue. At the present time, it seems clear that the 3 percent prevalence figure, which is based on IQ alone, must be reduced. However, the reduction will probably not be nearly as drastic as Mercer's liberal estimates suggest.

Sampling surveys have indicated several other interesting aspects about the prevalence of mental retardation. The variables of age, sex, and social class produce some striking differences in prevalence estimates.

## Factors Affecting Prevalence

*Age* There is marked variation in prevalence estimates of mental retardation by age. Surveys indicate a fairly dramatic rise during the school years, peaking in adolescence. Rates for infancy, early childhood, and adulthood are much lower. These findings point to the cultural relativity of mild mental retardation. Before entering school, the mildly retarded child functions on a par with his normal age peers. Neither they nor his family detect anything strikingly different about him, although he may sometimes be seen as a "little slow." Other factors (e.g., laziness, "problem child") are often used to explain any differences in his behavior. However, upon entering school, with its intellectual demands, the problem of low intelligence becomes more and more apparent. The intellectual demands are greatest during the high school years, given the need for abstract thinking. Accordingly, more referrals to special classes are made at this time than at any other academic level. The "storm and stress" of adolescence may also serve to heighten problems during this period. Upon termination or graduation, however, these individuals again tend to blend into the population—or more specifically, into their particular sociocultural context. In other words, except for the school years, these persons are not seen to be too much of a problem. Furthermore, it is precisely, and perhaps solely, the intellectual demands of school that are problematic. Thus, the school system is the social agency most responsible for identifying mild mental retardation.

## BOX 6.1

### Prevalence by Levels of Mental Retardation

As reported earlier, on the basis of the theoretical normal distribution of intelligence, approximately 2.27 percent of the population is expected to have IQs below 70. This figure can be broken down further to indicate the theoretical expectations by level of mental retardation. Of this 2.27 percent, 2.14 percent are expected to be mildly retarded, with only 0.13 percent moderately retarded. The combined figure for the profound-severe levels of mental retardation is 0.01 percent. Of course, these figures are based only on IQ and do not consider adaptive behavior. In addition, there is a considerable excess of actual cases over expectations in the lower end of the normal distribution of intelligence, primarily because of serious pathological conditions. This factor produces the traditional (actual) 3 percent prevalence estimate rather than the 2.27 percent prevalence (theoretical) estimate. Using the 3 percent figure, Kauffman and Payne (1975) indicate that it would break down into 2.3 percent mild, 0.6 percent moderate, and 0.1 percent severe-profound. The actual figures from various surveys are difficult to compare, because different IQ categories are used. However, they are all in basic agreement. In 1963, the National Association for Retarded Citizens estimated that the actual percentages for the four levels of mental retardation were 89.0, 6.0, 3.5, and 1.5, respectively. Conley (1973) estimated that there were 88.2 percent in the 50 to 70 IQ range, 8.3 percent in the 25 to 50 IQ range, and 3.5 percent below IQ 25. Several investigators (Dunn, 1973; Penrose, 1966) have concluded that the actual ratio of cases of mild to moderate to severe-profound mental retardation is 12 : 3 : 1, or 75, 20, and 5 percent, respectively.

There is another important aspect of these findings regarding age and prevalence. Not only are these children identified as mentally retarded almost exclusively during the school years, but even more striking, they are so labeled only during the school hours. Before and after school, in their family and neighborhood contexts, they are seen as normal. They are able to adapt in those situations which make none of the intellectual demands of school. They cease to be "different." This, as we have noted, is the phenomenon of the "six-hour retarded child." Many people feel it is inappropriate to label these children "mentally retarded" since they are presumably adapting during the rest of the day. Furthermore, since the ultimate criterion of mental retardation is adaptation, why label someone who satisfies this criterion most of the time? Some investigators believe it would be more appropriate to call these children "educationally handicapped" or "educationally disadvantaged," to distinguish them from persons who are mentally retarded 24 hours a day.

There are, of course, legitimate questions regarding the "six-hour retarded child." Are these children really adapting during the other 18 hours, or are we simply not looking close enough? Do they really blend into the population after graduation from school, or do they encounter frequent problems (e.g., getting and maintaining employment, general coping skills, psychological distress) wherein low intelligence is simply unrecognized as fully or partially responsible for their dilemmas? Perhaps most importantly, can anyone who has serious learning problems really adapt in our society, given the need for education to succeed and function effectively? Our discussion in the previous chapter about the societal perspective seems highly relevant here.

Whatever the case, this marked variation in the prevalence rates with age does indicate that the formal designation of "mental retardation" may often be a temporary (although perhaps quite harmful) affair. This highlights two important features about mental retardation. First of all, it indicates the folly of conceptualizing mental retardation in medical or disease terms. What strange disease occurs only between the ages of six and eighteen and then only between 9 A.M. to 3 P.M.? To stretch the point, what strange disease also disappears on weekends and over the holidays and summer vacations? This brings us to the second point. The phenomenon of the "six-hour retarded child" underlines the cultural relativity of mental retardation. As the situation (e.g., school) changes, so does the problem. It is precisely for this reason that the concept of mental retardation is so controversial and will always remain indefinite. Thus, there will never be any clear and easy way to determine mild mental retardation or estimate its "true" prevalence.

*Sex* As with practically all areas of exceptionality, more males than females are diagnosed as mentally retarded. The estimates vary considerably and also differ by IQ level. For example, the New York State Department of Mental Hygiene (1955) reported that the percentage of males was 45.6 percent for IQ 0 to 25, 50 percent for IQ 25 to 49, and 64.3 percent for IQ 50 to 74. Most studies (e.g., Peckham, 1974) suggest that the sex differences are greatest at the milder levels of retardation.

There are several possible explanations for these findings. One is that males have a much greater chance of inheriting sex-linked recessive conditions. This is analogous to the problem of color blindness, which is sixteen times more prevalent in males than females. The other explanation involves differences in cultural expectations for males and females and appears most relevant to the mildly retarded. Males are expected to achieve more and become self-sufficient, and there is relatively more concern when they are not seen to be progressing in this regard. In addition, and perhaps more importantly, an acting-out, disruptive, low-IQ male is more likely to be referred for special class placement than his usually better-behaved female counterpart of equally low IQ.

*Social Class and Race* There are marked variations in the prevalence estimates of mental retardation by both race and social class. An overwhelming disproportionate number of persons from some of the racial minorities (especially blacks and Mexican-Americans) and the lower classes are labeled mentally retarded.

Any discussion about race must take into account the fact that race and social class are inextricably intertwined and confounded with social class in the United States. This is so because the racial minorities come primarily from the lower classes. Given this situation, it becomes almost impossible to consider each of these factors separately. The controversy about racial differences in intelligence, and whether these differences are due to genetic or environmental effects, is incredibly complex and still unresolved. Furthermore, there are several almost insurmountable methodological problems in any such investigation of this issue. Therefore, at this time, it is unlikely that a clear and final solution will be forthcoming. However, the reader should be aware that social class and associated variables are clearly believed to be the predominant factor. We will consider social class and race together, with the primary focus on social class.

The marked variations in prevalence estimates by social class and race occur almost exclusively for mild mental retardation. The incidence of the more severe forms is proportionately the same for all social classes and races. (Actually, there is a slightly higher proportion among the racial minorities and lower classes, but this is considered to be related to factors like poorer general health, nutrition, and medical care, which are associated with lower-class status.) In other words, the pathological processes that produce severe mental retardation (e.g., single gene or chromosomal abnormalities, such as PKU and Down's syndrome) can happen to anyone and occur about equally for all racial groups and all social classes. The picture is much different, however, for the milder forms of mental retardation. In this case, there is an overwhelming contribution from the lower social classes and racial minorities. In fact, the case can be made that mild mental retardation is primarily a lower-class problem. Tarjan and his associates (1970, 1973) have estimated that a child from a lower-class environment has fifteen times the probability of being classified as mentally retarded as his age peers in the suburbs. Needless to say, this situation has much to do with the controversy regarding labeling, discrimination, and the "inappropriate" use of "white, middle-class" tests on lower-class, nonwhite children.

A vast amount of research and discussion have been devoted to this phenomenon, primarily in terms of social class characteristics. Some investigators suggest that the possible role of genetic factors cannot be discounted (e.g., issue of assortive mating among the social classes). Many other investigators have pointed an accusing finger at the "culture of poverty." However, no one has been able to untangle the myriad factors and to isolate and specify the major variable or variables. Robinson and Robinson (1976) describe the complexity of the situation by listing just some of the possible relevant factors.

> Social class represents a matrix of interrelated variables, both genetic and acquired. Among the distinguishing features of social classes are parental education and occupation, parental IQ and verbal behavior, family income, health status, childrearing practices, neighborhood and housing conditions, a variety of attitudes toward education, achievement and the possibility of controlling one's destiny, and so on. (p. 153)

The answer is probably that all these factors are involved in as-yet unspecified ways. The "environmental disadvantage" hypothesis is extremely popular in the field. The marked differences in the prevalence of mild retardation by social class are seen to be strongly related to this hypothesis. This is supported by the dramatic results of intervention studies like the Milwaukee Project (Garber and Heber, 1977), discussed in Chapter 8. However, there are limits to the environmentalist explanation.

For while it is true that the majority of the mildly retarded come from the lower classes, it is equally true (and perhaps more important to realize) that the vast majority of children from the lower classes are *not* mentally retarded. If the environment is all that disadvantaged, why isn't the effect much more pervasive? While certain environmental changes do appear to prevent some mild mental retardation, this does not prove that the condition is totally environmental. Rather, it suggests the importance of the dynamic-development view of intelligence, which stresses the interaction between the genes and the environment. Although there are limits, these studies have demonstrated that much can be done to prevent and ameliorate problems associated with low intelligence. Furthermore, they establish a foundation for a cautious but realistic optimism in this regard.

## Incidence versus Prevalence: Three Percent versus One Percent

Earlier, we mentioned some confusion in the literature between the terms "incidence" and "prevalence." Most of the studies talk about prevalence estimates, such as the traditional 3 percent figure. However, this is really an incidence estimate.

"Incidence" refers to the total number of people who will be classified as mentally retarded at any point in their lives. "Prevalence" refers to the total number of persons who are classified as mentally retarded at any given point in time. It is a fact that incidence rates are always higher than prevalence rates. For example, the total number of children who will ever have chicken pox (incidence) is much higher than the total number of children who have chicken pox at any particular point (prevalence). The confusion between these two statistical indices has much relevance to the argument, recently advanced by several investigators (e.g., Mercer, 1973; Tarjan et al., 1973) that the true prevalence of mental retardation is closer to 1 percent than to 3 percent. This is believed for two reasons.

The first reason concerns the employment of the "double screen" (IQ and adaptive behavior) in the diagnosis of mental retardation. The traditional 3 percent figure is based on psychometric criteria only (i.e., an IQ below 70). Mercer and others have suggested that many people with IQs below 70 do in fact adapt and thus are not mentally retarded. She found that when both IQ and adaptive behavior are assessed, the figure comes much closer to 1 percent. While the methodological problems of her study may somewhat undermine her conclusions, some of these individuals below 70 IQ may indeed be adapting. Thus, the traditional 3 percent figure must be reduced somewhat.

The other reason why the 1 percent figure is more accurate concerns the marked variations in prevalence estimates by age. Given the large number of "six-hour retarded persons," the prevalence and incidence rates will differ considerably. If we count all persons who have ever been labeled mentally retarded (incidence), the 3 percent figure is probably accurate. However, if we only want to know how many people are mentally retarded right now (prevalence), the 1 percent figure is more appropriate.

Given all the issues concerning the occurrence of mental retardation, two conclusions can be made. First, the true incidence of mental retardation is probably around 3 percent. In other words, approximately 3 percent of the population will be classified as mentally retarded at some point in their life. However, for a large portion of these people, this will be a temporary label, acquired during the school years only. Given this fact, some researchers suggest that these cases should be called "educationally handicapped" or "educationally disadvantaged." They would reserve the label "mental retardation" for persons with more chronic and pervasive adaptive impairments. The second conclusion follows directly from the first. The true prevalence of mental retardation is probably about 1 percent. Only about 1 percent of the population is classified as mentally retarded at any given point. The 3 percent figure is actually an incidence estimate rather than a prevalence estimate.

The confusion between incidence and prevalence estimates is not just an academic matter. From a social-administrative, program-planning, and funding point of view, it makes a big difference whether 1 or 3 percent of the population appears to need services for mental retardation. In absolute numbers for a population of 220 million people, we are talking about 6.6 million versus 2.2 million people requiring services now. However, while it is important to emphasize the lower figure from a realistic, social planning point of view, the present authors feel compelled to issue a warning regarding this change. The newer "corrected" estimate of 1 percent may suggest or imply that the population of the mentally retarded is actually shrinking or that there is much less of a problem than once thought. This is absolutely untrue. The number of people requiring services remains the same; we have simply revised our base-rate figures to reflect the actual state of affairs. Furthermore, the present authors seriously question the belief that these "six-hour" mentally retarded are in fact adapting the rest of the time. Closer inspection of these persons during their non-school hours as well as in their preschool and postschool years may reveal that they could indeed benefit from some type of continuing service and assistance. It is quite possible that the 1 percent figure reflects the insensitivity of our present social institutions, with the notable exception of the school systems, to problems in adaptation. Moreover, the complex nature of our society suggests that the problems for people with low intelligence will increase and become more pervasive (i.e., spill over to nonacademic areas) in the future. We shall have more to say about this possibility in the last chapter.

# CHAPTER 7

# Assessment

The practice of psychological testing in the United States is approximately 60 years old. It began with the development of intelligence tests for screening Army draftees for World War I and the advent of the Stanford-Binet Intelligence Test in 1916. A variety of tests followed. They flourished until the mid-1960s, when a strong negative reaction set in. While the reasons for this are complex, one of the central problems was that their misuse led to errors in the diagnosis of mental retardation. In this chapter, we will explore the assessment of mental retardation, considering the problems encountered, the tests used, and new developments in this area. First, however, let us discuss psychological assessment in general. This will provide a background against which the assessment of mental retardation can be viewed.

## PRINCIPLES OF PSYCHOLOGICAL ASSESSMENT

Maloney and Ward (1976) have differentiated between psychological testing and psychological assessment as follows.

### Psychological Testing

This refers to the process of administering, scoring, and interpreting psychological tests. This procedure is test-controlled, since test scores, by

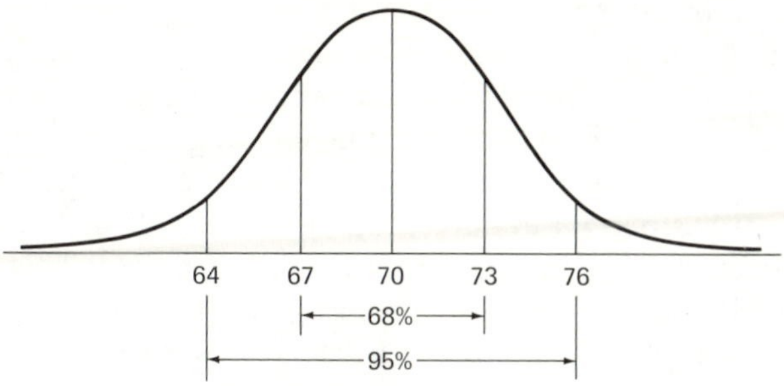


FIGURE 7.1

The standard error of measurement, illustrated with an IQ of 70, demonstrates the latitude in scores that a single IQ might reflect.

themselves, are used to make a decision. This historically has been a prevalent attitude in the diagnosis of mental retardation. An intelligence test is administered, an IQ score obtained, and if the individual scores below a certain cutoff point (for example, IQ 70), he is automatically called mentally retarded. This practice has led to a great deal of error and much concern on the part of parents, schools, civil rights groups, and the courts. There are many problems inherent in such an approach.

First, IQ is not constant. Both the tests (i.e., the issue of reliability) and how a person performs can vary over time. There are statistics (e.g., standard error of measurement) that indicate, in a sense, how accurate an IQ score is. This means that if we administered an IQ test to an individual 100 times (let's presume that there is no practice effect), on 68 tests his scores would be within 6 IQ points of each other ($\pm 3$). Results of the remaining 32 tests would be further above or below these limits. In 95 of the 100 trials the IQ scores would be within 12 IQ points. Figure 7.1 illustrates this idea. What is important here is that IQ is not an exact number, as it is often used. If we determined mental retardation solely by obtaining an IQ below 70, we would be misdiagnosing a certain number of cases. For very low IQs there is less chance of such an error, but for IQs just below 70 the error risk is quite high.

Another problem of the test-controlled approach is that test performance on IQ tests varies for a number of reasons. Persons who are very depressed may score lower than their potential. If a child's parents argued all night before he was tested, he may be tired, preoccupied, or upset and do poorly on the test. Any number of such possibilities may result in spuriously low IQ scores. One problem merits special attention: the issue of culture or ethnicity and IQ tests. Many of our IQ tests have been developed for and standardized on English-speaking, middle-class Americans. There is great concern about testing minority children with these tests, especially if they are bilingual or of a different language background. This concern has led to restriction of the use of certain tests. The Los Angeles Unified School District, for example, forbids the use of the Stanford-Binet Intelligence Test for any person with a Spanish surname. This is because the test is highly language-dominated (English) beyond the six-year age level. Other tests (as will be discussed later) may be partially or totally non-language and use motor performance tasks instead.

These few problems illustrate some of the many difficulties with the test-controlled approach and the inappropriateness of its use determining mental retardation. We simply cannot depend on an IQ score for this purpose. Further, mental retardation is a two-part diagnosis. Both an intellectual *and* an adaptive deficit are necessary. Thus, we must have some measure of adaptive ability as well. This will be discussed later in the chapter.

The solution to these problems is not simply to develop new tests, although our tests must be made as accurate as possible. Despite their accuracy, however, tests are simply tools; they can almost never be used alone to make clinical decisions. This is definitely true regarding mental retardation. To make such a diagnosis, we must use the process of psychological assessment.

## Psychological Assessment

This is a variable process which cannot be limited to a single set of rules. It is defined (Maloney and Ward, 1976) as a process of solving problems (answering questions) using psychological tests as *one* method of collecting data. This process involves three basic components; the problem, data collection, and interpretation. Let us consider each of these factors in diagnosing mental retardation.

*Determining the Problem* Before tests or other data collection can commence, the examiner must know what referral question he is attempting to answer. This breaks down into two parts. First, the examiner must know what the referral source (teacher, parent) is asking. The answer here might seem obvious, but it must be remembered that referral questions are often expressed in very vague terms. A parent may complain, for example, that the child "just doesn't seem to be doing as well as he should." Rarely does a parent ask specifically for an evaluation for mental retardation. In addition to clarifying the problem or referral, the examiner must know the content of the problem. This is critical in determining mental retardation. What it means is that the examiner must know the criteria of mental retardation, the general attributes of low intelligence, and various methods of assessing intelligence and adaptive behavior. This goes well beyond simply giving an intelligence test and obtaining an IQ score. The assessment of intelligence seems to be simple and straightforward, but the problem can be very complex—involving different cognitive abilities, differential performance under differing conditions, cultural differences, and so on. Thus, the examiner who knows how to administer an individual intelligence test in a standardized manner and how to interpret IQ as a deviation score, but is not well grounded in the issues surrounding the nature of intelligence—how it is differentially manifested and how this abstract idea relates to IQ—is not prepared to assess intelligence or mental retardation (Maloney and Ward, 1976). It is lack of this general knowledge that leads to many errors in the determination of mental retardation.

*Collecting the Data* After the problem has been clarified and the examiner knows the content area, the next step is to collect data. With mental retardation we immediately think of intelligence tests, but much more is necessary. As we have already stressed, psychological assessment is not test-controlled. *Any* relevant data are appropriate for the assessment process. Two types of data are important here. The first is the case history. If a child or an adult is mentally retarded, this will have been manifested throughout his life. It is not something that first becomes apparent when an IQ test is administered. Second, interview observations would include how he expresses himself, word usage, and the individual's own report of his experiences. In sum, data collection refers to using all possible data related to the problem.

*Interpreting the Data* We have broken the assessment process down into three steps. In actuality, however, these steps are not necessarily separated, nor do they occur in an orderly fashion. Interpretation of data actually occurs right from the beginning; the examiner does not passively collect data and then interpret it. Throughout the process, he makes observations, hypothesizes about what they mean, and collects additional data to determine whether his hypotheses are correct. What the examiner is attempting to do is to develop the most logical explanation for these observations. One possible explanation is mental retardation. However, even after mental retardation is determined, the assessment process should not be concluded. Having collected a variety of data, the examiner knows the individual's strengths and weaknesses and is in a unique position to make recommendations regarding training, prescriptive teaching, and so on. Assessment must continue through these stages.

## TESTS OF INTELLIGENCE

As discussed in Chapter 4, mental retardation must be manifested by deficits in both intelligence and adaptive behavior. These factors will be considered separately.

There is a great variety of intelligence tests; some of them take several minutes to administer, others several hours. There are dozens of different intelligence tests, some administered in groups, some individually. Although all of these devices are measures of intelligence, they have different purposes. Some brief group IQ tests, for example, may be used only for superficial screening of large groups. Only a small number of the available intelligence tests should be used to assess for mental retardation. All tests so used must be individually administered and well standardized. We will examine three of the more commonly used measures of intelligence.

### The Stanford-Binet Intelligence Scale

For years the Stanford-Binet was the only widely available and accepted test of general intelligence. As noted in Chapter 2, Alfred Binet, a French physician, developed the forerunner to this scale in the late 1890s. Several French editions were published in the early 1900s. The psychologist Terman at Stanford University revised Binet's scale and translated it into English. Terman's scale, which was the first broadly standardized and accepted test of intelligence, became available in the United States in 1916. For more than three decades, this was the only test which was widely accepted for the determination of mental retardation. The scale has been revised several times, with major revisions in 1937 and 1960 and an additional technical revision in 1972.

The construction of the Stanford-Binet is based on the mental age approach (see Chapter 3). Mental age expresses the cognitive ability of an average child of a given age. A mental age of nine suggests that the individual functions at a cognitive level comparable to average nine-year-olds, no matter how old he actually is.

The procedure for constructing a mental age test is fairly simple but involves a great deal of work. First, a number of tasks that are presumed to require or reflect intelligence are administered to a large number of children at various ages. Items for the final scale are selected for a certain year level if they have the following characteristics. First, roughly 50 percent of the children at that year level must pass the items and 50 percent fail. Second, progressively older children must have a progressively higher percentage of passing. Finally, progressively younger children must have a progressively lower level of passing. For example, one test at Year V involves copying a square. We would expect that roughly one-half of a randomly selected group of five-year-olds would pass the item, while more than 50 percent of a group of six-year-olds would pass and less than 50 percent of a group of four-year-olds would succeed.

When items fit the age-performance criteria, they are grouped together at year levels—usually six items (also called tests) at each year level. The Stanford-Binet begins at Year II and extends to the Superior Adult range. There are 20 year levels that consist of more than 100 separate tests. In the early year levels (II–V), the tests proceed at six-month intervals because intellectual growth is quite rapid in this period. Thus, there are six items grouped at Year II, II–6, III, III–6, IV, and IV–6. From ages five to fourteen, the tests proceed at one-year intervals, followed by an Average Adult level and three Superior Adult levels.

The test materials (see Figure 7.2) consist of a number of toy objects for the younger ages, two printed booklets containing a number of visually based tests, and a manual that contains numerous verbal tests. Although the kit is fairly large, most of the objects and materials are for use with ages below six. From this age on, the test is composed primarily of a question-answer format and could be administered with the manual alone.

Actually item content is quite variable, as shown by examples at several different year levels.

### Year II

1. Three-hole Form Board: This is a small board with cut insets for a square, a triangle, and a circle. The child is presented with the form board and is required to place the cutouts in the correct insets.
2. Identifying Parts of the Body: The child is presented with a large cardboard figure of a boy (1960 form) or girl (1972 form) and is asked to point to hair, mouth, feet, ear, nose, hands, and eyes. Correctly identifying four parts receives credit at Year II. This test is also used at Year II-6, where six parts must be identified.
3. Picture Vocabulary: This test consists of 18 small cards in a booklet. The child is asked to give the name of the object depicted on the cards in ink line sketches. Such objects as airplane, telephone, hat, ball, tree, horse, coat, umbrella, cane, arm, pocketknife, and leaf are used. At Year II, three items must be correctly named for credit. This test is also used at Years II-6, III, and IV, when progressively more items need to be recognized for credit.

4. Word Combinations: This item is scored "plus" if the child is able to combine at least two words in his language.

Year IV-6

1. Opposite Analogies: The child is asked to complete the following statements:

   (a) Brother is a boy; sister is a . . .
   (b) In daytime it is light; at night it is . . .
   (c) Father is a man; mother is a . . .
   (d) The snail is slow; the rabbit is . . .
   (e) The sun shines in the day; the moon at . . .

   Three of the above must be scored "plus" for credit at this level.

FIGURE 7.2

Materials used with the Stanford-Binet Intelligence Scale. (Courtesy of Houghton Mifflin.)

2. Pictorial Similarities and Differences: The subject is presented with six cards, which depict objects. One object on each card is different from the others, and the child is asked to put his finger on the different one. He must score three for credit at this level.
3. Three Commissions: The examiner plans for the test by setting various objects in the room. The child is then told: "Here's a pencil. I want you to put it on the chair; then I want you to shut (open) the door; and then bring me the box which you see over there."
   All three commissions must be executed in the proper order for credit at this level.
4. Comprehension III: The child is asked:

   (a) What do we do with our eyes?
   (b) What do we do with our ears?

   One item must be scored "plus" for credit at this level. Specific scoring standards are provided.

### Year VI

1. Vocabulary: The child is asked about how many words he knows. The examiner reads the word aloud and encourages a response. If the child is able to read, he is provided with a list of words, which total 45. This test is used throughout the rest of the test up to the Superior Adult Level. At the Year VI level, six words must be correctly defined. At the Superior Adult Level III, 30 words must be correctly defined. The less difficult words include "orange," "envelope," and "puddle," while more difficult words include "harpy" "casuistry," and "sudorific."
2. Differences: On this task, the child is asked to explain the difference between such objects as a bird and a dog or wood and glass. Three items are given, two of which must be correct for credit at this level.
3. Number Concepts: With 12 small cubes, the child is asked to give the examiner various numbers of blocks.
4. Opposite Analogies: The child is asked to complete sentences that the examiner reads aloud. For example, "An inch is short, a mile is . . ." Four of these sentences are administered, three of which must be correctly completed for credit.

### Average Adult

1. Vocabulary: This is the same test described at Year VI. A score of 20 correctly defined words is needed for credit at this level.

2. Ingenuity I: This test involves solving a series of verbally presented problems (subject cannot use paper and pencil). These problems involve obtaining various amounts of water with containers of different amounts. For example, "Get exactly 2 pints of water with a 3-pint and a 5-pint can."
3. Differences Between Abstract Words: This test involves asking the subject to explain differences between such abstract words as "character" and "reputation." Three such combinations are given, and two must be correctly answered.
4. Essential Differences: The subject is asked to tell the principal differences between various ideas or concepts, such as "work and play" and "ability and achievement." Two of three such items must be scored correct for credit at this level.

The test is administered in a way that is similar to all mental age tests. What this means is that the examiner begins testing at a level where it is expected that the individual will successfully complete all items. For an average six-year-old, we might start testing at Year IV–6 or V. Starting at a lower level is done to obtain a "basal" age—that is, the level at which the person is able to pass all items. It is presumed that the individual would also successfully complete all items below this level, so these easier tests are not administered. The examiner proceeds, giving items above the basal level until he reaches a level at which all items are failed. This is called the "ceiling age." The test is then discontinued, since it is presumed that the subject will fail the following items, which are progressively more difficult.

With the Stanford-Binet, no subject tries all the tests. He is given only the tests at age levels that are related to his level of intelligence. With average young children, the test takes from one-half hour to an hour to administer. At higher age levels, it may take one-half again as long to complete the test. For some atypical or disturbed children, and in some cases for very bright children, it may take up to two hours to complete the test; such children may continue to get one item correct at continuing age levels. This necessitates giving each successive series of tests until a ceiling age is reached (all items at that level are failed).

Each Stanford-Binet item, or test, is scored plus or minus. In other words, the person either receives credit or does not. The manual spells out the criteria for passing or failing each item. Credit in months is given for all items passed, and a total score is expressed in years and months. For example, using all six tests on the Stanford-Binet at each year level, a child passes all items at Year VII (this would be his basal age), four at Year VIII, two at Year IX, and fails all items at Year X (ceiling age.) The child's mental age would be eight years (ninety-six months). He would receive eighty-four months of credit for passing all items at Year VII ($7 \times 12$) and an additional eight months for passing four tests at Year VIII ($4 \times 2$) and four months at Year IX for passing two tests.

The test yields a mental age (MA), discussed above, and an IQ. Formerly, the IQ was obtained by dividing the mental age by the chronological age (CA) and multiplying by 100.

$$\frac{MA}{CA} \times 100 = IQ$$

Multiplying by 100 was done simply to change the score from a decimal to a whole number. This *ratio* IQ was criticized for a number of reasons. Mental age ceases to increase after a certain age. This varies with different tests, but it is usually felt that mental age levels off at about age sixteen. This does not mean that a person learns no more beyond that age, but that he has attained his basic cognitive and problem-solving abilities by that age. The ability to remember series of digits increases to about age 14 and then levels off, decreasing during later years. A mental age test thus becomes problematic to use with adults. There has also been a good deal of difficulty with mental age or ratio IQs (see, e.g., Matarazzo, 1972), since they are not constant over time and the degree of intelligence at different age levels is difficult to compare. For example, a child of ten with a mental age of twelve has an IQ of 120 ($12 \div 10 \times 100 = 120$) and is two years above his average peers. A three-year-old child with a mental age of four has an IQ of 125 ($4 \div 3 \times 100 = 125$) and is one year above his age peers. It becomes difficult to compare the magnitude of such scores from age to age. These and other problems led to dropping of the ratio IQ for most uses of the Stanford-Binet. In 1960 and 1972, new tables were developed for IQ determination that statistically corrected some of the quantification problems (Pinneau, 1960; Thorndike, 1972).

*General Considerations* The Stanford-Binet Intelligence Test is important historically for two reasons. First, for several decades it was *the* test of children's intelligence. Second, more recently, it has been the object of more criticism than any other major test of intelligence. The strongest criticism concerns the so-called cultural bias of the test. This criticism states that persons of certain culturally deprived, or even culturally different, backgrounds may perform lower on the Stanford-Binet, not because of low intelligence but because the test is biased toward a white, middle-class set of behaviors and attitudes. Examples of such bias follow.

Williams (1970) states that responses to such Stanford-Binet items as "What's the thing to do if another boy hits you without meaning to do it?" depend on the neighborhood of the child tested. Williams proposes that in many black neighborhoods, the correct response "Walk away" would mean suicide. In addition to allegedly biased items, it is also claimed that bias permeates the whole evaluation procedure. Typically, it is a white, middle-class examiner who evaluates black ghetto youths. In such situations, rapport may be strained and language use may be different. Educational experience also contaminates the situation. The Stanford-Binet has often been singled out for criticism because it becomes totally verbal beyond age six and is heavily weighted with educational problems. Also, early norms for the test were biased, using a majority of upper-middle-class subjects and excluding minority groups. The reaction against the scale has been so strong, as noted, that the Los Angeles City Unified School District does not permit its use with minority students.

Despite these problems, the Stanford-Binet still has great value as an assessment instrument. It remains an effective intelligence test with middle-class whites. It is also used extensively as an intelligence test for retarded adults, since tests like the Wechsler Adult Intelligence Scale do not allow for computation of IQs below the low 40s. With the Stanford-Binet, we can obtain very low scores by using the mental age format. For example, if we have a fifteen-year-old youth who obtains a mental age of three, we would obtain an IQ of 20 ($3 \div 15 \times 100 = 20$). The Stanford-Binet is also often used for young children, since such tests as the Wechsler Intelligence Scale for Children (WISC-R) cannot be used below the age of six.

## The Wechsler Intelligence Scales

Three different Wechsler scales have been developed for different age ranges. The Wechsler Pre-School and Primary Scale of Intelligence (WPPSI) is used for children aged four to six and one-half years. The Wechsler Intelligence Scale for Children-Revised (WISC-R) covers ages six to sixteen, and the Wechsler Adult Intelligence Scale (WAIS) covers ages beyond sixteen, with norms extending to more than seventy-five years. The WPPSI covers a restricted age range which partially overlaps with the WISC-R. Since this scale is less often used than the WISC-R and WAIS, it will not be considered in any detail.

The WISC-R (1974) and the WAIS are constructed in a similar fashion and have similar characteristics. Thus, the characteristics of both tests can be described simultaneously.

The WAIS and WISC-R consist of 10 (WISC-R) and 11 (WAIS) basic subtests, which are divided into verbal and performance tasks. Both of these scales yield three IQ scores: Verbal IQ, Performance IQ, and Full Scale IQ.

One of the major characteristics of the Wechsler scales is that they provide data regarding specific cognitive, perceptual, and motor abilities, in addition to IQ scores. Thus, each subtest deals with one specific area of information or ability. This approach allows for a profile type of analysis, wherein both the relative strengths and weaknesses of a person can be assessed and described.

The subtests are listed below, with a brief description of their content. (See also Table 7.1.)

Verbal Scales

Information: This test consists of 29 (WAIS) or 30 (WISC-R) items which cover a wide variety of content that persons in our society would have an opportunity to know without advanced or special schooling. Examples at various difficulty levels from the WAIS are: "What does rubber come from?", "How tall is the average American woman?", and "What is the Koran?"

Comprehension: This test consists of 14 WAIS items or 17 WISC-R items on which the subject explains what should be done in different situations, why certain practices are followed, or why certain conditions exist. Examples from the WISC-R at different difficulty levels are: "Why is it usually better to build a house out of brick than out of wood?", "Why are criminals locked up?", and "Why do we have elections by secret ballot?"

Arithmetic: These are all basic arithmetic problems which must be solved mentally and do not demand any arithmetic functions beyond the basics which are typically learned by the fifth or sixth grade. Extra credit is given for speed on some of the more difficult items. Examples from the WAIS are: "How much is four dollars and five dollars?", "How many hours would it take a man to walk twenty-four miles at the rate of three miles an hour?", and "A man bought some second hand furniture for two-thirds of what it cost new. He paid $400 for it. How much did it cost new?"

Similarities: This task consists of 14 items on the WAIS and 17 on the WISC-R. The subject is asked to note similarities between such ostensibly different items as "wheel and ball," "cat and mouse," and "pound and yard" (WISC-R items).

Digit Span: This test requires the subject to repeat increasing series of numbers read aloud. The subject is asked to repeat digits in the order presented and later in the reverse order.

Vocabulary: The subject is asked to define words which are read aloud and which he also reads from a sheet. Examples from the WAIS are: "winter," "slice," "assemble," "hasten," "domestic," "consume," "edifice," and "impale."

Performance Scales

Digit Symbol/Coding: This task involves the coding of novel marks or symbols with the numbers 1 to 9. A key is presented showing

TABLE 7.1

WISC-R and WAIS Subtest Descriptions

| Subtest Name | |
|---|---|
| **Verbal Subtests** | |
| Information: | Breadth of general information, long-term memory, experiential background |
| Comprehension: | Practical knowledge, social judgment, reasoning, logical solutions |
| Arithmetic: | Numerical reasoning, concentration, freedom from distraction |
| Similarities: | Abstract verbal reasoning, relationships, association of abstract ideas |
| Digit Span:* | Immediate auditory memory, freedom from distraction |
| Vocabulary: | Word knowledge, expressive vocabulary, verbal fluency |
| **Performance Subtests** | |
| Digit Symbol: Coding† | Speed, accuracy of symbol learning |
| Picture Completion: | Visual organization, alertness to details, general information |
| Block Design: | Spatial visualization, abstract reasoning, visual perception |
| Picture Arrangement: | Interpreting social situations, logical sequencing, visual organization |
| Object Assembly: | Reproduction from memory and perception of visual wholes, visual retention |
| Mazes:‡ | Visual perception, logical planning |

* This is an alternate test on the WISC-R.

† Digit Symbol on WAIS is essentially the same task as Coding on WISC-R.

‡ Alternative task on WISC-R not included on WAIS.

the number-symbol matching, and the subject must provide the appropriate symbols for a series of numbers. The task is timed, and the score depends on the number of items completed in the time allowed.

Picture Completion: This test involves 21 (WAIS) or 26 (WISC-R) cards on which there are pictures with an important item missing. The subject must tell what is missing.

Block Design: The subject is presented with red and white cubic blocks with solid red sides, solid white sides, and diagonally colored half-red and half-white sides. He is asked to reproduce designs presented on stimulus cards.

Picture Arrangement: Each item contains a series of cards with various pictures that must be correctly arranged to tell a sensible story. Pictures are cartoon-like drawings, and items cover a variety of content.

Object Assembly: This is essentially a puzzle test. Pieces are arranged in a standard order, and the subject is asked to put them together. The test is timed.

Mazes: (WISC-R only) This task involves a number of lined mazes. The subject is asked to begin at one point and draw a line through the maze to a finish point.

With each of the Wechsler scales, a manual is provided which specifies how items are to be administered and scored. Scoring for the Performance tests is fairly straightforward, since there is usually only one correct answer. For example, Block Designs can be correctly duplicated in only one way. This is also true with Verbal subtests, such as Arithmetic, Digit Span, and generally for the Information subtest. The Comprehension, Similarities, and Vocabulary subtests are more difficult to score since there is no single right answer. For these subtests the manual provides detailed scoring criteria, giving multiple examples. With the Wechsler scales, there is little disagreement in scoring between trained examiners. After the separate subtests are scored, the examiner changes the raw scores into scaled scores (a type of transformed score) and gets totals for the Verbal, Performance, and Full Scale sections. The IQs are obtained from Age Tables in the manual (discussed below).

The Wechsler scales are generally considered the best-designed and developed tests of intelligence. They are complex tests for which a great deal of data has been collected. We will summarize only a few salient features of these scales. The reader is referred to Matarazzo (1972) or Maloney and Ward (1976) for a more in-depth discussion.

The Wechsler scales provide a "deviation IQ," which differs signifi-

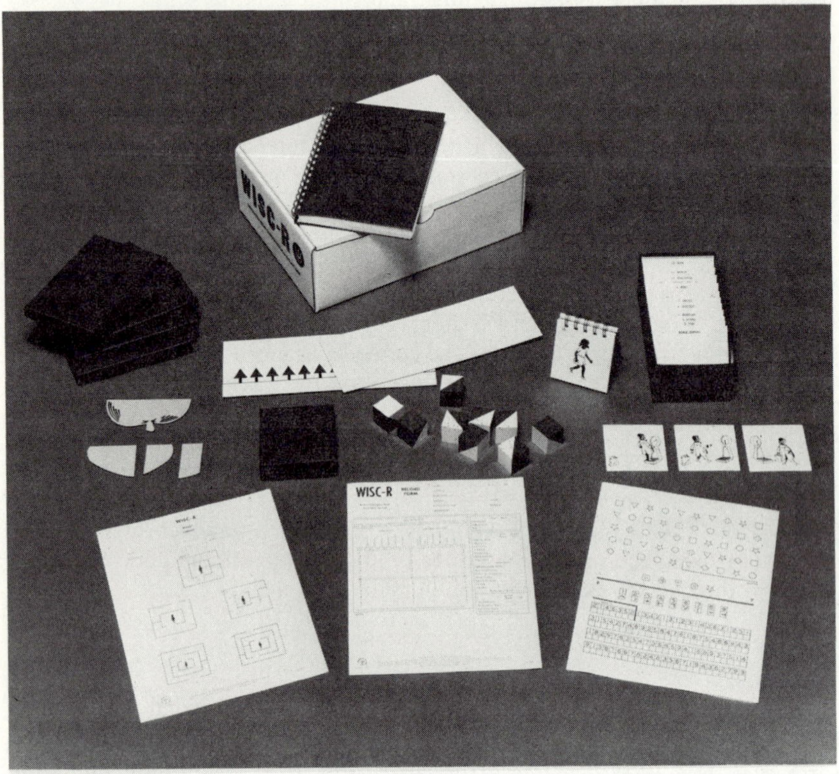


FIGURE 7.3

Materials used with the Wechsler Intelligence Scale for Children-Revised. (Courtesy of The Psychological Corporation.)

cantly from the ratio or mental age IQ. With the deviation IQ, an individual is compared to others of his age on the basis of how many items or problems he was able to solve correctly. A representative sample of the United States population was tested and its average performance determined. This performance received an IQ of 100. Persons who scored above or below this point receive higher or lower IQs respectively, depending on how much they deviate from the average. The exact IQs are determined by the normal distribution (see Chapter 3).

A second feature of the Wechsler scales is that separate IQ tables are used for different ages. With the adult scale, for example, there are separate tables for age ranges starting from 16–17 on up to 75 and over. This is important because on these tests, IQ compares an individual with persons of his own age group. An IQ of 120 for a person of 65 means that he is brighter than a certain percentage of persons his own age. Similarly, the same IQ for a person of 25 means that he is brighter than the same percentage of persons in his own age group. Thus, IQ means the same thing for persons of different ages even though the younger person in our example will actually solve more problems than the older one.

The Wechsler scales are unique in that they provide scores for the individual subtests and the three different IQs. These scores can be helpful clinically, since persons with different types of pathology often perform well on some tasks and poorly on others. With mental retardation, however, we expect a consistently low performance. The Wechsler scales also offer some help in determining whether tested low intelligence really suggests mental retardation or may result from cultural or language factors. In this regard, the person's performance on such tests as Block Design and Object Assembly may be viewed as a measure of ability that does not reflect specific education or language. These tests often are seen as more "culture fair" than, for example, the Comprehension or Information subtests, which can reflect specific values and education.

### The Leiter International Performance Scale

The Leiter International Performance Scale (LIPS) is not considered one of the standard tests of intelligence. It is, however, being increasingly used as a general measure of intelligence in certain situations because it is reported to be "culturally fair." In the Los Angeles City Unified School District, for example, it is the only acceptable intelligence test for children with Spanish surnames.

The LIPS is completely nonlanguage, and instructions can be given in pantomime. Additionally, none of the test material incorporates language (e.g., no printed words are used). A strong point is that it allows for considerable demonstration and assistance at the very early levels of the test to ensure that the person understands the task and has an opportunity to succeed. Although the examinee must complete the task on his own to receive credit, he may be repeatedly shown or helped on how to do it. Test materials consist of a response frame (see Figure 7.4) made of wood, paper stimulus strips, and approximately 200 blocks. The examiner places the stimulus strips on the response frame and then places a series of blocks in front of the subject. The subject must then place the blocks in the appropriate slot in the frame below the stimulus strip. Test content consists of problems in matching colors, duplicating designs, matching

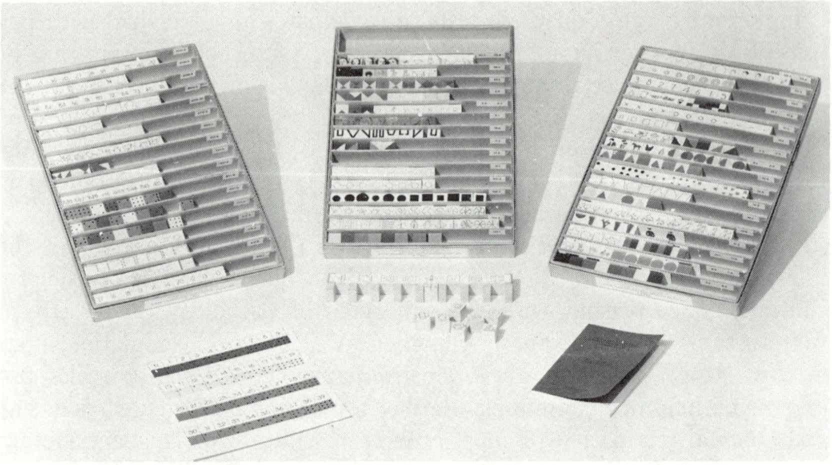

FIGURE 7.4

Materials used with the Leiter International Performance Scale. (Courtesy of Stoelting Company.)

shades of gray, estimating the number of dots in a given area, recognizing forms, and so forth. The test does incorporate number, perceptual, and abstract reasoning tasks, but no verbal material.

The LIPS is administered as a mental age test, and a basal and ceiling age are obtained. The IQ is obtained by the ratio method, using the formula MA ÷ CA × 100 = IQ.

The test manual gives directions for administration and scoring, which are objective and straightforward. The blocks must be correctly matched in order to pass the item. Each item gives a certain amount of mental age credit, and this credit is added in a manner similar to that of the Stanford-Binet.

Despite its new popularity, little actual research data are available on the LIPS. It was originally standardized on several ethnic groups in Hawaii and later used with African groups. Several more recent studies have compared the LIPS to general tests of intelligence, but there is much to be learned. Additionally, although this measure is being used in place of the Stanford-Binet and WISC for culturally deprived children, some data indicate that they may actually perform more poorly on the LIPS. Further relevant data are clearly needed.

Hundreds of different tests and methods are available for measuring intelligence. We have briefly reviewed only a few of these to give the reader some idea of how an IQ is obtained. It must be remembered that intelligence is only a hypothetical idea, not a real entity. The IQ is simply a test score which is believed to reflect the level of intelligence. For a variety of reasons, however, the IQ may be erroneously low. Sometimes the tests are inappropriate; at other times, the subject may score low for reasons other than low intelligence. The examiner must make certain that the IQ seems consistent with all other data available (interview, case history, etc.). As an additional safeguard against diagnosing mental retardation on the basis of an erroneously low IQ, the examiner must also determine that the subject has an adaptive deficit.

## MEASURES OF ADAPTIVE ABILITY

Prior to 1959, intelligence (actually, IQ) was the primary criterion for the diagnosis of mental retardation. In that year, the American Association on Mental Deficiency introduced the further criterion of adaptive behavior. The definition of mental retardation was also changed (Heber, 1959/1961; Grossman, 1973/1977) to include this feature. This two-dimensional definition protects against certain errors that had previously occurred. First, if a person scored low on an IQ test but was not mentally retarded, his adaptive ability would be unimpaired. Thus, even with low IQ, a person is not considered mentally retarded unless he also shows an adaptive deficit. Conversely, an adaptive deficit, in itself, would not indicate mental retardation. Consider, for example, the child with motor spasticity who needs help with dressing and eating but who is also quite bright. It would be erroneous to call such a youth mentally retarded despite his deficit.

However, while the addition of adaptive ability in diagnosing mental retardation was a much needed step, we still lack good broad scales of adaptive ability.

Before we examine adaptive behavior scales, it is instructive to define adaptive behavior and to explore some of its characteristics. Leland (1973) defines adaptive ability as involving three components:

(1) *Independent functioning,* defined as the ability of the individual to successfully accomplish those tasks or activities demanded of him by the general community, both in terms of critical survival demands for that community and in terms of the typical expectations for specific ages.

(2) *Personal responsibility,* defined as both the willingness of the individual to accomplish those critical tasks he is able to ac-

complish (generally under some supervision) and his ability to assume individual responsibility for his personal behavior. This ability is reflected in decision-making and choice of behaviors.

(3) *Social responsibility,* defined as the ability of the individual to accept responsibility as a member of a community group and to carry out appropriate behaviors in terms of these group expectations. This is reflected in levels of conformity, socially positive creativity, social adjustment and emotional maturity. (p. 92; adapted from Leland et al., 1968)

This definition emphasizes the individual's ability to respond to the demands of his environment and community. These demands obviously change radically as the individual develops. For the young child, adaptive ability is reflected in such behaviors as learning to walk, talk, and feed himself. Later, he must master toilet use, further communication ability, dressing, and so forth. As a child reaches school age, adaptive behavior is typically viewed as the ability to cope with, profit from, and successfully complete school tasks. For the adult, adaptive ability is primarily assessed by the capacity to function independently in the community, hold a job, effectively use money, and so forth. A second feature of adaptive ability is that these behaviors vary depending on the demands of a given individual's environment and community. Thus, what is seen as adaptive will vary from society to society and even from community to community. Certainly the adaptive demands of a complex industrial society are more stringent than those of an agrarian society. Thus, we can make no absolute statements as to what constitutes adaptive ability. It is a relative and variable phenomenon. This will be explored further in Chapter 11.

As we have stated, development of tests of adaptive behavior has lagged far behind intelligence tests in both technical quality and utility. This is probably because interest in this area goes back only about 15 years. Further, funding for development of scales in this area has been limited to use with institutionalized persons. This accounts for less than 5 percent of the mentally retarded population. Finally, the concept of adaptive ability has achieved only limited popularity and this is limited to institutional settings. It is clear, however, that further developments in this area are forthcoming.

In the next section, we will examine the construction and use of two adaptive behavior scales. These scales illustrate the two types of approaches (developmental versus inventory) used to assess adaptive behavior. The first measure, the Vineland Social Maturity Scale, is organized much like a Binet test. That is, it is based on normal development and measures an individual's adaptive behavior against age norms. In contrast, the second measure we will consider, the Adaptive Behavior Scales, is an inventory test, much like the format of the Wechsler scales with their various subtests. Here, skills and responsibilities in several areas relevant to adaptive behavior are assessed.

## The Vineland Social Maturity Scale

The Vineland Social Maturity Scale was developed by Edgar A. Doll (1936, 1942, 1953), a true pioneer and almost the only early proponent of evaluating the social competence or maturity of the mentally retarded. The Vineland was the first such scale developed and remains quite popular. From a psychometric point of view, however, it has serious developmental limitations (e.g., a small, restricted norm group), and reliability and validity are inadequate. The popularity of this scale stems from its early development and the fact that it summarizes and quantifies the complex phenomena of adaptive behavior into simple summary terms similar to mental age and IQ.

The Vineland scale is more of an interview than a test. It consists of a number of items which the examiner generally scores "plus" or "minus," based on data he receives from an interview with an *informant* (teacher, parent, etc.) who is well acquainted with the individual's daily behavior. The examiner may not even see the person who is evaluated. The scale consists of 117 items organized by age, ranging from infancy to adult life. Items are classified into eight categories: general self-help, self-help dressing, self-help eating, locomotion, communication, self-direction, socialization, and occupation. Table 7.2 presents items from Year II to Year IV level on the Vineland.

The scale is based on what the subject has actually done in his daily living, but partial credit may be given for tasks which he could potentially complete. The scale yields a "social age," which is similar in concept to mental age. Unlike mental age, however, it does not reflect intelligence alone. Social age (SA) divided by chronological age ($SA \div CA \times 100 = SQ$) yields a "social quotient." This number (SQ) has characteristics similar to IQ (i.e., mean = 100, similar distribution) but, again, it is considered to reflect social maturity rather than intelligence. It is assumed that a person may have a higher or lower degree of intelligence than social maturity, or vice versa. By comparing IQ and SQ, we can estimate the actual difference. The retarded person would, by definition, have to be significantly below average on both variables.

## The Adaptive Behavior Scales

After changing the criteria for mental retardation from intelligence alone to intelligence and adaptive behavior, the American Association on Mental Deficiency pressed for the development of appropriate adaptive behavior measures. The primary result was the Adaptive Behavior Scales (ABS), which were first published in 1969 and revised in 1974 (Nihira et al., 1969; Fogelman, 1974).

The Adaptive Behavior Scales is a behavior rating scale for both mentally retarded and emotionally disturbed individuals. It was designed to assess the individual's effectiveness in coping with the demands of his natural and social environment. It should be reiterated that this scale was developed for use with retarded and emotionally disturbed persons in

TABLE 7.2

Vineland Social Maturity Scale Items, Years II–IV

| Items* | | Activity | Life Ages† |
|---|---|---|---|
| | | II–III | |
| SHG | 35. | Asks to go to toilet | 1.98 |
| O | 36. | Initiates own play activities | 2.03 |
| SHD | 37. | Removes coat or dress | 2.05 |
| SHE | 38. | Eats with fork | 2.35 |
| SHE | 39. | Gets drink unassisted | 2.43 |
| SHD | 40. | Dries own hands | 2.60 |
| SHG | 41. | Avoids simple hazards | 2.85 |
| SHD | 42. | Puts on coat or dress unassisted | 2.85 |
| O | 43. | Cuts with scissors | 2.88 |
| C | 44. | Relates experiences | 3.15 |
| | | III–IV | |
| L | 45. | Walks downstairs one step per tread | 3.23 |
| S | 46. | Plays cooperatively at kindergarten level | 3.28 |
| SHD | 47. | Buttons coat or dress | 3.35 |
| O | 48. | Helps at little household tasks | 3.55 |
| S | 49. | "Performs" for others | 3.75 |
| SHD | 50. | Washes hands unaided | 3.83 |

* SHG, self-help general; O, occupation; SHD, self-help, dressing; SHE, self-help, eating; C, communication; and L, locomotion.

† Average age in years at which normal children are able to complete that task.

institutions. Revised scales (Lambert, 1974) have also been designed for use in schools.

The ABS is divided into two parts. Part One (see Table 7.3) is designed to evaluate abilities and habits in ten behavioral areas. These areas are considered important in the development of personal independence in daily living. Part Two (see Table 7.4) of the ABS was developed after ex-

TABLE 7.3

Adaptive Behavior Scale
Part One: Behavioral Domains

| | |
|---|---|
| I. | Independent Functioning |
| | A. Eating |
| | B. Toilet use |
| | C. Cleanliness |
| | D. Appearance |
| | E. Care of clothing |
| | F. Dressing and undressing |
| | G. Travel |
| | H. General independent functioning |
| II. | Physical Development |
| | A. Sensory development |
| | B. Motor development |
| III. | Economic Activity |
| | A. Money handling and budgeting |
| | B. Shopping skills |
| IV. | Language Development |
| | A. Expression |
| | B. Comprehension |
| | C. Social language development |
| V. | Numbers and Time |
| VI. | Domestic Activity |
| | A. Cleaning |
| | B. Kitchen duties |
| | C. Other domestic activities |
| VII. | Vocational Activity |
| VIII. | Self-direction |
| | A. Initiative |
| | B. Perseverance |
| | C. Leisure time |
| IX. | Responsibility |
| X. | Socialization |

tensive reviews of the social expectations placed on retarded persons, both in the community and in institutions. This part was designed to measure maladaptive behavior related to personality and behavioral disorders.

The authors (see Fogelman et al., 1974) list the following uses for the Adaptive Behavior Scales:

1. To identify areas of deficiency that individuals or groups have, in order to facilitate proper and useful assignment of curricula and placement in training programs.
2. To provide an objective basis for the comparison of an individual's ratings over a period of time in order to evaluate the suitability of his or her current curriculum or training program.
3. To compare ratings of the same individual under different situations, e.g., home, school, ward, etc., in order to study how different environmental factors influence his or her behavior.
4. To compare ratings by different raters in order to gain additional understanding of the relationships between certain raters and persons being rated, e.g., mother and child, father and child, teacher and child, therapist and patient, etc.
5. To provide a common medium of information exchange within, as well as between, organizations through a standardized reporting system.
6. To stimulate the development of new training programs and research.

TABLE 7.4

Adaptive Behavior Scale
Part Two: Content Areas

| | |
|---|---|
| I. | Violent and Destructive Behavior |
| II. | Antisocial Behavior |
| III. | Rebellious Behavior |
| IV. | Untrustworthy Behavior |
| V. | Withdrawal |
| VI. | Stereotyped Behavior and Odd Mannerisms |
| VII. | Inappropriate Interpersonal Manners |
| VIII. | Unacceptable Vocal Habits |
| IX. | Unacceptable or Eccentric Habits |
| X. | Self-abusive Behavior |
| XI. | Hyperactive Tendencies |
| XII. | Sexually Aberrant Behavior |
| XIII. | Psychological Disturbances |
| XIV. | Use of Medications |

7. To provide descriptions of groups of individuals which will facilitate making useful and realistic administrative decisions concerning programming and staffing needs. (p. 7)

The use of the ABS is easily illustrated, using a page from the 1974 Revised Scale (see Figure 7.5). These items deal with area IV of Part One (Language Development).

The ABS manual provides instructions for scoring the areas and items. Scores for various areas of ability are calculated, and various norm groups—such as institutionalized retarded children at different levels of intelligence—can be compared. Results from the ABS can be used for diagnostic and training purposes (e.g., to determine where the deficits are, how extreme they are, what habilitation procedures seem appropriate, etc.) as well as for deciding, for example, as whether it is best to institutionalize an individual.

The Vineland and ABS are two measures of adaptive behavior. Other scales exist, but will not be described here. What is important to remember is the concept of adaptive behavior rather than specific tests. The concept of mental retardation, both from a diagnostic and a treatment point of view, involves not only intelligence but how well the individual copes with and handles environmental demands. The addition of adaptive behavior in diagnosing mental retardation has been a very positive move. While we may or may not be able to promote significant changes in intelligence, we can definitely increase adaptive behaviors through training in a majority of cases. The adaptive behavior scales have clarified this goal and have helped to achieve it.

## RECENT TRENDS IN ASSESSMENT

Up to now, we have discussed assessment largely from a diagnostic/classification point of view. Assessment in this area is critical, since it deals with the often controversial issue of who is called mentally retarded. The problem of misdiagnosing and mislabeling certain people, particularly members of various minority groups, has led to vociferous calls for reform. Considerable energy has recently been expended to make the diagnostic process more precise and valid. Most important has been the work of sociologist Jane Mercer, who has proposed a new model for assessment. Her system, an elaboration and refinement of the traditional approach, will be discussed shortly.

Over the past decade, there has been an even more significant development in assessment practices. As mentioned above, the traditional ap-

FIGURE 7.5

Part IV Language Development of the Adaptive Behavior Scale.
Adopted from AAMD *Adaptive Behavior Scale:* American
Association on Mental Deficiency (1969; 1974).

## IV. LANGUAGE DEVELOPMENT

### A. Expression

[32] *Writing* (Circle only ONE)

| | | |
|---|---|---|
| Writes sensible and understandable letters | 5 | |
| Writes short notes and memos | 4 | ◯ |
| Writes or prints forty words | 3 | |
| Writes or prints ten words | 2 | |
| Writes or prints own name | 1 | |
| Cannot write or print any words | 0 | |

[33] *Preverbal Expression*
(Check ALL statements which apply)

| | | |
|---|---|---|
| Nods head or smiles to express happiness | ____ | |
| Indicates hunger | ____ | |
| Indicates wants by pointing or vocal noises | ____ | ◯ |
| Chuckles or laughs when happy | ____ | |
| Expresses pleasure or anger by vocal noises | ____ | |
| Is able to say at least a few words (Enter "6" if checked, regardless of other items.) | ____ | |

*None of the above* ____

[34] *Articulation* (Check ALL statements which apply—
if no speech, check "None" and enter "0" in the circle)

| | | |
|---|---|---|
| | | 4-number checked = |
| Speech is low, weak, whispered or difficult to hear | ____ | |
| Speech is slowed, deliberate, or labored | ____ | ◯ |
| Speech is hurried, accelerated, or pushed | ____ | |
| Speaks with blocking, halting, or other irregular interruptions | ____ | |

*None of the above* ____

FIGURE 7.5 (*Continued*)

[35] *Sentences* (Circle only ONE)

| | |
|---|---|
| Sometimes uses complex sentences containing "because," "but," etc. | 3 |
| Asks questions using words such as "why," "how," "what," etc. | 2 |
| Speaks in simple sentences | 1 |
| Speaks in primitive phrases only, or is non-verbal | 0 |

[36] *Word Usage* (Circle only ONE)

| | |
|---|---|
| Talks about action when describing pictures | 4 |
| Names people or objects when describing pictures | 3 |
| Names familiar objects | 2 |
| Asks for things by their appropriate names | 1 |
| Is non-verbal or nearly non-verbal | 0 |

A. Expression → ADD 32-36

B. Comprehension

[37] *Reading* (Circle only ONE)

| | |
|---|---|
| Reads books suitable for children nine years or older | 5 |
| Reads books suitable for children seven years old | 4 |
| Reads simple stories or comics | 3 |
| Reads various signs, e.g., "NO PARKING," "ONE WAY," "MEN," "WOMEN," etc. | 2 |
| Recognizes ten or more words by sight | 1 |
| Recognizes fewer than ten words or none at all | 0 |

[38] *Complex Instructions*
(Check ALL statements which apply)

Understands instructions containing prepositions, e.g., "on," "in," "behind," "under," etc. ___

FIGURE 7.5 (*Continued*)

Understands instructions referring to the order in which things must be done, e.g., "first do– then do–" ___ ○

Understands instructions requiring a decision: "If–, do this, but if not, do–" ___

*None of the above* ___

B. Comprehension ——→ ADD 37-38 △

C. Social Language Development

[39] *Conversation*
(Check ALL statements which apply)

Uses phrases such as "please," and "thank you" ___ ○

Is sociable and talks during meals ___

Talks to others about sports, family, group activities, etc. ___

*None of the above* ___

[40] *Miscellaneous Language Development*
(Check ALL statements which apply)

Can be reasoned with ___ ○

Obviously responds when talked to ___

Talks sensibly ___

Reads books, newspapers, magazines for enjoyment ___

Repeats a story with little or no difficulty ___

Fills in the main items on application form reasonably well ___

*None of the above* ___

C. Social Language Development ——→ ADD 39-40 △

IV. Language Development ——→ ADD *TRIANGLES* A-C □

proach is designed to diagnose and classify mental retardation. But this model has limited utility for continued treatment or for aid in developing programs for the mentally retarded. For these persons, a different approach is necessary. This is especially true today, given the optimism about enhancing the development of the mentally retarded. Assessment is now seen to be an integral part of such programs. This newer view of assessment is highlighted by the difference between the so-called "normative" and "clinical" approaches to assessment. This concept, along with some examples of clinical assessment approaches (e.g., diagnostic-prescriptive teaching, assessment of learning potential, and the functional analysis of behavior) will be discussed.

## Mercer's SOMPA Approach

Mercer (e.g., 1975), contending that IQ is a biased measurement for many minority or deprived children (1972, 1973a,b), proposed an alternate system known as SOMPA (a System of Multi-cultural Pluralistic Assessment). This system is designed to determine the present and potential level of functioning of children of English-speaking Caucasian (Anglo), chicano/latino, and black cultural backgrounds. An attempt has been made to eliminate test discrimination based on race, cultural heritage, or ethnic group. Mercer contends that the need for this system was demonstrated by research that indicated (1) a disproportionate number of children from minority and low socioeconomic families were being classified as mentally retarded in school and placed in special classes, (2) minority students labeled as mentally retarded have significantly higher IQ scores and fewer physical deficits than their Caucasian counterparts, and (3) school systems rely almost totally on individual intelligence tests as a diagnostic tool and do not consider the sociocultural background of the student when interpreting these scores (Mercer, 1973a).

SOMPA is based on what Mercer calls three conceptual models: the medical model, the social system model, and the pluralistic model. Each model is based on a different conception of abnormality and has different approaches to assessment. Mercer thus contends that each model provides a different "lens" through which the child's behavior can be viewed.

The *medical model* focuses on deficits or "symptoms" that indicate abnormality. These symptoms are considered to be a direct result of underlying pathology, which is generally biological or physical in nature. With this model, sociocultural factors are unimportant because the problem is an individual defect. Tests used with this model reflect these assumptions and attempt to measure physical characteristics. In SOMPA, Mercer uses several measures which fit these assumptions: the Physical Dexterity Test, the Bender Gestalt Test (a measure of perceptual-motor integration which incorporates drawing geometric figures), the Health History Inventory, a visual acuity test, and a measure that gives a ratio of height to weight. Again, all of the medical model measures generally relate to physical characteristics and are typically interpreted in a normative manner (i.e., compared to the average).

The *social system model* defines abnormality as social deviance—behavior which violates social norms. These norms can be role specific and social system specific. "Role specific" simply means that there are different norms for different roles (e.g., student, employee, daughter, husband). Each of these roles has different expected behaviors. As a result of the many different roles, there are many forms of deviation. For example, a child might be deviant in the role of student (e.g., slow learner) but not deviant in the role of daughter or babysitter. Different social systems also have different norms. Thus, the school, as a social system, focuses on academic behavior, while the family may not. The social system model is multidimensional and evaluative. It assesses both assets and deficits. In this regard, a child may be above or below average (the medical model focuses only on deficits).

Measures in SOMPA which reflect the social systems model are variable. A basic measure is the WISC-R (see above). This test is used (with the standard population norms) because it is believed to reflect the successful student role in the social system of the school.

A second social system measure is the Adaptive Behavior Inventory for Children (ABIC), which is used to reflect success in family, peer group, community, and nonacademic school roles. It also indicates self-maintenance and earner-consumer roles in the family. The ABIC is conducted through one interview with the mother and consists of questions regarding the various areas of content (e.g., family roles, peer group roles).

The *pluralistic model* assumes that all tests measure some form of learning. With this model, subnormality is defined as low performance on tests of learning *when compared to children of similar cultural backgrounds*. The model assumes that children of similar sociocultural backgrounds have had similar opportunities to learn the test material, have been similarly reinforced in that learning by major socializing agents (school, general society, home), and have had similar experience with test taking. Statistical procedures (multiple regression) are then used so that a child can be compared to other children with a similar sociocultural background. This approach avoids the problems of cultural bias and attempts to uncover potential ability in children that has been masked by cultural differences. SOMPA yields a score which Mercer calls Estimated Learning Potential.

Measures are profiled on separate charts—one for the medical model, one for the social system model, and one for the pluralistic model. (Data from one test could be used differently for the different models.) The results of each model are compared for interpretation. If the child performs similarly on all three models, interpretation can be made with a high degree of confidence. When findings differ, caution is needed before a definitive conclusion can be made. Case examples of Mercer's system are presented in Boxes 7.1 and 7.2.

## Normative versus Clinical Assessment

Haywood (1977) has made a useful distinction between normative and clinical assessment. The normative assessment model is based on the premise that a trait, such as IQ, is normally distributed and that its variations can be measured. Also, we can agree (arbitrarily) at what point a score is deviant. Thus, an IQ of 70 is defined as the cutoff for mental retardation. This type of assessment can be effectively used for policy-making (knowing how large groups of persons behave on some measure) or research, but it is not functional for educational or behavioral treatment programs. Haywood stresses that mental retardation has recently been defined in terms of behavioral/social deficits rather than a physical or structural deficit that inheres in the individual. The behavioral/social deficits have a variety of sources (causes), but four sources seem apparent: (1) deficiencies in intelligence—failure to develop significant cognitive skills, (2) deficiencies in adaptive behavior, which may be related to the expectations of others, (3) deficiencies in personality/motivation traits, which may combine with intelligence problems to further decrease learning, and (4) deficiencies in what Haywood calls the "person-setting interaction." This refers to deficiencies in a person's ability to determine appropriate behavior for different settings.

As we have said, there are effective normative tools for assessing intelligence and adaptive behavior. Certain normative tests can be used for personality-motivation assessment, but none of these are considered valid psychometric tools. There are no normative tests for assessing person-setting deficiencies. It becomes clear that with the expanded concept of mental retardation (behavioral, social deficits), normative assessment becomes less useful.

A final limitation of normative assessment is important. This relates to the fact that mental retardation is now considered to be a dynamic

## BOX 7.1

Fred: A Case Illustration of Mercer's SOMPA

Fred illustrates a case at the lower end of the continuum. He is a 7-year-old Black boy with a standard WISC-R score of 69, about the 2nd percentile on the standard norms. This score is low enough to make him eligible for classes for the mentally retarded in most public schools and indicates that he will probably have serious difficulty with the regular school program at his school level of functioning (SFL). His sociocultural modality scores are: Anglization, 1; Family Size, 3; Role Boundaries, 3; Efficacy, 3; and Source of Income, 0. Translating these scores into a verbal description, we find a family of six living in a four-room, rented dwelling. The family consists of five children: two full siblings to Fred, and two step-siblings. Fred's mother is divorced from her spouse, does not work outside the home and the family is on welfare. Fred's mother was born in rural Jamaica and speaks in an English dialect which is difficult to understand. She never finished high school herself but expects that Fred will finish college and has a high sense of efficacy and control over the future.

The average score for a child of Fred's sociocultural modality is 80.9. His score of 69 is about 12 points or 1.0 standard error below the mean for his sociocultural group and would place him in the 33rd percentile for his normative group. Although his estimated learning potential (ELP) is low, he does not appear to be mentally retarded. His very low school level of functioning (SLF) appears to reflect an impoverished family background and socialization by a mother who has relatively little familiarity with the dominant Anglo-American society. He needs an enriched education program which will acquaint him with the roles and skills needed in urban America. His educational program should probably be planned with this in mind, providing other aspects of the assessment confirm the diagnosis.

From J. R. Mercer, in M. J. Begab and S. A. Richardson (Eds.), *The Mentally Retarded and Society,* Baltimore: University Park Press, 1975.

## BOX 7.2

Peter: A Case Illustration of Mercer's SOMPA

Peter is a 7-year-old Anglo-American boy who scored 107 on the standard norms (WISC-R) (approximately the 68th percentile). We would predict that his academic performance will be above average. However, we see a slightly different picture using pluralistic norms. His sociocultural background received close to the maximum score on most factors: Anglization, 10; Family Size, 5; Occupation of Head, 7; Source of Income, 3; and Family Structure, 3. Peter comes from a relatively advantaged background. Translated into a verbal description, Peter lives with his mother and father and one other sibling. His father provides the family's income and is a nonacademic employee of the University of California. Peter's father has 4 years of education beyond high school and his mother has 1 year of college. They expect that Peter will graduate from college. Both parents spent their childhoods in Colorado. The father was reared in Denver, and Peter's mother was reared in a small town. The family has moved three times in the past 5 years and now lives in a six-room home which they are buying. Peter's mother feels that the family determines its own success or failure and can make plans for the future that will work out.

The average score for children from similar sociocultural backgrounds is 108.8. Therefore, Peter's score of 107 is average for a child of his sociocultural modality and places him at about the 44th percentile for his normative group. His school functioning level (SFL) is above average compared to the total population but his Estimated Learning Potential (ELP) is average when his sociocultural advantage is taken into account.

From J. R. Mercer, in M. J. Begab and S. A. Richardson (Eds.), *The Mentally Retarded and Society*, Baltimore: University Park Press, 1975.

developmental problem, not a static one. Thus, permanent classification is no longer appropriate for many of the retarded. Along with the reconceptualization of mental retardation as a developmental problem with behavioral/social deficits, the goal of intervention has changed. Its purpose now is to enhance or even to raise the level of the individual's development. Given these new directions, new or different assessment methods are needed. Examples of the new clinical assessment approach will now be presented.

## Diagnostic-Prescriptive Teaching Model

"Diagnostic-prescriptive teaching" stands for a variety of programs based on the premise that assessment and treatment must both occur in an interactive and ongoing manner. The process begins with an assessment of the person's strengths and weaknesses (diagnostic), followed by recommendations (prescriptive) for remediation (teaching) of his deficiencies. The focus on a person's assets as well as his liabilities is important because the areas of strength often suggest approaches for remediation of deficiencies. As the individual improves, the focus may shift to new deficiencies or deficiences at a different level, followed by new recommendations, and so on. The process is continuous and ongoing. It is not a static procedure, as is often the case in traditional psychometric assessment.

One such approach used in the classroom is a set of commercial materials known as DISTAR (Engelmann and Bruner, 1969; Engelmann and Carnine, 1970; Engelmann, Osborn, and Engelmann, 1969). These procedures apply to various academic areas. The child is first assessed to determine his level of achievement. This is followed by training or teaching, then more assessment, and so on. Assessment takes place every day, and the results of this lead to the next step of teaching. The children conduct and chart a good deal of the assessment themselves, and are able to compare immediately their present and past performances. Haywood (1977) speculates that the self-assessment and charting may also reinforce and further enhance the learning process.

The basis of all diagnostic-prescriptive teaching programs is to constantly evaluate the learning or intervention program. Assessment and intervention become completely intertwined and interdependent. Few standardized tests exist for such a model, since treatment or intervention can use many different procedures and materials. The course of intervention is dictated primarily by the individual—his level of development and his needs. Thus, assessment must be also geared to the individual, and must involve different procedures and methods at different times. With this type of assessment, we must depend more on the experience and expertise of the clinical examiner and less on standardized tests. While the examiner may use tests or parts of tests in his assessment, he can rarely rely totally on their use.

### Feuerstein's Learning Potential Procedure

Another new clinical approach to assessment in mental retardation is the work of Feuerstein (see, e.g., Feuerstein, 1972). His model, usually referred to as Learning Potential or the Assessment of Learning Potential, was developed as the result of more than two decades of work in Israel. This program was originally used to assess immigrants to Israel who were retarded from an academic point of view. Feuerstein's model and procedure allow learning potential to be assessed in such a way that specific deficits can be described. Consequently, teaching or remediation procedures will be indicated.

Feuerstein's program is based on a concept of intelligence referred to as "modifiability." This means that the individual can use previously acquired knowledge to adjust or adapt to new situations and to acquire information that can be applied to these situations. In this theory, learning and intelligence are intertwined. Learning takes place in two ways. First, the individual can learn through direct experience. For example, the young child may learn to avoid the stove after touching a hot burner. However, much direct experience is facilitated through the second type of learning, which Feuerstein refers to as "mediated." This learning occurs when significant others (e.g., parents) select, interpret, or mediate environmental experience for the infant or child. The child is made aware that he is learning something important. As Haywood et al. (1975) state, "The combination of sufficient mediated learning is the key to the development of the information-processing strategies valued in our culture and collectively named intelligence" (p. 115). In Feuerstein's approach, one of the primary causes for cultural-familial mental retardation (i.e., most mild mental retardation) is lack of appropriate or adequate mediated learning experiences.

To help develop learning strategies or sets, specific deficiencies must be assessed so that the child can begin to benefit from direct learning. For this purpose, Feuerstein (1970) developed the Learning Potential Assessment Device (LPAD). This program was designed to describe the amount and type of mediated learning that is necessary before permanent changes will occur. The purpose of mediation is to teach children to profit from their own direct experience with the environment.

While a description of the tasks and procedures of the LPAD goes beyond our present scope, certain differences in assessment are pertinent.

First, the examiner encourages the child to perform at his maximum. A specific attempt is made to increase motivation and performance. This is in contrast to traditional intellectual assessment, where the examiner is objective and uninvolved. Second, as the assessment proceeds, the examiner provides feedback regarding the child's performance. There is a constant interaction between child and examiner in the form of remarks, explanations, and concern. Finally, the most important difference between the LPAD and traditional assessment is that the LPAD leads directly to intervention or remediation procedures. For this purpose, Feuerstein's group has developed lengthy and elaborate exercises. Treatment is not only an integral part of the program, it is the final goal. This is in striking contrast to the traditional psychometric model, where assessment itself often appears to be the goal.

## The Functional Analysis of Behavior

One of the greatest breakthroughs in the area of treatment or remediation is the use of operant conditioning—or, more generally, "behavior modification." At this point, its use in assessment will be explored. Gardner (1971) has used the term "functional analysis" to refer to behavioral modification in an assessment framework. This simply means an evaluation of the functions of behavior. Traditional psychometric evaluation (e.g., intelligence tests) can be quite valid, but a low IQ in itself provides little useful data for developing an individual educational program. The functional analysis approach uses operant conditioning procedures to describe or delineate behavioral deficiencies. Then, specific treatment or remediation procedures can be designed.

Behavioral deficiencies are assumed to be an overt manifestation of intelligence. Functional analysis, however, is unconcerned with the idea of intelligence except as it places broad limits on behavior. Instead, stress is placed on the role of the environment in producing or reducing behavioral deficiencies. The conditions that are necessary to produce positive changes in behavior are emphasized. Environmental factors can be divided into two categories: "antecedent events" and "consequent events." Antecedent events are all of the relevant environmental characteristics that are present just before the behavior occurs. Consequent events are the relevant environmental changes (reinforcers) which occur as a result of the behavior.

With functional analysis, the examiner first describes the behavior in question. He then specifies the conditions (both antecedent and consequent) under which it occurs. Finally, the "functionality" of the behavior is checked out. This simply means that the examiner must somehow prove that the behavior in question is actually related to the observed environmental events. This is done by manipulating some of these events and observing behavioral changes. If the predicted changes occur, the functional analysis is probably correct. Let us illustrate this process. A child is described as a problem because he cries a great deal. Upon observation, it is determined that he cries more (or predominantly) when his mother is present. It is also observed that the mother immediately picks up the baby when he begins to cry. It can be hypothesized that the mother's behavior (e.g., picking up the baby) reinforces the baby's behavior (e.g., crying) when the mother is present. The functional connection between crying and the mother's presence is made. This can be checked by increasing or decreasing the mother's presence and observing consequent changes in crying. This is, admittedly, an oversimplified example, but it does illustrate the functional analysis approach. Again, the goal of this type of assessment is to design individual programs for positive behavioral changes. Assessment and treatment or education are inseparable.

There have been two recent trends in the assessment of mental retardation. First, there is the attempt to extend and refine traditional assessment practices. This is exemplified by Mercer's SOMPA procedure, wherein the child is viewed from many different vantage points. Second, there is an increasing emphasis on clinical assessment. With this model, assessment is an integral and inseparable part of the treatment process. Furthermore, it is an ongoing dynamic procedure, in contrast to the often static quality of traditional normative assessment. Diagnostic-prescriptive teaching, the assessment of learning potential, and the functional analysis of behavior all demonstrate that the ultimate goal of assessment is to aid in the treatment process.

Both of these recent trends in the assessment of mental retardation illustrate the much broader changes in psychological assessment over the past decade. The primary purpose of assessment in the past was diagnosis and classification. However, it is now recognized that a comprehensive assessment must take into account the many environmental influences on a person's behavior. Diagnostic and classification decisions made from one particular viewpoint may be irrelevant, inappropriate, or even erroneous from another viewpoint. This is not to imply that there are no such things as traits (e.g., intelligence) that have a certain generality across situations. However, it is asserted that the environment may modify the expression of traits and that at times the environment may be the predominant influence on behavior. Thus, we cannot assess only persons; we must also assess their environments. Since most people operate in many different environments, assessment must focus on the interaction between the person and his multiple environments. The importance of this interaction is highlighted by the ultimate goal of assessment, which is to aid in the intervention process. This process can only occur in an environmental context. Thus, we can no longer construe assessment as a static process whereby a person is evaluated in a vacuum. We must assess persons, environments, and their interactions. It is a complex, dynamic process.

According to Hobbs (1975b), this model of comprehensive and dynamic assessment is best conceptualized in "ecological" terms: "Human ecology is the study of the dynamic relationship between the individual and his unique set of environmental circumstances, at a particular period of time" (p. 113). The essence of this ecological approach is as follows:

> With this approach, the child is no longer the sole focus of assessment and intervention. Rather, the problem is seen as residing in the ecological system of which the child is an integral part. This system consists of the child and the settings and the individuals within these settings that are a part of the child's daily life. All parts of the system influence all other parts of the system. Physical and psychological as well as social factors are involved. Thus, assessments and interventions focus on the exchanges between the child, the settings in which he participates, and the significant individuals who interact with him. Each child's ecological system is unique. The objective is not merely to change or improve the child but to make the total system work. Change in any part of the system, or in several parts, may accomplish this purpose. And changes may be brought about through interventions affecting physical, psychological, or social functioning of one or more components of the system. (pp. 113–114)

## SUMMARY

Psychological assessment is a variable and complex process. First, it is not simply a matter of administering tests and making decisions based on the scores. Test scores are just one part of a complex procedure. A second point relates to the changing emphasis in the criteria for a diagnosis of mental retardation. It is obvious that, as these criteria change, so must assessment procedures. In recent years there has been an increasing emphasis on behavioral and social deficits and developmental disability. These changes must be reflected in assessment, and new assessment procedures must be used. Third, assessment is not limited to diagnosis and classification. Assessment is now becoming an integral part of remediation and education programs, where the results of assessment systematically guide intervention procedures. In addition, comprehensive evaluation demands assessment of persons, environments, and their interactions. Finally, assessment is not a test-controlled procedure. There are almost no situations where clinical decisions can be made on the basis of test scores alone. As Haywood (1977) indicates, we are witnessing a return to the skilled clinician who collects and weighs all of the relevant data before a decision is made. This point is especially important in light of the recent furor about culturally biased tests. If a test is inappropriate for certain persons, obviously it should not be used. Much of the problem in this area has resulted from poorly trained or inexperienced examiners who have used tests mechanically and inappropriately. Assessment cannot be done by some *a priori* formula. It is a dynamic process, which varies with the specific case.

# CHAPTER 8

# Etiological Factors in Mental Retardation

Most lay persons believe that mental retardation occurs as a result of damage to the brain or some other physical condition. This attitude stems from the fact that, historically, the prominent scientific perspective on mental retardation has been the medical or deficit model (Chapter 5). This model states that there is something wrong with the individual and implies that the reason for this defect is physical. This attitude was prevalent well into the 1940s. Mental retardation was felt to be a physical condition associated with low intelligence. In contrast, the present scientific concept of mental retardation is primarily descriptive, with little emphasis on etiological (causative) factors. When etiology is considered, less emphasis is placed on specific physical conditions. Studies have shown that 90 percent of the persons diagnosed as mentally retarded have no responsible, identifiable physical condition. In cases where the etiology is known, it is often found to be a complex set of interacting factors. Although many conditions can result in mental retardation (more than 250 have been identified), all of them combined result in only a small minority of the cases. It is this small proportion of the mentally retarded that had been the focus of lay and professional concern. In more recent years, however, there has been an increasing emphasis on the problems of the mildly retarded, who constitute the vast majority of all mentally retarded persons and who have no demonstrable organic pathology.

The objective of the present chapter is not to detail the various causes of mental retardation. It is of little concern to the average reader that the condition of porphyria (a metabolic disorder related to the function of the liver) causes mental retardation and what the characteristics and processes of that disease are. The objective of this chapter is to explore some of the more common causes that lead to mental retardation and the complexities involved.

Before we begin, however, there is one general etiological consideration that merits discussion. As Robinson and Robinson (1976) note, there is "a consensus among geneticists that intelligence as a trait or complex of traits depends for the most part upon polygenic modes of inheritance in constant interaction with a multiplicity of environmental factors" (p. 76). This "polygenic" model states that the genetic aspect of intelligence depends on the cumulative effect of a very large but unknown number of genes. Furthermore, there is a wide range of environmental contexts that interact with these genetic givens in promoting the development and expression of intelligence.

However, while this polygenic model is considered to hold true for almost all persons, there are some dramatic exceptions. They include most of the medical conditions considered in this chapter, and which typically result in severe forms of mental retardation. In these cases, there is something so drastically wrong with either the genetic makeup or the environment that the polygenic model becomes inoperative. This is most apparent in cases of severe retardation resulting from a single genetic defect or chromosomal abnormality. Although we have stated that intelligence is not the result of a single gene, sometimes a defect in just one gene or chromosome is so deleterious and pervasive in its influence that it overrides the action of thousands of other genes normally responsible for intelligence. As Robinson and Robinson (1976) further note: "By far the majority of profoundly retarded children are impaired not because of their polygenic inheritance and psychosocial environment but because of overriding damage by some single catastrophe in their genetic makeup or in their environment" (p. 77).

As mentioned before, this group of medical disorders accounts for only about 10 percent of the cases of mental retardation. What about the other 90 percent? Is the cause really "unknown" for this much larger group of the (primarily) mildly retarded? The polygenic model of inheritance provides a tentative answer. In these cases, the cause of retardation is not so much "unknown" as "unspeciable." The etiology of mild mental retardation depends on the confluence of a number of factors, including the genes, the environment, and motivational and personality variables. This interaction, and the relative importance or contribution of these multiple factors, are extremely complex and controversial subjects. For now, however, the following discussion of specific medical causes of mental retardation relates to only approximately 10 percent of the mentally retarded; it is not generalizable to the other 90 percent. Some consideration of the causes of mild mental retardation, particularly the importance of the environment, will be presented near the end of the chapter.

## PHYSICAL CAUSES OF MENTAL RETARDATION

A large variety of physical conditions can result in mental retardation. These conditions can be viewed from many different perspectives and classification systems. We could, for example, categorize conditions according to when the initial defect occurred. Some conditions are present at conception (genetic and chromosomal conditions), while others occur later in pregnancy. Other conditions occur at the time of birth (perinatal), and still others after birth in the later developmental period (postnatal). Classification could also be based on the physical process that causes impairment in the brain. Such processes include metabolic problems, trauma, and infections. In this chapter, we will follow the classification system proposed in the *Manual on Terminology and Classification in Mental Retardation of the American Association on Mental Deficiency* (AAMD) (Grossman, 1973/1977). This system is a combined temporal (when it occurred) and process (what process caused damage) approach to classification.

Before presenting the various etiological categories, let us review some facts regarding genetics. This is necessary since a number of genetic defects can result in mental retardation, and these conditions do not fall into any single disease category.

### Genetic Processes

*Genes* are extremely complicated submicroscopic units in the cells which determine heredity. The genes are located in a larger cell structure called the *chromosome*. Every normal body cell has 46 chromosomes. At conception, humans receive 23 chromosomes from the father's sperm and 23 from the mother's ovum. The 46 chromosomes form 23 identifiable pairs, which are duplicated in every body cell as the individual develops. There may be 1,000 or more genes located in pairs on the chromosomes. The genes carry biochemical information, providing patterns for the type of proteins the cell will produce. These proteins serve as enzymes, or catalysts, of the body's chemical reactions. These chemical reactions provide the basis for metabolism in the cells and for the growth and development of all tissues. A genetic defect can thus interrupt any of these complicated body processes. A genetic defect is a biochemical error resulting in a failure to produce an enzyme necessary for a specific biochemical reaction.

The term "genetic defect" refers to types of mental retardation which result from some genetic abnormality in the zygote. The "zygote" refers to the union of the egg and sperm cell at conception. At this point, then, genetic material (chromosomes and/or genes) is defective, and normal development becomes affected. Some, but not all, genetic defects are inherited. This means that one or both parents carried a defective gene which could be passed on to their offspring. Whether this will happen depends largely on the type and location of the defective gene. *Recessive* genes, which can cause such conditions as PKU, result in the defect in offspring only when the same recessive is contributed by both parents. This condition is known as "pairing." This is a rare phenomenon; PKU occurs in only about 1 out of 13,000 births. If only one parent cell carries the recessive gene, the offspring will not have the defect. However, the offspring may carry this recessive gene and pass it on to his offspring.

*Dominant* genes are more rarely the cause of mental retardation, since the defective trait has a much higher probability of being manifested, and the defective individual has a smaller chance of successful development or procreation. A dominant gene determines certain characteristics of the individual regardless of the nature of its homologous (paired) gene. Thus, it "dominates" its partner. Most of the genes governing enzyme patterning are dominant and, as stated above, dominant genes rarely result in severe mental retardation. There are several exceptions, however. Huntington's chorea (discussed later) usually develops in middle-aged persons who may have procreated and thus passed on the condition. (Note: Most conditions caused by dominant genes cause death of the fetus *in utero* or the individual is so impaired that he cannot procreate.) Another dominant gene condition, tuberous sclerosis, can have minimal effect on one generation and severe effects on the next one.

Other genetic defects are not inherited. The genetic material in the parent cells may be damaged by radiation or drugs and result in a defective zygote. It is also possible for a whole chromosome to be defective, as in the case of Down's syndrome (discussed later). Again, such a disorder is not inherited.

Later in this chapter, we will discuss several conditions which result from genetic defects. Some are inherited, others are not. It should be noted that, with the exception of Down's syndrome, noninherited genetic causes of mental retardation are rare. Furthermore, while the precise effect of a number of disorders cannot be specified, it presumably relates to the metabolism of the brain, as controlled and directed by the genes. Some types of environmental assault—infection, trauma, lack of oxygen—wreck havoc with the entire system.

## Infections and Intoxications

Certain types of infections, occurring both before and after birth, can damage the brain and result in mental retardation. Retardation can also result from certain toxins which destroy brain tissue. These toxins can occur at any time after conception.

*Prenatal Infections* *Rubella* and *syphilis* are the two most common types of prenatal infections that result in mental retardation. Both are maternal infections which are contracted by the fetus and result in brain damage.

Rubella (German measles) has been the subject of a great deal of research, especially since the rubella epidemic of 1964. This disease is usually not serious for children or adults, but it can severely damage the fetus. If the mother contracts rubella during the first three months of pregnancy, there is a fairly high risk of the baby being born with serious defects. These can be physical (e.g., cataracts) as well as neurological, and it is common for the baby to have several different defects. In the rubella syndrome, seriously affected babies are born deaf, blind, and mentally retarded. A recently developed vaccine has significantly decreased the incidence of congenital rubella.

In the past, syphilis was a major cause (relatively speaking) of mental retardation. Advances in treatment and widespread mandatory blood tests have sharply curtailed the prevalence of this disease. Syphilis rarely causes mental retardation in adults. However, maternal syphilis can damage the germ cell from either parent or can directly harm the developing fetus. The infection can result in spontaneous abortions, miscarriages, and stillbirths, as well as blindness, deafness, and mental retardation. The central nervous system is especially vulnerable to syphilis; at least half of the children of infected mothers have damaged central nervous systems.

*Postnatal Infections* This category includes viral and bacterial infections that occur after birth. They result in mental retardation by infecting and destroying the brain tissue.

Meningitis is an inflammation of the meninges, the protective covering of the brain and spinal cord. There are several forms of this disease, caused by different types of bacteria. Severity of the disease and prognosis are also variable. In the past, many forms of meningitis were frequently fatal, and the issue of mental retardation did not arise. Today, with more effective medical treatment, many children survive the acute phase of the disease but suffer permanent brain damage, which can range from mild to severe.

Encephalitis literally means "infection or inflammation of the brain." This disease can result from viruses, protozoan infections such as toxoplasmosis, lead poisoning, and many other causes. It can also result as a sequel to such diseases as measles, chicken pox, scarlet fever, and whooping cough. In these cases, an infection which is usually restricted to other body systems is transmitted to the brain, causing an inflammation. Encephalitis is popularly known as sleeping sickness, since one common form is characterized by lethargy, apathy, and increasing drowsiness. Many forms of encephalitis are caused by viruses carried by forest ticks, mosquitos, and other insects. Specific types of encephalitis are often named after an insect which inhabits a definite geographic region. For example, Semliki Forest encephalitis is due to a virus carried by mosquitos in the Semliki Forest.

In addition to mental retardation, encephalitis can result in other types of damage to the brain. Formerly, this disease was often fatal, but the percentage of fatalities has been significantly decreased by modern therapies. As with meningitis, a certain minority of these survivors have residual mental retardation.

More postnatal mental retardation results from infection than any other physical cause. It must be remembered, however, that we are speaking in relative terms; the percentage of cases due to *all* physical causes is small.

*Intoxicants* This category includes a number of conditions wherein foreign substances cause either malformation of the brain or destruction to a previously intact brain. One toxin which causes fetal malformations is Thalidomide. This sedative-type drug was popularly used in Europe in the 1960s. It was found to cause extreme congenital abnormalities when taken by a mother in early pregnancy. "Thalidomide babies" were characterized by dysmelia, or malformation of the limbs, often accompanied by mental retardation.

In *toxemia of pregnancy*, the fetus is poisoned by toxic by-products of a maternal disease. In this case, the pregnant mother may suffer from a bacterial infection. Bacterial products are absorbed into the mother's blood, which are then transmitted to the fetus. These toxins may not cause damage to the intact mature brain, but they can result in severe destruction or malformation of the developing fetal brain.

Numerous other toxins, both before and after birth, can cause brain damage. These typically cause inflammation, which leads to bleeding and results in permanent brain lesions. Heavy metals such as lead can cause such damage. Lead poisoning, known as "plumbism," has recently received a great deal of attention from lay and consumer advocate groups because of the high lead content in paints used for children's furniture and toys as well as house paint. New paints no longer contain lead, but the hazard still exists where old, peeling paint is within reach of young children.

## Trauma or Physical Agent

The brain can be damaged as a result of trauma (injury) or other physical or mechanical agents. This damage can occur during pregnancy (prenatal), at the time of birth (perinatal), or at some time after birth (postnatal).

Although prenatal injuries are rare, the fetal brain can be damaged by irradiation, hypoxia (lowered amount of oxygen), or direct injury to the fetus. At the time of birth, the infant may be injured by instrument delivery, excessively long or extremely short labor, and complicated deliveries such as a breech position. Brain damage occurs because of a lack of oxygen or by direct injury to the brain or its blood vessels.

Postnatal injuries can also result in brain damage and low intelligence. While the mature healthy brain can recover from relatively severe damage, serious injuries which are often accompanied by unconsciousness and coma can result in permanent brain damage. Postnatal hypoxia, shock, poisoning, or convulsions can also result in permanent brain damage.

Physical brain damage as a cause of mental retardation seems quite logical and is accepted by most people. However, the direct relationship between brain damage and intelligence is hardly clear or simple. For example, we might assume that if we removed a certain amount of brain tissue, a specifiable decrease in intelligence would result. This is not the case. Sometimes, the excision of even fairly large amounts of cortical brain tissue results in no marked changes in behavior. In other cases, destruction of small amounts of tissue results in severe and obvious deficits. Many variables affect the behavioral and intellectual deficits that will be observed in brain damage. Not only is the size of the lesion (the damaged area) important but also its location and type, the age of the individual at onset, and a host of other factors. Thus, it is impossible to generalize about the relationship between intelligence and brain damage. Careful medical, neurological, psychological, and other evaluations must be made before the effect of damage can be determined. It is also important to remember that recovery from brain injuries may take a year or more.

### Disorders of Metabolism or Nutrition

This category includes a number of disorders which involve the metabolism of food and growth. In the healthy individual, foods are broken down in an orderly and predictable fashion. In others, however, this metabolic process is faulty. This results in the production of toxins which either interfere with the development of the central nervous system and the brain or result in brain damage. These disorders can be classified into four general groups: (1) metabolism of fats, (2) metabolism of carbohydrates, (3) metabolism of amino acids, and (4) endocrine imbalances.

The disorders that result from faulty metabolism of fats are called neuronal lipid storage diseases. The word "neuronal" refers to cells of the nervous system; "lipid" indicates the fatty substances in foods; "storage diseases" means a storage problem of these fatty materials in the body. In these disorders, fatty substances are abnormally stored in the cells of the nervous system, and most importantly, in the central nervous system, resulting in damage to these cells. These disorders tend to be familial—in other words, usually caused by an inherited genetic defect.

Tay-Sachs disease is a lipid storage disease that typically has a very early onset and develops rapidly. It is transmitted by a single recessive gene and is much more common in families of Jewish background than others. The baby generally appears normal at birth, but after three to six months he may become apathetic and hypersensitive to light and sound stimulation. The disease progresses rapidly and usually involves convulsions, progressive blindness, spasticity, and a progressive intellectual deficit. The child typically dies by age two or three. Several additional diseases which are quite similar to Tay-Sachs are first noted at later ages. These diseases are referred to as amaurotic familial idiocy. In general, the later the onset of these diseases, the slower the progression. A lipid storage disease which first occurs at age six or seven has a longer, more gradual course than one that first occurs at age two. For example, Spielmeyer-Vogt disease is called the juvenile form and is first seen between three and ten years of age. This disease results in blindness, difficulties with balance and coordination, and convulsions. There is also a progressive deterioration in intellectual function. In both Tay-Sachs and Spielmeyer-Vogt disease, the physician is able to recognize identifiable deteriorations in the retina of the eye. In Tay-Sachs disease there is a characteristic cherry red spot. In Spielmeyer-Vogt disease there is a more scattered retinal deterioration known as "salt and pepper" degeneration. Both of these disorders result in severe brain damage, typically profound mental retardation, and frequently very early mortality.

While there are many lipid diseases, most of them are quite rare. Hurler's disease, however, has been popularized in many books on mental retardation. This disease is also called gargoylism, since the child's appearance is similar to that of the medieval gargoyles. There are abnormal deposits of lipid substances in the liver, heart, lungs, spleen, and brain. Some signs of this disease may be present at birth, but typically the characteristics develop in the first six months of life. The child has a large head with a protruding forehead far out of proportion in size to the body, which is stunted. Eyebrows tend to be heavy and bushy, and the nose is flat and saddle shaped. The child's features are typically coarse and heavy, with a double chin, thick lips, and a large tongue. At a later age, other abnormalities become apparent, such as changes in bone shape and structure, hand deformities, and limitations in movement. Moderate or more severe mental retardation usually occurs as a result of the disease, and mortality is premature.

The *carbohydrate metabolism disorders* refer to disorders in the digestion and breakdown of starches, sugars, and cellulose. One of the most common of these disorders is called galactosemia. Galactose is a substance obtained from lactose, or milk sugar, by the action of certain enzymes. When the body cannot effectively metabolize the galactose, it is found in high concentrations in the blood. This is the condition of galactosemia. The infant is normal at birth, but is unable to metabolize milk from any source. If the disease is identified early, the infant can be raised on a milk-free diet, and symptoms will diminish. It should be noted that the symptoms in this disease are extremely variable, reflecting different individual tolerances to the metabolic abnormality. In some cases, symptoms are fairly minor; in others, mental retardation and even death occur. Other carbohydrate metabolism disorders include glycogen storage disease, fructosemia, and hypoglycemia. Glycogen is a carbohydrate storage material for many animals, including humans. Associated with the malfunctions of glycogen storage in this disease is the development of toxic substances which damage brain tissue. In fructosemia, the body is unable to metabolize the sugars found in many common fruits. In some cases, this disease is harmless or asymptomatic, but in other cases, brain damage and mental retardation do occur. Hypoglycemia refers to a lowering of the glucose level in the blood. In recent years this has become a "popular" adult disease. Many persons complaining of fatigue, weariness, dizziness, lightheadedness, and so forth were diagnosed as having hypoglycemia. This, however, is not the same disorder that can result in mental retardation. The type of hypoglycemia that we are referring to occurs in early infancy and is associated with periods of dizziness, staring, and seizures. As the disease develops, general fatigue and weakness occur as well as disturbances in speech, vision, and intelligence. While it is known that this disease is a type of carbohydrate metabolism disorder, the exact mechanisms are unclear.

The *amino acids* are a large group of organic compounds, many of which are necessary for growth and the maintenance of life. They represent an end product in the metabolism of proteins. By far, the best-known metabolism disorder is phenylketonuria or PKU. This disorder was first described by Folling in 1934. It was reportedly first discovered by a physician noting a peculiar odor in the urine of two infant brothers who were severely retarded. Upon further evaluation, the metabolic disturbance was determined. It occurs in approximately 1 in 13,000 to 20,000 births. In this disorder, the body is unable to transform a protein called phenylalanine, which is present in most foods. As a result, a toxic material is developed which causes brain damage. Phenylketonuria is the result of a recessive gene. The discovery of this syndrome has been one of the greatest medical breakthroughs in mental retardation in recent decades. Not only has the source of this disease been identified, but effective prevention approaches have also been developed. Since brain damage results from the inability to metabolize phenylalanine, it was hypothesized that if this substance was eliminated from the diet, brain damage would not occur.

Basically, this hypothesis has been confirmed. However, the actual mechanics of dietary management are quite difficult. Because phenylalanine is present in most foods, the resulting highly restricted diets are unappealing to most children. Furthermore, a certain amount of phenylalanine is necessary for normal growth and development. Consequently, a diet must be constructed with just the right amount of phenylalanine. Too little of it leads to dietary insufficiency, loss of body protein, and cessation of growth, while too much leads to the problems of PKU. A blood test has been developed for the detection of PKU in newborn infants. Many states now require all infants to be tested for PKU right after birth. The possibility of early recognition and immediate dietary management has resulted in a significant decrease in PKU. The story of PKU is one of the most dramatic successes in the field of mental retardation.

Persons with PKU tend to have certain physical characteristics. The vast majority have less skin and hair pigmentation. About 90 percent are blond and blue-eyed. Many are microcephalic (significantly smaller than average skull) and have a peculiar, awkward gait. The mental retardation

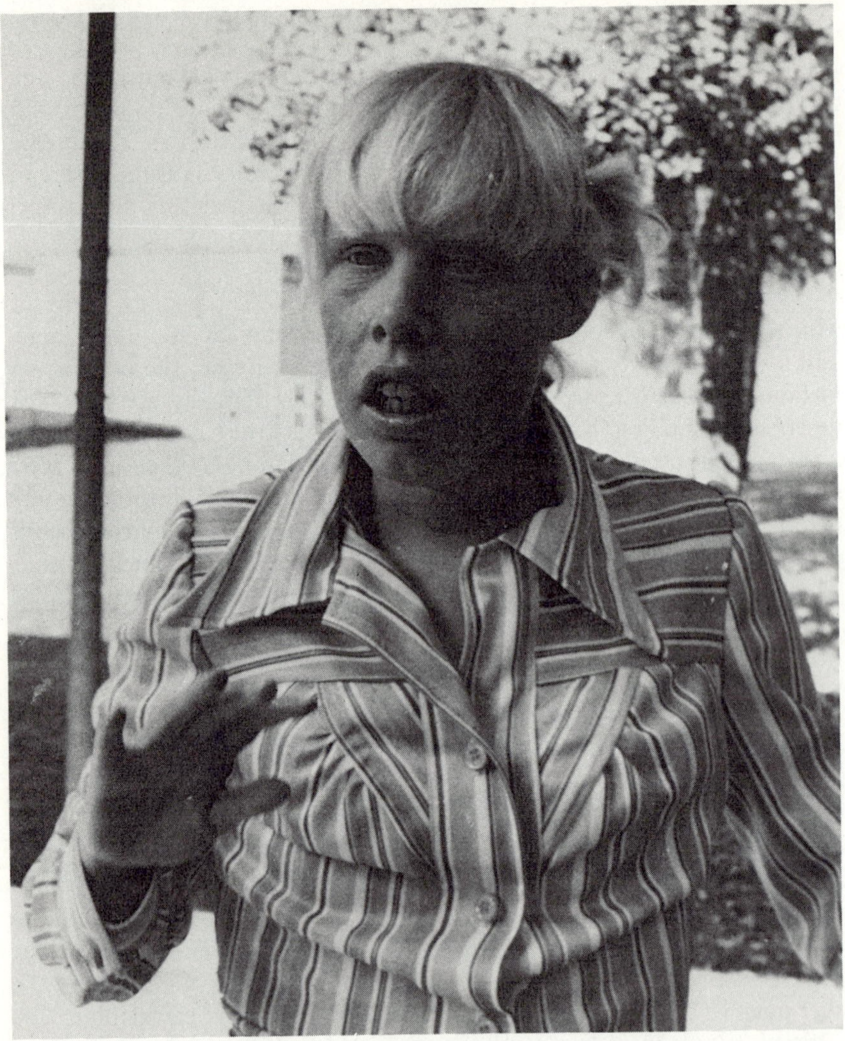

FIGURE 8.1

A case of phenylketonuria (PKU). Note the blond hair and light complexion.

in untreated PKU is usually severe, with most persons having IQs well below 50. The restricted diet often prevents severe retardation, but it remains unclear as to what proportion of PKU persons avoid significant brain damage. Recent data (see Sells and Bennett, 1977) indicate a minimal intellectual impairment for successfully treated PKU patients. A comparison of these patients with their normal siblings has indicated mean IQs of 94 versus 99 for the PKU and normal patients, respectively. Before the mechanisms of this disease became well known, many persons with PKU were erroneously diagnosed as having childhood schizophrenia or autism. These diagnoses were made because many PKU patients manifest odd and asocial behavioral patterns.

*Endocrine Disorders* This group of disorders results from malfunction of one of the endocrine glands, which include the pituitary, pineal, thyroid, parathyroid, pancreas, adrenal, and testicles and ovaries. All of these glands help to regulate metabolism and growth. Malfunction of any of these glands can be caused by genetic or environmental factors and can result in mental retardation.

The most common of these disorders is hypothyroidism, a decreased or total lack of function of the thyroid gland. The thyroid, located at the front of the neck, secretes a hormone called thyroxin, which regulates body metabolism. The primary thyroid disorder that results in mental retardation is called cretinism. (The reader should recall that Guggenbuhl, who founded the first institution for the mentally retarded in 1841 in Switzerland, worked primarily with cretins.) This can be a genetic or an acquired disease. The genetic form results from a recessive gene, the acquired form from a dietary lack of iodine. It is of interest that the soil of certain regions is low in iodine. Thus, foods grown there are also lacking in iodine. As a consequence, the diet of indigenous people is iodine deficient. This situation exists in many parts of the United States and other countries, where the deficiency is compensated for by the use of iodized salt.

In acquired cretinism, the fetus fails to fully develop thyroid tissue due to a maternal lack of iodine. Whatever the cause of thyroid deficiency, the symptoms are similar and noticeable at birth. The cretin baby typically has a large head, with excessively wide spaces in the frontal fontanel. (The fontanel is the soft space between the bones of the skull found in newborns and infants.) The nose is typically flattened, broad, and somewhat recessed toward the top or base. The forehead and cheek bones tend to protrude. The skin is usually very dry and scaly, and the forehead is wrinkled. Arms and legs are short, with excessive folds of the skin on the extremities. The skin has a gray, ashen, unhealthy appearance. The baby generally looks like an older person. During the first months of life, he is apathic, slow, and quiet. The stomach is large and somewhat protruding. The typical older person with cretinism is calm and quiet. There is no hyperactivity, anxiety, or other behavioral problems that appear in some other diseases. Although cretinism is an extremely complicated, multifaceted condition with several different causes, treatment is available. This demands careful evaluation and early identification of the condition. Hormonal treatments (e.g., thyroxin) are effective in reducing symptomology in a number of cases.

As indicated earlier, hypothyroidism is the most common endocrine disorder that can result in mental retardation. Other endocrine disorders can cause brain deterioration and low intelligence, but these conditions are quite rare.

### Gross Brain Disease (Postnatal)

This category includes a number of conditions that result from neoplasms or heredogenerative (inherited, usually degenerative central nervous system) disorders. The cause is unknown or uncertain.

A neoplasm is any type of tumorous or abnormal growth. Neoplasms in the brain can result in severe impairments of intellectual functioning. It is difficult to make any general statement regarding the relationship between neoplasms and intelligence. As we have mentioned, minor damage to certain parts of the brain can lead to severe losses, while even major damage to other parts of the brain sometimes causes unremarkable deficits. A similar case can be made for the effect of neoplasms. The type of neoplasm, its size and location all have a strong bearing on its effect on behavior. With some tumors, growth is extremely slow or may cease completely at some point. Thus, it is possible for a longstanding tumor to have relatively little effect on complex intellective behavior. Other tumors grow rapidly and can result in extreme deficits in a relatively short time.

The heredodegenerative diseases are a loosely grouped set of diseases genetically based and associated with a degeneration in the brain or central nervous system. *Neurofibromatosis* (Von Recklinghausen's disease) is caused by a dominant gene. This disease is marked by changes in skin pigmentation, with resulting brown patches or blotches, which can appear anywhere on the body. There are also tumorous growths on the skin, ranging in size from small, discrete dots or patches to large grotesque growths. The mental retardation in such patients is apparently due to tumors in the central nervous system which lower intelligence and produce seizures. The degree of involvement of the brain is quite variable, as is the resultant deficit in intelligence. Some persons with neurofibromatosis are of average intelligence, while others are severely mentally retarded.

Another disease in this category is *tuberous sclerosis*. The term "tuberous" refers to tubers, or nobby growths, while "sclerosis" indicates a hardening frequently found in the nervous system. Tuberous sclerosis is a familial (inherited) disease characterized by tumors on the lateral ventricles of the brain and hardened patches on the surface of the brain. It is marked frequently by progressive mental deterioration and epileptic seizures. There are also changes in skin pigmentation which may appear as coffee-colored blotches, underpigmentation, and certain butterfly rashes on the cheek, alongside the nose, and on the back. There may also be sclerotic patches in various internal organs and tissues. There are two forms of tuberous sclerosis. One type is severe and usually involves progressive mental deterioration. The other type may be much more mild and lead to no serious deficits in intelligence and behavior. In the latter form, even changes in skin pigmentation may not be noted. Although it is known that this disease is genetically transmitted, the exact mechanisms remain unclear.

Both neurofibromatosis and tuberous sclerosis are often grouped in a category of diseases called congenital ectodermoses. The ectoderm is the outer layer of the embryo from which the skin, nervous system, eyes, and various other tissues, such as the lining of the mouth, nose, and anus, develop. These disorders occur at a critical point in fetal development, which explains the distribution of tissue abnormalities noted above. The congenital ectodermoses are not limited to the two conditions mentioned here. As a group, they constitute less than one-half of 1 percent of all mentally retarded persons.

There are many other heredodegenerative diseases, all of which eventually result in mental retardation. A description of all of them would go well beyond the scope of this text. Furthermore, many of these disorders are quite rare. One condition, however, that does merit mention is *Huntington's chorea*. This condition is more common than many of the other disorders and results from a dominant gene condition. This disease may occur as early as four years of age, but is most common at later ages and often in adult and middle-age persons. The term "chorea" refers to a nervous disease characterized by involuntary and irregular movements of the muscles of the limbs and face. While these movements may appear well coordinated (i.e., not spastic or awkward), they are not under the control of the individual. The condition is also characterized by a progressive deterioration of intellectual functions.

### Unknown Prenatal Influence

The AAMD manual uses this category to cover all conditions that have an unknown or uncertain etiology and are present at the time of birth. These include primary cranial anomalies and other congenital defects of the brain. Cranial anomalies refer to atypical or abnormal development of the cranium, the bone cavity which surrounds the brain. Three such conditions are *anencephaly*, *microcephaly*, and *macrocephaly*. In these conditions, the suffix "cephalus" refers to the head, while the prefix refers to the size of the head—or, more specifically, the size of the brain. Anencephaly is characterized by partial or complete absence of the cerebrum (cerebral cortex), cerebellum, and the flat bones of the skull. This extremely rare condition is accompanied by severe intellectual deficits. Primary microcephaly is transmitted by an autosomal recessive gene and presents a characteristic clinical picture. As Grossman (1973) states: "The

FIGURE 8.2

A case of microcephaly. Note that the long hair masks the physical characteristics of the condition.

ear and nose are large, the nose joining the receding brow without a bridge, the scalp is redundant and furrowed, and the cranial vault is abnormally small" (p. 61). These persons usually have a small, cone-shaped skull, a curved spine often with a stooping posture, and typically severe mental retardation. These deformities often result in a monkeylike walking and hopping. A secondary type of microcephaly can occur as a result of adverse prenatal conditions, such as maternal infection (rubella), maternal alcoholism, and radiation. For example, follow-up studies of pregnant mothers (first trimester) who were near the epicenters of the atomic bomb explosions in Hiroshima and Nagasaki during World War II revealed a high proportion of children born microcephalic (Wood, Johnson, and Omori, 1967). The physical characteristics and degree of mental retardation are much more variable in secondary microcephaly.

The term "macrocephalic" means "large head." There are two types of this condition—primary and secondary. Primary macrocephaly is considered to be a congenital anomaly of the brain which may be familial. Patients with this condition are typically mentally retarded, epileptic, and sometimes have spastic paralyses. A secondary type of macrocephaly is a result of *hydrocephalus*. The term "hydrocephalus" means "water in the brain," which refers to an excess of fluid within the brain spaces known as ventricles. These ventricles contain cerebrospinal fluid, which also surrounds the spinal cord. Hydrocephalus typically involves a problem with the production, absorption, or the transmission of this fluid. In *primary* hydrocephalus, there is increased pressure within the brain and a disturbance in the absorption, formation, or circulation of cerebrospinal fluid. This condition typically begins soon after birth and causes an enlargement of the head before the sutures are fully closed. If it occurs after the skull has developed and the sutures have closed, there is a resulting increase of the pressure in the brain but no significant increase in head size. *Secondary* hydrocephalus refers to an increased amount of cerebrospinal fluid in the brain when the fluid has pooled in gaps left as a result of maldevelopment of the brain. In such cases, the cerebrospinal pressure is within normal limits.

Another method of classifying hydrocephalus relates to the cause of the increased cerebrospinal fluid pressure in the brain. In *communicative* hydrocephalus, there is an abnormally high production of cerebrospinal fluid or some difficulty in its absorption. In either case, there is an increased pressure of the fluid and often a resultant enlargement of the head size. In the *blocking* form of hydrocephalus, there is some obstruction in the transmission of the cerebrospinal fluid which again results in increased pressure and possibly an enlarged head size. Hydrocephalus can occur as a result of birth trauma, postnatal injury, tumor, infection, or other prenatal factors which often remain undetermined. In some cases, hydrocephalus may not result in an increased head size but simply in an increased pressure in the cerebrospinal fluid in the brain. In other cases, the head becomes extremely large and the cortex may be stretched to such an extent that it amounts to only a very thin layer beneath the skull with a large volume of cerebrospinal fluid in the middle.

The degree of mental retardation associated with hydrocephalus depends on the amount of damage to the cerebral cortex and other brain structures. In cases where the head is extremely enlarged, severe brain damage and significant intellectual deficits are common. In cases where the condition has been arrested, there may be no significant intellectual deficit. Operations for the treatment of hydrocephalus have been used for more than 20 years. This surgery typically involves shunting the cerebrospinal fluid out of the brain or absorption of the fluid by other systems. Drug treatments have also been used with some success. As might be expected, the success of these procedures is variable, depending on the initial cause of the hydrocephalus, age of onset, and how long the condition existed before treatment was begun.

The individual with significant hydrocephalus has certain characteristic physical features. The top of the head is extremely enlarged, with a protruding forehead. Hair placement is extremely thin, and the eyes may appear to be extremely widely spaced. In some cases, the head becomes so large that the individual is not able to hold it erect. Such individuals are bedridden or infrequently may have the head suspended by a sling mounted on a wheelchair. In these extreme cases, the individual also typically has paralysis of the lower limbs, visual defects, seizures, and a variety of other deficits. Premature death is very common in the more severe untreated cases.

## Chromosomal Abnormalities

This category includes a number of conditions which involve a disturbance in the chromosomal cell structure. The chromosome is the body within the cell that carries the genes, which are complicated, minute structures that determine the inherited characteristics of the individual. Thousands of genes are unevenly distributed among the 46 chromosomes found in all normal human cells. Syndromes associated with chromosomal aberrations (abnormalities) are numerous. The possible causes of such conditions include genetic mutations, radiation, drugs and other chemicals, viruses, autoimmune mechanisms, aged gametes (egg and sperm), and a number of other conditions involving thermal, temporal, geographic, and possibly economic factors (Grossman, 1973).

Down's syndrome is by far the most common chromosomal abnormality that results in mental retardation. Not only is there an easily recognizable physical syndrome, but it is also the largest single physical condition which results in moderate and severe mental retardation. This condition has been recognized for many years and was earlier referred to as mongolism. This name was given primarily because of the individual's slanted eyes and short stature, which appeared to be oriental. The condition was later more completely documented and specified by a Brit-

FIGURE 8.3

A case of Down's syndrome. Note the ear, eye, and facial characteristics, as described in the text.

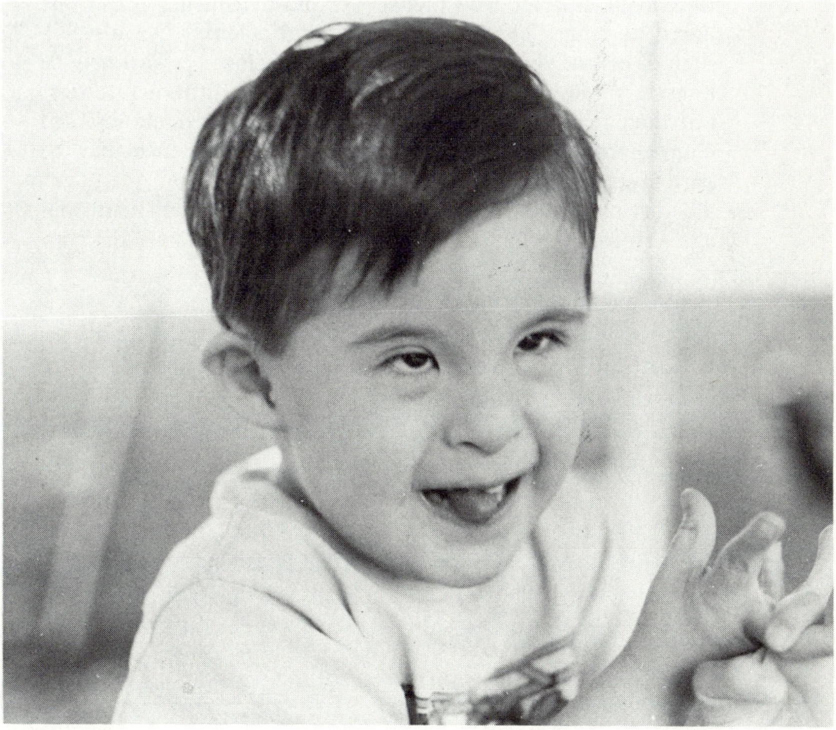

ish physician, Down, in 1866. In 1959, a third chromosome matching one of the 23 pairs was discovered. The specific pair involved was designated as #21, and the resultant condition is now called trisomy #21. Thus, the individual with Down's syndrome has 47 rather than 46 chromosomes, with extra material on the twenty-first chromosomal pair. While the transmission mechanism of Down's syndrome is known, the exact cause of this chromosomal abnormality is not fully understood. It is known, however, that one in every 660 births is affected and that the incidence of the disorder increases markedly with maternal age (see Table 8.1). Robinson and Robinson (1965, 1976) provide an excellent summary of the symptoms of Down's syndrome. Rarely, however, are all of these symptoms found in any given case.

1. Intellectual impairment, usually in the severe to moderate range of mental retardation (IQs ranging from the low 30s to the low 50s). However, there are also patients with both lower and higher IQs. School-aged children with Down's syndrome who were living at home have modal (i.e., most frequent) IQs in the 40 to 54 range. The majority of institutionalized Down's children of essentially the same age had IQs below 35. This may be a result of fewer learning experiences in the institutional setting, but there is also a greater probability for more severely retarded children to be institutionalized. Thus, the difference may be partially a result of a sampling bias.
2. The brains of Down's syndrome children are smaller than average, resulting in smaller skulls. Since they are shorter than av-

TABLE 8.1

Relationship between Probability of Occurrence of Down's Syndrome and Maternal Age*

| Maternal Age | Probability |
|---|---|
| 20–30 | 1 out of 1,500 |
| 30–35 | 1 out of 600 |
| 35–40 | 1 out of 300 |
| 40–45 | 1 out of 70 |
| Over 45 | 1 out of 40 |
| Population in general (mothers of all ages) | 1 out of 600 |

* Figures from M. C. Banker et al. *Will my baby be normal? Patient care*. April 30, 1972. Copyright 1972. Miller and Fink Corp., Darien, CT.

erage, their small head size may not be readily apparent, but as Robinson and Robinson (1976) indicate, the average fifteen-year-old Down's child has a head size similar to that of a normal two-and-one-half-year-old-child.

3. Down's children have a small skull in the lower ranges of the normal size which is flattened and shorter than it is wide. There is also an underdevelopment of the nasal bones of the skull, resulting in a flat bridge and a shallow, small, egg-shaped eye socket. The eyes are often slanting. There is a small chin, and ears that may look simplified and distorted.
4. Eye abnormalities include irregular pigmentation, with light-colored specks close to the outer border of the iris. There are often other congenital eye defects, including cataracts, poor vision, and pupil abnormalities.
5. There is often a delay in the eruption of the teeth, which tend to be small and abnormal in alignment.
6. There is often a large, fissured tongue, which tends to protrude from the mouth.
7. There is often a broad neck with loose skin at the sides.
8. There are short, broad, flat, square hands and feet with a shortened fifth finger, which tends to curve inward and often has only one crease. Also, there is often only a single crease across the palm of the hand and abnormalities in fingerprints.
9. The hair is often sparse, fine, and straight.
10. In approximately 40 percent of the cases, there is a congenital heart defect, often involving the valves and chambers. One-fourth to one-third of Down's babies do not survive the first few years of life.
11. Genital organs are frequently undeveloped, and there is a delay in the development of secondary sex characteristics. Girls with Down's syndrome usually begin menstruation at a normal age and it tends to follow a normal course. Sex drive is typically diminished in both sexes. A small number of women with Down's syndrome have reproduced, transmitting the syndrome to about one-half of the offspring. This is predictable since the chromosome pairs split in the production of ova, with about one-half of the eggs having a normal 21st chromosome and one-half with an extra chromosome (the latter leading to offspring with Down's syndrome).
12. The individual's stature is typically short, especially because of retarded growth during the first three years of life.
13. The skin is lacking in elasticity; it hangs loose and is easily roughened.
14. There are frequent speech disorders and a low-pitched, coarse voice.

Persons with Down's syndrome often also have metabolic irregularities and other physical conditions, such as leukemia. Although Down's syndrome is readily noticed at birth, the Down's baby has an essentially normal first year of life with socialization and motor development that is unremarkable. However, commencing with the second year, the intellectual deficits become more apparent. It is also during this time that the abovementioned physical characteristics become more pronounced. By the time the child is four or five years old, both the physical and intellectual characteristics of Down's syndrome are quite apparent. The aging process appears to be accelerated. Changes in skin, gums, teeth, and brain tissue typically seen in elderly persons are noted in Down's syndrome persons at ages 35 to 40. It is commonly believed that Down's children are more happy, cheerful, and easygoing than most other retarded children. Certain research data support this contention. Art Silverstein at Pacific State Hospital (1964) found that patients with Down's syndrome were considered more mannerly, responsible, cooperative, cheerful and, in general, better adjusted than other patients who were matched for intelligence and certain other variables.

Abnormalities in the so-called sex chromosomes have also been found to cause mental retardation. In *Klinefelter's syndrome,* males have an extra X sex chromosome and thus have an XXY arrangement. The extra X chromosome causes certain female secondary sex characteristics, such as breast development. There is also immature development of the male sex genitalia and sterility. Mild mental retardation typically results. *Turner's syndrome* is a sex chromosome disorder in females marked by an absence of an X chromosome, which results in an XO arrangement. As with Klinefelter's syndrome, there are abnormalities in secondary sex characteristics and resultant mild mental retardation.

## Gestational Disorders

Significant deviation in the normal gestational period of nine months increases the probability of mental retardation. The most common cases classified here are prematurity or postmaturity. "Prematurity" refers to the shortened gestational period and is defined as live infants delivered before 37 weeks from the first day of the last menstrual period. When exact dates are not known, prematurity is determined by an examination of the infant's level of development. Some studies have used the cutoff of 3½ pounds of birth weight to indicate prematurity. "Postmaturity" refers to infants whose gestation exceeds the normal time period by seven days or more. The extremity of the deviation in either direction increases the probability of birth complications and defects. A considerable body of research has developed on the causes and effects of prematurity. It is clear that there is a strong association between prematurity and low social class. Other contributing factors are extremes of maternal age, heavy cigarette smoking, and the mother's weight gain during pregnancy. As to effects, there is clear evidence of a high risk for adverse outcomes. In one study (Niswander and Gordon, 1972), it was found that the perinatal mortality rate was twenty-five times higher for low-birthweight infants than for larger infants. By the age of one year, the existence of definite neurological abnormality was more than three times higher in the low-birthweight group. In another follow-up study of 50 children (Drillien, 1967), 58 percent had IQs below 80 by age five and approximately 70 percent manifested some type of educational retardation or problem. In addition to impaired IQ, common problems of premature children include gross motor deficits, perceptual motor disturbances, and immature speech.

## FOLLOWING PSYCHIATRIC DISORDER

This category includes cases of mental retardation following a psychosis or other psychiatric disturbance in which there is no evidence of cerebral pathology. The relationship between severe psychiatric disorders and intelligence is a cloudy one. Several issues contribute to this complicated picture. First, in many serious psychiatric disturbances, there are gross abnormalities in behavior. In schizophrenic psychosis, for example, the individual's thought may become illogical, disorganized, or confused. With depression of psychotic proportions, the individual may become lethargic and unresponsive. In both of these cases, the administration of standardized psychological tests becomes quite difficult. Severe disturbance can result in erroneously low IQ scores which reflect the psychotic condition rather than intellectual deficit. Thus, one major problem in this area is the assessment of individuals who are psychotic. Typically we must wait until the acute phase of the disturbance has passed before an accurate assessment of intelligence can be made.

A second assessment problem in persons with major psychiatric disturbances is that some intellectual cognitive processes may decrease while others remain stable. For example, general information and level of word knowledge remain essentially intact. In contrast, the ability to think logically, to sequentially organize data and information, and to solve problems in ambiguous situations tend to decrease. Thus, with different types of assessment devices, we are apt to get significant differences in IQ scores. Despite the assessment problems in this area, the vast majority of persons who suffer even severe psychiatric disturbances experience no significant intellectual degeneration. Studies by Maloney and others (Maloney and Steger, 1972; Maloney, Steger, and Ward, 1973) demonstrate little decrease in general intelligence that can be attributed to the severity of the psychiatric disturbance. In one study (Maloney and Steger, 1972), patients coming to a large, urban, acute, general psychiatric facility were evaluated regarding intelligence, education, and a number of other variables. No differences in IQ were noted between patients diagnosed as psychotic (schizophrenia, manic-depressive illness, other depressive disorders, etc.) and nonpsychotic (personality disorders, neurosis, drug abuse, etc.). These data suggest that the severity of mental illness is not related to general intelligence. In the same study, a comparison was made between patients who were admitted to the hospital after their initial evaluation and those who were not admitted. Again, patients who were admitted were generally considered to have had a more severe psychiatric disturbance, while the patients who were not admitted had less severe conditions and were referred for outpatient follow-up. The IQ results of these two groups indicated no significant differences in level of intelligence. The authors concluded that the degree of psychiatric disturbance had no effect on general intellectual levels.

Low intelligence does result from some psychiatric disorders of childhood, such as childhood schizophrenia, autism, and even hyperactivity, but the relationship is unclear. Many such cases may have a neurological basis which is the cause of the low intelligence as well as the psychiatric symptoms. Research in these areas is unclear and often contradictory. It is important to recall that before the discovery of PKU, many children afflicted with this disorder were diagnosed as childhood schizophrenics. It is quite probable that many children now considered to have some severe psychiatric or emotional disorder may actually suffer from a still unrecognized disease. To complicate matters further, psychiatric conditions and diagnoses in children are often more unclear than in adults. Thus, it is difficult to make any summary statements regarding mental retardation and psychiatric disturbance. One thing, however, is clear: the earlier the disturbance occurs (providing it is of significant duration), the higher the probability that it will interfere with intellectual development. The child clinician always evaluates children regarding their development, socialization, intelligence, and all other relevant variables, and makes his recommendations or treatment formulations on an individual basis. In sum, the relationship between psychiatric disturbance and intelligence, especially in childhood, is a complex issue. Few general conclusions can be made.

## ENVIRONMENTAL INFLUENCES

This category includes cases with evidence of adverse environmental conditions and no sign of any other significant disease or pathology (Grossman, 1973). The AAMD guidelines for this type of condition have changed significantly over the past few years. It is instructive to review the criteria for this condition set forth in the 1961 AAMD manual. There, this category was entitled "Mental Retardation Due to Uncertain (or Presumed Psychologic) Cause with the Functional Reaction Alone Manifest." These criteria are similar to those of the 1973 manual, with the important difference that the primary subtype in the 1961 manual, which was referred to as "cultural-familial mental retardation," is no longer called by that name. The criteria for this condition were as follows: (1) an absence of reasonable indication of cerebral pathology; (2) evidence of retarded intellectual functioning in at least one of the parents and in one or more of the siblings where there are such; (3) some degree of cultural deprivation due to parental inadequacy. The term "cultural-familial" indicates the belief that both genetic and environmental factors are operating which together result in low intelligence. Heber (1961) states:

> There is no intent in this category to specify either the independent action of, or the relationship between, genetic and cultural factors in the etiology of cultural retardation. The exact role of genetic factors cannot be specified since the nature and mode of transmission of genetic aspects of intelligence is not yet understood. Similarly, there is no clear understanding of the specific manner in which environmental factors operate to modify intellectual functioning. (p. 40)

Thus, the 1961 criteria clearly indicate the presence of a genetic contributant to this condition.

In the 1973 manual, the syndrome name has been changed from "cultural-familial retardation" to "psychosocial disadvantage." Here, there must be evidence of subnormal intellectual functioning in at least one parent and one or more siblings where there are such. Further, these cases must usually be from impoverished environments, including poor housing, inadequate diets, and inadequate medical care. There may also be prematurity, low birth rate, and a history of infectious diseases. No single entity, however, appears to have contributed to this retarded development. In the 1973 manual there is no mention of a familial or genetic contribution to this condition. As Robinson and Robinson (1976) indicate, the 1973 specifications do not appear to be justified.

> Although there are plenty of environmental factors on which to pin much of the blame for cultural-familial mental retardation, it does not follow that deleterious genetic factors may not also be responsible, perhaps more significantly in some cases than in other ones. The 1973 position represents another swing of the pendulum in what seems to be an everlasting controversy about the contributions of heredity and environment to human capacities. (p. 168)

As we saw in Chapter 2, the attitudes regarding genetic and environmental factors have changed significantly throughout the history of mental retardation. Recent political and attitudinal influences may also have affected the changes in criteria. The present philosophy, illustrated by such concepts as normalization and developmental disability, deemphasizes the role of genetics in low intelligence and stresses the more optimistic view that if environmental factors are prominent, more change could occur.

The second category of environmental influences is sensory deprivation. This requires evidence of atypical parent-child interactions, such as maternal deprivation, or severe environmental restrictions, such as prolonged isolation during the developmental years. In this latter case, the term "attic children" has been used to refer to children who have been isolated in attics, closets, or back rooms for extended periods of their development. Actually, there are very few well-documented cases of this syndrome. One of the most recent was discovered in California in 1970. A summary of this case is used to illustrate this syndrome (see Box 8.1).

## ENVIRONMENTAL FACTORS AND INTELLECTUAL DEVELOPMENT

Throughout this text, we have stressed the combined effects of heredity and environment on intelligence. In this section, however, we will focus only on environmental issues.

As a background for this discussion, let us examine the *intelligence growth curve.* We know that the greatest amount of intellectual growth occurs in the earliest years of life. In fact, the rate is probably greatest during the first year of life. This has been demonstrated by child development expert Arnold Gesell (Gesell and Amatruda, 1947). Figures 8.4, 8.5, and 8.6 illustrate the growth in language functions, adaptive behavior functions, and personal-social functions in the first few years of life. The steepness of these curves readily demonstrates the high rate of growth in these areas during infancy and early childhood. Figure 8.7 illustrates the growth of intelligence throughout childhood and into adult life. It is clear that intel-

## BOX 8.1

### The Case of Genie

In November, 1970, the *Los Angeles Times* carried the headline "Girl, 13, Prisoner Since Infancy . . . the parents of a 13-year-old girl who still wears diapers and is unable to talk were accused . . . of keeping her a virtual prisoner in their Temple City home."

Thus begins the newest[1] case of an "attic" or "wild" child, the terms most frequently used to describe a person who from infancy or early childhood has had limited or minimal human contact and exposure to the environment.

Genie was discovered inadvertently when her mother took her to a local social service office. The mother, whose sight was extremely poor, was attempting to obtain aid for the blind. The social worker noticed that something was obviously wrong with Genie and contacted the police.

Genie was found to be suffering from extreme malnutrition. She had a pallid and sallow complexion and weighed only 59 pounds. Despite the fact that she was thirteen and one-half years old, she was only four and one-half feet tall. Her movements were extremely awkward, and she walked in an unsteady manner with an ambling, swaying gait. She seemed unable to stand erect and could not straighten her arm or leg joints. Genie had no speech whatsoever; her only verbal production was an occasional whimpering sound. She could not chew; she salivated copiously and frequently spat. She was extremely nearsighted and had great difficulty focusing on or seeing objects which were more than eight or ten feet away. She was also incontinent and had a pungent body odor.

Genie's bizarre story actually began long before she was born. Her mother was described as a cowed, passive, frightened woman who had once stated that her life ended when she married. Genie's father, who was 20 years older than his wife, was described as a twisted, sadistic, and antisocial man who frequently beat his wife and on many

[1] On April 18, 1978, a seven-year-old girl was discovered in Paramount, California, who has allegedly been kept in a 4 × 2½ foot, unlighted closet since age two. Her weight is between 20 and 30 pounds, and she is only 32 inches tall. She is obviously retarded.

occasions had threatened to kill her. Reportedly, he frequently stated that he disliked children and never wanted to have a family. Despite this dislike, after five years of marriage, Genie's mother became pregnant and gave birth to a baby girl. There was a good deal of turmoil and discord in the family at this time. The father reportedly beat the mother before the birth, which, however, was normal. After the baby was born, the father demanded that she be reared in the garage so that he wouldn't have to listen to her crying. The baby, although healthy at birth, finally died at two and one-half months from pneumonia and exposure.

Approximately one year later, a second baby was born. This one was male and reportedly had an Rh blood incompatibility. From the available data, it appears that this baby died when two days old, supposedly from choking on his own mucus. Approximately three years later, a second son was born. Although this boy also had an Rh blood incompatibility, his health was described as generally normal. His development was extremely slow during the first three years of life, and he showed clear adaptive difficulties with eating and other self-help skills. He walked and talked much later than average, and at the age of three he was not toilet trained. Again, it appears that the father constantly threatened the mother and forced her to keep the son quiet. When the boy was approximately three years old, the maternal grandmother interceded and took him to live with her. This apparently was a much more nurturing and healthy environment, and many of the boy's developmental problems were ameliorated.

Genie was born three years after the birth of this brother. She was born by caesarean section, as were her other siblings. She also had an Rh incompatibility, but this appears to have been corrected by a transfusion about a day after she was born.

Genie had her first pediatric evaluation when she was three months old. At this time, a congenital hip dislocation was diagnosed and a splint was prescribed. At subsequent visits to the pediatrician, at four and five months of age, she was found to be essentially normal for her age and sex. At six months of age she weighed about fourteen and a half pounds. However, when she was next brought back, approximately five months later, she had gained only a little over two pounds. At this time, she could sit up and balance herself, was alert, and had the normal primary teeth for her age. Her hip splint was removed, and physical therapy was recommended. Her father, however, refused this treatment.

Little is known of the details of Genie's first year and one-half of life. Her mother does report that she was not "cuddly" and that she did not coo and babble very much. She ate no solid food and even resisted "junior" foods. Genie's father apparently openly disliked her and did not allow her mother to spend much time with her. At 14 months of age, Genie developed pneumonitis and was taken to a pediatrician. This pediatrician did report possible signs of mental retardation, but because of her acute fever it was difficult to assess her development. The father apparently used the comment regarding her possible retardation to justify his subsequent isolation and abuse of his daughter.

Just before Genie was two years old, her paternal grandmother was killed in an automobile-truck accident. As a result of this accident, Genie's father became enraged and embittered, especially when the truck driver was acquitted of all criminal charges. The father subsequently moved the family to his mother's home. This move marked the beginning of what was essentially imprisonment and seclusion for the entire family. For Genie, who was less than two years of age, the situation was even more severe, for the move began a period of extreme abuse, neglect, and isolation. Genie spent most of her time in a small bedroom and was secluded from the rest of the family. Her father sewed a cloth harness by which Genie was essentially tied to a potty seat. In this apparatus she was unable to move her body but was able to move her fingers, hands, feet, and toes. Apparently she was tied in this fashion for hours on end, day after day. At night, she was removed from the harness but was then placed into another restraining device—a type of modified sleeping bag, also fashioned by her father. This sleeping bag was essentially a straitjacket in which she was unable to move her arms or legs. Not infrequently, she was forgotten and left in the potty seat harness throughout the night.

Genie's environment was almost completely devoid of sound. The bedroom in which she spent the most of her time was located at the rear of the house, adjacent to a bathroom and a second bedroom. The second bedroom had been the grandmother's bedroom. Genie's father would not allow anyone to enter it at any time, keeping it as a shrine to his mother. Consequently, no sounds ever emanated from this room. Occasionally Genie heard noises from the bathroom, but these were infrequent and limited to plumbing sounds. It is also noteworthy that Genie's father apparently could tolerate very little noise, so that even talking in the house was held to a minimum. Television and music were never played in the home. Genie's small room did have two windows, one of which was held open two or three inches all the time. She probably did hear some traffic noise but, again, her room was located at the rear of the house, away from the street.

Genie sometimes attempted to attract attention by making noise, but her father would not tolerate this and frequently beat her for it. A wooden stick was found in the room which apparently had been used by the father to beat her. As a result of these beatings over a long period of time, Genie repressed all vocalizations. Also, during these beatings her father never spoke to her. By his wife's report, he would make growling and barking noises in an attempt to scare her and also scratched her with fingernails that he let grow solely for this purpose. It is also reported that on occasion he would stand outside of her door, making these noises to warn her that he was there and if she did not stop what she was doing, he would come in and beat her. The actual details of Genie's existence are extremely brutal and abusive. From approximately two to thirteen and one-half years of age she lived in this manner.

Genie's mother was becoming increasingly blind. By the time Genie was 13, her mother was unable to dial the telephone. Genie's father would not allow her to call her parents, who lived in the area, or contact any other persons. When Genie was 13½ years old, her parents got into a violent argument and, finally, the wife was able to convince her husband to call her mother. Genie and her mother at last escaped to the grandmother's home. They stayed there for approximately three weeks, until the mother was advised to seek aid for the blind. It was on this trip that Genie's condition was inadvertently discovered. This ended Genie's isolation and began a new era in her life.

Genie's parents were charged with willful abuse and injury to the personal health of a minor—a felony. On the day of the trial,

Genie's father committed suicide, leaving a note that stated that "the world will never understand."

For the next eight months, Genie was hospitalized in Los Angeles and was treated intensively from a physical and psychological point of view. She was described as unsocialized and primitive, but also as alert and extremely curious about her environment.

In November, 1970, shortly after her admission to the hospital, Genie was administered the Vineland Social Maturity Scale and the Preschool Attainment Record. The results of both tests indicated that she performed approximately at the level of a one-year-old child. It should be noted that both of these tests reflect adaptive and social-competence abilities. In January, 1971, she was administered the Leiter International Performance Scale, on which she achieved a mental age of between four and five years. The results of Genie's testing suggested a great deal of scatter. In other words, she performed at fairly high levels on some types of tasks and very low on others. Many standard psychological tests could not be administered because they demand verbal interaction and Genie could say no words. She was extensively tested over the next five and one-half years.

Genie's prognosis was initially quite poor. Most of the professionals involved in the case felt that she would not be able to overcome the effects of her long years of deprivation and trauma. In her first six months in the hospital, however, Genie did manifest clear social and intellectual growth. She soon became dependent on the hospital staff and appeared to relate to them well. During her first months in the hospital, Genie was evaluated by many different professionals, primarily child development specialists and child clinical psychologists. As noted above, her performance was quite scattered. It became apparent that Genie performed better on tasks that are mediated by the right hemisphere of the brain and did poorly on tasks that are mediated by the left hemisphere. The left hemisphere is primarily involved in speech processes and logical associations. In this type of task, her development was quite poor. She did significantly better in such tasks as remembering faces, and in visual and tactile orientation. Also, she was quite efficient in finding her way around in physical space.

In June, 1971, Genie contracted German measles and had to be isolated from the other children in the hospital. The staff felt that this isolation might result in a major setback for Genie's development, and a decision was made to transfer her to a foster home. There, Genie had two foster brothers and a foster sister as well as the foster parents. Her adjustment in this setting was quite good. She was provided with a bedroom and a bathroom of her own and a large yard to play in. Her environment was different from the hospital environment in that the family made typical social demands on her and limits were placed on her behavior. She responded well to the foster family placement but did have some difficulty adjusting to the family dog. This was because Genie's father had made barking and growling noises to scare her. It is interesting to note that the father's barking and growling behavior first came to light after the foster mother found Genie clutching a picture of a wolf. When found, Genie seemed frozen in place with the picture in her hand and a look of terror on her face. After this episode, Genie's own mother was queried in some detail, and it was then that she reported the father's doglike behavior.

In January and March, 1973, two and one-half years after her discovery, Genie functioned at the six to seven and one-half year level on various psychological tests. Thus, in the first two years after her discovery, she had made significant gains in intellectual ability. She was using some language but still had significant problems in communicating fluently. She was given training in sign language, which further increased her ability to communicate.

By mid-1975, Genie had progressed significantly; nevertheless, she still had a severe developmental disability. She could now communicate, but only in limited fashion. She was able to read several words. She was described as rarely initiating play, although she did interact with other persons. Her social behavior was still often inappropriate; she would, for example, walk up to people and stare intently at them. Although she still had temper tantrums, these had decreased in both frequency and intensity.

Genie has made remarkable progress in many different areas. She has learned a number of self-help skills, has learned to communicate, and has learned to socialize and interact with other persons. However, her general level of intelligence and social competence remains significantly below average. She had been placed in TMR classes, which are for persons with IQs between 30 and 50. She is able to perform and act effectively in her immediate environment. It should be noted, however, that this environment affords Genie a good deal of protection, structure, and advice. She has been placed in several foster homes. At the present time she lives in a board and care facility, which provides for her needs and offers structured activities and supervision. At the time of this writing, she is clearly incapable of living on her own and coping with society. It is doubtful whether she will ever be able to do so.

---

lectual growth levels off at about 16 years of age and remains level for some time thereafter. These growth curves underscore the importance of the early developmental years in relation to intellectual ability. Thus, the quality of the individual's environment becomes a critical issue.

A great deal of clinical and laboratory data have been collected regarding the effects of early environmental experiences on intellectual growth. One of the pioneers in this area is psychoanalyst Rene Spitz, who studied children in two institutions. In both of these facilities, the infants received adequate food, and the hygiene and housing were considered excellent. Medical care was also more than adequate. In both institutions, the infants were admitted shortly after birth. Spitz (1945, 1947) reports that the institutions differed in one important factor: the amount of emotional interchange offered. In one institution, referred to as the "nursery," the infants were raised by their own mothers, who were prison inmates. In the second institution, referred to as the "foundling home," the children were raised from the third month by what Spitz refers to as "overworked nursing personnel"; one nurse had to care for from eight to twelve children. These studies showed that while the "prison babies" developed on at least an average intellectual level, the "foundling home" infants showed drastic decreases in intellectual development. The foundling home children "never learned to speak, to walk, to feed themselves. With one or two exceptions in a total of 91 children, those who survived were human wrecks who behaved either in a manner of agitated or of apathetic idiots" (Spitz, 1947, p. 168).

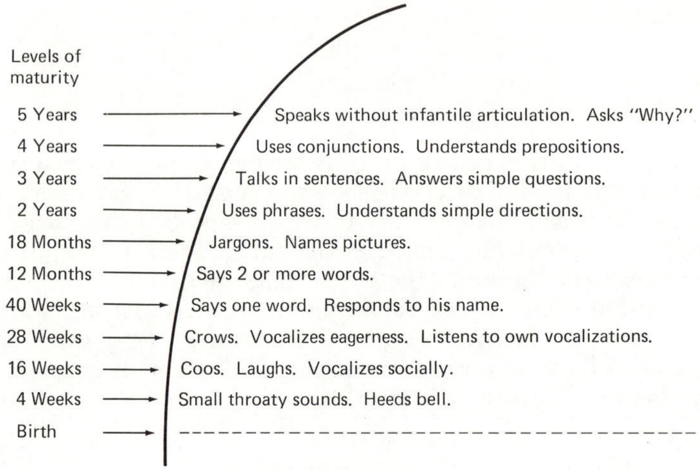
Levels of maturity
5 Years
Speaks without infantile articulation. Asks "Why?"
4 Years
Uses conjunctions. Understands prepositions.
3 Years
Talks in sentences. Answers simple questions.
2 Years
Uses phrases. Understands simple directions.
18 Months
Jargons. Names pictures.
12 Months
Says 2 or more words.
40 Weeks
Says one word. Responds to his name.
28 Weeks
Crows. Vocalizes eagerness. Listens to own vocalizations.
16 Weeks
Coos. Laughs. Vocalizes socially.
4 Weeks
Small throaty sounds. Heeds bell.
Birth

FIGURE 8.4

Developmental sequences of language behavior. "Language maturity is estimated in terms of articulation, vocabulary, adaptive use and comprehension. During the course of the developmental examination spontaneous and responsive language behavior is observed. Valuable supplementary information may also be secured by questioning the adult familiar with the child's everyday behavior at home." (Adapted from Gesell and Amatruda, 1947, p. 13.)

According to Spitz, the most impressive evidence is the mortality rates of the two institutions. Compared to the national average, the mortality rate for infants from the "nursery" was far lower. In a five-year observation period during which 239 children were each observed for one year or more, the nursery did not lose a single child through death. In the foundling home, on the other hand, 37 percent of the children died during the first two-year observation period. Spitz stresses that the infant mortality rate is only the most extreme consequence of the general decline, both physical and psychological, which is shown in children who are completely starved of emotional interchange. Spitz refers to this condition as "marasmus," which means "wasting away." While some investigators have criticized Spitz's study (e.g., Pinneau, 1955) because many details of the investigation were withheld to preserve the anonymity of the institutions, other data do tend to support Spitz's conclusion. Notable among these are studies done by Dennis (e.g., 1960) who observed children living in institutions in Iran. The general conclusion is that early deprivation has profound effects on the level of intellectual growth.

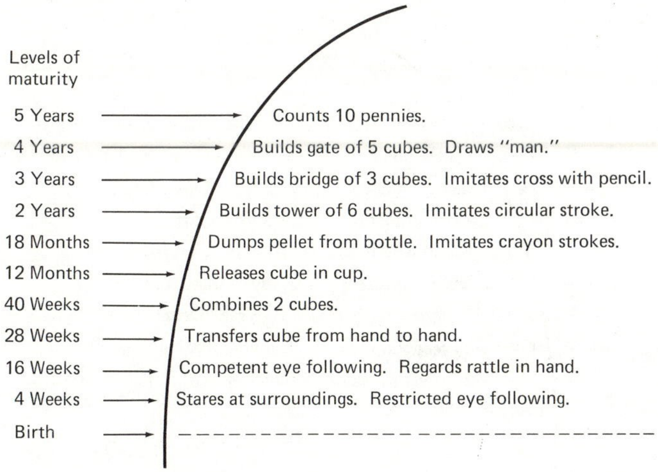
Levels of maturity
5 Years
Counts 10 pennies.
4 Years
Builds gate of 5 cubes. Draws "man."
3 Years
Builds bridge of 3 cubes. Imitates cross with pencil.
2 Years
Builds tower of 6 cubes. Imitates circular stroke.
18 Months
Dumps pellet from bottle. Imitates crayon strokes.
12 Months
Releases cube in cup.
40 Weeks
Combines 2 cubes.
28 Weeks
Transfers cube from hand to hand.
16 Weeks
Competent eye following. Regards rattle in hand.
4 Weeks
Stares at surroundings. Restricted eye following.
Birth

FIGURE 8.5

Developmental sequences of adaptive behavior. "To determine how the infant uses his motor equipment to exploit the environment we present him with a variety of simple objects. The small red cubes serve not only to test motor co-ordination, they reveal the child's capacity to put his motor equipment to constructive and adaptive ends. The cube tests create an objective opportunity for the examiner to observe adaptivity in action—motor coordination combined with judgment." (Adapted from Gesell and Amatruda, 1947, p. 12.)

These studies point out the critical need for an adequate amount of "mothering" and other types of stimulation during infancy and childhood. Spitz's studies point out the disastrous effects of extreme deprivation and the almost complete lack of mothering. These studies were done three decades ago, when orphanages and foundling homes were much more prevalent than they are today. Consequently, such extreme cases of deprivation are fortunately becoming more rare. However, what are the effects of less profound, but nevertheless significant, forms of deprivation and lack of experience in the early developmental years? Investigators have shown that children who are raised in extreme poverty show a disproportionately large amount of developmental retardation. It could be hypothesized that this retardation is a result of various organic diseases or causes, but no evidence of this has been found. It is strongly suggested (Bloom, 1964; Hunt, 1961) that the poor quality of the environment contributes to this slower developmental rate. In such homes there is some

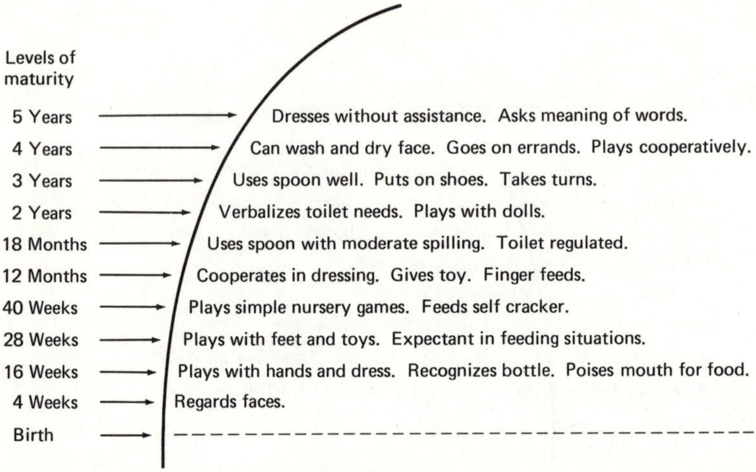
Levels of maturity
5 Years
4 Years
3 Years
2 Years
18 Months
12 Months
40 Weeks
28 Weeks
16 Weeks
4 Weeks
Birth
Dresses without assistance. Asks meaning of words.
Can wash and dry face. Goes on errands. Plays cooperatively.
Uses spoon well. Puts on shoes. Takes turns.
Verbalizes toilet needs. Plays with dolls.
Uses spoon with moderate spilling. Toilet regulated.
Cooperates in dressing. Gives toy. Finger feeds.
Plays simple nursery games. Feeds self cracker.
Plays with feet and toys. Expectant in feeding situations.
Plays with hands and dress. Recognizes bottle. Poises mouth for food.
Regards faces.

FIGURE 8.6

Developmental sequences of personal-social behavior. "Personal-social behavior is greatly affected by the temperament of the child and by the kind of home in which he is reared. The range of individual variation is wide. Nevertheless maturity factors play a primary role in the socialization of the child. His social conduct is ascertained by incidental observation and by inquiry. The chart illustrates types of behavior which may be considered in evaluating the interaction of environmental influences and developmental readiness." (Adapted from Gesell and Amatruda, 1947, p. 14.)

deprivation and lack of stimulation, but certainly not to the degree found in Spitz's foundling home study.

In poverty-stricken homes, the developmental deficit usually results in mild mental retardation. Children from such homes are considered at high risk for developmental or mental retardation. The identification of such high-risk children in the 1960s led to the development of programs to aid in their learning and development, most notably the Head Start program. This program was originally designed for preschool-age children. Its objective was to present experiences that would allow these children to "get a head start" on their schooling. Results from early Head Start programs (see, e.g., Cicirelli, 1969; Matarazzo, 1972) were disappointing. Participating children did not show the expected gains in development and learning abilities. Subsequent research demonstrated that the earlier such programs were instituted, the more effective they were.

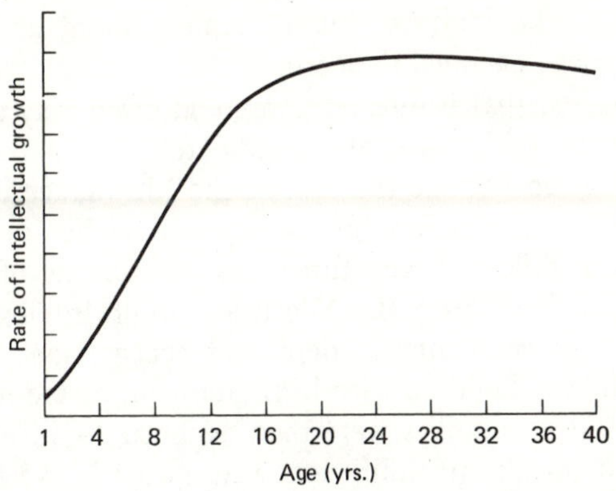


FIGURE 8.7

Illustrative curve of the growth of intelligence based on the repeated testing of the same individuals in the Berkeley Growth Study. (Adapted from N. Bayley. Development of mental abilities. In P. Mussen (ed.), *Carmichael's manual of child psychology*, Vol. 1, New York: Wiley 1970, p. 1176, Fig. 3.)

After Head Start, programs were developed for younger-age children. One of the most extensive and striking of these is the Milwaukee Project. This study investigated the efficacy of early, direct, intensive family rehabilitative therapy as a means of preventing mental retardation in families of high risk (Garber and Heber, 1977; Heber and Garber, 1973, 1975). In their early studies (Heber, Dever, and Conry, 1968), an attempt was made to find clues that would lead to the early detection of high-risk factors related to mild mental retardation. Two clues were found. First, although there is a higher incidence of mental retardation among the low socioeconomic classes, certain specific families among the most disadvantaged are disproportionately responsible for the number of mentally retarded children. From the high-risk survey area in Milwaukee (which had only 2½ percent of the city's population but 33 percent of the educable mentally retarded children), in one sample 45 percent of the mothers were responsible for nearly 80 percent of the children with IQs below 80. Second, these high-risk families could be identified by the low IQ of the mother. Mothers whose IQ was below 80 produced offspring who showed an intellectual growth curve distinctly different from that of the offspring of mothers who were of similar sociocultural background but of higher intelligence. The children of seriously disadvantaged mothers with IQs below 80 declined markedly in IQ level from normal to retarded between infancy and maturity. The high-risk infants were normal at birth; their intellectual development declined thereafter.

It was hypothesized that if intervention could occur very early, before the intellectual decline took place, the mental retardation could be prevented. This intervention became the task of the Milwaukee Project. The outline of the study is summarized by Garber and Heber (1977). Forty families, each with a child between three and six months of age and a mother with an IQ below 75 on the Wechsler Adult Intelligence Scale, were sampled from an economically depressed census tract area in the inner city of Milwaukee. Children with birth anomalies were not included in this sample. The forty families were then assigned to an experimental or control group. No significant differences were noted between these two groups on various measures of development in the early months of life.

The experimental group began a program lasting for six years. The program consisted of vocational and social education for the mothers and education for the children. Part of the program for the mothers consisted of job training with remedial education. Later work included parental counseling and family crisis intervention.

The children's educational program began shortly after they reached three months of age. The children were brought daily, year around, to a special neighborhood center, where specially trained staff and teachers worked with them. The children were placed in an elaborate educational program that was both extensive and innovative. The control group was assessed at the same regular intervals as the experimental group, but received no special training programs.

Significant results were obtained for both the mothers and the infants in the experimental group. The self-concept and self-confidence of the experimental mothers became more positive. They also changed the manner in which they interacted with their children. Not only were they more responsive to them, but they also became more verbal. Garber and Heber suggest that this change reflects their changed attitudes about their importance as parents. Control mothers, on the other hand, continued to have low self-confidence and viewed their children as just one more problem in life. They were also relatively nonresponsive in interacting with them. Garber and Heber indicate that the differences between the experimental and control children were even greater. On all assessment measures, the experimental children made strong gains. This is illustrated in Figure 8.8, adapted from Garber and Heber (1977), which shows mean IQ results for the two groups from approximately four years to nine years of age. At the end of this period, the control group had an average IQ of less than 80, while that of the experimental group was approximately 100.

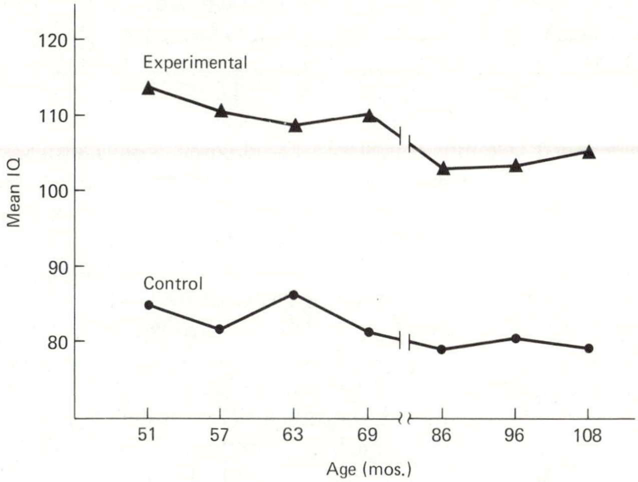


FIGURE 8.8

(Adapted from Garber and Heber, 1977, p. 125.)

The Milwaukee Project researchers sum up the results of their study as follows:

> It is our interpretation that early intervention into the lives of seriously disadvantaged families at risk for retardation with a direct, intensive and comprehensive rehabilitation effort can effectively prevent retardation, but it is important to note that neither are all such families doomed to failure nor can all such families be successfully helped.
>
> A more thorough understanding of the differences between disadvantaged families is necessary so that we can know to what extent certain families can mediate and extend the educational process of school, i.e., once given help to do so, and which families cannot, and so must have extended family support from outside. (p. 126)

## SUMMARY

In this chapter some of the causes of mental retardation have been presented. Although these causes are extremely variable and complicated, several conclusions can be drawn.

1. Low intelligence in mentally retarded persons is rarely the result of a single event or entity. Multiple variables interact to result in a certain level of intelligence. This is true even in cases where the cause of mental retardation is clearly known. For example, the cause of Down's syndrome (chromosomal aberration) is well understood. Despite this, however, children with Down's syndrome range from profound to mild mental retardation. Certain *physical* factors contribute to the final level of intelligence, but so do *environmental* variables, such as early experience, the home environment, and the child's learning experience. This is important to stress since it is tempting to be satisfied with a diagnosis rather than to consider the mentally retarded person as a unique individual.
2. Although there are several medical or clinical conditions that result in mental retardation, the vast majority of mentally retarded persons have no specific medical problem or known brain damage. While estimates vary, it is believed that less than 10 percent of the mentally retarded have a medical syndrome. Instead, the vast majority of these persons have a functional disorder.
3. Most mentally retarded persons are mildly retarded (IQs between 55 and 70). Most of the functionally retarded also fall in the mild range, while a majority of those with medical syndromes fall in the lower ranges of mental retardation. The lower the intelligence, the higher the probability of specific neurological damage.
4. Regarding the prevention or treatment of mild mental retardation, several conclusions seem warranted. First, it has been clearly demonstrated that the earlier the intervention, the higher the probability of success. This was substantiated by the early difficulty of Head Start programs to significantly improve the intelligence of mildly retarded youngsters. In these endeavors, an attempt was made to alter the learning experiences and environment of four- and five-year-old disadvantaged high-risk youngsters. It was quickly discovered, however, that intervention at this age was nonproductive. This led to the development of programs designed for even younger children. The Milwaukee Project has further demonstrated the need and efficacy of intervention at a very early age. Second, the growth rates of intelligence are the highest in the early years of life. There appear to be certain critical stages when intervention is most effective. When the child passes these stages, remediation or treatment becomes more difficult. This does not appear to be due to any permanent changes in the central nervous system or brain, but rather to the development of certain personality traits which are consistent with low intelligence, such as passivity and a tendency to be

anxious. Additionally, poor learning strategies are developed, and the child tends to expect to fail. All of these variables combine to develop a more chronic and stable low level of intellectual performance.

5. The cause of mild mental retardation is an extremely complex issue. In the vast majority of cases, it is not the result of a specific physical or medical entity and there is no demonstrable organic pathology. This is in contrast to the majority of the conditions considered in this chapter, wherein a single gene defect (e.g., PKU), chromosomal abnormality (e.g., trisomy #21), or severe environmental assault (e.g., infection, trauma, severe deprivation) may have overwhelming deleterious effects on the development and expression of intelligence. With healthy persons (including both normals and the mildly mentally retarded), it appears that a polygenic model of intelligence is most appropriate. Furthermore, as Robinson and Robinson (1976) state: "Polygenic modes of inheritance are fully consistent with a normal distribution of intelligence, and most cases of mild mental retardation can be accommodated within that normal distribution" (p. 76). However, it is also clear that social-psychological factors play a very significant role. This is shown by the fact that the majority of the mildly retarded are found in environments that are deprived in a number of ways. This brings us back to the original question: What causes mild mental retardation? Is it a result of deprivation or is it inherited? As the reader might expect, the answer appears to be, both. This follows from our conceptualization of intelligence as a dynamic, developmental phenomenon involving the interaction between heredity and the environment. This suggests that personality and motivational variables are both affected by intelligence and influence its development and expression. Thus, the statement that the cause of 90 percent of mental retardation (mostly the mildly retarded) is unknown is not exactly correct. The cause lies in the complex interactions of all of these factors.

Benton (1970) has developed a fairly inclusive multivariate model for the prediction of intelligence which can help us conceptualize the problem of mild mental retardation. (This model was also briefly discussed in Chapter 5.) According to his model (which we have extended somewhat), intelligence results from the interaction of multiple variables, each of which has several gradations. Included in this model are measures of cerebral, sensory-motor, emotional, motivational, and cultural statuses. For example, cerebral status refers to the integrity and efficiency of the central nervous system, especially the brain. That status is a function of the genetic inheritance and its interaction with the environment. The final level of attainment is determined by the quality of that critical interaction. The IQ test represents a vague, indirect, and relatively restricted and imprecise measure of that cerebral status. Cultural status refers to the environmental effect on the development of intelligence. Presumably, environments can be rated in terms of their stimulation value. Similar measures could be developed to rate the other relevant factors, such as emotional and motivational variables. The end result would be a complex equation that assigns various values to each of these factors.

What Benton's model suggests is that no one variable or factor necessarily leads to mental retardation. The major exception to this would be severe cerebral assault. This is the situation with the 10 percent of mental retardation that has a clear, specifiable cause. And these are the persons who are severely retarded; that one factor (e.g., defective gene) does exert an overriding influence on the development and expression of intelligence. However, even here, the role of the other factors (e.g., quality of environment, motivation) has an important moderating influence in the actual effects of these severe conditions. But in almost all other cases, it is the interactions among these many variables that become critical. Accordingly, the model allows for a wide range of possibilities. For example, a combination of low cultural status (e.g., deprived environment) and marginal cerebral status (e.g., less efficient nervous system) may be quite detrimental to cognitive growth, whereas low cultural status with superior cerebral status may be much less of a cause for concern.

Benton's model seems to account for much of the present data about mild mental retardation. While it is true that most of the mildly retarded come from deprived environments, it is equally true that the majority of persons within those environments are *not* mentally retarded. The proposed multivariate model offers a possible explanation for this situation. It is only when an individual from these deprived environments has additional deficits on one or, most likely, several of the other variables in the model (e.g., low cerebral status and/or poor motivation) that he becomes mentally retarded. All of these factors will be involved to different degrees in different cases. It is the individual of low cerebral, motivational, and cultural statuses who is clearly at risk for mild mental retardation.

Finally, this multivariate, interactive model must be viewed within a developmental framework. It is the developmental history of these interactive influences that is critical to intelligence. We cannot focus on cognitive factors alone; we must also address emotional, motivational, and environmental factors as well. This model provides a theoretical rationale for the need and efficacy of ventures like the Milwaukee Project. Given the dynamic, developmental nature of intelligence (and thus mild mental retardation), it is imperative that intervention efforts begin extremely early and focus on numerous factors in addition to purely cognitive ones. Mental retardation is much more than just low IQ; it involves personality and motivational variables as well. Accordingly, attempts at either prevention or remediation must also address these other factors.

# CHAPTER 9

# Social Psychological Factors

Mentally retarded persons have been the object of a vast amount of research. They have been compared to normals on general intelligence, learning speed, short-term memory, verbal reasoning, numerical reasoning, and an exhaustive array of other mental characteristics. Similarly, they have been compared on such physical characteristics as height, strength, head size, running speed, and myriad other traits. All of these studies are similar in their focus on characteristics of the mentally retarded and how they differ from normal persons.

In this chapter, we will look at mentally retarded persons from a slightly different perspective. We will consider how normal people respond to the mentally retarded person and what they expect of a person called mentally retarded and what general attitudes toward the mentally retarded are. This area of study is often ignored, but its importance is critical. What the general public feels about mental retardation has a great effect on such factors as the acceptance and success or failure of treatment and training programs, willingness to fund such programs (e.g., voting for certain issues), and professional development and education. All program, training, and treatment provisions for the mentally retarded are affected by public attitudes. Perhaps more importantly, these attitudes have a great impact on how mentally retarded persons are responded to and treated socially and interpersonally.

## SOCIAL ATTITUDES TOWARD THE MENTALLY RETARDED

Determining attitudes toward the mentally retarded may initially appear to be easy: simply ask a number of persons how they feel about the mentally retarded, what they expect the mentally retarded can do, and so forth. Unfortunately, the problem is much more complicated. Many variables affect the outcome or, in this case, the measured attitude. For example, if we ask people what they think of "mentally retarded" persons, we will get different results than if we ask what they think of "slow learners" or persons with a "developmental disability" or "mentally defective" persons.

The term we use to describe or label the object of the attitude (in this case, mentally retarded person) is the "referent." Even slight changes in the description of the referent or how the idea is presented can result in marked changes in the measured attitude.

To illustrate, let us examine the experimental method employed in various attitude studies. In some studies, subjects are asked simply to evaluate, or respond to, the concept of mental retardation in its most general form. They might be asked to describe or define what is meant by mental retardation with no additional information available. Other researchers have used a different approach. Instead of having subjects respond to an abstract idea (e.g., mental retardation), they determine how subjects feel about a particular mentally retarded person. This may be done by presenting a written description of a mentally retarded person, using a videotape, or having subjects personally relate to or work with a mentally retarded individual. There is a wealth of data to indicate that these differences in how the referent is presented do result in differences in attitudes (see, e.g., Gottlieb, 1975).

Differences in characteristics of the "respondent"—the individual whose attitudes we are measuring—can also have pronounced effects on the attitude we observe. Subjects who personally know a mentally retarded individual have different attitudes from those who do not. Many studies of attitudes toward the mentally retarded have attempted to relate differences in these attitudes to characteristics of the respondents. Although we cannot review all of these studies here, the point can be illustrated by using one variable: the sex of the respondent. Harasymiw (1971), after reviewing the studies in this area, concluded that women tend to have a more favorable attitude than men toward disabled persons in general. Greenbaum and Wang (1965) demonstrate a significantly more positive attitude toward mentally retarded persons by women. Also, women have been shown to have more awareness of the causes of mental retardation than men (Gottwald, 1970). Other variables, such as amount of education of the respondent, also make a difference, as do age and type of job.

Other more general issues also affect attitudes toward the mentally retarded. As was discussed in Chapters 4 and 5, the very concept of mental retardation varies from society to society. What is considered handicapping in one society or culture is not in another. Thus, it is not surprising that different societal variables affect public attitudes toward low intelligence. In more complex technological societies such as ours, even mild deficits are considered handicapping. In a more agrarian society, such levels of intelligence do not constitute a deficit; consequently, there are no corollary public attitudes.

This brief look at some of the factors that can affect attitudes or reactions to the mentally retarded illustrates how complex this area of study is. It also stresses the importance of caution in making any general con-

BOX 9.1

Factors Affecting Attitudes toward The Mentally Retarded

Many factors can have a great impact on attitudes toward the mentally retarded. Below are some of the characteristics of respondents and referents that can affect the development of these attitudes.

| RESPONDENT | REFERENT |
| --- | --- |
| Age, sex | Label—what he or she is called |
| Education, occupation | Severity of retardation |
| Socioeconomic status | Appearance and behavior |
| Personal knowledge of mentally retarded persons | Presence of physical defects |
| Degree or amount of contact | Physical ability |
| Tolerance in the society for deviance | Language usage |

clusion regarding attitudes toward the retarded. This must be kept in mind when we consider two related topics: stereotypes and the effects of labeling.

## Stereotypes

The term "stereotype" refers to a general social attitude toward a specific group of persons. English and English (1958), in their *Comprehensive Dictionary of Psychological and Psychoanalytic Terms,* define a stereotype as a "relatively rigid and oversimplified or biased perception or conception of an aspect of reality of persons or social groups" (p. 523). Guskin (1963) adds that a stereotype is a conception or set of ideas concerning a group or class of persons. He further divides the stereotype of the mentally retarded into three parts: (1) the content of the stereotype and the degree of agreement regarding these ideas, (2) the favorableness of the stereotype, and (3) the amount of distortion of the stereotype.

We could determine whether there is a stereotype of mental retardation and describe its content simply by asking people some general question, such as, Describe what mental retardation is and What are the chief characteristics of mentally retarded persons? This is the method that was previously described. The content of the stereotype would be the responses most frequently given to the term or concept of mental retardation. Recently one of the present authors asked an undergraduate class in mental retardation to answer several questions, one of which was, What is mental retardation? This was done on the first night of class, in order to minimize the effects of any learning or bias. Nearly 50 percent of the class stated that brain damage or an inherited genetic defect was one of the primary characteristics of mental retardation. Further, 80 percent mentioned an impairment in intellectual functioning, and approximately 10 percent indicated that mentally retarded persons "couldn't be helped," "couldn't make decisions," or were otherwise totally debilitated. The results of this brief, informal survey obviously cannot be generalized to the whole population. The fact that the respondents were college students enrolled in a class on mental retardation is a limiting condition. Nevertheless, it does appear that a stereotype of mental retardation was present. Guskin (1963) conducted a more formal study by interviewing 50 persons in the Nashville, Tennessee, area. An attempt was made to assure broad coverage of socioeconomic variables, age, and sex. Each respondent was asked to rate an average 18-year-old boy who had just finished high school, using a set of adjectives. They were then asked to rate an 18-year-old boy who had just returned home from a state training school for the "feebleminded or

TABLE 9.1

Terms Applied to the Mentally Defective*

| More Often | Less Often |
|---|---|
| Quiet | Talkative |
| Timid | Confident |
| Unintelligent | Bright |
| Abnormal | Normal |
| Strange | Ordinary |
| Helpless | Capable |
| Clumsy | Skillful |
| Unpleasant | Likable |
| Unfriendly | Friendly |
| Lazy | Ambitious |
| Irresponsible | Reliable |
| Sloppy | Neat |
| Careless | Careful |
| Nervous | Calm |
| Dissatisfied | Happy |
| Quick-tempered | Self-controlled |
| Inconsiderate | Good-natured |

* Terms are listed in the order of their discrimination between the normal and defective groups of boys.

mentally defective" on the same set of adjectives. The results of the study are summarized in Table 9.1.

Guskin's results indicate that there is a stereotype for mental retardation and gives some idea as to the content of the stereotype—quiet, timid, unintelligent, abnormal, strange, and so on. Another method for determining the content of the stereotype of mental retardation is to compare or rate different groups of people and state how similar or different they were. In this regard, Guskin (1963) asked a group of college students to rate 10 different boys on how similar they were to one another. The results of this study are summarized in Table 9.2.

## Stereotype Accuracy

After exploring some of the issues related to attitude development and looking at certain examples of stereotypes related to the mentally retarded, it is reasonable to ask, Which stereotype is most accurate? At first glance, this appears to be a realistic, legitimate question. However, when

TABLE 9.2

Judged Similarities between
Mentally Subnormal and Other Groups of Boys*

| | Mentally Subnormal Group Is Judged as | | |
|---|---|---|---|
| Other Groups | Similar | Not Sure | Different |
| Mentally ill | 28 | 2 | 5 |
| Emotionally disturbed | 20 | 4 | 11 |
| Delinquent | 18 | 3 | 14 |
| Worker's son | 8 | 6 | 21 |
| Crippled | 7 | 3 | 25 |
| Tubercular | 8 | 4 | 23 |
| Doctor's son | 2 | 5 | 28 |
| Athlete | 2 | 2 | 31 |
| Average | 1 | 1 | 33 |

* The mentally retarded are seen as similar to the mentally ill, emotionally disturbed, and delinquent boys but generally dissimilar to boys with physical disabilities.

we look closer, it becomes clear that the answer is elusive. Such a question involves two (possibly more) faulty assumptions: (1) There is some generality or constancy to a stereotype and (2) there is a broad and readily discernible commonality in persons diagnosed as having mental retardation. In the first case, we have already discussed the numerous factors that can affect attitude and stereotype development. It is clear that there is little constancy to the mental retardation stereotype. Second, there is no single common characteristic in persons diagnosed as mentally retarded. Some such persons are clearly physically and mentally disabled even to the casual observer. They may be incontinent, unable to talk, have further disabilities, and be totally dependent on others. On the other extreme, we have persons who are validly diagnosed as mentally retarded who are attractive, have no physical disabilities, and by all outward appearances—even in casual conversation—do not appear disabled in any sense. The stereotypes we have discussed do not accurately fit either of these extremes. Further, the stereotype or attitude often has much more consistency than the referent (mentally retarded persons) it is believed to represent. The term "mental retardation," or "developmental disability," is applied to a heterogeneous group of persons who simply cannot be grouped together and described as "timid," "quiet," "strange," or "similar to mentally ill." By definition they have intellectual and adaptive deficits, but these are complicated abstract ideas that often cannot be readily observed in either their physical demeanor or behavior.

The study of attitudes and stereotypes is important because it sheds light on the variables that affect their formation. Additionally, such attitudes can be assessed for their degree of distortion. This information is essential in designing programs to educate the public regarding the mentally retarded. More accurate public knowledge is especially important in light of recent attempts to "normalize" the experiences of the mentally retarded and integrate them into the community. This leads to the question, How can attitudes be changed?

## CHANGING ATTITUDES TOWARD THE MENTALLY RETARDED

The data from studies regarding attitude changes toward the mentally retarded (see, e.g., Gottlieb, 1975) are, unfortunately, inconclusive. Several of these studies (Cleland and Chambers, 1959; Cleland and Cochran, 1961; Kimbrell and Luchey, 1964) have focused on the effect of a guided tour through an institution for the mentally retarded on attitudes toward the mentally retarded. In this type of study, groups of persons (usually high school or college students) are pretested with an attitude scale or questionnaire. The groups then tour the institution and are again tested on the same questionnaire. These studies *do not* show a consistent increase in favorable attitudes toward the mentally retarded. In fact, in the Kimbrell and Luchey study, an increase in negative attitudes was noted. However, at the same time, there was an increase in positive attitudes toward the institution.

These results are not surprising when we examine a few variables. The studies in question do not provide data regarding the institutions, the type of program or ward visited, or the type of residents seen. Generally, however, severely or profoundly retarded persons are much more apt to be institutionalized. These patients frequently have physical deformities, are unable to talk, and are clearly severely disabled. This is especially true if the institutional tour includes a visit to the so-called "infirmary wards." The present authors have taken many groups on such tours, and the effect on the students is often dramatic—even to the point where the students discontinued the tour. This was not a response to mental retardation per se, but rather to such physical conditions as hydrocephaly or multiple handicaps. Even when such wards are not visited, institutional tours expose the public to the most severely retarded individuals. Resultant attitudes may indeed become more negative, probably because the tour presents mental retardation as a much more severe and negative condition than would be anticipated by most subjects. It must be remembered that only a small percent (less than 5 percent) of the mentally retarded are in institutions, and again, they are the more severely handicapped or disabled. If a tour was conducted in a productive work setting with mildly retarded individuals, would we also find no positive attitude change? The answer would seem to be no. We could go a step further and expose our experimental students to mentally retarded persons who live in the community, socialize, and live productive lives. Again, under such circumstances, we would expect positive attitude change. There is a scarcity of data in this area; further studies need to be done. On an informal level, the authors have witnessed such attitude changes on innumerable occasions. Many persons, in fact, believe that such persons "are not retarded." Again, it must be stressed that the vast majority of persons who fit the criteria for mental retardation are mildly retarded, do live in the community, and are frequently sociable and productive. When the public becomes aware of these facts, it seems clear that positive attitude changes will follow.

## THE SELF-CONCEPT AND MENTAL RETARDATION

"Self-concept" refers to how a person feels about himself and what traits he believes he has. The term also implies a certain stability over time. This is not to suggest, however, that it is a static phenomenon. Self-concepts change with experiences, both good and bad, with maturation, education, psychotherapy, and a host of other variables. These changes, however, are slow and gradual. Since self-concepts are a personal, individual phenomenon, we can make no general statements regarding what a self-concept includes or what has most importance. Some individuals may stress physical attractiveness or a sense of humor, while others see themselves as physically agile, intelligent, and popular.

For most persons, a self-concept includes a wide variety of traits. Thus, it makes little sense to ask, What is the self-concept of the mentally retarded? This would imply that there is one major characteristic that is more or less common to all mentally retarded persons. This, of course, is not the case. Mentally retarded persons have a variety of personal characteristics in addition to the fact that they are of low intelligence. It is important to ask, however, What effect does mental retardation have on self-concept? This question stresses that the effect of a person's low intelligence interacts with a number of other factors to result in his self-concept.

It has been suggested that the self-concept develops as a result of a person's experiences—more specifically, experiences with other persons and how they respond to him. This has been referred to as the "looking-glass self" because the self-concept reflects the responses of others. The process starts in early infancy, when the newborn cries and gets fed, later smiles and is cuddled, and so forth. His behavior has an impact on other persons, who respond to him in various ways. As the baby grows, the self develops when he learns that he is a distinct individual. The child thereafter learns characteristics of the self, and these become the self-concept. The careful observer can witness how this development takes place in young children. An example will illustrate this.

Eighteen-month-old Jeff plays in the old ashes in the fireplace, making a grand mess of himself and the room. He is reprimanded and scolded, "bad boy." Later, he is observed approaching the fireplace and saying, in an angry voice, "bad boy." If he continues to be reprimanded as "bad boy" for a number of different reasons, he will begin to develop a vaguely negative self-concept. Other persons respond to him as negative for what he does and, essentially, for the way he is.

### Self-Concept Experiences of the Mentally Retarded

As we have said, it is tempting to overgeneralize about *the* self-concept of the mentally retarded. It is also tempting to generalize about *the* experiences of mentally retarded persons. Obviously, such persons have a great variety of experiences. Some are pleasant, some are not. Some are normal, some are not. They do, however, have some fairly consistent experiences related to slow learning that most normal persons do not have. It is instructive to explore what these experiences might be at different levels of development. These comments will relate primarily to the experiences of mildly retarded persons, since, as we go lower in intelligence, the development of self is increasingly limited. At lower levels of intelligence, many interpersonal experiences have little effect on the development of self-concept. (This is not to imply, however, that persons of even very low intelligence do not profit from and enjoy interpersonal contact.)

*Infancy and Early Childhood* Mild mental retardation is often not recognized in infancy, and early development may apparently be quite normal. Even with the case of such conditions as Down's syndrome, where physical anomalies are quite obvious, development during the entire first year is essentially normal. As the child reaches certain developmental milestones (points at which specific skills or behaviors normally occur), the parent may notice that the child is behind or slow. In many cases, this causes little or no concern because development is typically not a smooth, continuous progression but is characterized by lags or spurts. Even children of superior intelligence have developmental lags where they seem to level off for a while, followed by continued development. When the mentally retarded child is consistently slow in a number of developmental skills (e.g., sits up at a later age, walks later, talks later, etc.), the parents may begin to feel that there is something wrong. At this point, the parents or significant others may begin to respond to him differently. The response may be negative and rejecting or overly protective or indulging. The nature of the response shapes the type of self-concept that will develop. The child may learn he is bad, useless, weak, incapable, good, lovable, or so on, depending on how he is responded to. It must also be noted that, although development is slow, many children are not recognized or responded to as mentally retarded by their families until later ages.

For the children who are recognized as mentally retarded, self-concept development is largely determined by how the family responds to them. This remains true during the early childhood years as long as the family is the primary source of interpersonal contact. As the child begins to play with other children, he may also be responded to as different from normal. This could vary a great deal, depending on how retarded the child is, how old and bright the playmates are, what they like to play, and so on. It is not uncommon that the mentally retarded child is rejected from play and may be called "dummy," "stupid," or some other derogatory name. Two points need to be stressed here. First, even with a protective, loving family, the child is apt to encounter such experiences. Second, this peer rejection is not simply a result of labeling (see next section). If the child's behavior is different and if he can't successfully engage in group games, he is vulnerable to peer rejection whether or not the peer group knows what his problem is (labels him). It is difficult for the mentally retarded child to avoid such experiences. In most cases, the fact of his low intelligence cannot be altered. The self-concept, however, can be altered. He can also learn (in addition to the fact that he has difficulty learning and is, in this way, different from others) that he is reliable, funny, hard-working, or has a host of other nonintellectual traits.

*School Years* When the mildly retarded child reaches school age, it is nearly impossible for him to avoid the fact that he is of below-average intelligence. If the child is in a normal class he will, by definition, perform at the bottom of the group and is apt to fail academically. These experiences must be somehow incorporated into the self-concept. Special class placement does not avoid this issue, since this is also a recognition of his learning problem. In the next section, we will review some of the research data on these issues. At this point, it is important to note that the mentally retarded child has these experiences and that they can affect self-concept development. Further, however, learning failures or difficulties are not a constant, continuing experience for the mentally retarded person in school. The child typically adjusts to his program, which is geared to his ability level, and learning difficulty as central to his experience diminishes.

*Adult Years* Since learning and, to a lesser degree, intelligence is closely related to school, it is difficult for the child not to be seen as "slow," "retarded," and so forth. This is not the case during the adult years. In many ways, mental retardation during these years can be seen as a silent handicap. For the average mildly retarded person, there is no physical stigma. The casual observer is not aware that such persons are mentally retarded. This presents a unique problem for these individuals since they themselves know they have trouble reading, writing, and making mathematical computations, and many other problems as well. At the same time, people are apt to expect them to complete such tasks. As a result, many mildly retarded persons try to avoid problem situations. They "pass" as normal—that is, they behave in certain ways under certain conditions to cover their handicap. An example will illustrate this point.

The authors do frequent consultations for the Superior Court and conduct evaluations on persons awaiting trial. During these evaluations, the issue of whether an individual is capable of understanding the waiver of his Miranda rights arises. These rights are usually stated by the arresting officer, who instructs the individual that he has the right to remain silent and to have an attorney present and that, if he does talk, the information may be used against him. The officer may hand a copy of these rights to the individual and ask him if he can read and understand them. In many cases, the arrested individual who is mildly retarded answers "yes" to avoid or cover the fact that he is unable to read and may not know what some of the words mean.

Consider also the mentally retarded person who accepts change for a purchase but cannot calculate whether it is correct. He may also give an incorrect amount (lesser) for a purchase and get a negative response from the clerk. Or, he may ask for directions or information about some product and be told, "It's right there [on a label or sign]—read it." These examples point up some of the difficulties of the mentally retarded adult who lives in the community. It is not difficult to imagine how limited intelligence could also affect interpersonal relationships, dating, and the like. These are all experiences which the mentally retarded person is apt to have and which do affect his self-development.

In this section, we have presented some of the experiences that a mentally retarded person might have. It is difficult for these persons to avoid some of these experiences, and it is presumed that such experiences affect the self-concept. These negative experiences are just one facet of the individual's total life; he has many other experiences, both positive and negative. Mentally retarded persons who are responded to by others as retarded must incorporate low intelligence into their self-concept. Realistic self-appraisal is considered desirable; in this regard, their low competence must be integrated into their self-concept. Two additional goals are indicated. First, the mentally retarded person must be helped to develop positive self-experiences. Second, as Anderson and Messick (1974) conclude: "Here is a case in which the goal is not necessarily to develop higher and higher feelings of worth, but rather to avoid any instances of extremely negative self-depreciation" (p. 289).

## LABELING

One of the most controversial topics in the field of mental retardation today is labeling. The negative effects of labeling have been stressed for some time (e.g., Dunn, 1968; Jones, 1972; Mercer, 1971). While it may seem convincing, or even logical, to assume that labeling a person as mentally retarded has negative effects, this is not supported by research data. Before we can draw any conclusions, however, several issues need to be explored. As we have noted in regard to attitudes, responses to mentally retarded persons are very complicated and have multiple determinants. This complexity is true of labeling as well. This becomes immediately apparent when we attempt to state what labeling means. At first glance, it may seem to be a simple, straightforward task. Labeling simply means calling a person mentally retarded. This answer, however, leads to a number of questions.

For example, does placement in a class for the educable mentally retarded constitute labeling? Does formal labeling, as done in the school or other institution, have a significantly different effect on the individual, compared to informal labeling (e.g., in peer groups)? If an individual identifies himself as mentally retarded, does this constitute labeling? Numerous similar questions could also be asked. Further, when we talk about the effect of a label on a mentally retarded person, we must keep in mind that at some level of intelligence labeling probably has no impact on him because he is unable to appreciate what the label means or even that it discriminates him from others. Thus, when we discuss labeling, we are typically referring to the labeling of mildly retarded school children by the school system.

It is pertinent to explore how the process of labeling takes place in such a setting. First, a child manifests some difficulty in his schoolwork and is then referred for evaluation. In other words, classes or groups of children are not tested in a blanket fashion, regardless of school performance, and placed in special classes and labeled as mentally retarded. When the child is evaluated, the psychologist responsible uses appropriate tests and evaluates adaptive behavior as well as intelligence. Finally, the children who perform below certain cutoffs in intelligence and adaptive behavior may be called mentally retarded and placed in a special class. The actual label of mental retardation (EMR, etc.) may or may not be used and may or may not be made public to the child or his peers. Given this sequence of events, how do we determine what effect the label itself has had? The child has performed poorly in his regular class and is then placed in a special class. How can we separate the effects of these variables from the effect of the label? These are some of the methodological problems that confront researchers in this area.

A second problem also needs to be mentioned. MacMillan et al. (1974), in an excellent review article, comment that "as authors discuss the labeling issue, there is frequent reference made to the 'devastating,' 'long-lasting,' and 'traumatic' effects of being labeled mentally retarded. Often, the authors fail to specify *what* is affected by the label" (p. 245, italics ours). Different studies use a wide variety of dependent variable measures. Some investigators use peer rejection as the dependent measure, while others use self-esteem or self-concept. MacMillan et al. (1974) also note that two different studies may both examine the effects of labeling on, for example, self-esteem but use different ways of measuring it. Several different measures are believed, or have been demonstrated, to be sensitive to labeling. These include self-concept, peer rejection, level of aspiration, expectancies by teachers, a variety of adult indices such as marital adjustment and job success, and the child's dislike of being labeled. With any of these measures, the researcher must make certain that any purported effect of a label is not confounded with other variables, such as special class placement, social awkwardness, and so on. Much of the published research has not separated such variables, and the results are consequently unclear. With these complexities in mind, we will look at the conclusions of MacMillan et al. (1974) regarding the effects of labeling on various measures.

*Self-Concept* No evidence has been found to indicate a direct relationship between self-concept and labeling. Most of the data on this issue are confounded with special class placement. Some of these studies (Borg, 1966; Jones, 1973, Mann, 1960; Meyerowitz, 1962) have shown a slightly lower self-concept in labeled children. Other studies (Drews, 1962; Goldberg, Passow, and Justman, 1961) have found a higher self-concept. Still other studies have found no difference. MacMillan et al. believe that these findings are difficult to interpret and do not warrant any specific conclusions.

*Peer Rejection or Acceptance* The hypothesis investigated in these studies is that children labeled as mentally retarded are less popular and less often selected by their peers for activities, friendships, and so on. Here, we must ask whether mentally retarded children are rejected because of their label or for other reasons, such as atypical or bothersome behavior, an inability to relate effectively in groups, and so on. Data from these studies, again, are inconclusive. In the studies that do show some peer rejection, it seems plausible that this is a response to their behavior rather than to their label per se.

*Self-Fulfilling Prophecy* The idea of the self-fulfilling prophecy has received a good deal of attention and popular acceptance. According to this idea, labeling, especially regarding intelligence, sets up certain expectancies regarding performance for teachers and others who might work with children or students. Two possible dynamics are involved. First, an individual who knows that the child is mentally retarded might communicate this to him, resulting in the child devaluing himself. This self-denigration results in poorer or different performance.

Second, the individual (teacher, etc.) may behave differently than he would if he did not know the child was mentally retarded. This somehow results in altered performance or perceived performance of the child. A number of researchers, most notably Dexter (1956, 1958, 1960, 1964), have strongly emphasized the impact of this phenomenon and concluded that much of the behavior of the labeled retarded is a result of other persons' expectations and treatment of them. One of the most often cited studies in this area is that of Rosenthal and Jacobson (1966, 1968), who investigated the relationship between teacher expectation and school achievement. They divided a group of children who were all at about the same level of achievement into two groups—an experimental and a control group. These groups were then randomly assigned to different classes, and the teachers were told they could expect outstanding performance from certain children (experimental group). Teachers were told nothing about the control group. At the end of the school year, the experimental children performed at a higher achievement level than did the control children. It is suggested that the teachers' expectations, in some subtle way, resulted in their relating to or teaching the children in a different manner. It is further suggested by many authors (e.g., see Smith, 1971) that these same expectations affect teachers and parents when they consider educational plans of children in light of IQ scores. We might expect more from a child with an IQ of 90 than one with an IQ of 80. Do these expectations actually affect the child's performance? Rosenthal refers to this self-fulfilling prophecy as the "Pygmalion effect."

Despite the popularity of this idea, it remains unclear as to how labels actually affect behavior. The Rosenthal-Jacobson studies have been criticized on a number of bases. MacMillan (1971, p. 6), after reviewing these studies, concludes, "If one could extrapolate so easily from the Rosenthal and Jacobson (1968) work . . . the problem could be solved immediately by simply labeling the children under consideration 'gifted' and thereby increase the teacher's expectancy for them to succeed." MacMillan et al. (1974) also cite the conclusion of Thorndike (1968) regarding the Rosenthal study: "Alas, it is so defective technically that one can only regret that it ever got beyond the eyes of the original investigators! Though the volume may be an effective addition to educational propagandizing, it does nothing to raise the standards of educational research (p. 208)." Thorndike here refers to the fact that the study was fraught with problems involving control groups, subject selection, teacher rating differences, generalization of the findings, and so forth.

Even from this brief discussion, it becomes clear that the available data on the effects of the labeling are unclear. Certainly they do not support the popular (e.g., Mercer, 1971) belief by many workers in mental retardation that labeling is always negative. In fact, some studies (e.g., Gersh and Jones, 1973) have demonstrated positive effects. Mentally retarded persons are sometimes rated higher in social acceptance when they are labeled. This may, at first, appear difficult to understand but several explanations, such as that of MacMillan et al., are available. Their conclusion rests on the theory of "cognitive dissonance," which states that a person's perception of another person, situation, and so on is largely determined by the perceiver's attitudes, beliefs, or expectations. These, in turn, are largely affected by what is generally considered "normal." When a person perceives some behavior that is considered deviant, unexpected, unexplained, abnormal, and so on, he is in a state of dissonance. A drive is then created to decrease the dissonance.

One way this dissonance can be reduced is by developing some other explanation for what is perceived. With a mentally retarded child, normal children may look at his behavior and see it as inappropriate to the normal standard. (The standard is an informal expectation of an individual or group.) Dissonance is created because the mentally retarded do not behave as expected. The normal child may respond by categorizing the mentally retarded person as "weird" or "odd" and then shun him. However, when the child is labeled mentally retarded, there is an explanatory (cognitive) device that decreases the dissonance. This may even result in a more positive, helping attitude on behalf of normal children. The data suggest that this does occur.

## Post-School Adjustment

Thus far, we have examined the possible effect of labeling primarily during the school years. However, it is also contended that the effects of labeling are lifelong. This can be determined to some degree by evaluating the adult adjustment of persons who were labeled mentally retarded in school. Many studies have been done on this issue, and it is impossible to summarize them here. However, several points need to be made. First, persons with critically low intelligence (IQ below 70) have more difficulty coping with a modern technological society such as ours. It would be quite surprising if students who were labeled EMR or TMR in school did not have more difficulty in later years with occupational-vocational pursuits. Behaviorally, however, the mildly retarded blend quite well into the general population. Guskin and Spiker (1968) conclude:

> It hardly seems necessary to do further research to demonstrate that the average educable mentally retarded adult does more poorly economically and socially than the non-retarded adult. Nor is there much point in continuing to demonstrate that the typical retarded individual makes a somewhat satisfactory adjustment to adult life and that few mentally retarded are a serious threat to the community. (p. 266)

The majority of data support this conclusion. Further, the mentally retarded person's lower level of functioning results from his lesser ability, fewer skills, and occasionally personality factors. Data do not indicate that labeling, by itself, has a primary effect on such adjustment variables.

## Reactions of Mentally Retarded Persons to Being Labeled

Thus far, we have examined a number of the alleged effects of labeling. Despite the difficulties of research design and interpretation of data, there is little evidence that labeling, alone, has significant effects on self-concept, others' expectations, postschool adjustment, etc. Ironically, the one area where labeling does appear to have a clear and negative effect has been the subject of little research. The data that are available, however, strongly indicate a broad negative response by mentally retarded persons to being called "mentally retarded." This is not surprising, since mental retardation is generally considered negative in our society. This negative reaction to being labeled occurs almost totally in the mild range. At the lower levels of intelligence, there is an increasing inability to understand what the label means and what it implies. One of the present authors asked a 21-year-old moderately retarded man if other youths called him names when he was in school. He responded, "Yeah, they called me M.R." When asked what this meant, he replied, "For a long time I thought it meant Mister." This is obviously not a typical case, but it does illustrate how labels might be misinterpreted even at the moderate range (IQs 40–55) of mental retardation. Even at lower levels, however, mentally retarded persons place importance on labels. This is illustrated by the terms "high grade" and "low grade," which are often used by institutionalized residents to refer to each other. When queried, many of those who used these labels did not really know what they meant. For many of the mildly retarded, however, there is a clear understanding of such labels and a strong feeling that they are derogatory. Consequently, they attempt to avoid such labels and try to give no information that might indicate their lack of intelligence, ability, and so on.

The negative response of the mentally retarded to these labels presents a difficult problem. They do have a handicap that cannot be ignored. It is strongly recommended that labels be used only when necessary—for administrative or classification purposes. Rarely do such labels need to be used in interacting with the mentally retarded person.

## SUMMARY

Up to the early 1900s, mental retardation, then referred to as "idiocy," "imbecility," "feeblemindedness," etc., was considered a form of extreme deviance and associated with physical abnormalities. The societal response to this condition was also extreme, resulting in inaccurate stereotypes of mental retardation. The recent (1960s on) professional reaction to labeling stems, at least in part, from a fear that these extreme attitudes refer to all mentally retarded persons. There has also been concern about the legal consequences of labeling and finally, a concern that labeling is a negative, dehumanizing experience for mentally retarded persons. Other more extreme claims about the devastating consequences of labeling have also been made. Research data, as we have seen, do not support these claims.

At this point, several conclusions can be drawn. First, in an abstract sense, labeling is neither good nor bad. When used to support the early stress on negative eugenics (restricting procreation of less intelligent persons), labeling could be considered bad. When used to support President Kennedy's proposals for advancement in the area of mental retardation, labeling became more positive. Second, as Begab (1975) points out, we must distinguish between labeling and classification. Labeling is a personal issue. A given individual is referred to as mentally retarded. Classification, on the other hand, is an impersonal procedure which has definite purposes. Such systems are needed to provide a basis for measuring incidence, prevalence, characteristics, and related information regarding the effectiveness of programs and treatment. Such data are also needed from a political-economic perspective when funding is contingent on the number of persons at different levels of mental retardation. Third, children or adults whose behavior is deviant (because of low intelligence) will be labeled by peers or others. While they may be called "weird," "odd," "out of it," or the like, they are nevertheless labeled. It may well be more humanistic to use formal labels which are at least standard and not derogatory.

Finally, although research findings do not suggest dropping labels, two points need to be emphasized. First, labels should be used only when there is some specific need and utility. This is because mentally retarded persons do not like to be called retarded, and every effort should be made to respect this desire. Second, what needs to be avoided at all costs is mislabeling. The more labeling becomes a routine practice, the higher the risk that individuals will be mislabeled. Such persons may then be referred to inappropriate programs, excluded from others, or in some other way treated inappropriately. This might occur, for example, when mental retardation is determined solely on the basis of IQ when, in fact, the person's performance was low for some nonintelligence reason.

We cannot conclude that labels are generally good or bad. The judicious use of labels can expedite certain administrative or program situations. In this sense, labels may be seen as positive. Indiscriminate use of labels may promote stereotyped attitudes; then the effect is always negative.

# CHAPTER 10

# Treatment Provisions for the Mentally Retarded

You would set them free?
So we can be free.
Where will they go?
Where we go.
*Burton Blatt* (1975)

Scores of books and thousands of articles have been written about the treatment of mental retardation. In fact, more is written about this topic than any other aspect of the field. This is because mental retardation today is seen as a significant, practical, social problem that demands immediate attention and intervention. Consequently, historically, as well as currently, treatment has been the focus of concern. The first two major books ever written on the subject of mental retardation (i.e., Itard, 1801; Seguin, 1846) were essentially treatment texts. While such important issues as etiology, definition, classification, and assessment are important in their own right, as well as critical to the treatment process itself, the major emphasis has always been and will continue to be on practical solutions here and now.

As mentioned in Chapter 1, it is impossible to summarize the vast and complex literature on the treatment of mental retardation here. Most introductory textbooks have resolved this dilemma in one of two ways: (1) they focus only on selected treatment provisions (e.g., special classes, institutionalization) or treatment procedures or techniques (e.g., behavior modification, diagnostic-prescriptive teaching) in some detail or (2) they devote several chapters to the whole subject of treatment, attempting to attain both breadth and depth. In either case, there is a focus on the specifics of the treatment process. In this text, we shall take a much broader conceptual approach. There are several reasons for this decision. First, consistent with our general approach, a conceptual orientation seems most appropriate for the introductory student. Detailed discussions of specific procedures tend to hinder the student's ability to see the overall picture. Also, the vast majority of students taking an introductory course will not work in this field. Accordingly, an overview of the problems and major issues in this area seems most useful.

Second, most discussions of the specifics of treatment must usually be preceded by coverage of the underlying theories. For example, many texts that present behavior modification approaches often include the underlying principles of learning theory. Such theoretical discussions are best handled in courses that deal specifically with these topics. Similarly, the application of such theoretical principles to a field like mental retardation is more effectively handled in advanced "methods" courses for students specializing in the area.

The third reason, however, was the major determining factor in our decision to take a general conceptual approach. We recognize that over the last decade or so, there has been a virtual revolution in the general philosophy that governs all treatment considerations. In the past, discussions about treatment were devoted almost entirely to specific treatment procedures, approaches, and issues from a purely scientific or technical perspective. There was often a focus on the "how to" aspects of the various techniques, as well as on an evaluation of their appropriateness and effectiveness. However, in the last decade, this approach has been overshadowed by a more general concern with various nonscientific and nontechnical issues. Today, a variety of philosophical, humanistic, ethical, and legal issues and concerns have become the most prominent considerations in the treatment of mental retardation. Given this situation, it seems appropriate to introduce the student to this new area. In fact, it was the very neglect of these nonscientific issues in the past that led to the problems that necessitated the current revolution. As we shall suggest later in the chapter, the case can be made that the emergence and prominence of these philosophical, humanistic, and legal concerns have had a much more profound impact on the treatment of mentally retarded persons than any specific treatment procedure or technique.

One final comment must be made. A focus on the specifics of treatment may suggest that there are treatment approaches or techniques that are used solely with the mentally retarded and are appropriate only for this group. This is not true. While there are certain methods that are utilized more frequently or intensively with this population, there are none that are limited exclusively to them. (A possible exception may be certain medical procedures for the treatment of some of the rarer conditions.) For example, although behavioral techniques are widely employed with the mentally retarded, they are also extensively used on nonretarded populations. Likewise, the concept of diagnostic-prescriptive teaching is considered appropriate for all areas of exceptionality, as well as the ideal model for general education. Finally, it should be noted that special classes, often incorrectly identified only with the mentally retarded, are also used with many other handicapped groups. (The recent trend toward mainstreaming has affected these other groups as well.)

This is not to suggest that the mentally retarded and other handicapped groups do not require special services. Obviously, they do. However, while certain procedures or methods may have to be adapted for each group, the general principles, methods, and procedures are the same for all. It is the adaptations, not the general models or principles, that are different. And these adaptations, while extremely important for each special group, should not be allowed to obscure their basic similarities.

In summary, at the most fundamental level, the treatment of the mentally retarded is no different from the treatment of anyone else, normal or handicapped. All education, training, and treatment is based on the assumption that every client is unique. Any and all of the numerous approaches, models, and techniques are to be utilized when and where appropriate, according to the client's needs. There is no one treatment approach to mental retardation, and no mystery or magic involved.

There is, however, an extremely important difference in the requirements of those who do the educating, training, and treating. While there are no differences in the general methods, models, or principles employed, the task is invariably more difficult and complicated for these special groups. It requires much more creativity and resourcefulness, not to mention healthy doses of perseverance and patience, a high level of frustration tolerance, and, perhaps most importantly, a capacity to derive satisfaction from even very small gains. Furthermore, the effective adaptation and application of the general principles and models to each of these special groups demands persons who are knowledgeable and aware of the special characteristics of the persons in each of these areas of exceptionality.

There is much talk today of abandoning special education, particularly in terms of self-contained "special classes." There is, however, no talk of abandoning special educators. There will always be a need for experts in the field of mental retardation who are able to creatively individualize habilitative, training, and educational programs. Our attempts to decrease the negative aspects of being a special (handicapped) person can succeed only to the extent that we increase the special qualities of those persons charged with their care and training.

## PHILOSOPHICAL AND CONCEPTUAL FOUNDATIONS OF TREATMENT

Over the last two decades, there have been several significant and far-reaching scientific and technical developments in the treatment of mental retardation. Dramatic medical breakthroughs have led to the possibility of eliminating or greatly reducing certain types of mental retardation. The best example of this is the dietary treatment of PKU. Future prospects look even brighter, particularly in the area of DNA technology and the possibilities of genetic engineering. The age-old hope of finding a "cure" for mental retardation is no longer a pipe dream with regard to some of the genetic and medical conditions causing it. Less dramatic but no less significant, the widespread application of behavioral technology has greatly improved the treatment possibilities of many mentally retarded persons, particularly the more severely retarded. We now realize that these persons are capable of functioning at a much higher level than ever thought possible in the past.

Two other nonscientific developments have had a pervasive and immediate impact on mental retardation. Both of these have been discussed in Chapter 2. The first is the tremendous upsurge of interest, commitment, and support to the field of mental retardation stemming from President John Kennedy's personal involvement and intervention. Mental retardation became a national priority, and a specific, highly energized, broadly comprehensive national plan of action was implemented. More than any specific treatment provision, modality, or technique, this factor has changed the lives of all mentally retarded persons. However, the second nonscientific development is perhaps the most significant of all. The field of mental retardation during the 1970s has been marked by its emphasis on the mentally retarded as *persons* and *citizens*. It was during these years that their human and legal rights became paramount, as well as the recognition of their dignity as persons. The courts had affirmed their rights as citizens; and the moral and humane corollary to these judicial actions, embodied in the principle of normalization, restored their human dignity.

As a result of these nonscientific developments, emphasis on the specifics of treatment has been superseded by legal, ethical, philosophical, and humanistic concerns. The most critical "treatment" consideration is that we "treat" the mentally retarded as persons. Thus, the field has experienced a change in perspective and orientation; the scientific approach to mental retardation has become humanized. This fact has had more impact on the treatment of the mentally retarded than any other factor.

The importance of these humanistic concerns was highlighted by our historical review in Chapter 2. We saw how the debacle of the early 1900s was the result of distorted conceptions and attitudes. Even the science of the day was often perverted for sociopolitical purposes. The resulting view of the mentally retarded as a social menace, perpetrators of all social ills and evils, and a blot on society had dire implications for their treatment. They became disenfranchised and dehumanized; they were no longer treated as citizens or persons. It was not until the last decade that this mistreatment of the mentally retarded was ended. There had finally been a change in people's conceptions and attitudes, a change that had to be prompted by the courts and reinforced and elaborated by the principle of normalization. From history we learn that the nonscientific concerns and issues have had the greatest impact on the treatment of mental retardation. And so it will be in the future.

The shift from scientific to philosophical-humanistic concerns indicates a critical and complex relationship between science and values. Mental retardation is one area where this becomes much more than an academic issue. Our understanding of this relationship has definite implications for the treatment of the mentally retarded.

## THE RELATIONSHIP BETWEEN SCIENCE AND VALUES

As was noted in Chapter 2, the rise of modern culture is often associated with the emergence of the scientific approach. However, there has always been a tension between the fields of science and those dealing with ethics or values. Many social commentators and critics have expressed alarm and discontent over the fact that the rise of science has been accompanied by a corresponding decline and often an ultimate rejection of other value systems and philosophical approaches, such as religion, traditional modes of authority, and cultural mores and codes of conduct. In their place, science has been enthroned as the major interpreter and illuminator of man's conceptualizations, policy forming, decision making, and behavior. In the pluralism that characterizes modern culture, the "objective," rational, empirical nature of science has seemed to offer the greatest promise of salvation. However, while there has always been some resistance to the dominance of science, this resistance has increased markedly in the last few decades. The value of science itself is being questioned, not to mention its role in policy and decision making. There are now increasing calls for man to turn to other modes of inquiry and value systems for illumination and direction. More and more, science is being reconceptualized as just one of many valid approaches to understanding and guidance in human affairs. In fact, there is a growing belief that science should be seen merely as a tool in decision making, not as an end in itself.

Mental retardation is a case in point. In this field, as in many others, numerous decisions are being made on a nonscientific basis. While science is still seen to be capable of providing relevant data on certain issues, there are other areas in which science is considered useless or irrelevant. In fact, some decisions are made in spite of apparently contradictory scientific data. In order to bring this somewhat abstract discussion down to a more practical, concrete level, we shall present several examples from the field of mental retardation.

*Special versus Regular Classes* Ever since the inception of special classes, there has been a long, often heated debate about their value. Numerous studies (of variable quality from a methodological point of view) have been conducted comparing EMR students in regular classes with those in special classes. As usually happens, the findings are complicated and often contradictory. As a result, it is extremely difficult to draw any firm conclusions. Nevertheless, several tentative ideas have emerged. In general, the findings suggest that EMR students in the regular classes perform at a higher academic level than their peers in special classes. However, the data also suggest that the social competence and adjustment, as well as the self-concepts, of EMR students in the special classes are better than those of their counterparts in the regular classes. This situation presents a dilemma for which science cannot provide an answer. Obviously, it is a question of values or priorities. If academic achievement is considered to be more important, then regular class placement is probably preferable. However, if greater value is placed on personal and social adjustment, special classes are more appropriate.

This example points out the complexity of the relationship between science and values. In this case, scientific data are potentially quite relevant. For instance, had the data indicated that both academic achievement and personal-social adjustment are better in one type of setting, the decision would be obvious. This example indicates that, while data may be useful and relevant, they often do not and cannot lead to a final decision.

The question of special versus regular class placement is further complicated by other issues. Given the principle of normalization and its educational corollary of "mainstreaming," a final decision has been made on a purely nonscientific basis. On philosophical grounds, it has now been decided that EMR children should live and be educated in a normalized manner. This has resulted in a movement to abandon special classes wherever possible, or at least to reduce their usage—both in terms of the numbers of students involved and the actual time per day that a student spends in such a class. In this case, the data of science are irrelevant to the issue. In fact, there is an implication here that data which indicated some negative aspects of regular class placement (e.g., lower levels of personal-social adjustment) should be disregarded in light of the overriding importance of living in a normalized environment. (Whether such negative data should, in fact, be disregarded is another relevant value judgment.) In short, the question of which classroom situation is better has been answered by the emergence of a value. The greater good of the principle of normalization is seen to outweigh all other considerations and findings.

*Labeling* Here, in the absence of any solid supporting data, a judgment has been made that labeling has overwhelming deleterious effects. In fact, some data even suggest that labeling may have beneficial effects. This issue is amenable to scientific inquiry, and the resulting data would be most helpful in arriving at a decision or policy. For example, if there are no demonstrable ill effects of labeling, then the argument for the abandonment of this practice loses much of its power. The labeling controversy is an example where decisions are being advocated or judgments made in the absence of scientific data, when in fact, such data are critical. In this case, science is quite relevant and should not be ignored.

*Deinstitutionalization* Since the mid-1960s, there has been a growing movement to depopulate the institutions for the mentally retarded. (There are now approximately 250,000 mentally retarded persons in public and private institutions across the country. The vast majority of these persons are the more severely retarded, with IQs usually below 50.) Several factors have contributed to the drive toward deinstitutionalization. First, the 1962

President's Panel report advocated a community orientation, which was further reinforced by the passage of the Community Mental Health Act of 1963. Second, the movement was given great impetus by the many horror stories and exposés regarding institutional conditions. Public outrage at the dehumanizing nature of such facilities led to immediate calls for reform, including the drastic action as closing all such institutional "warehouses." Several court decisions ordered the breakup of some of the larger facilities and also demanded that institutions document and demonstrate that their treatment programs were appropriate and effective. The final factor responsible for the depopulation drive was the principle of normalization, which in many ways is diametrically opposed to the idea of institutional treatment.

The results of this often emotional campaign have been less dramatic than expected. Many of the larger institutions have greatly reduced their populations, but often by simply transferring their residents to a number of smaller facilities. It also became apparent that many communities were not prepared for the influx of residents who were discharged from large institutions. Additionally, many of the smaller community placement facilities were no better, and in some instances, actually worse than the large institutions themselves. Gradually, the field of mental retardation began to recognize the excesses of this campaign. While it was generally agreed that the enormous institutions of the past (e.g., resident populations of 5,000 or more) should be abandoned, there was a growing realization that there is still a place for a central, multipurpose institution. This is especially true when considering the needs of persons with the more severe forms of mental retardation, which are often accompanied by complicated medical problems. These residents usually require highly specialized treatment services which cannot be adequately provided in the community.

Scientific data have played a relatively minor role in the movement toward deinstitutionalization. Although some data did indicate a poor quality of institutional care, this had none of the impact of photographs depicting deplorable conditions. No data were needed to "objectify" the obviously dehumanizing and degrading conditions of some institutions. This idea was erroneously generalized to suggest that all institutions were bad. This, of course, was not true; several institutions provided top-quality care. Although science had little to do with the deinstitutionalization movement, it became obvious that science would be quite relevant to an unemotional and reasonable resolution of the problem.

There are two primary issues related to institutional care and scientific data. In fact, it is hard to imagine any other mode of inquiry that could provide the necessary information for decision and policy making. The first issue relates to the optimal size of an institution in terms of numbers of residents. Empirical data from several sciences (e.g., psychology, sociology, architecture) will be required to come up with an answer to this question. The other factor is a determination of the type of institutional environment that facilitates or inhibits growth and development. This is an extremely complex subject that will require careful and intensive scientific investigation. Since some form of institution is necessary, what we need now are scientific data to tell us how to design and operate such facilities so that any potentially negative effects are minimized. The field has spelled out the general direction and goal; science is needed to work out the details.

The above examples indicate several things about the relationship between science and values. First, they demonstrate the ultimate futility of a totally scientific approach, since various nonscientific issues are often the sole or major basis for decision and policy making in the treatment of mental retardation. Second, these examples point out that scientific data may or may not be relevant to such decisions. Some of the critical issues about the treatment of the mentally retarded can never be decided on a scientific basis. However, it is also true that the emotional atmosphere surrounding some of these issues could benefit from the dispassionate scrutiny of science. While we cannot ignore the potential contributions of science, we also cannot wait for or expect science to answer some of the more critical fundamental questions about the treatment of mental retardation.

Given the prominence and impact of these nonscientific concerns in the treatment of mental retardation, it is important to further explore and investigate the related events, concepts, and principles. Much of this material has been mentioned or touched upon elsewhere. However, a more systematic discussion is required to emphasize the importance of these factors in the treatment of mental retardation.

## JUDICIAL AND LEGISLATIVE DECISIONS

The mentally retarded had their day in court in the 1970s, and they won. The courts have affirmed their status as citizens and their right to public education, to appropriate and effective treatment, to due process in placement and treatment decisions, and to the least restrictive alternative when limitations must be made. The result of all of these decisions, in addition to their effect on the mentally retarded, has been to make normal persons cognizant of and responsive to their rights. To a large extent, these judicial actions have done more for the treatment of mental retardation than any other single factor.

By order of the courts, and in anticipation of other orders, legislatures at all levels of government have begun to enact laws and provide the accompanying funds to carry out judicial mandates that relate to treatment, placement, and other programs. In many instances, these legislative initiatives have gone beyond the judicial orders, and represent genuine and far-reaching attempts to treat the mentally retarded as full-fledged citizens and human beings. The most prominent and extensive of such legislation was the Education for All Handicapped Children Act, PL 94–142, passed in 1975. This act mandates, among other things, that all disabled children, regardless of their degree or type of handicap, must receive a public education. Furthermore, these services must be shown to be both appropriate and effective for the client. This legislation will have a massive impact on the education and training of all handicapped children, including the mentally retarded. In addition, special educators will be held accountable for the quality of their efforts. This will necessitate evaluative research and will spur new research aimed at developing better alternatives to present programs and practices. The net effect will be to advance the treatment of the mentally retarded. Once again, it is nonscientific events and factors, such as judicial and legislative actions, that appear to have the most profound effect on our treatment of mental retardation.

These judicial and legislative actions insure that treatment practices are legal and do not violate a person's rights. But they cannot specify the goals, content, or process of treatment. To find out about the means and ends of treatment, we must look elsewhere. It is here that the principle of normalization becomes important.

## THE PRINCIPLE OF NORMALIZATION

Aside from the legal initiatives, the most influential factor in terms of treatment is the principle of normalization. It is the spirit behind the letter of the law. This principle affirms that the treatment of the mentally retarded is to be guided by the realization that they are first and foremost fellow human beings who are to be afforded their human dignity. As the major governing treatment principle, it specifies both the means and the end of the treatment process. Very simply, it states that the first and last goal of treatment is to provide experiences and living conditions which are as normal as possible. Equally significant, this principle also spells out the means of working toward this goal; that is, the treatment consists of whatever steps are necessary to give the mentally retarded a normal life. Furthermore, in working toward this goal, we must use normalized procedures and techniques as much as possible. Several examples will help clarify what we mean by means and ends. Because the principle of normalization is most dramatically illustrated from an institutional perspective, the examples will be drawn from this setting. The generalizability of this principle to other settings and populations will be discussed later.

According to normalization, the ultimate goal for any resident in an institution is return to his own family's home or placement in a community setting, such as a family care facility, where a number of residents (usually fewer than ten) live and are cared for. But whenever institutionalization is necessary, either temporarily or permanently (especially with the more severe, medically involved cases), there is a host of subgoals that implicitly follow from the principle of normalization. Some of these goals refer to the institutional settings, while others pertain to the residents themselves.

In terms of the institution, it should be made to look as normal as possible. "Normal" in this case means "homelike," since institutional living is not considered normal. Accordingly, community toilet areas and large sleeping dorms, for example, should be individually partitioned to afford some privacy. Walls should be painted and decorated other than with the typical drab "state" gray or green. Draperies should replace bars and heavy-duty screens on windows. Carpets should be installed, and steel chairs and metal lockers should be replaced with more homelike furnishings. The changes that can be made are limited only by the imagination and dedication of workers in the institutions. What is most important here is the change in attitude that has resulted from the goal of making these facilities more normal. In the past, no one gave much thought to the appearance and condition of such places, other than in terms of health and safety standards and ease of operation and maintenance. With the principle of normalization, however, we are finding that much can be done to create an atmosphere that is more human and homelike. Nor are these changes merely for cosmetic purposes; ultimately, they relate to the whole issue of treating the mentally retarded with dignity. Part of the reason many of the older institutions were referred to as "warehouses" was that they looked like warehouses—barren, impersonal, cold buildings that stored people. There was absolutely nothing homelike about them. It is easy to see how such an environment contributed to a perception of the inhabitants as less than human. They were clearly not being treated like persons in terms of their living conditions. The reverse, however, should also hold true. If the environment is humanized, the inhabitants will be thought of and responded to in equally human terms.

The goal and subgoals of normalization with respect to the residents themselves are even more numerous and important. Perhaps the major factor responsible for the dehumanization of the mentally retarded has been a press toward institutional expediency. The main goals often appeared to be to run the facilities as cheaply and efficiently as possible and for staff convenience. By their very nature, institutions have a group rather than an individual orientation. This is related to the issues of expediency and efficiency. Exceptions to the rule are rarely tolerated, yet it is precisely such exceptions that constitute an individualistic orientation. The net result of the emphasis on groups, expediency, and efficiency was incredible regimentation. All residents wore state-issue clothes because the laundry (always in a separate building) couldn't be bothered with separating white clothes from colored fabrics and didn't have a "delicate cycle" on their huge washers and dryers. Everyone had to get up at the same time in the morning, and the entire morning was geared to the arrival of the food trucks (the kitchen was also in a separate building). It usually proved much more efficient for the staff to wash and dress the residents rather than "fool around" trying to train a resident "who wanted to return to bed anyway." In order to prevent "accidents," all residents were herded into the community toilets right after breakfast. Afterward, each resident was then handed a toothbrush from a cannister of 50 toothbrushes. All the toothbrushes were the same and all were state property. There was no time for ridiculous "personal extravagances" such as a personal toothbrush when there were so many residents and such a tight schedule to follow. Throughout the day, residents traveled with their groups from area to area and activity to activity. (However, this was a vast improvement over the older systems, where there were often no activities whatsoever.) If a resident didn't feel like participating in a particular activity, he might be considered to be a "behavior problem." Such personal preferences and deviations simply couldn't be accommodated by a system where group unity and group routine were of paramount importance for efficient and orderly operation. Meals were almost always served cafeteria style, with the food placed in the neat, built-in sections of the tray. There was no such thing as raiding the refrigerator; residents did, however, "steal" food from their peers. And there was never the opportunity to eat in the living room or den while watching television. At night, everyone showered at the same time in the group showers (again, the staff often found it more efficient to do the washing themselves) and then went to bed in a huge dormitory at the prescribed hour. There were no bedtime stories and no exceptions for residents who wanted to stay up a little later. All in all, if nothing else, it was certainly a predictable, orderly existence. And it was also highly efficient. It was not, however, particularly human, joyful, or normal.

The present authors are well aware that institutions must be organized somewhat along group lines and must be concerned with efficiency and expediency. Tax dollars can only be spread so far. But while these are valid considerations, they should not be primary, as they have been in the past. By their very nature, institutions will have more routine and regimentation than is typically found in home environrents. It is the overemphasis of these efficiency factors and the almost total neglect or even awareness of humanistic considerations that is the problem. The major effect of the principle of normalization is to foster a much more humanistic orientation. And our priorities have been reordered accordingly. Concern with human rights and dignity is now considered to be far more important than the balancing of our budgets, although this factor can obviously never be ignored. But we now recognize that it is incumbent on us, given the inherent negative aspects of institutions, to spend some extra effort and money to ensure that certain basic human requirements are met and maintained.

This simple change in our priorities, perspective, and attitudes has already borne considerable fruit. Residents now wear "normal" clothes. The simple addition of small washers and dryers in the living units would allow for even greater freedom and diversity in this regard. (The institutional laundry can still take care of all the linen, etc.) The doors to many of our institutions have been unlocked, where appropriate and reasonable, and residents are allowed to move around the grounds. Parents and friends are no longer restricted to visiting only on certain days and at certain hours. They can come at any reasonable time, including daily if they wish. Residents now have personal possessions and an easily accessible, individual place to store them (i.e., they do not need to depend on a group leader with a key to a large cabinet). And there is much greater flexibility in terms of getting up, going to bed, foods eaten, and so forth. In short, the lives of these persons have become somewhat more normalized, human and we hope, joyful.

This increase in flexibility, of course, demands considerable judgment on the part of the staff. There must be some limitations for all and different limitations for different residents. But it is the decision to rely on such judgment rather than a rigid adherence to rules and routines that highlights the breakthrough. We now allow many exceptions to the rule, recognizing that it is just such exceptions that demonstrate our awareness and responsiveness to these people's rights and dignity. While much more progress still needs to be made, we do appear to be heading in the right direction. A few more examples will illustrate how the principle of normalization works.

*Physical Appearance* Many of the severely mentally retarded often have physical stigmata (e.g., microcephaly, trisomy #21) which reduce their attractiveness and emphasize their abnormality. Accordingly, we must make efforts to minimize these features. This means, for example, that medically unnecessary (the economic criterion) but cosmetically indicated (humanistic orientation) surgery and procedures should be carried out. However, the efforts don't always have to be this drastic. Simple attention to the type of clothes some residents should wear and how their hair should be styled (by a qualified stylist) can have considerable benefit. Also, some of the severely mentally retarded have awkward gaits that are not physical in origin. These residents should be taught to walk in a more normal fashion. Again, most people have simply never given any thought to these factors, with their obvious implications for how the mentally retarded are perceived and responded to.

*Dress* It is normal to be able to dress oneself. If a resident is unable to dress, this immediately becomes one of the goals of training. But if a resident already knows how to dress or has been taught to do so, this is not the end of the line. He or she must then be taught how to dress appropriately and how to coordinate their clothes. Ultimately, they should then be taught how to select and purchase their own clothes, as well as how to care for and clean them. The point here is that normalization is always forward looking. There is always a next step, which becomes a new goal after successful completion of previous goals. One further comment about dress shows the impact of this principle. Preferences in clothing are considered normal. Even though a resident may be unable to dress him- or herself, he or she should have some choice regarding what they want to wear. In the past, such preferences were usually ignored, with the staff making all decisions. Now it is recognized that such preferences should be honored whenever possible and appropriate, no matter what the resident's degree of retardation or skill in dressing. It is simply another dimension that needs to be considered.

*On Fish Aquariums* Prior to several years ago, a proposal to have fish aquariums in residential units would have been met with derision. "They'll break it; it won't last, etc." But protestations notwithstanding, they were introduced. And while they do occasionally get broken (as in normal environments), they have lasted a lot longer than anyone thought possible.

In addition to making the environment more normal looking, these aquariums provide stimulation for the residents, who can now learn about the habits of fish and the importance of cleaning the tanks and taking care of the fish.

A similar comment can be made about pets. Health and other regulations now prohibit the keeping of pets in state hospitals. While there are some obvious reasons for such rules, perhaps some way could be found to allow pets and still maintain the standards, given a genuine interest in doing so. In the past, there was simply no reason to try to modify such regulations or question their importance. The principle of normalization has now supplied the motivation to examine the wisdom of many of our standard practices.

Both of the above examples indicate how, for a variety of reasons, we tend to prohibit a normal existence for the mentally retarded. There has been an overconcern with their ability to "break things" or "hurt themselves." The net result is extreme overprotection and restriction in their lives. Not only is such restriction abnormal, but it also precludes natural opportunities for learning about the world.

*On Furniture and "Soilers"* An example of how the principle of normalization should be realistically applied is the issue of what type of furniture is appropriate in a unit where there are many profoundly retarded residents who soil themselves. Normalization states that residents must be trained not to soil and that the furniture should be homelike. Obviously, however, the more normal the furniture, the greater the problem when and if a resident does soil it. Much good furniture would be ruined in a relatively short time. The answer to this problem in the past was both expedient and efficient. Long, unattractive steel benches, which were easy to clean, were bolted to the walls. There are several problems with this kind of solution. First, the environment is not normal. Second, and perhaps more important, there is less reason to try and teach the residents not to soil, for little damage can occur. Also, it is much easier to clean the benches than to engage in a more difficult training program. The principle of normalization has now provided the motivation to begin concentrating on both aspects of this task, the behavior and the furniture. But it can be done in a steplike, reasonable fashion. The long benches should, of course, be immediately replaced by more normal-looking furniture (e.g., chairs, settees, couches), which, however, are made of materials that are easy to clean. As training progresses, even more normal type of furniture can be gradually introduced. The point here is that there is an interaction between behavior and the environment. If we don't try to normalize behavior, we are obviously restricting the possibilities of providing a normalized environment. However, it is also true that if we don't attempt to normalize the environment, there is often little reason or motivation to attempt to normalize behavior. Both aspects of the situation must be worked on.

This particular problem points out an additional reason why a focus on treatment specifics or procedures alone is extremely shortsighted. What difference does it make whether toilet training method A is better than method B when the resident's normal environment consists of a community toilet area and a dayroom of long steel benches? In a normal environment, there is a clear difference between the bathroom and the livingroom. Not so in many of our institutions. And the case can be made that training by either method would be facilitated by a clearer distinction between aspects of the resident's environment.

## Community Exposure and Experience

Perhaps the most direct implication of normalization for institutionalized persons is the demand that they receive community exposure and experience. As mentioned earlier, institutionalization is considered to be the antithesis of normalization. Accordingly, the ultimate goal is to move every resident into some type of community setting. Whether or not this objective is met or even possible in every case, it is what we must strive to achieve. The decision about whether this goal is realistic or possible is made after we have tried to accomplish it, not on some *a priori* basis. Whether or not the goal is achieved, however, normalization specifies that all persons must be provided with community experiences as part of their treatment program.

For those residents who will eventually return to the community, the rationale is obvious. From both a logical and a commonsense point of view, how can a person learn to live in a community setting if he is never exposed to such settings? The only way to adequately prepare the person for community living is to provide frequent community exposure.

But even with those residents who will never live in the community, the principle still applies. In this case, the goal of community placement is conceptualized in terms of the "least restrictive alternative." This principle is invoked in all cases where restrictions are necessary. The fact that a person will never be able to live in the community does not mean that he should receive no community experiences. His right to live as normal an existence as possible dictates that frequent community experiences be provided. Furthermore, the limits to the kind and frequency of exposure are dictated by what the resident can tolerate, not what he can "benefit from." This latter criterion has been used repeatedly to exclude community visits on the grounds that the resident is so severely impaired that, for example, he doesn't understand what is going on. First, just going out and doing something different is part of normalized existence. Second, there are multiple levels of experience for any particular situation. For example, residents are often taken to county fairs. Many lay people question the value of such trips for severely and profoundly mentally retarded persons. The main value is that it breaks their normal routine. They also get to experience large crowds, people laughing and talking, strange foods, sights, sounds, and experiences (e.g., rides). While they may not appreciate these things at the same level as normal persons, they are experiencing something new and different. We should not be making value judgments about the quality of their appreciation. Of course, reasonableness applies here also. We might not take profoundly retarded residents to an O'Neil play. But a rock concert or a puppet show might be quite appropriate. Obviously, some judgment and discretion are required as to where to take them. But there is no decision as to whether or not we should take them out into the community. It is an issue of "where," not "if." And we must be very careful not to be overly judgmental about the benefit or value of the "where."

An anecdote is relevant here. Both of the present authors have sat in on numerous meetings where the staff have reported on the behavior of residents while on community outings. While there are always residents who pose difficult management problems in such situations, it has often been observed that many of the residents behave much more appropriately on such outings than they do in their units. Some staff have even commented that "they almost seem to know that they should act differently." These observations should not be too surprising. We have repeatedly suggested that the environment has a definite influence on one's behavior. There may be a curious paradox here. We spend much time and energy trying to get the residents to behave appropriately in the abnormal, regimented, dull, and often stultifying environments we have provided for them. Perhaps some of their "inappropriate" behavior is a protest against such conditions. The fact that they behave much better in normal environments says something about them and our entire approach to treatment. To the extent we make their environments and existence more normal, the problem of dealing with inappropriate behavior may be greatly reduced.

This example, once again, demonstrates how a sole focus on treatment specifics often leaves much to be desired and may needlessly complicate our task. For example, we have developed elaborate but often time-consuming programs for dealing with the maladaptive behaviors of residents. If a more normalized existence would eliminate many or even some of these problems, we could concentrate more on increasing their positive skills. Furthermore, part of their problem may be our problem. There is a legitimate question of just how inappropriate their behavior is, given the inappropriate conditions under which they are forced to live. What is the point of being "good" in a "bad" environment? Normalizing their environments, both in terms of their residential units and providing frequent community experiences, may be far more important and effective than the number of programs we use to modify their behavior.

One other factor must be considered. Even if we are successful in teaching the mentally retarded to behave in the units, we may have made little or no progress toward the goal of teaching them to behave and live in a more normalized environment. The purpose of training is not to teach residents to live in an institution; it is to prepare them for life in the community. The resident whose major misbehavior occurs primarily on community outings is a case in point. One solution, often advocated in the past, is simply never to take him out. But this solution is no longer acceptable. We must simply adjust our training program with such a resident. For example, we may have to make arrangements to take him out alone, without his group, when it will be easier to manage any problems that occur. Or we must provide more staff just to work with him when he does go out with the group. But even if these adjustments are not effective, the next step is not to just leave him in the unit at all times. On the contrary, opportunities to go about the hospital grounds should be provided. If long trips prove problematic, then short trips should be undertaken. The point is that we must restrict as little as possible and only as much as is necessary. Furthermore, the goal of moving the resident forward is always uppermost and must constantly be kept in mind.

## On the Importance of Normalization

The new student in the field of mental retardation may not fully appreciate the impact of normalization on the treatment of the mentally retarded. It seems so reasonable and obvious. But such was not the case in the past; this explains why the principle has been embraced so enthusiastically. It was not that there was an active effort to mistreat or dehumanize the mentally retarded. We simply never thought about their rights and dignity as persons. We focused on programs and the mechanics of treatment without paying attention to these more important humanistic concerns. The courts and the principle of normalization have reversed our thoughtlessness and neglect and fostered a much more humanistic orientation. Treating the mentally retarded as full-fledged citizens and persons has become the major treatment goal and consideration. Treating them as normally as possible has become the guiding principle for achieving this goal. Prior to the emergence and enunciation of this principle, the field of mental retardation had no overall blueprint that specified both where we were heading and how we should get there in terms of treatment of the mentally retarded. More than anything else, the principle of normalization has provided a sense of direction. Although this principle is very general, it stresses that we must always be thinking in terms of small, discrete steps or subgoals which lead to the ultimate goal of normal existence. It thus supplies the necessary sense of direction that gives meaning and purpose to the specifics of the treatment process.

In addition, the profound change in our orientation and attitudes toward the mentally retarded has led to a genuine, dedicated effort to change our treatment practices accordingly. And as was noted before, the mere fact that we treat the mentally retarded more normally may lead to definite advances in their treatment and some diminution of our problems in teaching and training them in nonnormalized environments. Ultimately, and somewhat paradoxically, it may prove to be the most expedient and efficient way of "treating" them.

## Some Problems with Normalization

The principle of normalization is so obvious and reasonable that it is easy to champion. In fact, it is almost impossible to oppose. Nevertheless, there has been some criticism. Most of it relates to the extreme, excessive, and often absurd and rigid manner of implementing this principle. One example is that of voting. Because normal citizens can vote, some people have suggested that even severely and profoundly mentally retarded residents should also be allowed to vote. The fact that they lack the requisite skills to vote intelligently is countered by the fact that normal voting patterns are not necessarily that rational or intelligent. While there may be some legitimacy to this, it does not provide a justification for letting the severely retarded vote (The issue of the mildly retarded voting is a much more difficult problem.) Thus, although we could easily train many of the severely retarded to operate voting machines, there appears to be no point in doing so. Nor does the principle of normalization suggest this.

This example, however, does point out another potential problem with the principle of normalization. Its purpose is to treat all persons "normally"—that is, with respect and dignity. This does not, however, mean that all persons can behave normally, or for that matter, are normal. Although we must always strive to achieve the goal of normalcy, we cannot ignore the fact that some people have limitations which preclude their behaving in a normal fashion and living in a normal environment. The campaign to depopulate the state hospitals is relevant here. The large institutions should be broken up and many of the residents could and should be moved to community settings; this much seems clear. The institutions themselves could also be greatly modified so as to be more normal and human. However, the suggestion that all institutions be totally closed down is both unrealistic and inappropriate. Some of the more severely retarded are so impaired mentally and physically that they require institutional care. It would not be normal for them to live in a normal environment. They are clearly abnormal in the general, nonevaluative sense of the word; and accordingly, they require and must live in a nonnormal environment to live at all. At some critical point, their requirements for existence supersede even the principle of normalization. We are, of course, referring here to the letter rather than the spirit of this "law."

One final problem with the principle of normalization merits discussion. It is, however, an extremely complex problem and one which is difficult to present in a precise manner. It concerns the application of this principle to noninstitutionalized persons. We mentioned earlier that it was with the institutionalized mentally retarded that this principle has its most obvious and dramatic impact. This is because institutional existence is the antithesis of normalized existence, in terms of both the potential for normalcy in an institutional setting and the capacities of the residents themselves. The problem is obvious in both an environmental and a behavioral sense. And it is in such an obvious situation that the sense of direction provided by the principle of normalization is most clear. But what about the application of this principle to the noninstitutionalized mentally retarded—who, by the way, are much less severely handicapped and far greater in number? With the notable exception of the concept of mainstreaming, which is the educational counterpart of normalization, the sense of direction and application possibilities are much more vague. Part of the problem is conceptual. To the extent that these people are less handicapped, they are already, by definition, more normal. To the extent that they require fewer specialized services, they are treated in a more normal fashion (which may not, in fact, be beneficial). Furthermore, while there is no problem in defining normalcy when dealing with the more extreme cases or environments, the definitional problem becomes critical with the less extreme, "more normal" cases.

There is no clear answer to this problem. Two points, however, seem worthy of consideration. First, as we shall suggest in the next chapter, the problem of mild mental retardation is precisely the "normal" environment these people must live in. On closer analysis, we see that the normal environment is actually overwhelming in its complexity. It is the attempt to live a normalized existence that proves problematic. In fact, we will suggest that it is quite normal for persons of low intelligence to experience considerable difficulties in coping with our modern, complex, technological society. Once again, we have another paradoxical situation. What constitutes the ideal goal for the more severely mentally retarded (i.e., a normal existence) becomes anathema for those at the milder levels of retardation.

The second point is mentioned more as a caution in terms of our overall perspective. Because normalization is most relevant and obvious when applied to institutionalized persons, the enthusiasm generated by this principle has been directed primarily to this group and setting. While this is reasonable, it runs the risk of furthering an all too familiar and chronic problem with the field of mental retardation. Once again, the focus is on the more dramatic but much less frequent problem of severe mental retardation, with less concern given to the less dramatic but for more pervasive problem of mild mental retardation.

## SCIENTIFIC CONCEPTIONS OF MENTAL RETARDATION

Thus far, we have been talking about the ways in which a humanistic orientation affects the treatment of the mentally retarded. These nonscientific, philosophical, legal, and value considerations are often of much more importance than scientific and technical concerns. However, there is one aspect of the scientific approach to mental retardation that has important implications and often a dramatic impact on our treatment practices and considerations. This is the scientific concept of mental retardation itself. One's view of the problem has a definite bearing on how one approaches its treatment. Our historical review of the field (Chapter 2) has clearly shown how the treatment of and provision for the mentally retarded has changed with the different scientific conceptualizations of the problem. When mental retardation was seen as basically incurable (e.g., early 1900s), little treatment effort was put forth. When mental retardation was seen as modifiable (e.g., pioneer era and since 1950), treatment pursuits received much more interest and effort.

### Present Scientific Conceptions and the Treatment of the Mentally Retarded

Mental retardation is no longer seen as a permanent, incurable condition. This is especially true of mild mental retardation. With all degrees of retardation, there is much more emphasis on the modifiability of the condition, with prognosis closely related to things like motivation, training opportunities, and the environment. There are two reasons for the emphasis on the potential changeability of mental retardation. The first is the recognition of the cultural relativity of this condition. The second is the view of mental retardation as a dynamic developmental disability.

*Mental Retardation and Societal Variables* The most important recent influence on the scientific concept of mental retardation is the social system perspective. As discussed in Chapters 4 and 5, this view is in contrast to the traditional psychological perspective. According to the traditional view, mental retardation is a problem of the individual. It is obvious that the treatment approach emanating from such a view would be totally directed at the individual. Efforts to remediate his deficiencies would be the major concern. At present, most of our current treatment methods are directed toward just such individual treatment. A much different approach however, is suggested by the social system perspective. According to this view, mental retardation is created and defined by the society. Treatment must therefore focus on the society and not the individual. Changes in the fabric of society, its level of demand and expectations, and its tolerance of deviation become the focus of concern.

In short, we have two different scientific conceptualizations of the problem which result in two drastically different treatment approaches. One approach focuses on the individual, the other on the society. As we suggested in Chapter 5, the apparent tension between these approaches dissolves somewhat when they are considered to be complementary views of the same problem. They both have something to contribute to our understanding and treatment of mental retardation. For this reason, the present authors have proposed a third conceptual possibility, the societal perspective, which integrates and extends the individual and social system views. The societal perspective suggests that the treatment of mental retardation must be concerned with both the individual and the society.

*Mental Retardation as a Developmental Disability* The concept of developmental disability has been considered in Chapters 4 and 8. Several points merit reiteration. The fact that mental retardation is now construed as a dynamic, developmental problem underscores the possibilities for change. This is in marked contrast to the older view of this problem as a static, genetically determined given. Since mental retardation is now seen as something that *develops,* there is a direct implication that it can be altered throughout the developmental period. Correctly timed interventions may avoid the condition or, at the very least, minimize its severity. Furthermore, even after the condition has occurred, there is still considerable potential for modification and remediation.

Another aspect of the developmental view is the inclusion of personality and motivation variables. That is, intelligence, personality, and motivation all interact with each other, affecting both the development and expression of behavior. Since mental retardation is more than a mental problem, its treatment must therefore be concerned with more than intellectual and cognitive deficits. The motivational and personality deficits must be addressed as well. There is little point obsessing about which of three methods for teaching reading to the mentally retarded is most effective when many of these individuals are passive, expect to fail, and are almost totally unmotivated to learn. The view of mental retardation as a dynamic developmental disability requires the treatment of mental retardation to be much more holistic than in the past. Services will need to be available throughout the life cycle and should be broadly comprehensive, encompassing much more than just mental problems.

*Mental Retardation as a Psychosocial Challenge* In the past, mental retardation was thought of in medical, disease-oriented terms. This view is prevalent among many lay persons and some professionals even today. Even our use of the word "treatment" has medical connotations. It implies that there is some disease that accounts for the person's condition. However, while this medical model has some relevance to the more severe (but much rarer) cases, it is totally inappropriate for conceptualizing the much more pervasive problem of mild mental retardation. This condition is best thought of as resulting from a variety of factors, most of which are not medical. In fact, the major determinant is the complex interaction between the demands of the environment and the characteristics of the individual. In essense, it is a state of behavioral impairment or inadequacy. These persons have psychosocial deficits or problems. They have been unable to learn the personal and social skills required for normal living. In this sense, there is no need to look for underlying pathological causes. The problem is ultimately a learning problem, and the treatment must therefore be broadly educational in nature. In the final analysis, mental retardation represents a "psychosocial-educational" rather than a "medical-treatment" challenge.

Schools and educators have always borne most of the responsibility for treating the mentally retarded, for they have had to deal with the pervasive problem of mild retardation. Since we have construed the problem as a psychosocial-educational challenge, this is as it should be. In this context, the concept of education for the mentally retarded has recently been greatly expanded beyond the three Rs. At the most fundamental level, the purpose of education is to prepare the student for life. For the normal child, education focuses on the formal, academic subjects. This is appropriate because much of their personal and social development occurs informally and spontaneously. But such is not the case with the mentally retarded. Not only do they have greater difficulty with formal education but, more importantly, they do not pick up these other personal and social skills in the manner of normal persons. As a consequence, their education for life has a much different focus. What is really "special" about the education for the mentally retarded is the formal instruction and training in personal and social development. Thus, they receive instruction in self-help skills, how to get along with people, deal with their feelings, get and maintain a job, spend leisure time, and the like. The mentally retarded need education and training in all aspects of living. They need to be prepared for life in the broadest and most fundamental sense of the word "education." Furthermore, there is a greater recognition that the developmentally disabled have a lifetime need for this broad range of services.

## PREVENTION AND AMELIORATION

The issue of treatment provisions for the mentally retarded can be broken down into two broad goals: prevention and amelioration. The first deals with ways of preventing mental retardation from occurring in the first place. The second concerns ways of coping with mental retardation once it has occurred. Most discussions of treatment focus on amelioration. This is where the concern with specific approaches, methods, and techniques comes into play. However, one could certainly argue that prevention deserves at least as much emphasis as amelioration. In fact, the case can be made that it is a more important concern, for to the extent that we are able to prevent the problem from occurring, the less need we have for ameliorative services. In many helping professions, some tension is created by the fact that the goals of prevention and amelioration are often seen as competing. An example from the field of medicine will clarify this problem.

Medical care is a multi-billion dollar industry. We have a massive force of people, equipment, and facilities committed to the problem of treating medical illness. No one questions the value or necessity of this enterprise. However, the cost of our medical care system is becoming so prohibitive that more and more people are suggesting a greater stress on prevention. The real problem is how to divert enough funds and resources to this preventive effort, given the already pressing service burden. The need to treat current medical problems almost precludes the possibility of launching a serious and significant preventive effort. This issue also has sociopolitical overtones. There is evidence that much of the physical and mental illness that occurs is associated with the "culture of poverty." From this perspective, the tension between prevention and amelioration translates into the familiar question, Should we try to treat the problems associated with poverty, or should we get to the root of the problems and clean up the slums? Obviously, these problems are extremely complex and present no easy answers.

The issue is similar with mental retardation but even more complicated. Mental retardation is primarily a socially defined, culturally relative problem. Given this definition, the questions of prevention and amelioration are more difficult to deal with. Some comments about the preventive aspects, however, do merit attention.

First, the prevention of severe mental retardation is quite similar to the medical issues discussed above. This is the one clear area where the medical model does have considerable relevance. Preventive efforts here will thus depend on developments in genetics research as well as the elimination of the environmental causes of severe retardation, such as infectious and toxic agents. But these cases account for less than 15 percent of the mentally retarded. This leads to the question, What can be done about the prevention of the much more frequent condition of mild mental retardation? Given the cultural relativity of the problem, how can the concept of prevention be applied at all? Since the culture is part of the problem, massive changes in the culture would be required. Not only is this not feasible, but, more importantly, it would perhaps be undesirable. Furthermore, since the basic issue is the interaction between the individual and the society, the problem may be ultimately progressive. As society becomes more complex, coping will become more difficult. In short, talk about drastic reduction of mild retardation may be unrealistic. This is not to suggest that the many instances of mild retardation associated with adverse environmental conditions may not be preventable. However, it does suggest that the disappearance of all mild mental retardation is an impossible dream. For the very nature of the problem—low intelligence in our complex modern society—precludes total prevention.

The implications of the concept of developmental disability for treatment have been discussed. The same issues apply to prevention. In both cases, intervention must occur early to be most effective in minimizing the resulting developmental disability. Most theories of development include a "critical periods" hypothesis. According to this hypothesis, there are certain critical time periods in development when the effects of experience, either positive or negative, are most pronounced. If these periods are missed during attempted intervention, the prospects for making basic changes are greatly reduced. It must be emphasized that significant changes and modifications, both before and after these critical periods, are always possible. But the very nature of development indicates that possible change becomes more limited the further from the critical period it is attempted.

This situation poses a very difficult problem. Research data and theories indicate that we must intervene early to maximize the possibilities of preventing or ameliorating mental retardation. From a pragmatic point of view, therefore, we should be investing most of our energies in very young children, either to prevent disabilities from occurring or to minimize their effects when they have occurred. This raises the question about all those who are already mentally retarded, who are adults or are beyond the critical periods. A massive effort to prevent or ameliorate mental retardation in the very young, although theoretically advantageous from a long-range point of view, could be accomplished only by diverting energy from older persons currently receiving much needed services. Once again, we are faced with a question of values.

## PRAGMATISM, REALISM, AND VALUES: A RECONSIDERATION

Obviously, we cannot do it all. We are, therefore, forced to make some difficult decisions about our allocation of limited resources. These decisions will be based on certain pragmatic and realistic considerations, as well as on our sense of and system of values. The possible competition between the goals of prevention and amelioration is just one case in point. To the extent that we work vigorously to achieve one of these goals, the other must suffer. Today, the field of mental retardation appreciates the importance of early intervention for both prevention and amelioration more than it has at any other time in its history. And it has always been a child-oriented field. But the developments of the 1970s have raised other issues that have now brought the neglected mentally retarded adult into the limelight. What should we do: focus on prevention or amelioration, the young or the old, the severely retarded or the mildly retarded?

There are other issues and questions. Even if we learned nothing new about mental retardation, we could be doing much more in terms of treatment and prevention by simply applying more of our resources and energies to what we already know. Some people are waiting for breakthroughs that will dramatically advance the treatment of mental retardation. There is the belief that more knowledge will eventually solve the problem. But, to a large extent, both the present and the future for the mentally retarded depend more on what we *do* than on what we *know* or will come to know. In the field of mental retardation, our lack of concern and commitment has always been more problematic than our lack of knowledge.

The real problem goes far beyond mental retardation. Take, for example, the Education for All Handicapped Children Act (PL 94-142), which has been rightfully hailed as a necessary and significant development in the treatment of all handicapped children. To carry out the mandates of this act will be a mammoth undertaking. Where will the money come from? Our nation is already straining to carry out its present obligations and other legitimate priorities. Who will suffer if we do this job well? Report after report indicates that our systems of public education for the normal child are failing dismally. Is the cause of special education being advanced at the expense of general education? Maybe what was needed was an Education for All Children Act.

There are no final, "correct" answers to these difficult questions and problems. Ultimately, they concern issues of values and can be resolved only on this basis. In keeping with the theme of this chapter, the present authors will conclude with some value statements of their own.

The main point of this chapter is that the intense focus on, and preoccupation with, the specifics and mechanics of treatment has been inadvertently detrimental to the mentally retarded. How we could have been so concerned with treatment and yet treated the mentally retarded so poorly is hard to understand. What is clear is that in the process of treating the mentally retarded, we have inexcusably neglected a host of philosophical, legal, ethical, and humanistic considerations. As a result of recent court decisions and the emergence of the principle of normalization, our previous errors have been rectified, if not forgiven. Our science has also become humanized. We have finally come to realize that the single most important consideration is to "treat" the mentally retarded with the dignity and respect they deserve as citizens and persons.

The mere fact that this situation has arisen and that it has been necessary to reaffirm and guarantee the human and legal rights of these persons tells us something about how we should proceed in the future. The burden of proof is clearly on us. We must continue to ensure that the mentally retarded are treated properly. Without these special efforts, we normals have a tendency to become somewhat careless, thoughtless, and forgetful about such important matters.

As to the allocation of scarce resources and the unavoidable and difficult value tensions that result, we would make the following observations. There are some who suggest that the ultimate measure of a society is how it treats its less fortunate members. By this criterion, we have fared badly in the past. At present, however, we appear to be doing somewhat better. How we will measure up in the future is obviously the most important question, both for us and for the mentally retarded. Our scarcest resource may be a system of values. One of the best attributes of the mentally retarded is that they challenge our sense of and commitment to values. How they have been and will be treated in the future ultimately says much more about our values and problems than theirs.

# CHAPTER 11

# The Adaptive Deficit

Even a cursory review of this text would indicate that the field of mental retardation is broad and complex, characterized by many philosophical, scientific, and technical issues and complicated by often conflicting data. This would seem to imply that the idea of mental retardation could not be readily summarized. This, however, is not the case. *Mental retardation is simply a* CONCEPT *which indicates that some persons, because of low intelligence, have difficulty coping with the demands of society.* The concept of mental retardation thus involves both the individual and the society in which he lives. To understand mental retardation, we must understand both of these components.

In considering the individual, we must remember that mental retardation is generally not a medical or physical condition and is not even limited to *mental* retardation. It is a much broader concept which includes deficits in learning, memory, motivation, ability to use resources, and certain personality characteristics. Many professional discussions of mental retardation focus on technical issues, such as whether 1 or 3 percent of the population is mentally retarded. These issues, while important from a programing perspective, tend to lose sight of the basic fact that cutoff points (IQ scores) for mental retardation are arbitrary and do not necessarily indicate which persons have difficulty coping as a result of low intelligence.

An individual with an IQ of 72, for example, may not technically fit the AAMD definition of mental retardation but may, nevertheless, have severe problems coping and living in society. While the technical definition of mental retardation does not apply to such an individual, the general concept of mental retardation should. Such cases present a dilemma. Should we raise the cutoff point for mental retardation? For a number of reasons, this is probably not a good solution. Further, it would simply substitute one arbitrary cutoff score for another. The solution really lies in recognizing that many persons of low intelligence have difficulties coping with societal demands. While low intelligence may not be the total cause of these difficulties, it does play an integral role.

Much of the literature implies that persons are either mentally retarded or normal. Little attention is devoted to persons whose IQ is above 70 but who are, nevertheless, of below average intelligence. Such persons may be described as being of "marginal intelligence" (Maloney and Ward, 1976). These also include persons whose tested intelligence is below IQ 70 but who demonstrate no impairment in adaptive behavior. (It is felt that these persons have a lower potential for coping-adaptive behavior since, in an intellectual sense, they have a limited range of coping strategies.) We also include persons whose tested IQ is above 70 and possibly even above 85 (but still below average) and who may or may not demonstrate adaptive impairments. The term "marginal intelligence" was used not as a diagnostic category but rather as a general concept to indicate a high-risk population. Thus, marginal intelligence refers to a large number of persons who are of borderline or low-average intelligence and who have marginal ability to cope successfully with the demands of society. The concept of marginal intelligence focuses on the intellectual difficulties of these persons. As we have already discussed, the coping problems of many persons of low intelligence are not simply related to intelligence but to other issues, such as personality variables, lack of information, and so forth. Consequently, the term "adaptive deficit" is introduced to refer to much broader coping problems. These problems are directly related to the nature and complexity of the demands of the society. Let us consider this critical issue.

## SOCIETAL COMPLEXITY

An in-depth analysis of today's complex American society cannot be undertaken here. It is clear, however, that society continues to become more complex at an *accelerated* rate. Extreme changes can be noted in almost every facet of society. This is primarily the result of technology, which feeds on itself, making more technology possible. The net effect of this is that change and technology continue to accelerate, with resulting increases in complexity. Toffler (1970) has proposed the term "future shock" to refer to the deleterious effects that constant rapid change has on modern man. One facet of technology, automation, has a unique effect on persons with adaptive difficulties. The general effects of automation have been widely discussed, but the relationship between adaptive deficits and automation has not been adequately emphasized. The majority of jobs that have been "automated out" involve work skills that were usually within the capacity of persons with an adaptive deficit. This has caused more competition for the remaining jobs and a concomitant demand for higher adaptive ability.

In other areas of modern society, such problems as insurance contracts, tax computation and reporting, legal restrictions, and so forth have all become increasingly difficult. In fact, "truth in lending" laws have been enacted and consumer groups formed to help people decipher common business transactions and to protect themselves from deceptive market practices which turn this complexity to unfair advantage. Even freeway systems and printed bus schedules are so complex that they confuse persons of even average or above-average intelligence. Thus, it seems reasonable to anticipate that persons of lower coping ability would have more difficulty in such a society.

Robinson and Robinson (1976) have compared the effect of being mentally retarded in our society to that of being a traveler in a foreign country where a different language is spoken. If one has no knowledge of the language or customs, the ability to handle even the practical affairs of daily living is greatly hampered, and life becomes a very difficult, often frustrating chore. Although marginal facility with the language will increase one's adaptability, the traveler still has an adaptive deficit in many areas of functioning. What we are suggesting here is that our complex technological society is becoming more and more like a foreign country to persons of below-average intelligence.

## High-Risk Individuals

The term "adaptive deficit" refers to persons who have difficulty coping with the demands of the society. As mentioned earlier, such persons have below-average intelligence, but this is only one of many variables that produce the adaptive deficit. It is important to examine the other factors as well. One such category of factors is personality. This is a group of nonintellectual attributes which decrease adaptability or increase the adaptive deficit.

*Motivation* A certain degree of motivation is necessary for most accomplishments. It can be said that persons with higher levels of achievement or productivity also have stronger motivation. The opposite is also true. Persons with weaker motivation tend to succeed less and achieve less. This holds true regardless of level of ability. The development of motivation is difficult to understand, but it is clear that experience plays an important role in how it develops, to what degree, and how it is directed. With this in mind, it is instructive to look at the individual of below-average intelligence. In many cases, such persons have difficulty coping with such early societal demands as education. A child with an IQ of 85 would typically have to work harder and longer to learn academic subjects than one with an IQ of 110. It is reasonable to expect that many persons of below-average ability may become less and less motivated to conquer such subjects. Learning becomes more and more difficult and time-consuming and, more importantly, means competing unsuccessfully with persons of higher intelligence. Similar situations occur in other life experiences as well. This may well result in a decrease in motivation, especially in areas related to academic or broadly intellectual problems. If motivation does lessen, it would have two primary effects. First, the individual would tend to learn less during the critical developmental years; second, he would attempt to do less in later years.

*Expectancy* The "expectancy set" refers to the development of motivation. When the marginally intelligent or mentally retarded child attempts and fails to solve problems at a higher rate than his peers, he may come to expect that he will fail. Again, if such a set becomes ingrained in the developmental years, it is apt to remain throughout the adult years. Like motivation, such a set causes the individual to attempt fewer problems and to expect to fail more often than average.

Decreased motivation and expectancy are just two personality variables that might be expected in persons of lower intelligence. Additionally, such persons may be more passive, more deferent, and more other-directed (look to others for feedback, approval, etc.). All of these personality characteristics serve to increase the problems of low intelligence. Thus, we have a person who is lower than average not only in intellectual ability but also in other traits necessary for effective coping. A variety of other factors also contribute to the adaptive deficit. While these factors are nonintellectual they tend to develop from the experiences of less intelligent persons. Let us explore some of these traits.

*Lack of Interpretive Skills* In our modern Western society, such skills as reading, writing, and arithmetic are necessary for effective coping.

Less intelligent persons do more poorly in these areas. Further, the lower the intelligence, the poorer the performance. What is extremely important to note, however, is that such persons perform *at a much lower level than would be expected on the basis of IQ alone*. This suggests that deficits in this area result from more than intelligence level alone. Here, again, if we look at the developmental history of less intelligent persons, we see that their academic and other learning experiences have been often difficult and unrewarding, and, consequently, what they have learned has been poorly developed. Additionally, these persons tend to practice such skills as reading much less often than brighter persons. This further increases their difficulty. Lack of these skills tends to compound the difficulties of less intelligent persons.

*Lack of Knowledge of, and Ability to Use Societal Resources* Modern society is characterized by a great number of programs and agencies which have been designed to aid us in a variety of problem areas. Such resources are found in medicine, housing, legal counseling, financial aid, job training, job procurement, etc. Despite the increasing number of such services and resources, however, many persons of low intelligence do not effectively use them. This relates to a number of factors that we have already discussed. While motivation and personality traits do play a role here, lack of such skills as reading and writing becomes extremely important. Without these skills, the average individual would find it hard to determine what resources or services were available and how they could be obtained. These services and resources have been specifically designed to aid persons in coping with the problems of society. Yet, paradoxically, those who most need them often have the greatest problem obtaining them.

The above discussion shows how the coping difficulties of below-average persons may be greater than might be expected on the basis of IQ level alone. This is true both for persons who are mentally retarded and for those in the marginal area of intelligence (IQ 70 to 90) and who are not considered to be mentally retarded. Numerous studies have found, for example, that the reading and arithmetic skills of persons with mild mental retardation and borderline intelligence are much lower than would be expected on the basis of their intelligence. Why should this be the case? As we have suggested, additional developmental deficits have occurred.

Our discussion in Chapter 3 about the dynamic developmental nature of intelligence is relevant here. According to this view, both the development and the expression of intelligence are dynamically related to personality, motivational, and other nonintellectual factors. Furthermore, each of these factors affects the growth and development of the others. Severe problems in any one of these areas results in corresponding difficulties in the others. The net result is a person more deficient than would be predicted on the basis of intelligence level alone. The new term for mental retardation—"developmental disability"—which focuses on the interactive, dynamic, and developmental nature of the problem, is also appropriate in this regard.

Therefore, many persons of low intelligence are at high risk for developing certain negative attitudes and expectations, low motivation, a passive personality, inefficient problem-solving strategies, and poor use of information and resources. All of these deficits compound the problem of low intelligence and result in an even more severe coping deficit than might be expected. This deficit goes well beyond a simple cognitive deficiency and involves a broadly ineffective strategy of coping with the world. The net effect is what the present authors call the "adaptive deficit."

## THE ADAPTIVE DEFICIT

The "adaptive deficit" refers to persons of below-average intelligence who also manifest a variety of nonintellectual deficits which, in combination, seriously limit or impair their ability to adapt in our society. There are three basic components of the adaptive deficit. They are (1) low intelligence, (2) a variety of other nonintellectual deficits, and (3) the interaction between the individual and the society in terms of its complexity and demands. We shall briefly discuss each of these in turn.

### Low Intelligence

The term "adaptive deficit" is employed only with those persons having both coping deficits and low intelligence. Persons of average intelligence who may also manifest coping difficulties are not included. Such persons may also have physical or personality problems.

The term "adaptive deficit" also includes all persons considered to be mentally retarded. However, it also goes beyond this. In fact, the notion of adaptive deficit was formulated by the present authors to account for persons of low intelligence who were not mentally retarded. This includes persons with IQ below 70 but without the necessary impairment in adaptive behavior. Also included are persons above 70 IQ who are not considered mentally retarded. Both of these latter groups are considered to be "at risk" for adaptive difficulties. There is some confusion between the terms "mental retardation" and "adaptive deficit" that requires clarification.

In order to be diagnosed as mentally retarded, a person must have an IQ below 70 and a demonstrated impairment in adaptive behavior. If either or both of these requirements are not met, the person cannot be called mentally retarded. But does this mean that the person has no problems related to low intelligence? Unfortunately, this is the erroneous impression that it often created. While these persons may not be technically retarded, they may still manifest serious coping difficulties. Thus, the adaptive deficit includes both mentally retarded people and also the far greater number of people who have less severe but nevertheless serious coping problems that are related to low intelligence.

There is no attempt to specify the upper IQ cutoff for the adaptive deficit. As noted above, persons of average intelligence are not included. In terms of guidelines, we refer back to our earlier discussion of marginal intelligence. There it was suggested that an IQ of 85, or possibly even 90, might be appropriate. However, no absolute figure is given here for two reasons. First, the adaptive deficit is proposed only as a concept, not as a new diagnostic category or label. Thus, specific criteria are neither necessary nor appropriate. Second, the nature of the third component of the adaptive deficit—namely, the match between the individual and the society—precludes a precise upper limit. By definition, this will vary with the environment as it interacts with the individual. In terms of our modern complex society, the present authors suggest that an IQ of 85, and possibly even 90, is worthy of consideration.

### Additional Nonintellectual Deficits

These include but are not limited to deficits in motivation and personality, lack of information and skills, and an inability to obtain and/or use resources. For any given individual, any of these nonintellectual factors may be more important than low intelligence itself. In any case, it is the cumulative effect of all of these deficits, in addition to low intelligence, that produces a coping deficit. The result is a broadly impoverished individual.

### Match between the Individual and the Society

The adaptive deficit occurs as a result of the interaction between the individual and the requirements of the society. The more complex and demanding the society, the more coping ability is needed. It is this factor that makes it impossible to define any specific upper IQ cutoffs. Theoretically, the upper limit can change upward or downward, depending on the demands of the society. Practically speaking, however, the present authors strongly suggest that the problem is progressive, given our complex technological society.

There is a great similarity between the concept of the adaptive deficit and the concept of mental retardation, as discussed in Chapter 4. More will be said about this similarity at the end of this chapter. However, perhaps the major difference between the two concepts is that the adaptive deficit goes well beyond mental retardation, particularly in terms of the upper IQ cutoff and the resulting huge increase in the number of people potentially involved.

## DIMENSIONS OF THE PROBLEM

Mental retardation includes only some of the people who are experiencing difficulties in coping with society. It is a widely recognized formal diagnosis, and there is a tendency to presume that if a person is not formally mentally retarded, he generally has no problems related to low intelligence. As we have suggested, this idea is not only erroneous but prevents services from being rendered to persons who could well profit from them.

The difference between the Heber and Grossman definitions of mental retardation in terms of the upper IQ limit is extremely relevant here. When the IQ of 85 was the upper cutoff (Heber), approximately 16 percent of the population was potentially mentally retarded. However, when the upper limit was lowered to an IQ of 70 (Grossman), the projected figure on the basis of the normal curve dropped to approximately 2¼ percent. In terms of an assumed United States population of 220 million people, the difference between these two definitions is approximately 35 million versus 5 million. Of course, particularly with the larger figure, there would also have to be a manifest impairment in adaptive behavior before these persons could be called mentally retarded. But this is a technical issue related to diagnosis. We are not concerned here with formal diagnosis but with recognition of a problem, no matter what it is called. Furthermore, we are not advocating that a new label or category be formulated. We merely wish to emphasize that, in the 1960s, it was felt that an IQ as high as 85 might qualify for consideration of mental retardation. Yet, in the 1970s, with a mere stroke of a pen, approximately 30 million people were automatically eliminated from such consideration. Did their potential problems related to low intelligence simply disappear during the intervening years? Did their objective life situations and experiences change as a result of a newly published set of criteria?

The reasons for this technical change in the AAMD definition were discussed in Chapter 4. We, along with others (e.g., Robinson and Robinson, 1976), question the wisdom of this change. However, we do want to emphasize here that the changed AAMD criteria may suggest that low intelligence (IQs of 70 to 85) is not problematic. What we are trying to counteract is the erroneous but frequent assumption that if a person is not mentally retarded, he has no problems related to low intelligence. The consequence is that many persons with problems of adaptation and coping related to low intelligence may be ignored by the system and afforded few or no relevant services.

Throughout this chapter and, in fact, throughout most of this text, we have stressed that intelligence has no neat dividing line. Practically speaking, we cannot divide the distribution of intelligence into two groups —persons who are mentally retarded and persons who are normal. Such a dichotomy contradicts the normal distribution of IQ. But just such an artificial dichotomy is implied in much of the thinking and discourse concerning mental retardation. As we have stated (1976):

> . . . if you are not mentally retarded, then intelligence is not that important, or a cause for much concern. The present authors believe that the most unfortunate thing about such mental retardation research is that it downplays the importance of intelligence in daily living for millions of people who do not carry the label of mental retardation but who clearly have intellectual deficiencies. At both lay and professional levels, if you are not obviously retarded, then the explanation for your problem performance is to be found in intrinsic (motivational) or extrinsic (environmental) causes, but not with the variable of intelligence. (p. 240)

The notion of the adaptive deficit attempts to bypass such artificial and harmful distinctions by emphasizing that low intelligence, particularly that above the mental retardation level, is still problematic in our modern, complex society. Furthermore, this low intelligence interacts with other factors (such as personality, motivation, and ability to use resources) to produce a definite problem in coping and adaptation.

Thus, the notion of the adaptive deficit is a nondichotomous, noncompartmentalized concept which describes or explains problems in coping with a complex, demanding society. These problems can stem from a variety of sources (physical, emotional, etc.), but here we are referring only to adaptive difficulties related to intelligence. This group probably accounts for the majority of persons with significant coping difficulties. It would be extremely difficult to estimate the number of such persons, since this is apt to vary over time and to include many persons identified by other labels or concepts. The scope of the problem is enormous. This is indicated, to some extent, by studies which show significantly lower than average intelligence in persons manifesting many social disturbances (e.g., persons using mental health facilities, serving prison terms, and receiving welfare support). These findings are not surprising. Indeed, they are quite logical, since we would expect an increase in such problems in persons with a basic coping difficulty. Furthermore, these findings may be seen as validating the concept of the adaptive deficit. This relationship between adaptive difficulties and social disequilibrium can be illustrated by examining one problem area with which the authors are familiar.

### The Adaptive Deficit in a Psychiatric Setting: An Illustrative Case

Over the past several years, mental health services have expanded greatly into areas with a high percentage of persons of lower socioeconomic background, poor education, poor job stability, and low occupational level. Much attention has focused on adapting traditional methods of treatment, devising new methods of intervention, and developing new personnel resources for dealing with the broad mental health needs encountered in community-based programs. In the midst of these expanding services and programs, there has been an almost total lack of awareness concerning the relevance and consequences of low intellectual ability or mental retardation among many of the persons receiving these services. This continues despite clear statements of the need of such awareness (e.g., Hobbs, 1963; Maloney and Ward, 1976).

To evaluate this issue, the present authors and colleagues (Maloney and Steger, 1972; Maloney and Ward, 1976; Maloney, Steger, and Ward, 1973) have reported findings and discussed the results of studies which describe the intellectual characteristics of patients coming to the Psychiatric-Evaluation Clinic of the Los Angeles County-University of Southern California Medical Center. (This is the major emergency psychiatric facility serving the Los Angeles area, where approximately 1,200 persons are seen monthly for emergency psychiatric services.) The initial sample consisted of 195 patients, who were seen in the clinic in May 1970 and who were selected on a time-sampling basis. These subjects were shown to have a significantly low level of intelligence, as indicated by a mean IQ of 84. This study clearly demonstrated that the low intelligence of the sample was not simply a function of mental illness. For example, patients diagnosed as psychotic were essentially at the same level of intelligence as patients diagnosed as nonpsychotic. Additionally, patients who were admitted to the hospital had the same general level of intelligence as patients who were seen in the outpatient clinics. These data indicate that the intelligence results were not simply a result of mental illness. (If this were true, we would expect lower intelligence in the more disturbed patients.) Additionally, the samples showed that the patients were significantly below the national average in years of school completed, amount of income (nearly half of them were unemployed), and occupational level or type of job. Later studies also showed that the patients were significantly below average in literacy skills, especially reading. Two later studies done at the same institution produced almost identical results. Approximately 33 percent of the patients had IQs below 75, while only 10 percent had IQs of 100 or above. Despite these data, only 0.5 percent of the patients in the initial sample were seen as having problems related to low intelligence. In other words, in only 1 of the 195 cases was intelligence mentioned as part of the clinical picture.

Based on these studies, the authors made two conclusions. First, a significant number of persons visiting this psychiatric facility may have problems related to low intelligence. Second, low intelligence was typically ignored from a clinical point of view. There are three reasons for this minimal concern. First, clinicians appear to feel that low intelligence in psychiatric settings is merely the result of mental illness interfering with intellectual processes and not actually an intellectual deficit. As we noted above, the present studies do not support this contention. The second factor deals with the bias toward viewing patients in terms of the medical model, where psychiatric illness is expected. In the present studies, every patient coming to the clinic was given a psychiatric diagnosis, even though many of these diagnoses were extremely vague (e.g., chronic undifferentiated schizophrenia, adjustment reaction, etc.) and poorly documented. Finally, very few clinicians in psychiatry, social work, or even psychology have had any significant academic or clinical work with low intelligence. As a result, clinicians are not skilled in detecting low intelligence in mental health clients or recognizing the effects of low intelligence in everyday life. Most clinicians (as well as most lay persons) have a stereotyped image that subnormal intelligence poses problems only for the severely retarded. The person with the adaptive deficit who may be encountered in the community mental health setting, however, is generally of borderline intelligence or mildly retarded.

Accurate identification of such persons who manifest an adaptive deficit is extremely important. When such deficits are not clearly recognized or identified, the patient is often given a wrong psychiatric diagnosis. For example, the diagnosis "chronic undifferentiated schizophrenia" is frequently used to refer to persons who are not coping well, who have made only a marginal adjustment, and who may, at the time, manifest no clear symptoms of schizophrenia. If such persons are diagnosed as schizophrenic and treated with many antipsychotic medications, the result may be a further decrease in both their ability and their level of adaptation. Both authors have found that therapists have frequently requested assessment consultations on their patients who are not improving with medication treatment. After an extensive evaluation, low intelligence and the general inability to cope are the only clearly identified problems. If these persons were accurately identified as having adaptive deficits, more appropriate treatment and disposition might follow.

We are not contending that the majority of psychiatric patients coming to community facilities have primary intellectual problems. We do believe, however, that a significant number of such persons may have an adaptive deficit rather than a mental illness. The case of the adaptive deficit in a psychiatric setting is meant only to illustrate the types of problems we are trying to present. We have discussed this problem in some detail simply because both of the authors work in such a setting and were able to closely observe this phenomenon. The authors have also consulted in a number of penal settings. Here again, the story is almost identical. The general level of intelligence is significantly below average, and many of the inmates have adaptive difficulties. These problems, however, are almost totally unrecognized.

## THE ADAPTIVE DEFICIT AND MENTAL RETARDATION

As mentioned earlier, there is much similarity between the concepts of the adaptive deficit and mental retardation; in fact, the former is basically an extension of the latter. Mental retardation is a formal concept that has been operationalized for various pragmatic reasons and purposes (legal, economic, educational). It is a social-administrative concept that has been formulated so that important practical decisions can be made. The adaptive deficit is a much more informal concept. There is no attempt to formalize and operationalize it by proposing new labels or categories and setting specific cutoff points. Our purpose is to make people aware of a neglected problem that involves literally millions of people.

Let us examine the parallels between the concepts of mental retardation and the adaptive deficit. First, in both cases, there is a focus on low intelligence. Second, both concepts are ultimately concerned with clear behavioral problems. Third, both concepts see these deficits as being associated with low intelligence. The *associative* rather than the *causal* relationship is emphasized. Finally, the cultural relativity of mental retardation is part of the concept of the adaptive deficit. In fact, the interaction between the individual and the society is at the heart of both concepts. In defining either mental retardation or the adaptive deficit, one must consider the characteristics of both the individual and the society.

The term "adaptive deficit," however, emphasizes the recognition of a problem that goes well beyond mental retardation. The adaptive deficit is seen as the model of which mental retardation is the most extreme example. The adaptive deficit can be thought of as going beyond mental retardation, both in breadth and in depth. This needs further clarification.

We must broaden the meaning of "mental" in the term "mental retardation." Traditionally, mental retardation has dealt with a deficit which was presumed to be primarily or exclusively intellectual. However, throughout this text, we have emphasized the growing recognition that mental retardation is much more than this. Personality and motivational factors are now seen to be intrinsically involved. Furthermore, the new concept of developmental disability, which stresses the dynamic, developmental nature of mental retardation, states that all of these factors have an interactive effect in terms of both the development and expression of intelligent behavior. The concept of the adaptive deficit follows this trend, emphasizing the role of these nonintellective deficits in producing a general inability to cope.

In terms of depth, the concept of the adaptive deficit goes beyond that of mental retardation in not arbitrarily excluding persons with IQs above 70. In fact, as mentioned earlier, the notion of the adaptive deficit was conceived to cover those not in the range of mental retardation, but who nevertheless have a serious problem of low intelligence.

Therefore, the concept of the adaptive deficit includes all persons with significant coping deficits which involve low intelligence. Again, a specific upper cutoff cannot be given since we are talking about a match between an individual's capacities and the societal context. Further, we are interested in stressing the need for recognizing a problem, not in developing another arbitrary classification category.

To summarize much of the preceding discussion and reemphasize its major points, we wish to refer to our previous text:

> Recognition of a problem is the first step toward solution. That, essentially, is what the present chapter is about. The authors contend that we have lost sight of just how problematic low or marginal intelligence is in our complex, technological society. With all of the polemics currently raging about the *variable* of intelligence (group and racial differences and the concomitant heredity-environment issue), the central aspect of its "normal" *variability* has been neglected. And

this neglect has serious implications for the lower portion of that normal variation.

There are several reasons for this neglect. First, the present-day concern with egalitarianism as well as human and civil rights has made the assertion or affirmation of differences unfashionable and, in some quarters, downright unpatriotic. Second, and related to the political infusion implied in the first reason, the controversy surrounding such differences has become so overly emotional and vitriolic that any discussion about intelligence has been rendered essentially unintelligible. Consequently, many have simply preferred to avoid the issue or, in some instances, dismiss it altogether. Third, and by far most important from a professional-conceptual point of view, consideration of the variable of intelligence has been neatly compartmentalized into the category of mental retardation. For all practical purposes (and it is just such practicalness we are concerned with here), what was once viewed conceptually as a *continuous* variable has become a *dichotomous* variable. Intelligence has become an all or none phenomenon; a person is either intelligent or retarded, and there is no point in looking at differences in degree to see if such differences are related to anything else. The explanation for poor performance, if one is not mentally retarded, is perhaps craziness, probably laziness. The possible causative, interactive, or compounding effects of low intelligence (above and beyond obvious, legitimate mental retardation) have simply been ignored.

. . . Nowhere is the problem more clearly brought into focus than in the new "social system perspective" of mental retardation. This perspective suggests that mental retardation is a relative problem, with social and cultural antecedents, and represents a major shift from the traditional, more absolutist, disease-oriented conceptions. The demands a society places on its members are at least as important as the abilities those members bring to it. This newer formulation opens the door to a broader consideration of the concept of ability in interaction with the environmental context. It forces an examination of this relationship for more than just the mentally retarded. It suggests that given the present complexity of our environment, and even modest projections of increasing future complexity, low intelligence, over and above obvious mental retardation, is and will become increasingly problematic for both the people involved and society in general. (Maloney and Ward, 1976, pp. 254–256)

## CONCLUDING REMARKS

This discussion of the adaptive deficit was intended to make explicit an underlying theme that runs throughout this book and is alluded to in the title—*Mental Retardation and Modern Society*. The title was chosen to emphasize that mental retardation, particularly in its milder form, is fundamentally a modern phenomenon. Our modern, complex society has "created" the problem of mild mental retardation. This fact points to the cultural relativity of the problem and underscores why the definition of mental retardation must take both the individual and society into account. The same can be said for the concept of the adaptive deficit. It, too, is largely a function and product of modern society.

This book is not and cannot be concerned merely with the specific, arbitrarily defined (in terms of IQ) phenomenon of mental retardation. Instead, it deals with the general problem of the interaction between persons of low intelligence and our complex, modern society. This problem cannot be arbitrarily delimited by a set of artificial cutoff points, as we have done with the formal diagnostic category of mental retardation. Rather, it is best thought of as an interacting set of continua, one depicting the status or competencies of the individual and the other the demands of the society. Furthermore, society will probably continue to increase in its complexity and demands; thus, the nature of the problem is progressive. Our technological, computerized, efficiency-oriented society has formed the background for both the acute and chronic problems of low intelligence. Adaptation will become more and more problematic for those persons with this generalized adaptive deficit, and the "at risk" group will continue to expand.

What professional groups are addressing or even cognizant of the problems of this enormous group of people? Unfortunately, at present, none. It is our conviction that the field of mental retardation is both the logical starting place for thinking about this pervasive problem and the natural and obvious choice for providing many of the services. For the very factors basic to the concept of mental retardation (i.e., its intrinsic cultural relativity, the problem of low intelligence) are directly relevant and applicable to this neglected segment of society. It is for this reason that we have discussed the adaptive deficit in this text.

However, this exhortation runs contrary to the attitudes of many in the field of mental retardation. In fact, for a variety of reasons, there has been a major effort to "shrink" the field of mental retardation. We feel this is an error. In focusing solely on the particular problem of mental retardation, the field has lost sight of the more general problem of which it is simply the most extreme example—namely, adaptation as a function of the interaction between the individual and society. The field of mental retardation needs to broaden, not limit, its scope. We are not advocating the creation of even more formal labels and categories. We are suggesting that, for many of these persons, low intelligence is a significant problem which is not recognized and for which no help is available. We are primarily concerned here with publicizing an enormous problem that remains neglected, and we hope that this will produce an appropriate response. A true understanding of mental retardation should lead naturally to the notion of the adaptive deficit, which extends our ideas of mental retardation beyond any artificial cutoff points to their logical conclusion in the context of our complex, modern society.

# References

American Association on Mental Deficiency. The right to life. *Mental Retardation,* 1973, *11*(6), 66.

American Psychological Association. Psychology and mental retardation. *American Psychologist,* 1970, *25,* 267–268.

Anderson, S., & Messick, S. Social competency in young children. *Developmental Psychology,* 1974, *10,* 282–293.

Banker, M. C., Lambden, M. A., Lunch, H. T., Mickey, G. H., Roderick, T. H., Van Pelt, J. C., & Fosnot, H. Will my baby be normal? *Patient Care.* April 30, 1972. Miller and Fink Corp., Darien, CT.

Barr, M. W. *Mental defectives: Their history, treatment and training.* Philadelphia: Blakiston, 1904.

Bayley, N. Mental growth during the first three years: A developmental study of sixty-one children by repeated tests. *Genetic Psychology Monographs,* 1933, *14,* 1–92.

Bayley, N. Development of mental abilities. In P. H. Mussen (Ed.), *Carmichael's manual of child psychology* (Vol. 1). New York: Wiley, 1970.

Begab, M. The mentally retarded and society: Trends and issues. In M. Begab & S. A. Richardson (Eds.), *The mentally retarded and society: A social science perspective.* Baltimore: University Park Press, 1975.

Belmont, J. M., & Butterfield, E. C. What the development of short term memory is. *Human Development,* 1971, *14,* 236–248.

Benton, A. L. Interactive determinants of mental deficiency. In H. C. Haywood (Ed.), *Social-cultural aspects of mental retardation: Proceedings of the Peabody–NIMH Conference*. New York: Appleton-Century-Crofts, 1970.

Bergmann, G. The logic of psychological concepts. *Philosophy of Science*, 1951, *18*, 93–110.

Binet, A., & Simon, T. Méthodes nouvelles pour le diagnostic du niveau intellectuel des anormaux. *L'Année Psychologique*, 1905, *11*, 191–244.

Binet, A., & Simon, T. Le developpement de l'intelligence chez enfants. *L'Année Psychologique*, 1908, *14*, 1–90, 245–366.

Binet, A., & Simon, T. Le mesure du developpement de l'intelligence chez les jeunes enfants. *Bulletin de la Societe Libre pour l'Etude Psychologique de L'Enfant*, 1911.

Binet, A., & Simon, T. The development of intelligence in children. *Training School Bulletin, No. 11*, 1916. Reprinted in J. J. Jenkins & D. G. Paterson (Eds.), *Studies in individual differences*. New York: Appleton-Century-Crofts, 1961.

Blanton, R. L. Historical perspectives on classification of mental retardation. In N. Hobbs (Ed.), *Issues in the classification of children* (Vol. 2). San Francisco: Jossey-Bass, 1975.

Blatt, B. Understanding people with special needs. In J. M. Kauffman and J. S. Payne (Eds.), *Mental retardation*. Introduction and personal perspectives. Columbus, Ohio: Merrill, 1975.

Blatt, B., & Kaplan, F. *Christmas in Purgatory: A photographic essay on mental retardation*. Boston: Allyn & Bacon, 1966.

Bloom, B. S. *Stability and change in human characteristics*. New York: Wiley, 1964.

Bohr, N. *Atomic theory and the description of nature*. Cambridge: Cambridge University Press, 1934.

Borg, W. R. *Ability grouping in the public schools*. Madison, Wis.: Dembar Educational Research Services, Inc., 1966.

Boring, E. G. Intelligence as the tests test it. *New Republic*, June 6, 1923, 35–37.

Cattell, R. B. *Abilities: Their structure, growth, and action*. Boston: Houghton Mifflin, 1971.

Cicirelli, V. *The impact of Head Start: An evaluation of the effects of Head Start on children's cognitive and affective development*. Springfield, Va.: U.S. Dept. of Commerce Clearinghouse, 1969.

Clark, E. G. An epidemiologic approach to preventive medicine. In H. R. Leavell & E. G. Clark (Eds.), *Textbook of preventive medicine*. New York: McGraw-Hill, 1953.

Cleland, C. C., & Chambers, I. L. The effect of institutional tours on attitudes of high school seniors. *American Journal of Mental Deficiency*, 1959, *64*, 124–130.

Cleland, C. C., & Cochran, I. The effects of institutional tours on attitudes of high school seniors. *American Journal of Mental Deficiency*, 1961, *65*, 473–481.

Conger, J. J. The meaning and measurement of intelligence. *Rocky Mountain Medical Journal*, June, 1957.

Conley, R. W. *The economics of mental retardation*. Baltimore: Johns Hopkins University Press, 1973.

Crissey, M. S. Harold Manville Skeels. *American Journal of Mental Deficiency*, 1970, *75*, 1–3.

Crissey, M. S. Mental retardation: Past, present, and future. *American Psychologist*, 1975, *30*, 800–808.

Crosson, J. E. A technique for programming sheltered workshop environments for training severely retarded workers. *American Journal of Mental Deficiency*, 1969, *73*, 814–818.

Darwin, C. *The descent of man* (2nd ed.). Philadelphia: Mckay, 1874.

Dennis, W. Causes of retardation among institutional children: Iran. *Journal of Genetic Psychology*, 1960, *96*, 47–59.

Dentler, R. A., & Erikson, K. T. The functions of deviance in groups. *Social Problems*, 1959, *7*, 98–107.

Dexter, L. A. Towards a sociology of the mentally defective. *American Journal of Mental Deficiency*, 1956, *61*, 10–16.

Dexter, L. A. A social theory of mental deficiency. *American Journal of Mental Deficiency*, 1958, *62*, 920–928.

Dexter, L. A. Research on problems of mental subnormality. *American Journal of Mental Deficiency*, 1960, *64*, 835–838.

Dexter, L. A. *The tyranny of schooling: An inquiry into the problem of "stupidity."* New York: Basic Books, 1964.

Diebold, J. *Beyond automation*. New York: McGraw-Hill, 1964.

Dingman, H. F., & Tarjan, G. Mental retardation and the normal distribution curve. *American Journal of Mental Deficiency*, 1960, *64*, 991–994.

Doll, E. A. *The Vineland Social Maturity Scale: Revised condensed manual of directions*. Vineland, N.J.: Vineland Training School, 1936.

Doll, E. A. The essentials of an inclusive concept of mental deficiency. *American Journal of Mental Deficiency*, 1941, *46*, 214–219.

Doll, E. A. Social age as a basis for classification and training. *American Journal of Mental Deficiency*, 1942, *47*, 49–57.

Doll, E. A. *Vineland Social Maturity Scale: Manual.* Circle Pines, Minn.: American Guidance Association, 1947.

Doll, E. A. *The measurement of social competence: A manual for the Vineland Social Maturity Scale.* Minneapolis: Educational Testing Bureau, 1953.

Down, J. L. Observations on an ethnic classification of idiots. *London Hospital Reports,* 1866, 3, 25. *Journal of Mental Sciences,* 1867, 13, 121–123.

Drews, E. M. The effectiveness of homogeneous and heterogeneous grouping in ninth grade English classes with slow, average and superior students. Unpublished manuscript, Michigan State University, 1962.

Drillien, C. M. The incidence of mental and physical handicaps in school age children of very low birth weight. II. *Pediatrics,* 1967, 39, 238–247.

Dugdale, R. L. *The Jukes: A study in crime, pauperism, disease and heredity.* New York: Putnam, 1877.

Dunn, L. M. Special education for the mildly retarded–Is much of it justifiable? *Exceptional Children,* 1968, 35, 5–22.

Dunn, L. M. (Ed.). *Exceptional children in the schools: Special education in transition* (2nd ed.). New York: Holt, Rinehart, and Winston, 1973.

Edgerton, R. B. Mental retardation in non-Western societies: Toward a cross-cultural perspective on incompetence. In H. C. Haywood (Ed.), *Social-cultural aspects of mental retardation: Proceedings of the Peabody–NIMH Conference.* New York: Appleton-Century-Crofts, 1970, 523–559.

Ellis, N. R. The stimulus trace and behavioral inadequacy. In N. R. Ellis (Ed.), *Handbook of mental deficiency.* New York: McGraw-Hill, 1963.

Ellis, N. R. Current issues in mental retardation. Position paper of the American Psychological Association. Division on Mental Retardation: *Division 33 Newsletter,* 1975, 2(1), 1–2.

Engelmann, S., & Bruner, E. C. *DISTAR reading: An instructional system.* Chicago: Science Research Associates, 1969.

Engelmann, S., & Carnine, D. *DISTAR arithmetic: An instructional system.* Chicago: Science Research Associates, 1970.

Engelmann, S., Osborn, J., & Engelmann, T. *DISTAR language I: An instructional system.* Chicago: Science Research Associates, 1969.

English, H. B., & English, A. C. *A comprehensive dictionary of psychological and psychoanalytic terms.* New York: Longmans, Green and Co., 1958.

Esquirol, J. E. D. *Mental maladies.* Trans. E. K. Hunt. Philadelphia: Lea & Blanchard, 1845. Originally published (Maladies mentales) 1838.

Estabrook, A. H. *The Jukes in 1915.* Washington, D.C.: Carnegie Institution, 1916.

Farber, B. *Mental retardation: Its social context and social consequences.* Boston: Houghton Mifflin, 1968.

Fernald, W. E. The burden of feeble-mindedness. *Journal of Psycho-Asthenics*, 1912, 17, 87–111.

Fernald, W. E. A state program for the care of the mentally defective. *Mental Hygiene*, 1919, 3, 566–574.

Feuerstein, R. A dynamic approach to the causation, prevention and alleviation of retarded performance. In H. C. Haywood (Ed.), *Social-cultural aspects of mental retardation: Proceedings of the Peabody–NIMH Conference*. New York: Appleton-Century-Crofts, 1970.

Feuerstein, R. Cognitive assessment of the socioculturally deprived child and adolescent. In L. J. Cronbach & P. Drenth (Eds.), *Mental tests and cultural adaptation*. The Hague: Mouton, 1972.

Flavell, J. H. *The developmental psychology of Jean Piaget*. Princeton, N.J.: Van Nostrand, 1963.

Fogelman, C. (Ed.). *Manual for the AAMD Adaptive Behavior Scale: 1974 Revision*. Washington, D.C.: American Association on Mental Deficiency, 1974.

Folling, A. Über Ausscheidung von Phenylbrenztraubensäure in den Harn als Stoffweckselanomalie in Verbindung mit Imbezillität. *Atschrift für physiologische Chemistrie*, 1934, 227, 169–176.

Galton, F. *Hereditary genius: An inquiry into its laws and consequences*. London: Macmillan, 1869.

Galton, F. *Inquiries into human faculty and its development*. London: Macmillan, 1883.

Garber, H., & Heber, R. The Milwaukee Project: Early intervention as a technique to prevent mental retardation. *The University of Connecticut Technical Papers*. Storrs, CT.: The University of Connecticut, 1973.

Garber, H., & Heber, R. The Milwaukee Project: Indications of the effectiveness of early intervention in preventing mental retardation. In P. Mittler (Ed.), *Research to practice in mental retardation: Care and intervention* (Vol. I). Baltimore: University Park Press, 1977.

Gardner, W. I. *Behavior modification in mental retardation*. Chicago: Aldine-Atherton, 1971.

Gersh, K., & Jones, R. L. Children's perceptions of the trainable mentally retarded: An experimental analysis. Unpublished manuscript. Ohio State University, 1973.

Gesell, A., & Amatruda, C. S. *Developmental diagnosis: Normal and abnormal child development* (2nd ed.). New York: Hoeber-Harper, 1947.

Ginzberg, E. The mentally handicapped in a technological society. In S. Osler & R. Cooke (Eds.), *The biosocial bases of mental retardation*. Baltimore: Johns Hopkins University Press, 1965.

Ginzberg, E., & Bray, D. W. *The uneducated*. New York: Columbia University Press, 1953.

Goddard, H. H. Feeble-minded children classified by Binet method. *Journal of Psycho-Asthenics*, 1910, 15(1), 17–30. Reprinted in M. Rosen, G. R. Clark, & M. S. Kivitz (Eds.), *The history of mental retardation: Collected papers* (Vol. 1). Baltimore: University Park Press, 1976.

Goddard, H. H. *The Kallikak family: A study in the heredity of feeblemindedness*. New York: Macmillan, 1912.

Gold, M. W. Stimulus factors in skill training of the retarded on a complex assembly task: Acquisition, transfer and retention. *American Journal of Mental Deficiency*, 1972, 76, 517–526.

Goldberg, M. L., Passow, A. H. & Justman, J. The effects of ability grouping. Unpublished manuscript. Teachers College, Columbia University, 1961.

Gottlieb, J. Public, peer, and professional attitudes toward mentally retarded persons. In M. J. Begab & S. A. Richardson (Eds.), *The mentally retarded and society: A social science perspective*. Baltimore: University Park Press, 1975.

Gottwald, H. Public awareness about mental retardation. Research monograph, *Council for Exceptional Children*, 1970.

Gray, S. W., & Miller, J. O. Early experience in relation to cognitive development. *Review of Educational Research*, 1967, 37, 475–492.

Greenbaum, J. J., & Wang, D. D. A semantic-differential study of the concepts of mental retardation. *Journal of General Psychology*, 1965, 73, 257–272.

Greenberger, M. (Ed.). *Computers and the world of the future*. Cambridge, Mass.: MIT Press, 1962.

Grossman, H. J. *Manual on terminology and classification in mental retardation: 1973 revision*. American Association on Mental Deficiency. Baltimore: Garamond/Pridemark Press, 1973.

Grossman, H. J. *Manual on terminology and classification in mental retardation: 1977 revision*. American Association on Mental Deficiency. Baltimore: Garamond/Pridemark Press, 1977.

Guilford, J. P. *The nature of human intelligence*. New York: McGraw-Hill, 1967.

Guilford, J. P., & Hoepfner, R. *The analysis of intelligence*. New York: McGraw-Hill, 1971.

Gunzberg, H. C. *Social competence and mental handicap*. London: Bailliere, Tindall, & Cassell, 1968.

Guskin, S. Social psychologies of mental deficiency. In N. R. Ellis (Ed.), *Handbook of mental deficiency*. New York: McGraw-Hill, 1963.

Guskin, S. L., & Spicker, H. H. Educational research in mental retardation. In

N. R. Ellis (Ed.), *International review of research in mental retardation* (Vol. 3). New York: Academic Press, 1968.

Halstead, W. C. Biological intelligence. In J. J. Jenkins & D. G. Paterson (Eds.), *Studies in individual differences.* New York: Appleton-Century-Crofts, 1961.

Harasymiw, S. J. Relationship of certain demographic and psychological variables toward the disabled. *Research Development and Evaluation Bulletin, Series I, Attitudes toward the disabled.* Boston: Boston University Press, 1971.

Haywood, H. C. Experiential factors in intellectual development: The concept of dynamic intelligence. In J. Zubin & G. Jervis (Eds.), *Psychopathology of mental development.* New York: Grune & Stratton, 1967.

Haywood, H. C. Labeling: Efficacy, evils and caveats. Paper presented at the Joseph F. Kennedy, Jr., Foundation International Symposium on Human Rights, Retardation and Research. Washington, D.C., October 16, 1971.

Haywood, H. C. Intelligence, distribution of. In *Encyclopaedia Britannica* (15th ed.). Chicago: Benton, 1974. (Macropaedia, Vol. 9, 672–677).

Haywood, H. C. Alternatives to normative assessment. In P. Mittler (Ed.), *Research to practice in mental retardation: Education and training* (Vol. II). Baltimore: University Park Press, 1977.

Haywood, H. C., Filler, J. W., Shifman, M. A., & Chatelanat, G. Behavioral assessment in mental retardation. In P. McReynolds (Ed.), *Advances in psychological assessment* (Vol. III). San Francisco: Jossey-Bass, 1975.

Haywood, H. C., & Stedman, D. J. *Poverty and mental retardation.* Staff position paper prepared for President's Committee on Mental Retardation, 1969.

Hebb, D. O. *The organization of behavior: A neuropsychological theory.* New York: Wiley, 1949.

Hebb, D. O. *Textbook of psychology* (3rd ed.). Philadelphia: Saunders, 1972.

Heber, R. A manual on terminology and classification in mental retardation. (Monograph supplement.) *American Journal of Mental Deficiency.* Washington, D.C., 1959, 64.

Heber, R. A manual on terminology and classification in mental retardation. (Monograph supplement, 2nd ed.) *American Journal of Mental Deficiency.* Washington, D.C., 1961.

Heber, R., Dever, R., & Conry, J. The influence of environmental and genetic variables on intellectual development. In H. J. Prehm, L. A. Hamerlynck, & J. E. Crosson (Eds.), *Behavioral research in mental retardation.* Eugene, Ore.: University of Oregon Press, 1968.

Heber, R., & Garber, H. The Milwaukee Project: A study of the use of family intervention to prevent cultural-familial retardation. In B. Z. Friedlander,

G. M. Sterritt, & G. E. Kirk (Eds.), *Exceptional infant: Assessment and intervention* (Vol. 3). New York: Brunner/Mazel, 1975.

Hobbs, N. Statement on mental illness and mental retardation. *American Psychologist*, 1963, *18*, 295–299.

Hobbs, N. (Ed.). *Issues in the classification of children* (2 vols.). San Francisco: Jossey-Bass, 1975a.

Hobbs, N. *The futures of children*. San Francisco: Jossey-Bass, 1975b.

Howe, S. G. On the causes of idiocy. Report of Commission to inquire into the conditions of idiots of the Commonwealth of Massachushetts. Boston: *Senate Document No.* 51, 1848, pp. 1–37. In M. Rosen, G. R. Clark, & M. S. Kivitz (Eds.), *The history of mental retardation: Collected papers* (Vol. 1). Baltimore: University Park Press, 1976.

Hunt, J. M. *Intelligence and experience*. New York: Ronald Press, 1961.

International League of Societies for the Mentally Handicapped, October 24, 1968. Quoted in: Finch, R. H. *MR69: Toward progress: The story of a decade*. Report of the President's Committee on Mental Retardation. Washington, D.C.: U.S. Government Printing Office, 1969.

Ireland, W. W. *On idiocy and imbecility*. London: Churchill, 1877.

Itard, J. M. G. *De l'éducation d'un homme sauvage*. Paris: Goujon, 1801. (The wild boy of Aveyron. Trans. by G. & M. Humphrey. New York: Appleton-Century-Crofts, 1932.)

Jensen, A. R. How much can we boost I.Q. and scholastic achievement? *Harvard Educational Review*, 1969, *39*, 1–123.

Jones, R. L. Labels and stigma in special education. *Exceptional Children*, 1972, *38*, 553–564.

Jones, R. L. Educational alienation, fatalism, school achievement motivation and self concepts in mental retardates. Unpublished manuscript. University of California–Riverside, 1973.

Kanner, L. *A history of the care and study of the mentally retarded*. Springfield, Ill.: Charles C. Thomas, 1964.

Kauffman, J. M., & Payne, J. S. *Mental retardation: Introduction and personal perspectives*. Columbus, Ohio: Merrill, 1975.

Key, W. E. *Feebleminded citizens in Pennsylvania*. Philadelphia: Public Charities Association of Pennsylvania, 1915.

Kimbrell, D. L., & Luchey, R. E. Attitude change resulting from open-house guided tours in a state school for mental retardates. *American Journal of Mental Deficiency*, 1964, *69*, 21–22.

Lambert, N., Windmiller, M., Cole, L., & Figueroa, R. AAMD *Adaptive Behavior Scale: Public School Version, 1974 Revision*. Washington, D.C., American Association on Mental Deficiency, 1974.

Leiter International Performance Scale. Chicago: Stoettling Co., 1948.

Leland, H. Adaptive behavior and mentally retarded behavior. In G. Tarjan, R. K. Eyman, & C. C. Meyers (Eds.), *Sociobehavioral studies in mental retardation*. Washington, D.C.: American Association on Mental Deficiency, 1973.

Leland, H., Nihira, K., Foster, R., Shellhaas, M., & Kagin, E. Conference on measurement of adaptive behavior, III. Parsons, Kansas: Parsons State Hospital and Training Center, 1968.

Locke, J. *The philosophical works of John Locke* (Vol. 1). J. A. St. John (Ed.), London: G. Bell, 1905.

MacMillan, D. L. Special education for the mildly retarded: Servant or savant? *Focus on Exceptional Children*, 1971, 2, 1–11.

MacMillan, D. L. *Mental retardation in school and society*. Little, Brown, 1977.

MacMillan, D. L., Jones, R. L., & Aloia, G. F. The mentally retarded label: A theoretical analysis and review of research. *American Journal of Mental Deficiency*, 1974, 79, 241–261.

Maloney, M. P., & Steger, H. G. Intellectual characteristics of patients in an urban community mental health facility. *Journal of Consulting and Clinical Psychology*, 1972, 38, 299.

Maloney, M. P., Steger, H. G., & Ward, M. P. The Quick Test as a measure of general intelligence in an urban community psychiatric hospital. *Psychological Reports*, 1973, 32, 823–827.

Maloney, M. P., & Ward, M. P. *Psychological assessment: A conceptual approach*. New York: Oxford University Press, 1976.

Mann, M. What does ability grouping do to the self-concept? *Childhood Education*, 1960, 26, 357–360.

Masland, R., Sarason, S., & Gladwin, T. *Mental subnormality*. New York: Basic Books, 1958.

Matarazzo, J. E. *Wechsler's measurement and appraisal of adult intelligence* (5th ed.). Baltimore: Williams & Wilkins, 1972.

McCandless, B. R. Relation of environmental factors to intellectual functioning. In H. A. Stevens and R. Heber (Eds.), *Mental retardation*. Chicago: University of Chicago Press, 1964.

Mercer, J. R. Social systems perspective and clinical perspective: Frames of reference for understanding career patterns of persons labeled mentally retarded. *Social Problems*, 1965, 13, 19–34.

Mercer, J. R. The meaning of mental retardation. In R. Koch & J. C. Dobson (Eds.), *The mentally retarded child and his family*. New York: Bruner/Mazel, 1971.

Mercer, J. R. IQ: The lethal label. *Psychology Today*, 1972, 6, 40–43, 92, 94.

Mercer, J. R. *Labeling the mentally retarded.* Berkeley: University of California Press, 1973a.

Mercer, J. R. *The myth of 3% prevalence.* In G. Tarjan, R. K. Eyman, & C. E. Meyers (Eds.), *Sociobehavioral studies in mental retardation.* Washington, D.C.: American Association on Mental Deficiency, 1973b.

Mercer, J. R. Sociocultural factors in educational labeling. In M. Begab & S. A. Richardson (Eds.), *The mentally retarded and society: A social science perspective.* Baltimore: University Park Press, 1975.

Meyerowitz, J. H. Self derogation in young retardates and special class placement. *Child Development,* 1962, 33, 443–451.

Moore, A. *The feeble-minded in New York.* New York: State Charities Aid Association, 1911.

New York State Department of Mental Hygiene, Community Mental Health Research Unit. *Report of a special survey of suspected referred mental retardation.* Syracuse, N.Y.: Onondaga County, New York, 1955.

Nihira, K., Foster, R., Shellhaas, M., & Leland, H. *Adaptive Behavior Scales.* Washington, D.C.: American Association on Mental Deficiency, 1969. Revised 1974.

Nirje, B. The normalization principle and its human management implications. In R. B. Kugel & W. Wolfensberger (Eds.), *Changing patterns in residential services for the mentally retarded.* Washington, D.C.: President's Committee on Mental Retardation, 1969.

Niswander, K. R., & Gordon, M. *The women and their pregnancies* (Vol. 1). Philadelphia: Saunders, 1972.

Pearson, K. *The life, letters and labour of Francis Galton.* Cambridge: Cambridge University Press, 1914.

Peckham, C. *Mentally handicapped children. National Children's Bureau Tenth Annual Review.* London: National Children's Bureau, 1974.

Penrose, L. S. *The biology of mental defect* (2nd rev. ed.). New York: Grune & Stratton, 1966.

Pinneau, S. R. The infantile disorders of hospitalism and anaclitic depression. *Psychological Bulletin,* 1955, 52, 429–452.

Pinneau, S. R. Revised IQ tables. In L. M. Terman & M. A. Merrill, *The Stanford-Binet Intelligence Scale.* Boston: Houghton Mifflin, 1960.

President's Committee on Mental Retardation. *The six-hour retarded child.* Washington, D.C.: U.S. Government Printing Office, 1970.

President's Panel on Mental Retardation. *A proposed program for national action to combat mental retardation.* Washington, D.C.: U.S. Government Printing Office, 1962.

Rivera, G. *Willowbrook: A report on how it is and why it doesn't have to be that way.* New York: Vintage Books, 1972.

Robinson, H. B., & Robinson, N. M. *The mentally retarded child: A psychological approach*. New York: McGraw-Hill, 1965.

Robinson, N. M., & Robinson, H. B. *The mentally retarded child: A psychological approach* (2nd ed.). New York: McGraw-Hill, 1976.

Roos, P. Parents and families of the mentally retarded. In J. M. Kauffman & J. S. Payne (Eds.), *Mental retardation: Introduction and personal perspectives*. Columbus, Ohio: Merrill, 1975.

Rosen, M., Clark, G. R., & Kivitz, M. S. (Eds.), *The history of mental retardation: Collected papers* (2 vols.). Baltimore: University Park Press, 1976.

Rosenthal, R., & Jacobson, L. Teacher's expectancies, determinants of pupils IQ gains. *Psychological Reports*, 1966, *19*, 115–118.

Rosenthal, R., & Jacobson, L. *Pygmalion in the classroom*. New York: Holt, Rinehart & Winston, 1968.

Sarason, S. B., & Doris, J. *Psychological problems in mental deficiency* (4th ed.). New York: Harper & Row, 1969.

Sattler, J. M. *Assessment of children's intelligence*. Philadelphia: Saunders, 1974.

Sells, C. J., & Bennett, F. C. Prevention of mental retardation: The role of medicine. *American Journal of Mental Deficiency*, 1977, *82*, 117–129.

Seguin, E. *Hygiène et éducation des idiots*. Paris: Baillière, 1843.

Seguin, E. *Traitement moral, hygiène et éducation des idiots et des autres enfants arriérés*. Paris: Ballière, 1846.

Sequin, E. *Idiocy: Its treatment by the physiological method*. New York: William Wood, 1866.

Silverstein, A. B. An empirical test of the mongoloid stereotype. *American Journal of Mental Deficiency*, 1964, *68*, 493–497.

Simon, H. A. *The shape of automation for men and management*. New York: Harper & Row, 1965.

Skeels, H. M., & Dye, H. B. A study of the effects of differential stimulation on mentally retarded children. *Proceedings and Addresses of the American Association on Mental Deficiency*, 1939, *44*, 114–136.

Smith, R. M. *An introduction to mental retardation*. New York: McGraw-Hill, 1971.

Spearman, C. *The abilities of man: Their nature and measurement*. New York: Macmillan, 1927.

Spiker, C. C., & McCandless, B. R. The concept of intelligence and the philosophy of science. *Psychological Review*, 1954, *61*, 255–266.

Spitz, R. A. Hospitalism: An inquiry into the genesis of psychiatric conditions in early childhood. *Psychoanalytic studies of the child* (Vol. I). New York: International Universities Press, 1945.

Spitz, R. A. Hospitalism: A follow-up report. *Psychoanalytic studies of the child* (Vol. II). New York: International Universities Press, 1947.

Staats, A. W. Intelligence, biology or learning? Competing conceptions with social consequences. In H. C. Haywood (Ed.), *Social-cultural aspects of mental retardation: Proceedings of the Peabody–NIMH Conference*. New York: Appleton-Century-Crofts, 1970.

Stern, W. L. Über die psychologischen Methoden der Intelligenzprufung. Ber V. Kongress *Exp. Psychol.* 1912, *16*, 1–160. American translation by G. M. Whipple. The psychological methods of testing intelligence. *Educational Psychology Monographs, No. 13*. Baltimore: Warwick & York, 1914.

Tarjan, G. Some thoughts on sociocultural retardation. In H. C. Haywood (Ed.), *Social-cultural aspects of mental retardation: Proceedings of the Peabody–NIMH Conference*. New York: Appleton-Century-Crofts, 1970.

Tarjan, G., Wright, S. W., Eyman, R. K., & Keeran, D. V. Natural history of mental retardation: Some aspects of epidemiology. *American Journal of Mental Deficiency*, 1973, 77, 369–379.

Terman, L. M. *The measurement of intelligence*. Boston: Houghton Mifflin, 1916.

Terman, L. M., & Merrill, M. A. *Measuring intelligence*. Boston: Houghton Mifflin, 1937.

Terman, L. M., & Merrill, M. A. *The Stanford-Binet Intelligence Scale, second revision*. Boston: Houghton Mifflin, 1960.

Terman, L. M., & Merrill, M. A. *The Stanford-Binet Intelligence Scale, third revision*. (With 1972 tables by R. L. Thorndike.) Boston: Houghton Mifflin, 1973.

Thorndike, R. Review of R. Rosenthal & L. Jacobson: Pygmalion in the classroom. *American Educational Research Journal*, 1968, 5, 708–711.

Thorndike, R. 1972 Norms Tables for the Stanford-Binet Intelligence Scale. In L. A. Terman & M. A. Merrill. *The Stanford-Binet Intelligence Scale*. Boston: Houghton Mifflin, 1972.

Toffler, A. *Future shock*. New York: Random House, 1970.

Tredgold, A. F. *A textbook of mental deficiency* (6th ed.). Baltimore: William Wood, 1937.

Wallin, J. E. Prevalence of mental retardates. *School and Society*, 1958, 86, 55–56.

Wechsler, D. *The measurement of adult intelligence*. Baltimore: Williams & Wilkins, 1939.

Wechsler, D. *Wechsler Intelligence Scale for Children*. New York: Psychological Corporation, 1949.

Wechsler, D. *The Wechsler Adult Intelligence Scale*. New York: Psychological Corporation, 1955.

Wechsler, D. *Manual for the Wechsler Preschool and Primary Scale of Intelligence*. New York: Psychological Corporation, 1967.

Wechsler, D. Intelligence: Definition, theory and the IQ. In R. Cancro (Ed.), *Intelligence: Genetic and environmental influences*. New York: Grune & Stratton, 1971.

Wechsler, D. *Wechsler Intelligence Scale for Children–Revised*. New York: Psychological Corporation, 1974.

Williams, R. L. Black pride, academic relevance and individual achievement. *Counseling Psychologist*, 1970, 2, 18–22.

Wolfensberger, W. *The principle of normalization in human services*. Toronto: National Institute on Mental Retardation, 1972.

Wolfensberger, W. Citizen advocacy for the impaired. In D. A. A. Primrose (Ed.), *Proceedings of the Third Congress of the International Association for the Scientific Study of Mental Deficiency*. The Hague, The Netherlands: September 4–12, 1973. Warsaw: Polish Medical Publishers, 1975.

Wood, J. M., Johnson, K. G., & Omori, Y. In utero exposure to the Hiroshima atomic bomb: An evaluation of head size and mental retardation twenty years later. *Pediatrics*, 1967, 39, 385–392.

Zeaman, D., & House, B. J. The role of attention in retardate discrimination learning. In N. R. Ellis (Ed.), *Handbook of mental deficiency*. New York: McGraw-Hill, 1963.

Zigler, E. Mental retardation: Current issues and approaches. In M. L. Hoffman, & L. W. Hoffman (Eds.), *Review of child development research* (Vol. II). New York: Russell Sage Foundation, 1967.

Zigler, E. The nature-nurture issue reconsidered. In H. C. Haywood (Ed.), *Social-cultural aspects of mental retardation: Proceedings of the Peabody–NIMH Conference*. New York: Appleton-Century-Crofts, 1970.

Zigler, E. Cognitive-developmental and personality factors in behavior. In J. M. Kauffman & J. S. Payne (Eds.), *Mental retardation: Introduction and personal perspectives*. Columbus, Ohio: Merrill, 1975.

# Index